Disparate Measures

Disparate Measures

The Intersectional Economics of Women in STEM Work

Mary A. Armstrong and Susan L. Averett

The MIT Press
Cambridge, Massachusetts
London, England

The MIT Press would like to thank the anonymous peer reviewers who provided comments on drafts of this book. The generous work of academic experts is essential for establishing the authority and quality of our publications. We acknowledge with gratitude the contributions of these otherwise uncredited readers.

This book was set in ITC Stone Serif Std and ITC Stone Sans Std by New Best-set Typesetters Ltd. Printed and bound in the United States of America.

Library of Congress Cataloging-in-Publication Data

Names: Armstrong, Mary A., author. | Averett, Susan L., author.
Title: Disparate measures : the intersectional economics of women in STEM work / Mary A. Armstrong, Susan L. Averett.
Description: Cambridge, Massachusetts : The MIT Press, [2024] | Includes bibliographical references and index.
Identifiers: LCCN 2023015940 (print) | LCCN 2023015941 (ebook) | ISBN 9780262048866 (hardcover) | ISBN 9780262377959 (epub) | ISBN 9780262377942 (pdf)
Subjects: LCSH: Women—Employment—History—21st century. | Women scientists—Employment. | Women's rights. | Diversity in the workplace.
Classification: LCC HD6053 .A76 2024 (print) | LCC HD6053 (ebook) | DDC 331.4—dc23/eng/20211117
LC record available at https://lccn.loc.gov/2023015940
LC ebook record available at https://lccn.loc.gov/2023015941

10 9 8 7 6 5 4 3 2 1

For
Angelika von Wahl
and
Albert L. Folks, Rebecca N. Folks, and Natalie R. Folks

Contents

Acknowledgments

Teachers come first. I am deeply grateful to Jean Fox O'Barr and Eve Kosofsky Sedgwick for their brilliant tutelage, inspirational work, and friendship.

Boundless thanks to Susan Averett, coauthor and data wizard. Susan, you are 100 percent brilliance, 100 percent work ethic, and 100 percent fun.

I am grateful to my long-time collaborator Jasna Jovanovic and to magnificent colleagues and friends Kathryn Rummell, Andrea Nash, Susan Basow, Dana Cuomo, Tara Gilligan, Wendy Wilson Fall, Jennifer Stroud Rossmann, Petra Schäfter, Almut Sülzle, Katja Stamm, and Karen Anderson. Wendy L. Hill has made—and keeps right on making—wonderful things happen. Dar Williams gave me the best pep talk ever. Sandra Laursen has been unfailingly generous and encouraging. I am grateful to Kelly Mack, vice president for undergraduate STEM education and executive director of Project Kaleidoscope at the American Association of Colleges & Universities, who long ago took a chance on an unusual intersectional project. Thank you to the National Science Foundation's ADVANCE program for past funding support.

During the 2021–22 academic year, I was a visiting researcher at the Center for Interdisciplinary Women's and Gender Studies (Zentrum für Interdisziplinäre Frauen- und Geschlechterforschung, ZIFG) at the Technische Universität, Berlin. My thanks to center director Sabine Hark and the ZIFG faculty for hosting me.

My parents, Ellen and William Armstrong, remain inspiring examples. I cherish their legacy of unfailing kindness, generosity, and integrity.

Sharing life with someone as brilliant, supportive, kind, and fun as my partner, Angelika von Wahl, is cause for daily celebration. And celebrate we do. Micki, mein ganzes Herz hängt an dir.

—*Mary Armstrong*

I am forever grateful to H. Elizabeth Peters for taking me on as a doctoral student. She has always been a supportive mentor and adviser. She fostered my interest in women and their economic well-being. I am also deeply indebted to my coauthor on this volume, Mary Armstrong. Her lucid prose and lively ideas propelled this book forward. Working in partnership with Mary taught me the joy of interdisciplinary collaboration. In addition, Laura M. Argys offered her wise counsel. She and I met in graduate school and have collaborated on many projects over the years. My career has been richer and more rewarding because of Laura. I am also beholden to Saul D. Hoffman, who, early in my career, gave me the opportunity to coauthor the textbook *Women and the Economy: Family, Work and Pay* with him. This textbook changed the trajectory of my career, and I am grateful for his mentorship. My late father, Robert C. Averett, inspired me to earn a PhD, and when I was not sure of a major, he suggested I study economics. I know he would be proud of the accomplishment that this book represents. My late mother, Victoria A. Averett, a feminist before her time, was a continuous source of support, encouragement, and love. My mother-in-law eagerly awaits a copy of this book, and I am grateful for her enthusiasm. Most important, my husband of over thirty years, Albert L. Folks, has been unfailingly supportive of my career as we raised two lovely daughters, Rebecca N. Folks and Natalie R. Folks.

—*Susan Averett*

The authors thank the Office of the Provost at Lafayette College for support during this project. We are also grateful to our Lafayette student research assistants: Taylor Corsi made invaluable contributions to this book in its early stages, and Tafita Rakotozandry assisted with some of the programming at a critical phase. Our original editor at the MIT Press, Emily Taber, was a consistent cheerleader for this project. She provided many insightful comments that greatly improved this work. Three anonymous reviewers provided helpful and detailed comments that both improved our work and solidified our faith in the urgency of this project. We thank them.

Introduction: True Lies—The Narratives of STEM Diversity

> More or less severe manpower shortages are noted in most scientific and specialized fields. . . . However, women graduates provide a potential source of scientific talent that can be utilized more fully. . . . The greater use of women will be urged.
> —"The First Annual Report of the National Science Foundation, 1950–51" (National Science Foundation 1951), 18–19

In the twenty-first century in the United States, the science, technology, engineering, and mathematics (STEM) workforce is dominated by white men. Gender disparities in STEM have been demonstrated and acknowledged to the point of truism, and they have been analyzed and criticized from just about every possible disciplinary and institutional vantage point. Federally funded programs have taken aim at them. Higher education efforts are sharply focused on changing them. Nonprofit organizations push back against them. Businesses loudly bemoan them. Millions of dollars from many different sources have been invested in understanding and undoing them. And just about every actor and organization trying to transform the US STEM workplace can attest to the difficulty of changing them.

Disparate Measures is very much a part of these efforts. But while we agree that US STEM fields are dominated by white men, our goal is not to further corroborate the now obvious lack of diversity in STEM fields. Rather, our interests lie in innovatively examining the economic promises of STEM and the viability of those promises, particularly for women from historically (and currently) disadvantaged populations. Decades of intensive inclusivity work have made a more diverse US STEM workforce a national goal and transformed STEM careers into particularly desirable and sought-after occupations. Seen as part economic driver and part social remedy, STEM jobs are commonly understood to benefit everyone, especially women and particularly women from underrepresented groups. The public discourses of STEM promise a great deal. But what do diverse women actually find when they work in STEM occupations? What do STEM jobs really deliver— and for whom? Those questions are at the heart of this book.

Our detailed look at these questions shows that the promises of STEM are partly true but also partly false. Often touted as a panacea for stalled social mobility, STEM work is less a cure than a selective analgesic, less a solution than a formula for partial relief. This book demonstrates that when compared to women not working in STEM, women working in STEM are indeed economically elevated by their occupations—yet when compared to white men in the same STEM occupations, women's second-class status is usually reaffirmed. The STEM work realities of many women are characterized by lower overall wages, sizable wage gaps, and lower-paying, lower-status STEM jobs. Yes, doing STEM work pays well for women, including women from historically disadvantaged groups, but not nearly as well as it pays for white men.

These patterns mean STEM work is not just a solution. It is also a problem. *Disparate Measures* grapples with this problem by exploring the constricted economic benefits experienced by diverse women working in STEM. In addition, rather than simply pointing to the occupational and earnings data associated with standard diverse groups, we place our work within two theoretical frameworks that are necessary for understanding and intervening in these patterns. The first is *intersectionality*. Intersectionality holds that social identity categories are always partly constituted and shaped by intersections with other identity categories and by dynamics that are determined in the context of local power relations. The second framework is *critical data studies*, an approach that acknowledges that self-evident identity categories are in fact generated via historical processes and that data about these categories are products of social actions, not reflections of objective truth. Acknowledging that identity categories are inherently intersectional in their meanings and neither self-evident nor naturally countable complicates the use of quantitative data. But embracing that complication opens up new pathways for action and ultimately provides insights that better reflect women's STEM realities and experiences.

As we interrogate the entrenched belief that a diverse STEM workforce will bring about economic abundance for the women who participate in it, we also engage with the vexing questions associated with trying to measure the fortunes of diverse groups. Who do we (the usually invisible analyzers of data) automatically name when we speak of underrepresented women in STEM? When we say we want to open up STEM work for everyone, who has been left out? And how do we analyze occupational and earnings data on historically evolving, intersecting identities in order to consider the data associated with diverse groups in a more capacious way? These challenges around inclusivity, social identities, and quantitative data have long lain submerged beneath the many other challenges of STEM inclusivity work. *Disparate Measures* brings them to the surface.

In this introduction, we contextualize the familiar goal of diversifying the US STEM workforce by unpacking the ways in which fostering broader STEM field participation is driven by intertwined national-level narratives about combating social stratification and strengthening the US economy. We illuminate how these cultural narratives work together to naturalize the cultural script that STEM careers are a form of individual opportunity that will effectively promote the US economy while automatically advancing women from historically disadvantaged groups, particularly women of color. We further situate our work within STEM inclusivity research, clarifying why we focus on diverse women working in the wider US STEM labor force (and not on the more familiar areas of STEM education and academic STEM jobs).

In chapter 1, we introduce the concept of *intersectional economic analysis* and discuss the challenges of engaging with quantitative economic data as both intersectional and nonobjective. We offer a model that works to engage realistically with the complexities of data based on various salient social identity categories, arguing that data on diverse women in STEM is most valuable when we first (1) understand the factors that have historically (re)formed any given identity category and shaped the resultant data and (2) recognize the specific labor-force issues associated with that group. Carefully attending to the ways data are shaped by both identity-category histories and group-specific workforce factors is crucial for creating a multidimensional and meaningful economic picture of the diverse STEM workforce.

In chapter 2, we describe our data choices and offer a reality check on women in the US STEM labor force. We explore how STEM work stacks up against non-STEM work in the US and examine how women (as a generic group) fit into the larger STEM economy. In what STEM occupational areas do women tend to work? What are women's STEM earnings overall? This broadly contextualizing overview compares women and men in STEM and also introduces the concept of STEM-related jobs. Throughout *Disparate Measures*, we make important distinctions between conventional STEM work and STEM-related work, with the latter indicating jobs that are not always classified as STEM but that involve science and technology expertise. These jobs, which are strongly associated with the health professions and occupied mostly by women, are an important but often overlooked part of the larger US STEM economy. Chapter 2 provides a robust gender-centered context for our closer examinations of various groups of women working in STEM fields.

These closer examinations are spread across the eight intersectional case studies that make up chapters 3 through 10. Together, these chapters comprise the core of *Disparate Measures*. Each focuses on an intersectional group of women and addresses how the identity category in question has historically shifted and consequently shaped category-related data. They also examine how that group has been situated within the US labor force and (when possible) the US STEM workforce, as well as what forms of bias and workforce challenges have been associated with each group. For every intersection we examine, we provide data on participation patterns and annual earnings for conventional STEM and also STEM-related work. Every case study pushes intersectional work further by identifying additional salient intersections and examining them in the context of both STEM and STEM-related jobs. Each case study concludes with highlights of our findings for that group of women.

Our case studies intentionally emphasize and prioritize race and ethnicity, working to expand on the standard women-of-color aggregate approach whenever possible. We address the category histories, labor-force contexts, and STEM workforce participation and earnings of Black women, Native American and Alaska Native women, Asian and Pacific Islander women, and Hispanic/Latina women. Four more case studies illuminate and explore often neglected identities that are (to different degrees) still emergent within the STEM inclusivity literature—foreign-born women, women with disabilities, lesbian/bisexual/trans women and gender-nonbinary people, and mothers.

Finally, chapter 11 offers a wide-ranging discussion of our significant findings. This chapter outlines seven big-picture recommendations that suggest ways we might begin to reorient ourselves conceptually relative to promoting equity for a diverse STEM workforce. Emerging from our data-driven, intersectional economic analyses, these recommendations focus on how we can better recognize current STEM equity issues and rethink the patterns of economic disadvantage faced by many women in STEM jobs.

True Lies: The Narratives of US STEM Diversity

For several decades, the subject of broadening STEM field participation has merged with national conversations about the economy until STEM diversity has come to be seen as critical to driving STEM innovation and US economic competitiveness and to advancing the economic fortunes of women and historically underrepresented groups. These entwined connections have become largely axiomatic: a more diverse STEM workforce is understood to be a (perhaps *the*) lever that will foster STEM innovation, boost US global competitiveness, and serve economic justice by positively impacting historically underserved individuals and communities.

But these ostensibly self-evident connections between the US STEM economy and the increased well-being of historically underrepresented groups are in need of rigorous critical analysis. In order to understand the seemingly obvious mutually beneficial connections among STEM fields, the economy, and underrepresented groups, we must look more closely at the particular assumptions underpinning these familiar cultural claims—and ask what it means for underrepresented groups when such assumptions become economic and social truths.

We have identified three widely held, closely interwoven suppositions that structure this national logic of mutual benefit—that is, that a diverse STEM workforce will elevate both STEM excellence and the economy while also advancing the fortunes of the diverse workers involved:

1. *STEM jobs promote new and powerful economic opportunities for women and underrepresented groups.* This claim suggests that broadening the participation of women and historically disadvantaged groups in STEM occupations will increase their economic opportunities and social mobility. It is assumed that such participation will have positive, widespread, and sustainable group-level effects;

2. *Diversity in STEM fields supports STEM excellence and the US economy.* This claim reflects concerns that the US is falling behind in terms of STEM

excellence and a belief that STEM diversity will support innovation in STEM and long-term US global competitiveness. It is tacitly understood that US dominance in global capitalism via STEM is a desirable, shared goal.

3. *There is a looming STEM workforce crisis that the US must forestall or address.* This claim points to a burgeoning economic catastrophe that will be brought about by a lack of qualified US workers for a growing number of STEM jobs. Increasing the participation of women and other groups will ensure that the US does not run out of the scientists and engineers needed to buttress the STEM workforce specifically and the US economy generally.

These narratives circulate through shared national narratives about how to promote both social justice and economic opportunity for specific groups, and they shape our understanding of how to increase educational and workforce diversity and decrease social stratification. STEM diversity now forms a complex bridge between concerns about economic opportunity for women (especially women from underrepresented groups) and concerns about US competitiveness. Yet the actual experiences and relative earnings of women from historically underrepresented groups working in US STEM jobs remain a persistent blind spot in the circulation of these interconnected assumptions and ideas. Sustained attentiveness to intersectional issues is critical for seeing past this blind spot.

STEM = Social Change: New Economic Opportunities for Diverse Women

Taking a closer look at the three core national narratives about STEM diversity can help clarify some of the issues that arise when we uncritically link the power of STEM work both to social mobility and economic opportunity for (underrepresented) women and to a robust, competitive US economy. In terms of the role played by STEM fields in *promoting economic opportunity for women and underrepresented groups*, we can look to the surge in efforts by nonprofit organizations focused on connecting girls and younger women to STEM as one example. Such efforts reflect (among other concerns) a growing sense of urgency around linking young women to the economic opportunities that STEM fields are understood to represent. Well-established and widely respected organizations such as the Girls Scouts of the United States of America have pivoted strongly toward STEM and now focus substantively on promoting STEM skills and careers. In 2017, the Girl Scouts made a pledge to lead 2.5 million girls into the STEM pipeline (shorthand for educational tracks that often lead to STEM work) by 2025 (Girl Scouts of the United States of America 2017). The organization Girls Who Code focuses on the tech sector, a key opportunity area in terms of both job availability and salaries. In the words of founder and CEO Reshma Saujani, Girls Who Code was started "with the belief that computing skills are a critical path to security and prosperity in today's job market. That access to a computer science education could bring women into a thriving innovation economy and give families a real shot at the middle class" (Saujani 2017). Black Girls CODE, a tech initiative focused on girls and youth of color founded by Kimberly Bryant in 2011, highlights the beneficial connections between tech jobs, economic mobility, and social justice: "Together, we are creating stronger economies and more equitable societies" (Black Girls CODE 2021). When it comes to STEM work, strong economies and just societies are understood to go hand in hand.

Fostering economic justice and opportunities for the women of tomorrow is the driving force behind many organizations that work to prepare girls for higher-paying STEM occupations. These organizations have sophisticated, complex missions focused on multiple, highly laudable goals for girls and other underserved groups. Efforts at connecting girls to STEM pathways are also aimed at increasing self-efficacy and confidence and at providing critical opportunities to fulfill intellectual potential and develop leadership. Organizations such as Black Girls CODE make positive differences in structurally disadvantaged communities in the US, and they deserve both high praise and practical support for their work.

Our point here, however, is that these groups are premised on leveraging STEM careers to create new forms of economic advantage. Access to STEM work is identified as a uniquely powerful way to shift persistent patterns of disadvantage for women and girls, especially those who belong to historically underrepresented and underserved populations. Social mobility and social justice are seen as fundamentally linked, and STEM careers are widely accepted as one of the best bridges between the two.

But an awkward question remains to be addressed: when diverse women cross the bridge into STEM careers, what do they find on the other side? We argue that they find the "true lies" of STEM. While these women generally earn more than other working women like them earn, they are also likely to earn less than white men. STEM careers are indeed a road to better wages—but they are also a road to well-disguised wage inequality, depending on the comparison. And while gender pay gaps are a familiar part of generic discussions about the US workforce overall, there is a notable absence of national conversations about pay gaps in STEM fields. Instead, pay differences in STEM remain masked by the utopian economic promises now culturally attached to STEM work.

STEM Excellence and the US Economy Depend on a Diverse STEM Workforce

In terms of *diversity in STEM fields supporting STEM excellence and the US economy*, one of the most powerful illustrations we can provide is the National Science Foundation's (NSF) steadily increasing investment in STEM diversity. For decades, the NSF has invested millions of dollars in broadening participation in the US STEM workforce and has justified these expenditures by connecting STEM diversity to STEM excellence and hence to a stronger US economy. The NSF ADVANCE program, which focuses on promoting equity and inclusivity for women (particularly women from underrepresented groups) in academic STEM careers, has been a leader in this effort, awarding over $350 million to more than two hundred US institutions of higher education between 2001 and 2020 (National Science Foundation 2021). In recent years, NSF has increased its focus on historically Black colleges and universities and Hispanic-serving institutions as well. A NSF program called INCLUDES (Inclusion across the Nation of Communities of Learners of Underrepresented Discoverers in Engineering and Science) illustrates how diversity in STEM and excellence in STEM are fundamentally linked together and welded to a vision of a stronger US economy. INCLUDES is

> a comprehensive national initiative to enhance U.S. leadership in science, technology, engineering, and mathematics (STEM) discoveries and innovations focused on NSF's commitment to diversity, inclusion, and broadening participation in these fields. . . . Significant advancement in the inclusion of underrepresented groups in STEM will result in a new generation of STEM talent and leadership to secure our nation's future and long-term economic competitiveness. (National Science Foundation 2020)

Nothing less than "our nation's future and long-term economic competitiveness" depends on STEM diversity. The stakes are high, and the links among increased STEM diversity, STEM excellence, and US global competitiveness are now matters of significant taxpayer investment.

The NSF's interest in STEM diversity has been accompanied by similar interest from the private sector. The logics of social mobility and potential economic opportunity through STEM are often intertwined with the logics of competitive capitalism and good business. Unsurprisingly, it is easy to find partnerships between corporations and STEM-focused social justice and economic opportunity initiatives. Through these partnerships, nonprofit organizations receive the resources they need to run outstanding programs for underserved individuals. Simultaneously, corporate entities offer their participation as both evidence of the company's values (equity) and sharp business practices (profit). "Doing good" (supporting social and economic opportunity via STEM and other diversity initiatives) and "doing well" (increasing corporate competitiveness and profits) orchestrate easily within this model. The language of ethical and social responsibility around STEM diversity dovetails smoothly with private-sector and corporate interests in higher profits in the modern (information and global) economy.

One example of this dynamic is AT&T, a corporation that works closely with Girls Who Code and contributes over $1 million annually to that organization (Girls Who Code 2020). The company also supports STEM initiatives associated with the Girl Scouts and Black Girls CODE (AT&T 2021a). In the context of these substantial commitments, the company's 2020 diversity, equity, and inclusion webpage banner statement offers a mix of the values and business equation that rationalize such partnerships:

> At AT&T, inclusion is how we unleash the power of diversity, and equity leads to equality for all. We strive each day to foster a sense of belonging and empowerment in our workplace, create relevant marketing for our customers, listen before engaging in our communities and work as a team alongside our diverse suppliers. We innovate with the community in mind and focus our Diversity, Equity & Inclusion practices on five pillars: our employees, our communities, our customers, our content and our suppliers. (AT&T 2021b)

AT&T is committed to diversity and inclusion in principle ("equality for all," "sense of belonging for all") but makes clear that commitment is also good business ("create relevant marketing," "work as a team alongside diverse suppliers") and a way to "unleash power." Michael Dell, CEO of Dell Technologies, offers a succinct version of this ethics plus business logic: "I have always believed diversity is power. It is how we win, and win the right way" (Dell Technologies 2021).

Such statements are notable for their ordinariness, not their rarity. Businesses typically have public diversity statements that describe inclusion as supporting humane values and improving competitiveness via more effective marketing, better customer relations, and improved products. Pairing the goal of increased profit with the innovation generated by diverse teams is now a common practice, and there is nothing technically incorrect about the juxtaposition. There is no evidence to indicate that the individual benefits of opportunity are canceled out if they are publicly touted as driving profit. And inclusivity is indeed "good business": many studies report that diverse teams drive better financial outcomes (Eswaran 2019; Hunt et al. 2018; Sheppard 2018).

However, while businesses often promote diversity—including and perhaps especially STEM diversity—as a way to boost profits, such a pairing is rarely examined with any care. The seamless connection between fostering opportunities for underrepresented individuals and increasing corporate profits has become an unreflective one, with the latter simply justifying the former. The equation is now so normative it is simply proffered as an obvious win-win: doing the ethical thing (creating an equitable workplace) just happens to be doing the lucrative thing (maximizing the talent pool to amplify both performance and profit). Yet this approach has not always been the ground zero of STEM diversity efforts. As Lorenzo Baber (2015) points out, in the 1980s and 1990s, early narratives around STEM equity strongly echoed the discourses of the civil rights movement and were primarily focused on systemic prejudice and (non)meritocracy. And while those issues remain central to many scholars and practitioners today, arguments based on the principles of equity and access are now often overshadowed by profit-based arguments aimed at "strengthening the U.S. advantage in science and technology in the face of growing global competitiveness" (Baber 2015, 252).

Embedded in the now seemingly self-evident linkage of STEM diversity with stronger profits and products, the value of diversity in STEM has become welded to economic competitiveness in general, any company's bottom line specifically, or both. But this automatic equivalency deserves more thoughtful consideration. In the most obvious sense, some of these pairings might simply give us pause. BP's chief scientist Angela Strank's outspoken support for STEM diversity (in *Forbes* magazine) in order to ensure the future of Big Oil is less appealing when we consider the impact of fossil fuels on the climate emergency and the level of harm climate change will have—ironically enough—on women worldwide, especially in the Global South (Nagel 2015; Sharma 2018). And we are likely to recoil when the head of global commercial development for pharmaceutical giant Mylan—now infamous for ballooning the price of the broadly needed and historically affordable EpiPen—notes the importance of involving women in STEM so the company can reach its "bold mission: to provide the world's 7 billion people access to high quality medicine" (Gulfo 2017).

But problems with the linkage between STEM diversity and profits go beyond these disturbing examples. When arguments for STEM diversity shift away from an understanding of equity and access as values sufficient unto themselves and toward corporate profits, support for broader participation becomes vulnerable to any organization's sinking economic fortunes. In a worst-case scenario, the failure to innovate or compete successfully once parity across diverse groups has been reached might be understood to show that diversity does not automatically result in business success and therefore is not worth the effort. Far more perniciously, when the argument that diversity equals innovation and profit is made uncritically, the (normalized) structural inequalities that have created and sustained a lack of diversity—historical and systemic forms of disadvantage, explicit and implicit bias, patterns of microaggressive behavior, forms of unrecognized and unearned privilege—remain unacknowledged within a feel-good story that connects social mobility for historically disadvantaged groups with increased business success.

This approach leaves the underpinnings of systemic inequity and discrimination—racism, sexism, homo- and transphobia—intact. And with that infrastructure unexamined and in place, historically privileged groups remain privileged and historically underrepresented groups remain embedded in forces that have been (and will continue to be) unaddressed. Diverse workers may be good for business, but history shows that business has not necessarily been good for them—and our national conversations about STEM opportunities reflect little awareness of that latter fact (Acker 2006). Yes, diversity is power. But for whom? And to whose advantage?

Our point here is not that there are often startling contradictions between stated corporate values and actual effects (a point that would hardly be new). And equity-driven, nonprofit initiatives are neither naïve nor helpless in the context of corporate support. In 2017, for example, Black Girls CODE declined over $125,000 from Uber, with founder Kimberly Bryant citing Uber's intersectional "issues with gender" as well as "certain inequitable practices with people of color" (Connley 2017). But we do want to suggest that it is time to reconsider promoting a diverse STEM workforce primarily through arguments about national economic competitiveness and increased corporate profit and to imagine reframing the advantages of STEM diversity more humanely and capaciously (McGee and Robinson 2019).

STEM Diversity and the STEM Shortage

Finally, it also is instructive to examine what might be the longest-lived and most persistent way we commonly link STEM diversity with the US economy, and that is the claim that there is a looming STEM workforce crisis that the US must forestall or stop. Any person who is even minimally attentive to US cultural conversations around science and technology is likely to recognize the narrative of impending disaster that interminably circulates around the US STEM workforce. We have long been panicking about the shortage of trained US STEM professionals and the economic losses that will result from that shortage. Indeed, the twenty-first century began with both the National Science and Technology Council and the National Science Board issuing reports calling for increased vigilance around educational innovation in STEM and STEM-related employment needs (National Science and Technology Council 2000; National Science Board 2003). Many more studies followed, focusing on likely STEM worker scarcity and a shortage of trained STEM talent in the US, with alarming reports from the National Academy of Sciences (2007, 2010) (*Rising above the Gathering Storm: Energizing and Employing America for a Brighter Economic Future* and *Rising above the Gathering Storm, Revisited: Rapidly Approaching Category 5*) having particular impact. Under the Obama administration, a report from the President's Council of Advisors on Science and Technology (2012) estimated a future deficit of trained STEM professionals, positing an almost inevitable (national and economic) crisis. A report from the New American Economy Research Fund (2017) (a bipartisan group seeking immigration reform) warned of a "persistent and dramatic shortage of

STEM workers." In 2021, the US Department of Defense (2021, 102) cited the "national STEM shortage" as a looming crisis for military readiness and national security. All told, the twenty-first-century story of US STEM occupations is anxiety-ridden and powerfully fixated on an impending shortage of STEM workers.

But despite its dominance, that narrative is also hotly contested. An active counterargument seeks to complicate what has become the self-evident problem of a lack of US STEM workers. Robert N. Charette points out why it is so difficult to make claims around a STEM job deficit or surplus, noting that the National Science Foundation and the Department of Commerce define STEM jobs differently and thus reach different conclusions about the size of the STEM workforce and associated future needs (Charette 2013). Taking Charette's work further, Yi Xue and Richard C. Larson demonstrate the heterogeneity of the STEM labor market and show how the answer to "surplus or shortage?" can vary across occupational domains (such as academia and industry) as well as across specific types of STEM occupations (Xue and Larson 2015). These studies illustrate why it is difficult to be certain what the truth is—or, put another way, why it is relatively easy to calculate future STEM jobs as both a deficit *and* a surplus.

The STEM (non)crisis is a powerful example of how definitions and choices around a seemingly constant variable (STEM) can drive diametrically opposed findings. The simple question "What counts as a STEM field?" throws open the issue of a national STEM shortage, rocking the foundation on which many STEM diversity arguments (and other arguments, from educational pipeline funding to immigration reform) are built. In addition, the question of STEM job deficit and job surplus is also significant because arguments for broadening participation in STEM have come to depend on the threat of a STEM workforce deficit. The narrative that there is a dire need for skilled workers to support the US economy and fill STEM jobs and that plenty of untapped talent resides in US populations of women and underrepresented groups plays an enormous role in justifying educational and corporate diversity initiatives, providing validation, momentum, and support for efforts focused on promoting social mobility through STEM access. In short, when it comes to STEM diversity, narratives promoting the value of STEM diversity now at least partially rely on the threat of a STEM workforce deficit. Much depends on a dire need that only missing US populations can fill. But we must consider what we gain—and what we risk—when a core rationale for investing in STEM diversity relies on an entirely debatable economic crisis.

Our argument here is a call to be more carefully cognizant of the connections we make and their consequences when we predicate STEM diversity on the STEM shortage. If calls for STEM diversity depend heavily on a STEM crisis, then they are (like calls for diversity because it supports US innovation and corporate profit) subject to revocation in the very terms on which they rest. In 2014, Michael Teitelbaum's wide-ranging *Falling Behind? Boom, Bust, and the Global Race for Scientific Talent* traced nearly a century of episodic US STEM workforce emergencies, arguing that the ongoing sequence of STEM crises has been and continues to be the cyclical product of interest-group politics, faulty data collection, and misaligned understandings. Teitelbaum's argument posits that there is not (and probably never has been) a US STEM crisis, only new versions of the same national debate (Teitelbaum 2014).

For our purposes here, the central interest is not the back-and-forth of the crisis/no crisis debate but the importance of recognizing that once we are locked into the specific terms of a crisis debate, the stakes become exceptionally high for those who rely on the STEM shortage to justify interest and investments in increasing access to STEM fields. If the STEM crisis debate is a matter of how we produce data and define STEM, what happens to efforts to promote the participation of women and underrepresented groups when those data and definitions change? Like the premise that diversity is good for business, the STEM shortage argument places STEM diversity initiatives on surprisingly shaky and easily eroded ground.

Behind the STEM Curtain

The US STEM workforce stands at the center of a complex crossroads of national conversations and debates about the importance of diversity, innovation, and excellence in science and technology and about US economic and corporate competitiveness. To talk about diversity in STEM is to talk about many large and important things at once—possible economic opportunities for historically underserved groups, innovation and the discovery of new knowledge, increased corporate profits, US workforce capacity, a stronger (or weaker) US economy, and the shape of modern global capitalism.

Weaving together the various tangled strands of current thinking about STEM diversity is the idea of the future. The many narratives of STEM diversity are all oriented toward the idea of progress, and they are therefore necessarily forward-looking. Resources are focused on the potential economic elevation of women and historically (currently) disadvantaged groups, the future competitiveness of the US economy, and the forestalling of the always just-around-the-corner shortage of STEM workers. Ideas about STEM diversity in the twenty-first-century US also have a powerful relationship to temporality because of the belief that something called *diversity* will make things (markets, cultures, societies) better tomorrow. This is partly because the idea of progress (however defined) is inherently optimistic and always about making the future different from—and better than—both yesterday and today.

But this eternally forward-focused approach signals other factors, as well. First, it reminds us that the actual diversification of US STEM occupations has slowed and, in some cases, badly stalled (Fry, Kennedy, and Funk 2021). As the epigraph to this introduction suggests, years of effort have turned into more than half a century of frustration. The diversification of the STEM workforce has progressed in some areas but flattened for women and people of color in many high-paying and in-demand areas of STEM work (Kennedy, Fry, and Funk 2021). These failures partially explain why narratives of STEM diversity are stuck in the future tense.

Second, this fixation on the future distracts from the critical issues faced by diverse women who are in the STEM workforce *right now*. One useful way to conceptualize this blind spot in STEM diversity work is to consider the classic (and flawed) STEM education metaphor of the leaky pipeline. This familiar image invites us to imagine women and disadvantaged groups moving along educational pathways toward a successful STEM-oriented future—if we can only find ways to keep them in the groove over time. Over the past few years, the image of the pipeline has been critiqued for its failure to interrogate the pipe itself and, for example, the many ways that STEM teaching and learning are problematic and embedded in white supremacist, colonialist, and misogynistic concepts and practices (Cannady, Greenwald, and Harris 2014; Lord et al. 2019). STEM education has been revealed to be a decidedly nonneutral process.

In many ways, our critique of STEM diversity narratives parallels these critiques of the educational pipeline image. The current discourses that hold up STEM careers as a panacea for everything from social stratification to a shaky US STEM economy simultaneously mask significant questions about the nature of the STEM workforce itself: Who does which kinds of STEM work? How much do they earn in comparison to dominant groups? What specific forms of systemic disadvantage await different kinds of people working in the STEM labor force?

We are in agreement with the claim that "more research is needed on scientific careers outside of academia" and recognize that, like the mythical STEM education pipeline, the STEM workforce is not a neutral entity (Fox, Whittington, and Linkova 2017, 707). The occupational patterns and earnings of diverse women working in STEM tell us something important about STEM inclusivity because they illuminate what happens *after* people arrive in the STEM workplace. There are many loud national discussions about broadening participation in STEM, but little is said about the economic experiences of those who surmount the obstacles and finally come to work full-time in these jobs. What happens after the STEM dream comes true? As we close this chapter and move to a deeper discussion of identity categories and the challenges of intersectional data, we begin to foreground the economic realities of the diverse women working in STEM through whom these many narratives circulate.

1   Intersectional Economic Analysis: Theory and Praxis

> Our categories are important. We cannot organize a social life, a political move-
> ment, or our individual identities and desires without them. The fact that catego-
> ries invariably leak and can never contain all the relevant "existing things" does
> not render them useless, only limited.
>
> —Gayle Rubin, "Of Catamites and Kings" (2006, 479)

In this chapter, we explore the pitfalls and advantages of deploying quantitative data intersectionally. We offer the concept of *intersectional economic
analysis* as a way of embracing the tensions between quantitative economic
data (which rely largely on clear-cut social-identity categories) and intersectionality (which purposefully and productively blurs the boundaries
between such categories). Intersectional economic analysis coordinates
conventional single-identity-based economic data with an intersectional
perspective in order to illuminate the lived economic realities of women
working in STEM.

This approach means that *Disparate Measures* takes on the high-wire act
of historicizing and destabilizing identity categories while simultaneously
and strategically deploying those categories to reach new insights. Even as
we show how various social-identity categories are constructed and subject
to change, we also acknowledge that such categories matter: they shape
and perpetuate deeply entrenched forms of both unearned advantage and
systemic disadvantage, erase some people and highlight others, drive policy, and determine the distribution of resources. Our purpose, therefore, is
not only to expose the challenges of combining intersectionality and economic data but to demonstrate the value of this hybrid approach. Intersectional economic analysis pushes past overly optimistic, deafening cultural

narratives about the economic benefits of STEM jobs by attempting to think about difference, identity, and data outside the box—and bring along some of the box, as well.

Intersectionality: Difficulties and Definitions

Intersectionality is a theoretical and critical practice historically rooted in Black feminisms. The term came into popular use via seminal essays by Kimberlé Crenshaw in 1989 and 1991, but its origins stretch back through the history of Black (and women-of-color) feminist thought from the nineteenth century forward (Anzaldúa 1987; Collins 1990; Combahee River Collective 1983; Cooper 1892; Crenshaw 1989, 1991; A. Davis 1981; Lorde 1984; Murray 1987). Intersectionality has emerged as a leading approach to articulating the systemic invisibilities and violences to which women of color, particularly Black women, have been and continue to be subject. It is in this context that we acknowledge the intellectual and political labor of Black feminists and other feminists of color who have developed—and continue to transform and critique—intersectionality as a form of critical theory and resistance.

Intersectionality is not easy to define, and there is an expansive body of scholarship debating its conceptual content, practical applicability, use and misuse, and discursive dominance within both gender studies specifically and the US academy in general. A good deal of contemporary work on intersectionality is now meta work as scholars grapple with what intersectionality is, is not, could be, and has (not) become (Bilge 2013; Cho, Crenshaw, and McCall 2013; Collins 2019; Collins and Bilge 2020; May 2015; Nash 2013, 2019; Patil 2013). Overall, the concept represents a "somewhat confused theoretical landscape" (Choo and Ferree 2010, 145) that "does not always offer a clear set of tools" and methods for research (Rice, Harrison, and Friedman 2019, 409). Approaches differ across disciplinary contexts and conventions, as well (Cho, Crenshaw, and McCall 2013). Apprehensions about incoherence (What is it? How do we do it? Who gets to say?) are amplified by concerns about carelessness and cooptation. Intersectionality has been called a "buzzword" (K. Davis 2008) and "an article of feminist faith" (Nash 2015, 74) employed by academic feminists to signal (institutional and intellectual) legitimacy but often used in totalizing and inadequate ways (May 2015).

Where does this leave an interdisciplinary project like this book, whose interests focus strongly on the value and necessity of intersectional interventions? First, intersectionality's power has never been more apparent. It persists as a key point of reference and remains a core framework for thinking about the social operations of race, gender, difference, identity, and power. Post-intersectional perspectives abound yet nonetheless still summon intersectionality to the fore. Second, definitional clarity is critical for any intersectional project. There are many perspectives on intersectionality and many ways to approach it methodologically, and it is unacceptable to simply summon the concept and go forward. Hence, as we move toward the idea of intersectional economic analysis for women in STEM work, we begin with an overview of how intersectionality is conceived in *Disparate Measures*.

We understand intersectionality as an analytic of power that illuminates often unseen experiences within real-world contexts (that is, a real world of interlocking, interdependent systems of racism, misogyny, heteronormativity, ableism, and colonialism). An intersectional approach means no aspect of identity—especially one associated with persistent structural disadvantages—can be understood in isolation. Rather, the meaning of any social identity is always molded by other salient aspects of identity. Hence, intersectionality would hold that workplace bias against women with disabilities would be different from bias against men with disabilities because gender would affect how *disability itself* is experienced and perceived (and, as is shown in chapter 8, that is indeed the case) (Coleman, Brunell, and Haugen 2015; Louvet 2007).

An intersectional approach destabilizes single-identity categories, reconceptualizing them as mutually constitutive and dynamically interactive. These interfaces are also understood to be highly contextual: synergistic identities do not exist in a vacuum but are shaped by their specific locations. For example, a working-class Black lesbian living in rural Georgia in 1972 (one year before the American Psychological Association declassified homosexuality as a pathology) would experience health care differently than a working-class Black lesbian living in Los Angeles in 2022. However, an intersectional approach would not analyze health-care injustice for these populations by "adding up" information on separate groups (for example, by combining information about working-class people *and* Black communities *and* lesbian populations). Instead, it would examine intertwined systemic obstacles experienced by working-class Black lesbians themselves in those times and places. So, while the outcomes of these intersectional analyses might differ because of context (time and place), in both cases the working-class Black lesbian experience of health care would move from margin to center—and new information and insights would proceed outward from that specific location.

Finally, we see intersectionality as inherently attuned to a critique of social, political, and cultural systems and as a mechanism for change. *Disparate Measures* is closely in line with how Sumi Cho, Kimberlé Williams Crenshaw, and Leslie McCall (2013) describe intersectionality—an "analytical tool to capture and engage contextual dynamics of power" (788). We see this tool as one that links our work to Patricia Hill Collins's description of intersectionality as a heuristic for rethinking the operations of social power with the goal of "criticizing existing knowledge and posing new questions" (Collins 2019, 35). Our understanding of intersectionality is welded to advocacy and activism because our purpose in seeking fresh insights into forms of structural injustice is to better identify, engage, and disrupt them.

While intersectionality illuminates social identities and systemic disadvantages in ways that are sophisticated and valuable, it is also a demanding approach. Several challenges frame our project. First, it has long been noted that intersectionality is inherently reductive, with points of analysis shrinking as desired levels of specificity are sought (Chang and Culp 2002). In many ways, intersectionality's "infinite regress" is a source of analytical strength because it produces new insights across new domains (K. Davis 2008, 77). Its capacity to center the often hidden experiences of vulnerable groups and expose new aspects of power make it extremely productive. However, the right moment to stop taking more aspects of identity into account—especially marginalized ones—is not always obvious. Intersectional analysis tends to focus on smaller groups, raising the question of when and how to articulate any intersectional group, especially via quantitative data.

Second, intersectionality runs against the grain of familiar conventions for working toward social justice in a liberal state. The modern idea of social justice in the US has been shaped largely by identity politics and group-based protections. The feminist movement, the civil rights movement, the gay and lesbian movement, the disability rights movement: all these are familiar examples of people fighting to secure (among other things) protections for a group. Such movements experience their own internal conflicts about group identity, feature shifting coalitions and alliances, and struggle with the problem of reproducing injustice through other social hierarchies. However, the twenty-first-century US has inherited an *ethnic model* in which people are socially categorized into naturalized groups that then seek justice categorically. As a result, US cultures of diversity and social justice trend toward the inclusion and/or protection of specific groups.

Intersectionality is at odds with traditional liberal identity politics. At its core, intersectionality takes issue with a logic that group unity equals group uniformity, which compresses identities into single, discrete entities, hiding the important asymmetries of power within (Hancock 2007). Since its inception, intersectionality has been explicitly defined *against* identity politics: "The problem with identity politics," Crenshaw has written (1991, 1242), "is not that it fails to transcend difference, as some critics charge, but rather the opposite—that it frequently conflates or ignores intragroup differences." The challenge in enacting intersectionality lies in deploying intersectional approaches within discursive and political structures designed to articulate and accommodate single-category groupings.

The history of STEM diversity efforts in the US testifies to the dominance of identity politics as well as the need for and the difficulties of taking a truly intersectional approach. As one would expect, inclusion in the US (STEM) workplace has generally followed the larger pattern of adding new groups as the larger culture deems them worthy of attention and justice. In 1990, for example, the disability rights movement and the Americans with Disabilities Act (ADA) brought people with disabilities in STEM into public focus—and the National Science Foundation began collecting data and organizing disability inclusion efforts right around that time. The recent emergence of LGBTQ+ issues into the STEM diversity literature marks new inclusion efforts linked to populations that until recently (2020) have been legally unprotected at the federal level and almost entirely ignored within STEM diversity research. New rights (however precarious they may be) bring new visibility and protections, and STEM diversity narratives change as culture and politics push new groups forward. Such changes are positive, but they do not indicate an increase in intersectional thinking or approaches.

Perhaps the closest that STEM diversity work has come to a form of intersectional thinking is the intersection of gender and race. Given the systemic racism of STEM (and US) cultures, it is unsurprising that early attempts to promote women in STEM (particularly in higher education) often considered gender without attending to race. This pattern was noted as early as 1976, beginning with the groundbreaking *The Double Bind: The Price of Being a Minority Woman in Science* by Shirley Mahaley Malcom, Paula Quick Hall, and Janet Welsh Brown and has continued as an important theme. Women in STEM who do not have white privilege have been subject to "intersectional invisibility," often falling through the cracks between the separated concepts of gender and race (Purdie-Vaughns and Eibach 2008). And when they are recognized, these women are often (to use Crenshaw's term) "conflated" into a group called women of color, an aggregation that elides their many important differences. This trend pulls gender plus race intersectionality back toward yet another homogenizing group-identity model and shapes the data in ways that occlude specific and important experiences (Sharpe 2019).

The limits presented by single-category thinking are also powerfully entwined with data, particularly data's representative (demographic) function in the US STEM workplace. As Cheryl B. Leggon (2006, 325) has explained, the intersectional failure to think about gender and race for women in STEM "is due in part to the way data on the science work force have been traditionally collected: by race/ethnicity OR sex, but not by race/ethnicity AND sex. This both reflects and reinforces the invisibility of minority women in science." This widespread reliance on single-identity-category data as a mechanism that both shapes workplace diversity goals *and also* measures progress toward them illuminates a core challenge for intersectional approaches to women in STEM: large-scale, systemically focused efforts around diversity in STEM are often held hostage to single-category data—and to the kind of thinking that makes it seem self-evident that such data both fully represent diverse people and should function as both the definition and measure of progress. A data-driven focus on demographic representation determines how historically marginalized groups are protected (once they are deemed worthy of attention). These marginalized groups (such as Hispanics and people with disabilities) are placed within workforce diversity frameworks (that is, added to a diversity statement or plan), and policies are designed to address them. They can be counted, and their underrepresentation can be noted. Tracking the recruitment, retention, and advancement of specific populations in workplaces and businesses often becomes an organizational fixation, and demographic measurement serves as both metric and solution.

Single-group data fit institutional and business strategies well. But a reliance on conventional demographic groups and "master categories" (Warner 2008) such as gender and race makes large-scale intersectional efforts difficult to enact at the institutional level (Armstrong and Jovanovic 2017; Ferree 2009; Hankivsky and Cormier 2009; Hankivsky et al. 2012; Verloo, 2006). Such efforts are often hampered by the structural challenges of implementing intersectionality at the policy level because the focus is usually on single-identity groups and on using single-category-based demographic data to define and measure success (Armstrong and Jovanovic 2015; Leggon 2006). Standard social identity category approaches to STEM diversity (in the workplace and in higher ed, as well) clash with intersectionality, which is attuned to the complex interactions across mutually constituted groups. This problem repeats itself across STEM diversity work. How do we work with identity categories—race, ethnicity, ability, sexual orientation, gender identity—when the solo deployment of these categories repeats forms of exclusion, often erasing the most vulnerable groups? How do we pursue a potentially infinite number of intersectional groupings, especially when processes for articulating, assessing, and solving inequality rely on data for single-group categories?

Intersectional Data Trouble

An intersectional approach to the economics of women in STEM occupations demands that we confront a paradox: identity-based data can be both a way forward and a roadblock. It offers a way to measure the real situation so we can knowledgeably work toward change, and it pigeonholes people in ways that obscure the real situation. Intersectionality puts identities in motion, productively disturbing the perceived boundaries between them, but quantitative data nails identities down, hardening those boundaries. Conventional identity-based data can misrepresent representation itself, obscuring historically marginalized groups while appearing to offer comprehensive information on diverse populations. Yet when we move toward the most vulnerable populations, we encounter vexing issues—first, the challenge of selecting those populations (which specific intersections and why?) and, second, the infinite regress of intersectionality, which means samples get smaller and smaller. Such small data loses power as a compelling form of evidence and, in some contexts, risks exposing vulnerable individuals.

These conundrums suggest that identity-based quantitative data may be the nemesis of intersectional research. Since the 1990s, arguments about identity, data, methods, and social power (the "paradigm wars") have flickered across the social sciences and continue to echo in ongoing debates about research methods oriented in social justice (Bryman 2008; Oakley 1999). Compelling evidence illustrates how difficult it is to combine intersectional analysis with quantitative data, and researchers working with quantitative data as their primary method have struggled to integrate intersectional perspectives. Recently, Greta R. Bauer and her colleagues (2021) reviewed over seven hundred research studies attempting to deploy quantitative applications intersectionally, and their results reveal some deeply concerning patterns. These patterns include the widespread absence or misinterpretation of the central theoretical tenets of intersectionality, a failure to clearly define intersectionality, the frequent use of overly simplistic methods, and—perhaps most disturbing—the frequent inclusion of identity variables not salient to social position and power. Clearly, the current work of deploying quantitative data intersectionally by using standard quantitative methods is not going well.

Meanwhile, critical data studies (CDS), an interdisciplinary area of inquiry that has emerged over the past decade or so, has generated resonant critiques that have helped denaturalize quantitative data itself (Gieseking 2018; Iliadis and Russo 2016; Wernimont 2019). Reflecting theoretical frameworks from areas such as gender studies and science, technology, and society (STS) studies, CDS interrogates data as a social act embedded in systems of power (such as surveillance practices, national security practices, and personal data capture), including dynamics of predictive decision making that can perpetuate or even amplify social injustice (Brayne 2017; Eubanks 2018). CDS is often attuned to how data intersect with historically marginalized communities, how big data and data systems can be tools of oppression and control (Benbouzid 2019; Noble 2018; O'Neil 2016), and how they can be turned toward the pursuit of social justice (Data for Black Lives 2021; Taylor 2017). CDS often works against normative demographic data, especially when its proponents argue that conventional demographic categories and the quantitative data associated with them fail to capture the complex realities of identity and experience, such as those associated with LGBTQ+ (lesbian, gay, bisexual, transgender, and Queer) populations (Ruberg and Ruelos 2020). Data associated with demographic categories are understood to be insufficiently capacious, and to function as agents in the rigid (re)production of categories, playing a role in the management and perpetuation of interlocked social hierarchies. In other words, data can produce normative identity categories as well as measure such categories. CDS demands we turn a critical eye to data's origins, the complex and hidden choices embedded in them, their connections to both surveillance and predictive decision making, their role in the production of identity groups, their relationship to the deployment and (non)distribution of power, and their false posture as value-free, objective forms of knowledge.

There is much to grapple with when it comes to taking an intersectional approach to the economics of STEM work via conventional demographic data. Data offer a boundary conundrum where the interactive, contextualized categories of intersectionality come up against the rigid, discrete groupings on which both standard demographic data and conventional forms of diversity work rely. Evidence (Bauer et al. 2021) also indicates that attempts to use standard quantitative methods for intersectional research often fall short across myriad domains, confirming the difficulties of using quantitative methods intersectionally. Finally, critical work on data denaturalizes data and demographic categories, suggesting identity categories are created by data, not just reflected by them, and that objective data (often invisibly and therefore all the more powerfully) are a form of control that shores up the surveillance state in the name of concepts like security and health. All these challenges raise important issues with which intersectional economic analysis must grapple.

Deploying Quantitative Data: The American Community Survey

We support calls for new approaches to the concept of classification and the work of demography, and a feminist, antiracist, Queer reorientation of how (big and small) data are collected, represented, distributed, and employed (Data for Black Lives 2021; D'Ignazio and Klein 2020; Ruberg and Ruelos 2020). We also believe, however, that the pressing need for economic justice for women in STEM occupations makes it necessary to examine this group intersectionally using quantitative category-driven economic data. We have therefore bypassed the kinds of qualitative data that make intersectional analysis easier (interviews, focus groups, ethnographies), as well as radically reframed approaches to data, such as those suggested by Queer and Queer Black data scholars (Gieseking 2018; McGlotten 2016). Instead, we have chosen to work mainly with data from the American Community Survey (ACS), the conventional US Census Bureau product that shapes the majority of our case studies. Why?

We turn to the ACS for data for several reasons. Originally developed as a way to simplify a decennial census form that had become increasingly long and unwieldy, the ACS went into full production in 2005 and is administered to about three million US households annually. Its standard demographic questions use the same racial and ethnic categories as the decennial census survey, and it asks detailed questions about occupations and earnings. This means that the ACS can produce large samples that reflect specific questions about both identity and STEM work and can generate a great deal of information about the people who are working in what kind of STEM job and what they earn.

One reason for using ACS data, therefore, is simply this: the cultural narratives of US STEM diversity that we wish to test are fundamentally economic, and the ACS offers a deep look at the economics of STEM work. Claims that STEM jobs provide equalizing economic opportunities for (all) women require us to believe in the inherent financial advantages of STEM work. In order to test these assertions, it is necessary to examine both STEM job distribution (who is doing what in STEM?) and the wages being earned by different groups of STEM workers (who is earning what in STEM?). Questioning the glowing but dubious promises of STEM work requires data that enables us to speak back against the narrative that STEM jobs really do—or really will—bring (diverse) women into a state of economic and social equity.

There are several additional reasons that we work with ACS data when possible. First, it would be difficult to find a more deconstructed and debated set of identity-based categories than those used by the US Census Bureau (which the ACS deploys). The evolving identity categories used by the Census Bureau—unlike many forms of large-scale demographic data— have been subject to ongoing public scrutiny and historical study for more than half a century (Alterman 1969; Anderson 2015; Anderson and Fienberg 1999; Nobles 2000; Perlmann 2018; Schor 2017). There is no shortage of debate about the terms that should be used to describe various identities and the characteristics (including race, sexual identities, and immigrant status) that belong in the demographic mix. Indeed, US Census Bureau categories have long been used as examples of how social identities are deployed in service to political (racist, xenophobic, nationalist) ends. Our commitment to being explicit that data are embedded in power and politics makes the ACS a good choice.

Second, in order to reach our goals, we need economic data associated with STEM work that can actually be deployed intersectionally. As we have noted, the issue of infinite regress and ever-dwindling sample sizes methodologically haunts many intersectional projects. Small sample size impacts both data viability and (potentially) the privacy of individuals. There is no better source than the ACS for looking at the wage and occupation-related data for smaller, intersectional populations of women in STEM. Multiple years of ACS data (representing over three million US households per year) allows us to look closely at STEM participation and earnings patterns for many women whose experiences are usually masked by intersectional invisibility. In particular, the robust sample size of the ACS enables us to illuminate differences among women commonly conflated into the grouping "women of color." Myriad other specific populations become visible as well, such as women with disabilities in engineering professions, foreign-born women of color in the physical and life sciences, or even patterns of STEM work for women from different Native nations. This does not mean that designations such as *with a disability*, *foreign-born*, and *Native* are not compromised or contrived. And ACS data does not speak to STEM workplace experiences (like discrimination and bias). But the scale of ACS data allows us to challenge cultural assumptions about women and the economics of STEM work in innovative and highly specific ways.

Third, ACS data provides us with a useful although somewhat double-edged sword in terms of giving our work broader intelligibility. The ACS enjoys a level of viability in contexts in which quantitative data are commonly used. It is standard for conventional economic analyses of the US labor force and commonly deployed in the demographics-obsessed world of STEM inclusivity. Anyone familiar with STEM diversity literatures will recognize the ritualistic, quantitative data–driven statements about proportional (under)representation that frame and justify diversity work. If our intersectional analyses are audible across these domains, they may better promote change. As David Gillborn, Paul Warmington, and Sean Demack (2018, 160) point out in the context of antiracist work, "quantitative methods are well placed to chart the wider structures within which individuals live their everyday experiences, and to highlight the structural barriers and inequalities that differently racialized groups must navigate." Quantitative data from surveys like the ACS may enable stronger interventions.

One final factor powerfully frames our decision to deploy ACS data (and other forms of conventional data). We will not entirely abandon a quantitative approach if it might (even imperfectly) shed new light on systemic injustices, nor are we willing to cede such approaches to those who uncritically deploy data. While we agree qualitative data are more subtle and easily tuned to intersectional work, entirely rejecting quantitative data leaves important arguments unchallenged. Quantitative measures and the contrived categories on which they rely are flawed, but there is also danger in throwing the wage-gap baby out with the quantitative bathwater. We hesitate to reject a lever that has the potential to productively disturb the STEM diversity industry and upend the fantasy that STEM work is an unproblematic road to economic justice for all women.

As feminist scholars, we are acutely aware of the limits of the master's tools relative to the master's house and of engaging with systems that are structured by (and depend on) an intertwined matrix of racism, colonialism, misogyny, and homophobia. While we historically contextualize category-based quantitative data and show how systemic disadvantages permeate the US labor force, our presentation of ACS data nonetheless reproduces conventions that can reinforce the appearance of neutrality. Traditional formats for figures and tables, along with the source citations attached to them, reflect normative data presentations, offering visual signals that reinforce the impression of total objectivity (D'Ignazio and Klein 2020; Hullman and Diakopoulos 2011). Although *Disparate Measures* actively frames its data, there is always the risk that our analyses may be uncritically perceived and made to stand as truth, furthering the very issues associated with quantitative data that we seek to avoid.

We take this risk from a vantage point that aligns with an insight from feminist STEM studies pioneer Evelyn Fox Keller (1995, 11), who writes that "Judgments about which phenomena are worth studying, which kinds of data are significant—as well as which descriptions (or theories) of those phenomena are most adequate, satisfying, useful, and even reliable—depend critically on the social, linguistic, and scientific practices of those making the judgments in question." This reflexive approach to data—long promoted by feminist scholars—suggests a useful parallel between data and STEM fields themselves. Neither can ever be objective, but both wield tremendous power, and both can have value if they are consistently contextualized and reflexively used. And that is precisely what intersectional economic analysis attempts to do.

Enacting Intersectional Economic Analysis

At the level of implementation, our approach to enacting intersectional economic analysis has been influenced by Gillborn, Warmington, and Demack's (2018) work on QuantCrit (quantitative critical theory). Claiming that "statistical analyses have no inherent value but can play a role in struggles for social justice," the authors examine how quantitative data and methods can be merged with critically informed social justice projects (158). They use critical race theory (CRT) to "set out some principles to guide the future use and analysis of quantitative data," all of which recognize the centrality of systemic injustice in social life and commit to addressing the non-neutrality and non-naturalness of numbers and identity categories (158). Keeping these principles in mind, as well as the theoretical and methodological issues we have presented, our approach to intersectional economic analysis for women in the US STEM labor force is built around three basic steps.

1. Not Facts, Artifacts: Identity-Category Data in Contexts of History and Power

Quantitative demographic data are powerful forms of representation that resonate with objectivity and authority. The categories on which conventional demographic data are based often serve as self-evident representations of neutral reality. However, these categories and the data attached to them do not reflect facts. They are instead artifacts—of sociocultural values and priorities, state violences, political interests, attempts at liberation, and embedded asymmetrical structures of power. Taking identity-based data at face value reinforces the naturalness and self-evidence of what is neither natural nor self-evident—and leaves the workings of power unseen and undisturbed.

Intersectional economic analysis for women working in STEM therefore centers on the premise that because quantitative demographic data are cultural acts embedded in asymmetrical systems of power, use of such data must be framed by acknowledgments of those systems. Drawing on the feminist practice of situating knowledge, we sketch out identity-category histories for each intersectional case in this book. These overviews are necessarily limited in detail and scope (in many ways, we are barely scratching the surface of these complex histories). And they also are shaped by our own identities and epistemological frameworks (Fine 2006; Haraway 1988). Notwithstanding these constraints, these short histories offer valuable insights into some of the power dynamics that have shaped conventional identity categories, illuminate some of the logics behind them, and expose the longitudinal instability of the data they generate.

We denaturalize the identities we examine, exposing some of their origins and permutations: How has an identity been contrived and (re)built over time? What trajectories of power have shaped the collection of data based on that identity, tweaking the demographic process (and the data itself)? We consider what makes any given identity particular as a social category: Is it common over the lifespan (like disability) or relatively rare (like Native identity)? Is it rigid in definition (foreign-born) or a matter of self-identification (Hispanic)? Has it been obsessively tracked and redefined in order to shore up systemic injustice (like Blackness has been differently deployed to advance the national project of white supremacy)? Or has demographic erasure served the needs of power better (as in the case of LGBTQ+ populations)? While it is impossible to offer truly complete histories of these categories (it would take several books to fully chronicle the history of categories like Black or LGBTQ+), every case study begins by articulating at least some of the most distinctive factors that would otherwise silently shape the quantitative data we deploy.

2.   Experientially Real: Women in the Twenty-First-Century US STEM Labor Force

Socially salient identities—Blackness, Queerness, disability, and so on—are as experientially real and consequential as they are historically constructed. Our intersectional methodology is located in the space where social realities are "definitively there as well as in constant flux" (MacKinnon 2013, 1020). Before diving into specific quantitative data, our intersectional economic analysis for women working in STEM also considers patterns around the current lived workplace experiences of women associated with historically disadvantaged groups. This analytical focus on the local is a core principle of intersectionality. It is also a common theme of critical data studies, which recognizes the value of "engaging with data settings instead of simply data sets" (Loukissas 2019, 23).

Intersectional economic analysis takes data settings seriously, situating the groups we examine within cultures of the twenty-first-century US labor force and, when possible, in STEM workplace research. We first contextualize intersectional groups of women within the larger framework of their labor-force participation, as well as the factors that have shaped associated trends. We then explore the research on that group's current workplace experience. What specific stereotypes are likely in play? What particular forms of bias and systemic disadvantage tend to affect this group and how? What (if any) protections exist relative to discrimination? Qualitative data and an array of interdisciplinary scholarship are built into our work at this juncture, enabling us to trace how power flows within the current US labor force relative to the lived experiences of the diverse groups of women that participate in it.

As we orchestrate labor-market and workplace contexts, we include the research on STEM work whenever possible, outlining the STEM-specific workplace issues that emerge for particular intersectional groups of women. What does the existing scholarship tell us about forms of systemic bias for women in STEM fields? What kinds of intersectional disadvantages shape different women's STEM workplace experiences? The dearth of focused intersectional research on women's experiences of the STEM workplace becomes readily apparent at this stage. Research on some groups of women working in STEM (such as lesbians, bisexual women, and trans women) is just emerging from near total silence, while scholarship on some other groups (such as women with disabilities in STEM) remains almost nonexistent.

3. "Scrupulously Visible Political Interest": Using Quantitative Data Intersectionally

After we have denaturalized demographic data categories and recognized their workplace contexts, we use conventional quantitative data to examine the occupational distribution and earnings of diverse women in STEM. At this point, our QuantCrit approach reflects postcolonial theorist Gayatri Chakravorty Spivak's 1985 concept of strategic essentialism. Strategic essentialism recognizes the inherently constructed nature of social identities, as well as their role in maintaining asymmetries of power. It also suggests such identity categories may be productively deployed if political goals are made explicit, such as when categories are used in a context of "scrupulously visible political interest" (Spivak 1996, 214).

Our political interests are visible ones. *Disparate Measures* is a feminist, antiracist, anti-ableist, Queer-positive, anti-colonialist intersectional project. We use intersectionality theory to critique unjust power by exposing its inner workings and uncovering new knowledge in the service of change. We are openly suspicious of cultural narratives that promise justice for diverse women through STEM work or equate workplace diversity initiatives with increased profit for companies and equal opportunities for diverse women workers. We are invested in debunking these narratives, which misrepresent the lived realities of STEM work for women and perpetuate a toxic myth that the US STEM marketplace can simply will itself free of the misogyny, racism, homophobia, and other forms of injustice in which it has historically been grounded.

As we strategically use quantitative data, our work is intentionally situated in a place of honesty and ambiguity: we recognize both the limits and the urgency of the comparisons we make. Because we have contextualized the data in ways that are both critically and locally engaged, our data analyses stand as representations of intersectional moments, not as permanent truths about identities or social categories or types of STEM work. When we deploy conventional quantitative data intersectionally, evolving and very different kinds of identities are temporarily held still at a particular point in time. And we understand that, as we do so, we become agents in reproducing the categories we both use and question.

Ultimately, the work we do takes place in the spirit of Patricia Hill Collins's (2019) description of intersectionality as a heuristic tool. Our goal is to challenge the existing knowledge of glib narratives about STEM work and demonstrate how intersectional economic analysis opens up new questions about women, STEM work, and power. As we add intersectional comparisons, our goal is not to totally clarify but rather to deeply complexify. The difficult theoretical and methodological terrain that links intersectional analysis with quantitative data has value not only because it offers new insights but because it productively raises new questions and challenges.

2 Gender and STEM Work: A Particular Economy

> The literature on salary gaps in STEM is relatively thin, and much of it refers to specific fields or to academia only.
> —Shulamit Kahn and Donna Ginther, "Women and Science, Technology, Engineering and Mathematics (STEM): Are Differences in Education and Careers Due to Stereotypes, Interests, or Family?" (2018, 784)

As our examination of the theoretical and methodological terrain of *Disparate Measures* demonstrates, quantitative data are structured by (usually invisible) choices. In this chapter, we unpack the data-specific choices that we have made and discuss the decisions behind our empirical work. These include the parameters that shape our general data sample of workers in STEM and the ways that we approach the important and widely debated issue of defining STEM occupations. We also discuss the inclusion of STEM-related occupations (largely health-care jobs) in our work.

After establishing constraints and definitions, we offer a gender-based comparative overview of the current situation for women working in US STEM occupations. What does the US STEM workforce look like when seen through the lens of the gender binary? What STEM jobs do women generally trend toward (and away from) when they work in STEM and STEM-related occupations? What do women's STEM wages look like? Our purpose here is to establish a baseline around STEM workforce participation and earnings relative to binary gender identity and develop a suitably complex starting point from which we can move toward the deeper intersectional analyses that comprise the eight case-specific chapters to come.

Data and Definitions: Our Sample

Because intersectional analyses tend to focus on smaller populations and the groups we examine here are generally underrepresented in STEM, having a large number of data points is critical for this project. Our sample pools ACS data specific to the years 2012 to 2019, a timeframe that enables us to avoid confounding our view of the STEM workforce with the labor-market changes brought about by both the Great Recession and the COVID-19 pandemic. Because upward of three million individuals are surveyed annually via the ACS, this eight-year interval contains over twenty million observations and creates a very robust sample. We use the publicly available data extracts from the Center for Economic and Policy Research (2021). Despite this large sample size, our data are shaped by certain priorities and limits. And for some groups of women—lesbians, bisexual women, and mothers—the ACS does not provide the most useful data. In order to learn more about these intersections, we use other data sources, as described in chapters 9 (lesbians and bisexual women) and 10 (mothers).

Age range and work type are also important variables within our data. In terms of age groups, our analysis focuses on a sample of individuals who are age twenty-five to sixty-four and thus most likely to be finished with formal schooling but not yet retired. In selecting this age range, commonly designated as prime working years, we align our sample with the range most commonly used by economists. In terms of work type, we have restricted our sample to individuals working both year-round and full-time. These restrictions are linked directly to our interest in gender-based analysis. Because women are far more likely than men to work part-time, limiting our sample to year-round, full-time workers allows us to make more accurate comparisons between men and women. We have appropriately weighted our sample, as well.

We have not limited our sample in terms of academic degree type or educational level. While it is likely that many STEM workers have STEM degrees (that is, working engineers will probably have engineering degrees) and advanced degrees may be common, people transition to STEM jobs via many different routes (Rothwell 2013; Sassler et al. 2017). A narrow focus on only four-year degree holders who majored in a STEM field will likely result in an undercount of those actually working in STEM. In particular, given demonstrated patterns of systematic bias in STEM education, limiting our sample to four-year degrees or STEM-specific training may negatively affect the representation of women and other historically underrepresented groups working in STEM.

Two broader issues fundamentally impact our data at the meta level. We have limited our study to a specific population—women who have made it into full-time STEM work. This focus distinguishes *Disparate Measures* from the large body of STEM diversity research that is dominated by the framework of higher education, which, for example, examines who is earning what STEM degree or who persists and thrives in higher education STEM work (such as academic faculty) (Laursen and Austin 2020; Rosser 2017; Stewart, Malley, and LaVaque-Manty 2007). Looking at individuals who actually work in a broad array of STEM occupations is a key strength of our analysis and differentiates us from the majority of (no less important) studies of STEM equity.

Because we focus solely on the economic outcomes of women in STEM occupations, some women—women who trained in STEM but are not in the STEM workforce *and* women who have worked in STEM but opted out—are not visible in *Disparate Measures*. These missing women comprise an important group, and the attrition of women from STEM careers is a significant problem. It matters that the gap between STEM expertise and working in STEM is a gendered one: women who earn STEM degrees transition less often to a STEM career than men do (Sassler et al. 2017). This gap appears to be particular to STEM work itself: compared to women in other professional careers, women leave STEM jobs at higher rates (Glass et al. 2013). The usual predictors of job retention (advanced training, longer job tenure, job satisfaction, and aging) do not increase women's commitment to STEM jobs, even though these factors improve retention in other professional fields (Glass et al. 2013). And many women who leave STEM jobs do not leave the labor force altogether, which suggests that the issue may not be work but STEM work (Glass et al. 2013; Harris 2019). Women's weak persistence in STEM jobs is rightly the subject of considerable research (e.g., Blickenstaff 2005; Glass et al. 2013; Harris 2019; Kahn and Ginther 2018; Sassler et al. 2013, 2017; Seo, Shen, and Alfaro 2019; Xu 2017). We recognize this scholarship as vital for thinking holistically about the STEM workplace and—ultimately—the economics of STEM work.

A second fundamental limitation is the ACS's binary approach to the category of gender. The gender binary (identifying either as a woman or as a man) remains perhaps the most monolithic and intractable of identity systems. Although working with conventional quantitative data on gender is easy (in the sense of being uniformly available and accessible), gender-nonbinary, genderqueer, and intersex individuals are invisible within most demographic data sets. The gender binary is deeply naturalized, and the uncritical use of binary gender data repeats assumptions made by survey developers while furthering the erasure of nonbinary people.

This issue points to one of the most troubling aspects of using conventional quantitative category-based data—a lack of alternative ways of working with the gender binary simultaneously as a salient social category and as a constructed and often violently enforced one. Feminist data scholars have noted that the binary nature of data makes the gender binary especially difficult to break but that it is possible to develop more capacious ways to collect and visualize data that includes Queer gender identities (D'Ignacio and Klein 2020). Data sets like the ACS are not flexible in this regard, however, and we recognize this as a persistent disadvantage of using such data. As digital humanities scholar Miriam Posner (2016, 34) points out, "we frankly have not figured out how to deal with categories like gender that are not binary or one-dimensional or stable." As we proceed with our intersectional work, we acknowledge the limits of gender-binary–based data and the importance of the research focused on disrupting the stranglehold that the gender binary has on conventional quantitative data (Guyan 2021; Ruberg and Ruelos 2020). In chapter 9, we address this issue again, providing a discussion of the experiences of gender-variant individuals in the STEM workplace.

Finally, we want to highlight that we have kept our data parameters as consistent as possible throughout the entirety of *Disparate Measures*. Unless otherwise noted, the data decisions we have detailed here apply to both the sample we use in this chapter and to all the intersectionally specific chapters that comprise the remainder of the book. In addition, whenever a comparison is made between two groups, the findings for those groups are statistically different unless otherwise indicated. Such cases are rare.

Who Does What? Gendered Distributions across the STEM and STEM-Related Workforces

There is no single definition of what constitutes a STEM occupation, but it is an issue of some debate and considerable importance. As we discuss in the introduction, definitions of the STEM workforce play a significant role in cultural narratives around STEM diversity and the STEM shortage (Teitelbaum 2014). And the definitional possibilities are many. The National Science Foundation provides a commonly used definition that includes the social sciences (such as economics and political science), while other US government agencies (such as the Department of Homeland Security) use a narrower definition that excludes most social sciences (Granovskiy 2018). The National Academies of Science, Engineering, and Medicine use the STEMM acronym, which reflects their inclusion of medicine as a STEM field. And some agencies have suggested entirely reframing the issue. For example, the National Science Board (2015) has proposed a shift to STEM subworkforces and a reorientation of how we define and label STEM jobs.

Disparate Measures uses the occupational categories defined as STEM by the Standard Occupational Classification Policy Committee (SOCPC) and approved by the US Office of Management and Budget. These commonly used categories are based on Census Standard Occupational Classifications. They dovetail nicely with our use of ACS data, but the primary reason we have adopted this listing is that it offers a taxonomy of current STEM jobs that is reasonable and widely accepted. According to these classifications, in 2019 there were an estimated 100.9 million individuals between age twenty-five to sixty-four working full-time and year-round in the US. Of these workers, 8.6 million worked in STEM fields.

Another reason that we deploy SOCPC designations is that they help us navigate a significant gray area of jobs associated with but not always consistently labeled as STEM. The SOCPC usefully categorizes such occupations as STEM-related. The majority of STEM-related jobs are in the health-care professions, and it is a heterogeneous group in several ways. There is disparity in the level of required on-the-job engagement with scientific or technological practices, as well as significant variations in both the requisite levels of scientific or technical knowledge and length of formal training.

STEM-related occupations are important for several reasons. First, most STEM-related jobs could arguably be categorized as STEM work, and hence including STEM-related work in our analysis provides a stronger overall picture of the US STEM workforce. Second, these jobs comprise an important and steadily growing segment of the labor force. Third, as is shown throughout *Disparate Measures*, STEM-related work patterns and wages are a critical part of the larger picture of STEM work for women. In 2019, there were 7.3 million individuals age twenty-five to sixty-four working full-time and year-round in STEM-related jobs; 5.2 million of these individuals were women.

Overall, in 2019, about 16 percent of all US workers age twenty-five to sixty-four were working (full-time and year-round) in either conventional STEM or STEM-related jobs. Focusing on this same group of individuals over the years of our sample (2012 to 2019), we find that 10.4 percent of men work in STEM jobs compared to 4.3 percent of women. These numbers are essentially reversed in the STEM-related fields, where only 3.5 percent of men work in these jobs compared to 11.6 of women who report a STEM-related job. Women are, therefore, less than half as likely as men to work in conventional STEM occupations but more than three times more likely than men to work in STEM-related occupations.

Figure 2.1 provides another way to look at gender in conventional STEM and STEM-related occupations. Although women comprised 43.8 percent of the total US labor force, only 25 percent of STEM job holders were women. The story is very different in the STEM-related fields, where women comprise 71 percent of STEM-related workers. Relative to their participation in the overall workforce, women are severely underrepresented in STEM jobs and strongly overrepresented in STEM-related occupations. The reverse is true for men.

In order to better understand the occupational and earnings data picture for women in STEM, we now turn to a more granular look at the kinds of conventional STEM and STEM-related work women do. Our goal is to examine conventional STEM and STEM-related participation yet also avoid the precise (and enormous) task of addressing a plethora of individual occupations. In pursuit of a refined yet reasonably generalized approach, we have collapsed all conventional STEM jobs into four broad but fairly common groupings—computer/math, physical/life sciences, engineering, and STEM managerial (following Langdon et al. 2011; a full listing of the occupations within each group is included in appendix A). It is both noteworthy and unfortunate that these categories exclude teachers of STEM. This is because the ACS does not provide information regarding the specific subjects taught by individuals who identify themselves as teachers.

STEM-related work does not fall quite as neatly into occupational groupings as conventional STEM work does. We have therefore taken an approach

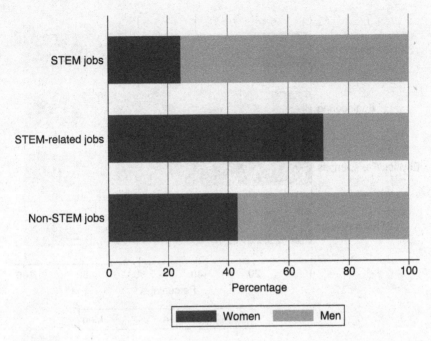

Figure 2.1
Percentage of men and women working in conventional STEM, STEM-related, and non-STEM jobs, individuals age 25–64 working year-round and full-time. *Source:* Data from the American Community Survey, 2012–2019.

that clusters STEM-related work more by job type (as opposed to occupational field). This approach enables us to identify some important variations within STEM-related work, particularly across nursing jobs. Because so many women work as nurses and because nursing work is internally characterized by significant differences in educational requirements, activities, responsibilities, and wages, we have disaggregated nursing occupations into two categories—vocational (licensed vocational nurse/licensed practical nurse) and professional (registered nurse). The resulting STEM-related occupational clusters are manager/other, therapist, vocational nurse, professional nurse, professional (including physicians/dentists), and medical support. (A full listing of the occupations within each group is included in appendix B.)

Figure 2.2 shows the proportion of men and women in each of the four conventional STEM occupational clusters. Although women are only 25

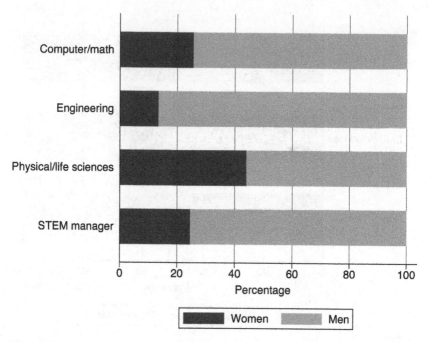

Figure 2.2
Percentage of men and women within STEM occupations, individuals age 25–64 working year-round and full-time. *Source:* Data from the American Community Survey, 2012–2019.

percent of all STEM job holders, they are sharply underrepresented in engineering, where they make up merely 14 percent of all engineers. On the other hand, women make up over 40 percent of those employed in the physical and life sciences. Overall, these data align with documented patterns of occupational segregation within STEM (e.g., Harris 2019).

Figure 2.3 shows the proportion of women in each of our six STEM-related occupational groupings. Although women make up 43.8 percent of the overall US workforce, they comprise 71 percent of all STEM-related workers. Within this 71 percent, women are underrepresented in the managerial positions in this category (60 percent are women) and as medical professionals (only 44 percent are women). Women dominate nursing work: well over 80 percent of nurses (both professional and vocational) are women. These patterns demonstrate that significant occupational segregation exists in the STEM-related fields, as well.

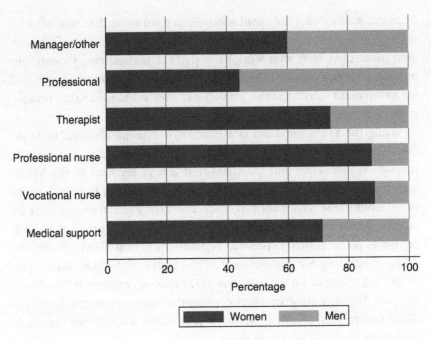

Figure 2.3
Percentage of men and women within STEM-related occupations, individuals age 25–64 working year-round and full-time. *Source:* Data from the American Community Survey, 2012–2019.

Who Gets What? Gender and Wages across the Conventional STEM and STEM-Related Workforces

How do women fare economically in STEM and STEM-related jobs? One way to answer this question is to calculate the STEM premium. Generally speaking, a wage premium describes the average amount that the wages of people in one occupation or group are greater than those of another occupation or population. A wage premium is a comparative measure that shows economic advantage. The example of the STEM premium is often used to demonstrate the economic benefits of working in STEM fields and frequently serves as a key data point in cultural narratives that extol the benefits of STEM work for women. When we calculate a STEM premium for women in STEM (using regression analysis to adjust for education, age, industry, marital status, citizen status, veteran status, and region of the country), we find that they earn about 30 percent more than women who work in non-STEM occupations. Men working in STEM earn about 24 percent more than men who work in non-STEM occupations. Overall, our analysis confirms an often cited fact: when compared to the women and men who don't work in STEM, women and men working in STEM occupations earn more money.

While the STEM premium is a normative measure attached to STEM diversity work, the same is not true for STEM-related work. This missing measure is instructive and illustrates that a large segment of the STEM-associated workforce has not been regularly included in larger conversations about STEM wages. For this chapter and the eight intersectional case studies that follow, we have calculated a STEM-related premium (which compares earnings in STEM-related occupations to non-STEM occupations while controlling for conventional STEM work). The STEM-related premium is 27 percent for women. The STEM-related premium is 25 percent for men. Together, these numbers confirm the relative economic benefit of STEM-related jobs, showing that these jobs confer a significant economic advantage to people who hold them.

The conventional STEM and STEM-related premiums make it clear that STEM is an economically powerful choice for women, at least when we make an intragender comparison—that is, when we compare women in STEM to women not in STEM. But when we shift the comparative framework and compare women in STEM to men in STEM, we see a different picture. Figure 2.4 presents annual median earnings for women and men across three sectors of the US economy (non-STEM jobs include both non-STEM and non-STEM-related work). Because the median value is less affected by outliers than the average value, median earnings are the preferred comparison when calculating wage gaps. Accordingly, *we use median earnings to make wage comparisons throughout this book*. An awareness that we use median and not average earnings throughout *Disparate Measures* is important for understanding tables in which we show earnings across the subgroups (clusters) of conventional STEM and STEM-related occupations. In addition, because we use data from 2012 to 2019, we have adjusted earnings for inflation by using the Consumer Price Index. Throughout *Disparate Measures*, all earnings are expressed in 2019 dollars.

In this new comparative context, another story begins to unfold. In all three categories, women earn significantly less than men—and the

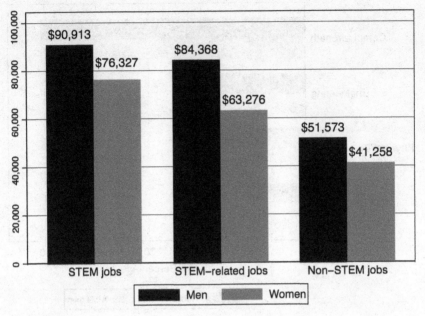

Figure 2.4
Median earnings of women and men by STEM, STEM-related, and non-STEM jobs, individuals age 25–64 working year-round and full-time. *Source:* Data from the American Community Survey, 2012–2019.

difference is greatest within STEM-related occupations, the category that women dominate (see figure 2.2).

Closer Comparisons: Occupational Distributions and Earnings of Women and Non-Hispanic White Men in STEM

Our comparative look at the occupational patterns and wages of women and men in conventional STEM and STEM-related work suggests there is much more to learn about the economics of gender and STEM. Accordingly, we have refined our analysis by focusing our comparison on the non-Hispanic white men in our sample. We have selected this group as our comparative baseline (both here and throughout *Disparate Measures*) for several reasons. First and foremost, white men best reflect entrenched systemic privilege. This group faces the least amount of structural and historical disadvantages overall and is most likely to effectively illuminate differences. In addition, white men

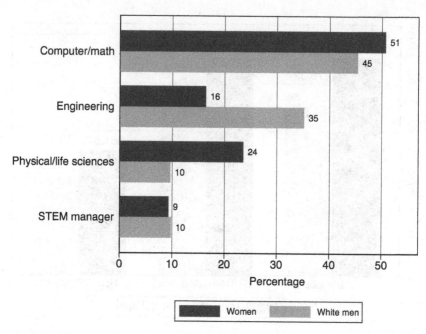

Figure 2.5
Distribution of women and non-Hispanic white men across STEM occupations, individuals age 25–64 working year-round and full-time. *Source:* Data from the American Community Survey, 2012–2019.

have historically (and disproportionately) dominated the conventional STEM workforce, making them de facto representatives of STEM work. We focus on non-Hispanic white men to avoid the confounding effects of ethnicity and circumvent any effects the inclusion of Hispanic/Latino men might have on the wages for non-Hispanic white men: Hispanic/Latino men are a relatively small part of the STEM workforce but experience a pay gap of a meaningful 16 percentage points relative to non-Hispanic white men in STEM.

Figure 2.5 presents the distribution of women and non-Hispanic white men across the four occupational groupings for conventional STEM work. Just over half (51 percent) of women working full-time in STEM careers are in the computer/math fields; this is true for 45 percent of white men. White men are more likely to be in engineering than women (35 percent compared to 16 percent), and women make up their shortfall in engineering by greater participation in the physical and life sciences. About 10 percent of both groups are in the STEM managerial positions.

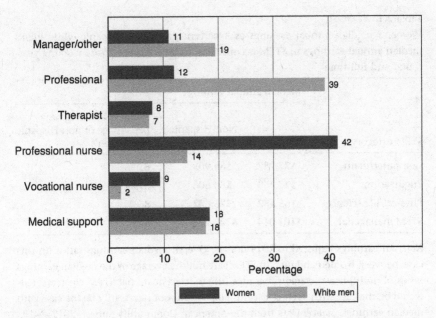

Figure 2.6
Distribution of women and non-Hispanic white men across STEM-related occupations, individuals age 25–64 working year-round and full-time. *Source:* Data from the American Community Survey, 2012–2019.

The distribution of women and non-Hispanic white men across STEM-related fields is shown in figure 2.6, which indicates that 39 percent of white men are in the professional fields while only 12 percent of women are in these jobs. As expected, women in STEM-related jobs most often choose nursing careers: 42 percent are in professional nursing, and another 9 percent are in vocational nursing. Men are far less likely to be in nursing: 14 percent of men in STEM-related fields are professional nurses, and only 2 percent are vocational nurses. Roughly equal percentages of women and men are in medical support and work as therapists. Figure 2.6 also shows that bars with equivalent numbers are not always the exact same length. This is because we round to the nearest whole number. Instances of this can be seen on occasion throughout this book.

How does all of this play out in terms of comparative earnings? Table 2.1 breaks down median earnings for women compared to non-Hispanic white men within conventional STEM categories. As a baseline, the overall wage ratio of all women working year-round and full-time to all men working

Table 2.1

Women's median annual earnings as a percentage of non-Hispanic white men's median annual earnings in STEM occupations, individuals age 25–64 working year-round and full-time

| STEM category | Median annual earnings | | Women's earnings as a percentage of non-Hispanic white men's |
	Women	Non-Hispanic white men	
Computer/math	$77,782	$89,903	87%
Engineering	$77,288	$88,606	87%
Physical/life sciences	$65,382	$75,632	86%
STEM managerial	$101,014	$120,226	84%

Note: All earnings adjusted to 2019 dollars. Overall median earnings ratios (in this case, between women and men in STEM) are not the average of the median earnings ratios of multiple associated subgroups (the four occupational STEM clusters). This would be the case with average earnings but would not necessarily be the case with median earnings. *Source:* Data from the American Community Survey, 2012–2019.

year-round and full-time is 80 percent. Within STEM jobs, women earn 84 percent of what non-Hispanic white men earn.

The message here is both clear and important: when we compare women working in conventional STEM to women who do not work in those fields (the STEM premium), we see the advantages of STEM work for women. But when we shift the comparison and compare women working in conventional STEM to non-Hispanic white men in those fields, we see that *these women lag significantly behind these men with a wage gap that always exceeds 10 percent regardless of STEM field.* The economic engine of STEM work fails to bring women's median earnings to parity with men's, a fact that undermines some of the stories told about STEM work.

What is the case for STEM-related work? While the overall percentage of women in STEM-related occupations surpasses that of men (because so many women are in these jobs), a close examination of pay indicates that for some STEM-related occupations women fare even more poorly relative to white men. Overall, women's median earnings in STEM-related jobs are 75 percent of men's STEM-related earnings. This again underscores that when we compare women to other women (in this case, in STEM-related work compared to non-STEM-related work), the former do quite well. When compared to non-Hispanic white men, they fall short.

Table 2.2
Women's median annual earnings as a percentage of non-Hispanic white men's median annual earnings in STEM-related occupations, individuals age 25–64 working year-round and full-time

STEM-related category	Median annual earnings		Women's earnings as a percentage of non-Hispanic white men's
	Women	Non-Hispanic white men	
Manager/other	$65,386	$86,437	76%
Professional	$110,757	$168,350	66%
Therapist	$66,454	$76,327	87%
Professional nurse	$70,230	$75,761	93%
Vocational nurse	$41,416	$45,457	91%
Medical support	$43,615	$53,635	81%

Note: All earnings adjusted to 2019 dollars. *Source:* Data from the American Community Survey, 2012–2019.

Table 2.2 also indicates the substantially broad spectrum of job types—and consequent strong variations in wages—associated with STEM-related work. This differentiates STEM-related work from the conventional STEM jobs, which are not as dramatically different from each other in job type and pay. The highest-paid occupation in the STEM-related group for both women and white men is the medical professional occupations, which are heavily dominated by men (see figure 2.3). Within these occupations, women earn only 66 percent of what men earn. This is a difference in annual median earnings of nearly $58,000, an amount that exceeds the median annual earnings (for both men and women) in the two lowest-paid STEM-related categories of vocational nursing and medical support.

Perhaps predictably, women do relatively well in the professional nursing category, earning 91 percent of what white non-Hispanic men earn. Women are well represented in nursing professions (see figure 2.3, which illustrates that more than 80 percent of nurses are women), but their stronger earnings are likely partially due to the unusually strong presence of unions in this field. In 2019, 18.3 percent of registered nurses and 11.5 percent of licensed practical and licensed vocational nurses were covered by union contracts. As a comparison, in that same year, 11.6 percent of the total US workforce was covered by a union contract (Hirsch and Macpherson

2003, updated 2019). Unions tend to have more rigid pay structures and more transparency around wages, leaving less room for individual decision making with regards to salary (Fins, Heydemann, and Tucker 2021).

Even when we take the strong variations across STEM-related work into account, the overall wider pay gap experienced by women in STEM-related work is sobering and instructive. In STEM-related work, women experience a pay gap even more severe than the pay gap that exists for them generally in the workforce. This fact signals that, despite the dominant presence of women overall, the world of STEM-related work is not characterized by pay equity.

What's Ahead: Intersectional Case Studies for Women in STEM Work

When analyzed across the gender binary, STEM wages are fundamentally inequitable. In no conventional STEM or STEM-related occupational grouping do the median annual salaries of women reach those of men, a pattern that holds for jobs where women are strongly represented (such as computer/math work) and jobs where women dominate outright (such as nursing). The data also show that when it comes to occupational distribution, women and men trend toward different kinds of STEM and STEM-related jobs. In short, both the wages and the work of women in STEM differ greatly from men in STEM.

As revealing as it is, however, this gender-centered analysis is also incomplete. Looking at STEM work and wages solely through the lens of the gender binary masks the effects of the many significant differences that exist among people who identify as women. It is in this context that we now direct our efforts toward an intersectional economic analysis of how gender intersects with other salient aspects of identity to shape the economic story for women in STEM work. In the eight case studies that follow (chapters 3 through 10), we engage in critically informed intersectional analysis to unmask what is hidden by a gender-binary–only approach.

The eight case studies in *Disparate Measures* explore the interface of gender (identifying as a woman) with an array of identities both well-established and emergent. In the US, demographic data are commonly collected and made available around five standard racial/ethnic groupings—White, Black, American Indian/Alaska Native, Asian/Pacific Islander, and Hispanic/Latina. As the data stories we provide for the four non-White identity categories demonstrate, these categories are shifting products of politics and power and have substantially changed over time. They do not represent US racial and ethnic diversity in any comprehensive, objective, or coherent way. They also comprise the grouping women of color, an amalgamation we have prioritized for closer exploration. The goal of exploring intersections of gender with race, racism, ethnicity, and ethnocentrism is at the heart of our work.

Emergent categories reflect identities that are also consistently and routinely subject to forms of bias and structural injustice but that do not have comparable data histories or STEM-specific workforce literatures. The four identity groupings we have selected for intersectional analysis—foreign-born status, disability, lesbian/bisexual/trans/gender-nonconforming identities, and motherhood—are less well-established in both survey instruments and STEM diversity work. Some of these groups—lesbians, bisexual women, trans women, and mothers—are fundamentally gendered in that they are comprised only of people who identify as women. But these identities are not truly new. Rather, they have more recently become recognized as identity groups worthy of protection or as groups on which data may be collected and research conducted.

In accordance with the theoretical and methodological parameters of intersectional economic analysis outlined in chapter 1, every case study in this book briefly overviews how each identity has evolved as a demographic category in the US. This process reveals the constructedness of the categories themselves, showing how the collection of data on these groups has unfolded as a social act and not as the recording of a natural fact. Second, we review the current research on forms of STEM workplace discrimination and bias associated with each identity group. These two steps place each intersection in a context that reveals some of the key asymmetries of power that circulate around and through it. Only after establishing this context do we use quantitative data to compare occupational distributions and wages across conventional STEM and STEM-related work for each intersectional group of women.

The identity-specific contexts we develop not only provide a critical framework for our intersectional data but also help us identify additional intersections that are salient for every group in question. For example, because of the importance of nation-specific affiliations for Native people (what the ACS terms tribal identities), we intersectionally explore STEM participation and wage differences for Native women who belong to the Cherokee and the Navajo nations. Because the research on disability in the workplace shows that the experience of ableism is strongly affected by disability type (in ACS terms, cognitive disabilities compared to physical disabilities), we examine the differences between the occupational distribution and wages for women with cognitive disabilities in STEM and women with physical disabilities in STEM. These kinds of case-specific intersectional explorations take the economic analysis of women in STEM work into new and important territory.

This contextualized approach makes each case study unique. Even as we have sought to reveal the contingent nature of identity categories and explore different points of intersection for different groups, we have also made these eight case studies consistent relative to the data itself. Our data consistently focus on women age twenty-five to sixty-four who work full-time and year-round. We use the American Community Survey whenever possible and merge the same years of data (2012 to 2019) in order to provide adequate sample sizes. In every case, we offer a picture of the job distribution of women in both conventional STEM and STEM-related work using the same occupational clusters. And when we establish the median wages of women in conventional STEM and STEM-related jobs, we use non-Hispanic white men as our main comparison group in every case. All these shared characteristics stabilize our data across many different examples, lending maximum coherence to these eight very different case studies and making cross-case comparisons possible.

It is our hope that our readers will consider and appreciate the uniqueness and particularities of every one of the following intersectional case studies for women in conventional STEM and STEM-related work. Each renders visible the roles of history and power across identities that are rarely acknowledged in terms of the STEM workforce—or any workforce. We are hopeful that readers will also be inspired to read and think across case studies and will compare and contrast the data and analyses we offer. In every intersectional comparison we make, our goals are to challenge others to reconsider the familiar narratives of STEM opportunity, raise more incisive questions about different groups of women in the STEM workplace, and inspire further research.

3 Black Women in STEM

Who Is Black in the US?

In many ways, the category of Black functions as ground zero for the question of who is counted by whom—and how and why—in the United States. As a perfect example of how identities, data, power, and politics drive each other, the origin of the US census itself lies at the center of this identity category, marking where an emerging representative democracy intersects with the legal enslavement of (some) people. The straightforward, data-driven ethos of the US Constitution's three-fifths compromise (the 1787 agreement to include three-fifths of the enslaved population in calculations used to seat the first House of Representatives) offers grim testimony about how racial categories and data shape and are shaped by distributions of power, political forces, and social hierarchies (including other races). In thinking about the data associated with Black people in the US, especially Black women, this first measure of the US Black population tells a story of demographically shaped, data-driven racialized violence and dehumanization that echoes powerfully today.

The journey from the three-fifths compromise to the 2020 decennial census category of Black or African American is a long one, and it involves more than two centuries of political, cultural, and scholarly debates about identity categories, race, and Blackness (Pew Research Center 2020). A considerable amount of scholarship has focused on the morphing census category of Black, forming a substantial body of historical-critical work on this important topic (Davis 2010; Guterl 2009; Nobles 2000; Prewitt 2013; Schor 2017; Strmic-Pawl, Jackson, and Garner 2018). For a case study like this one, which uses census data to examine the experiences of a specific Black population, it is necessary to acknowledge that the roots of the American democratic system and related demographic endeavors are planted in the genocidal practices of kidnapping, enslaving, and trading Black people and in all the abusive practices and carnage associated with those activities and their aftermath. The first demographic data for Blacks in the US reflect a foundational, entrenched commitment to denying Black people full humanity while securing the supremacy of white-identified people.

And for a long time, US census demography served as a powerful partner in this larger enterprise. Given its origins, it is unsurprising that for much of the history of the census, racial classification efforts focused powerfully on "controlling people of color and protecting Whiteness" (Strmic-Pawl, Jackson, and Garner 2018, 1). As part of the work of "controlling people of color," early census demography was also conducted in concert with settler colonial processes of racially categorizing Native people, a group whose unstable relationship to the project of a Black/white divide has its own (complex and also connected) history (see chapter 4). The racial history of Native people in the US therefore unfolds alongside and closely in relation to changing ideas about Blackness (Wolfe 2016).

Looking at the census and expanding out from the single original category of slave (in use from 1790 until 1840), the census offered its first descriptors of Blacks as people and not property in 1805. At that point, while the institution of slavery continued to shape the categories (Black and Black slave), additional new categories (such as mulatto) marked the beginning of the racial taxonomies that would replace slave as a racial identity. After emancipation, census categories multiplied as degree of Blackness became the point of focus. This peaked with the categories "black, mulatto, quadroon, octoroon" in 1890, signaling the escalating efforts of a society fixated on managing Blackness relative to whiteness.

At the turn of the century, obsessive management of racial categories in the service of constructing a society hierarchized through racial differences shifted from the proliferation of new categories to the one-drop concept (the state of Tennessee adopted the first one-drop legislation in 1910). The one-drop rule—that those individuals with any Black ancestry must be formally categorized as Black—determined Black identity through the principle of hypodescent, elevating whiteness as a monoracial form of absolute difference and purity (Davis 2010). The one-drop rule was far more efficient than the ongoing production and maintenance of many new nonwhite census identities such as mulatto, octoroon, and so on. It became a powerful mechanism articulated via the Jim Crow laws that structured and enforced American racial apartheid/segregation, primarily in the US South. In addition, the ongoing cultural and legal fixation with delineating Black racial identity relative to white identity cut across and affected other racial groupings. For example, the one-drop rule essentially erased the Native identities of Black Native people by automatically and unequivocally categorizing them as (only) Black.

Since the mid-twentieth century, the US census has moved slowly but surely toward another way of conceptualizing race categories. As Karen Humes and Howard Hogan note (2009, 118), in 1950 the Bureau of the Census publicly stated that the "concept of race as it has been used by the Bureau of the Census is derived from that which is commonly accepted by the general public. It does not, therefore, reflect clear-cut definitions of biological stock, and several categories obviously refer to nationalities." The waning of the one-drop rule and its focus on biology signaled a change in which race was slowly becoming understood to be a form of personal and cultural identity. In 1960, the census ceased the practice of officially imposing racial categories via trained census enumerators. Since then, respondents have answered race-related questions themselves by either choosing from the available racial identities or describing themselves under the other race option. The effect of the civil rights movement on the official collection of race-related data is apparent, as well. In 1973, the US Commission on Civil Rights pondered the value of such data, stating "racial and ethnic classification can be justified only if the data produced have a legitimate use in terms of combating discrimination, planning programs, or conducting program evaluation" (Graae 1973, 38).

The use of Blackness as a category at once both definitionally necessary for and deeply threatening to whiteness has nonetheless persisted. The fundamental primacy of the Black/white dyad is reflected in the fact that the US census has revised the ways it categorizes people who are both Black and white more than any other group in its history (Brown 2020). Despite profound shifts in the meaning of race as a census category (from a biological to a cultural category) and a documented increase in more careful thinking about what it means to collect racial data, government interest in maintaining whiteness as a single category persisted until the beginning of the twenty-first century. Not until the year 2000 did the decennial census finally allow respondents to select multiple racial identities.

The issue of Black identity itself continues to remain in motion on the census. The relatively new term *African American* (which was subject to much debate within the Black community as its use became more widespread in the later 1980s) was included in 2000 when the category description was redefined as Black, African American, or Negro (Pew Research Center 2020; Wilkerson 1989). The term *Negro*, which first entered the census in 1930, was removed in 2020 (Pew Research Center 2020). Also in 2020, in an unprecedented change, the census asked for additional data from respondents identifying as Black or African American via a new text box with the instructions "Print, for example, African American, Jamaican, Haitian, Nigerian, Ethiopian, Somali, etc." This expansion of the census race question has yet again changed the category of Black, potentially mixing ethnic and national identities into the (already unstable) category of race. Unsurprisingly, given the historically codependent/oppositional relationship of Black and white, a similar text box—using different examples—was concurrently added to the category white. It remains to be seen what effects these additions to the census might have on our understandings of race, Blackness, whiteness, and other identity categories.

The story of the census category Black is sobering and powerful, and it readily demonstrates the ways in which identity categories—and the data associated with them—both create and reflect social hierarchies. It is also a reminder that as we now turn toward the current data on the Black population generally and on Black women specifically, we are examining a snapshot that uses categories that are specific to our contemporary moment and still subject to (often unacknowledged) decisions about both terms and parameters. And as we see again in the most recent census, data associated with the category Black (or any racial identity) will likely morph again in the future as categories and the collection of related data continue their inevitable process of change.

American Community Survey (ACS) data indicate that 13.5 percent of the US population identified as Black in 2019. Although distinctly a minority group, the US Black population is significantly larger than the other racial populations explicitly enumerated by the census, excluding whites. In 2019, Asians comprised 6.7 percent and American Indian/Alaska Natives 1.4 percent of the US population. In all of these percentages, we have counted all respondents who identified with a particular group, including those who selected multiple racial identities. In addition, our calculations regarding the Black population—as well as our calculations throughout this case study—do not include Blacks who also identify as Hispanic. In order to avoid the confounding effects of race and ethnicity, we focus on non-Hispanic Blacks. In 2019, 5 percent of the Black population identified as both Black and Hispanic, and Hispanic Blacks are also subject to the personal, social, and economic effects of anti-Black racism (Holder and Aja 2021). This smaller population is included in chapter 6, Hispanic Women/Latinas in STEM.

Despite an historically obsessive interest in Blackness, the ACS does not effectively capture the Black population. People who identify as Black are chronically undercounted—and while the US Census Bureau officially designates all racial and ethnic minorities as "hard to count," Black people have typically fared the worst among US communities of color (Hale 2020; National Urban League 2020). In 2012, the Census Bureau itself estimated that the 2010 decennial census "undercounted 2.1 percent of the Black population," a number similar to the 2000 census undercount of Black people (estimated at 1.8 percent) (US Bureau of the Census 2012a, 2012b). Recent reexaminations of the 2010 census suggest that the undercount was more severe than officially estimated and that as many as 3.7 million Black people may have been overlooked (Edney 2020). As predicted by both demographers and census activists (Elliott et al. 2019; Owens 2020; Schuster, Osherov, and Chung 2020), the combined effects of the COVID-19 pandemic and census interference and obstruction by the Trump administration further amplified the Black undercount in the 2020 decennial census (now estimated at 3.3 percent) (Khubba, Heim, and Hong 2022).

Along with being consistently undercounted, the US Black population is also distinguished by the presence of a small but demographically significant foreign-born Black population: almost 10 percent of non-Hispanic Blacks reported being foreign-born in 2019. This population has also been steadily growing over the last several decades and has increased fivefold since 1980 (Anderson and López 2018). In terms of broadly defined origin areas, about half of the 2019 foreign-born Black population in the US originated in Latin America. Immigration from Africa has more than doubled over the last two decades, however, and African immigrants accounted for 47 percent of the foreign-born Black population in that year. As we consider Black women in STEM work, it is worth noting that 61 percent of the foreign-born Black population held US citizenship in 2019, compared to 51 percent of other immigrants, and the group is also more likely to be English-speaking than other immigrant groups.

The presence of a foreign-born Black population also helps explain the nomenclature of this case study and our preferred use of the term *Black*. Given that the number of foreign-born Black people living in the US is growing and not all US-born Blacks have African ancestry, *African American* cannot serve as an accurate term for all Black-identified people living in the US or even for all Blacks born in the US (see Agyemang et al. 2005 and Simms 2018 for a longitudinal look at usages of the terms *African American* and *Black*). Therefore, when describing data associated with Blacks born in the US, we continue to use the term *US-born* rather than *African American*. This level of inclusivity is critical not only because it is more accurate but also because the anti-Black racism that drives systemic discrimination is experienced by all Black people living and working in the US, regardless of their place of birth. And this population also includes many individuals outside our particular sample (for example, Hispanic-identified Blacks, a group that is addressed in chapter 6).

As we look at Black women's current participation in US STEM fields, we do so in a context that acknowledges the constructed nature of racial categories in general and the specific characteristics of Black as a US census category at this moment in time. The current census data on Black women have the following distinctive attributes: the data are (1) *self-selected* (the category is chosen by the individual in question, as all US census racial categories have been since 1960), (2) *racialized* (the category is understood as a distinctly racial identity, as opposed to an ethnicity, such as Hispanic), (3) *relatively substantial in size* (the category is the largest population among nonwhite racial groups), (4) highly likely to be *undercounted* by the census, (5) *strongly linked to US-born status* (about 91 percent of non-Hispanic Blacks reported being born in the United States in 2019), and (6) characterized by a relatively *small but growing foreign-born population*.

Black Women in the US Labor Force

Any responsible analysis of Black women in the US labor force must begin by acknowledging that systemic disadvantage and discrimination have always been central to Black women's working experience in the US, regardless of occupation. The literature makes clear that the history of Black women in the US workforce has been molded by a complex system of entrenched disadvantages (Harley et al. 2002; Jones 2009; Wallace 1980). The development of the US economy itself is tightly linked to forms of anti-Black racism and discrimination that have characterized US history more broadly, and the modern workforce emerged not only from industrial and entrepreneurial innovations but also out of stratification patterns shaped by the social fault lines of gender and race (among other categories). In this context, Black women's labor story is historically and currently specific to Black women as Black women—not only as women or women of color. As Joan Acker (2013, 117) argues, "Women from different racial and ethnic groups were incorporated differently than men and differently than each other into developing capitalism." Ever since Black women entered the labor force, they have encountered what labor historian Jacqueline Jones (2010, 2) describes as "a fundamentally different kind of prejudice, compared to their white counterparts."

The complex intersectional disadvantages experienced by Black women have come with persistent and often devastating economic effects. The experience of work is negatively compromised for Black women in many ways—overt and implicit anti-Black racism, sexism, microaggressions, tokenism, marginalization, job segregation, negative stereotypes, sexual harassment, and other forms of discrimination and bias—that have been and remain routine parts of the workplace experiences of Black women (Catalyst 2004; Mays, Coleman, and Jackson 1996; McKinsey & Company and LeanIn. org 2019; Reskin 1999). Studies show that these findings are consistent for Black women pursuing and working in STEM fields, as well (Bywater et al. 2017; Gutiérrez y Muhs et al. 2012; McGee and Bentley 2017). The economic consequences of these patterns are grim. As Nina Banks (2019) summarizes, "The black woman's experience in America provides arguably the most overwhelming evidence of the persistent and ongoing drag from gender and race discrimination on the economic fate of workers and families." This "overwhelming evidence" is that Black women's paid work experiences have been both systemically compromised and intersectionally shaped at the core and that Black women's disadvantages as Black women have long been both substantial and compound. This evidence also makes clear that intersectional economic analysis specific to the participation and earnings of Black women in STEM is urgently necessary.

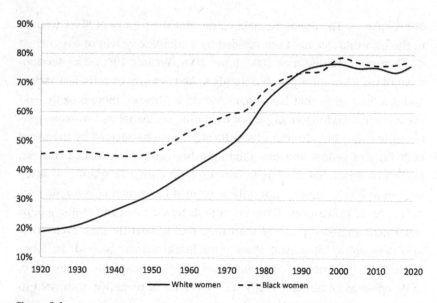

Figure 3.1
US labor-force participation rates: Black and white women age 25–54 years, 1920–2019. *Sources:* Years 1920–1970 adapted from Boustan and Collins (2015, appendix table A1); 1975–2019 from the US Bureau of Labor Statistics.

Much like the census's management of Blackness relative to whiteness via changing racial categories, the availability of labor-force participation data for Black women similarly testifies to the management and surveillance of Blackness and Black people as a matter of long-standing official interest in the US. Ongoing data collection focused on any specific group illustrates the important ideological work performed by that category, and the exceptionally lengthy availability of data on Black workers highlights the role that Blackness and its dependent partner whiteness have played in defining racial identity, experiences, and hierarchies. Figure 3.1 provides a look at Black women's US labor-participation rates over the last hundred years. We have employed Leah Boustan and William J. Collins's (2015) historical data combined with data from the US Bureau of Labor Statistics to provide a century-long snapshot of Black women's labor-force participation and capture a longitudinal yet reasonably contemporary view.

When we examine Black women's modern work participation in the US labor force over the past century, it is clear that Black women have historically had consistently higher rates of labor-force participation than white women. Since the late 1970s, more than half of Black women in the US have participated in the labor force, and their overall rate of participation generally has exceeded that of white women. The reasons behind this high level of participation are not mysterious. Black women have worked at high rates because their circumstances have demanded it. Economic disadvantage and restricted opportunities have characterized Black life in the US, and Black women's survival—and the survival of Black communities—have often depended on their earnings.

The anti-Black racism that has formed the economic history of Black women and amplified their workplace participation is in part linked to patterns of economic disadvantage associated with working Black men. Historically, Black men have had higher rates of unemployment and lower earnings than white men. While it is both heterosexist and stereotypical to assume all Black women are or wish to be in partnerships with Black men, a significant number of Black women are in such relationships. For example, in 2014–2015, 88 percent of Black women in marriages or partnerships reported that their partner is a Black man (Livingston and Brown 2017). For the many Black women married to or in partnerships with Black men, the patterns of economic disadvantage experienced by many Black men have made it necessary for Black women to work (Banks 2019). The compound and persistent disadvantages experienced by many Black men in the labor force at least partially drive patterns associated with Black women's labor participation.

Working in tandem with the labor-force disadvantages of Black men are the effects of mass incarceration. Black men in the US are incarcerated at significantly greater rates than both Hispanic and white men (Gramlich 2020), a pattern that has been explicitly connected to other racialized projects of social control (Alexander 2010). This insidious, entrenched dynamic has been shown to have profoundly negative effects on Black communities and families (Pettit and Gutierrez 2018). Mass incarceration of Black men is another systemic factor in Black women's labor participation and contributes to the relatively high likelihood of Black women being household breadwinners. As of 2017, 80.6 percent of Black mothers in the US were breadwinners, meaning that they were either the sole earner or earned a minimum of 40 percent of overall household income (DuMonthier, Childers, and Milli 2017). And while there are many different kinds of single status (such as never married, separated, divorced, widowed, and partnered) and nonmarried status does not necessarily indicate the absence of a partner, Black women are also much less likely to be married compared to women from other racial or ethnic groups: in 2019, 28 percent of Black women age eighteen and over were married, compared to 56 percent of white women. The number of Black women who raise children alone is also high relative to other nonwhite racial and ethnic groups. Responsibilities connected to both breadwinner status and solo parenting often place added pressure on Black women in terms of workplace participation.

Although Black women's actual engagement in the US workplace has been (and remains) necessarily high, the rewards of that engagement have been (and remain) remarkably low (Banks 2019; Frye 2018; Matthews and Wilson 2018). There is a network of complex and intertwined factors—historical and political, social, and structural—that contribute to this fact. The paid work of Black women, both historically and currently, is disproportionately composed of low-paying, low-skill work. For example, in 2017, 28 percent of employed Black women in the US worked in service occupations, low-paying jobs that also often lack crucial benefits (DuMonthier, Childers, and Milli 2017). Black women's labor overall is strongly segregated across occupations in ways that reflect racial and gender inequalities: they are consistently "segregated into lower-paying jobs while white men are segregated into higher-paying jobs" (Matthews and Wilson 2018). Perhaps unsurprisingly, pay ratios between these groups are extreme: in 2019, non-Hispanic Black women (age twenty-five and older, working full-time and year-round) made sixty-three cents for every dollar earned by non-Hispanic white men. And even though the educational attainment of Black women has steadily increased over the past half century, that increase has been insufficient to make up for the job instability, lower wages, discrimination, and poorer benefits that plague working Black women specifically and the Black community more broadly.

Economic historian Claudia Goldin (1977, 97) attributes these grim patterns in part to the "legacy of slavery" inherited by many Blacks who were born in or who grew up in the US. The literature confirms that Blacks in the US not only experience poor labor-market outcomes but are also particularly vulnerable within the labor market (Goldin 1977; Weller 2019). The systemic discrimination and disproportional unemployment faced by many Blacks in the US is directly or indirectly rooted in centuries of unequal and reduced opportunities. After more than 150 years, enormous formal/institutionalized obstacles and informal/social barriers remain fundamental variables in the economic fortunes of many Black women in the US. These obstacles—sharecropping debt schemes, Jim Crow laws, aggressive voter suppression, racialized systems of policing and criminal justice, mass incarceration, and a culture of white supremacy shaped by both systemic anti-Black racism and denial of that racism—all combine to form the historical arc of what Tompkins has named "the never-ending afterlife of enslavement" (2021, 471). This "afterlife" is as economic as it is cultural, social, political, and institutional. And while not all people who are Black identify as African American and not all Blacks in the US are direct inheritors of US systems of slavery and Jim Crow, the culture of US anti-Black racism reaches into the experience of all Black people—African American, US-born, and foreign-born—in the US labor force.

Finally, in considering the factors related to Black women's labor, we note that a history of working (and having to work) has normalized paid work for Black women in ways that are culturally significant, making such work an integral part of many Black women's social identities (Braun, Vincent, and Ball 2008; Reynolds 2001). While the normalization of paid work does not translate into occupational opportunity or strong earnings, it may help shape labor-force participation patterns.

How do these patterns connect to the experiences of Black women working in STEM occupations? The research on Black women in STEM has two distinguishing characteristics. First, it has been historically shaped by a women-of-color approach that combines women from several nonwhite racial groups and (usually) Hispanic/Latina women. While both effective and politically necessary, this approach often folds Black women into an amalgamated cluster where intersectional patterns specific to their experience have been lost. Second, the literature on women of color in STEM has historically focused on educational fields, and therefore the research specific to Black women in STEM has done so, as well (see Ireland et al. 2018 for a review). There are now an enormous number of studies on the experiences of women of color (both students and faculty) in academic STEM. Only a few of these studies, however, attend to differences among the workplace experiences of women academic STEM professionals from different racial and ethnic groups (notably, Williams 2014).

There is also a small but emergent body of work on Black girls and women (students and faculty) in nonacademic STEM careers. These studies of Black women in STEM careers tend to focus on specific occupations—for example, studies on engineering (Ross and Godwin 2016) and artificial intelligence (Floyd 2021). This scholarship also tends to focus on coping mechanisms and shows that STEM occupations are inhospitable climates for Black women. This is not surprising: the Black population of both women and men working in STEM report high levels of race discrimination (62 percent), unfair treatment in hiring (43 percent), and reduced opportunities for advancement (37 percent) (Funk and Parker 2018).

Overall, there is not enough scholarly work focused on Black women's experiences in the STEM professions and not a robust literature on the specific and unique challenges confronting Black women working in STEM. This absence of research on Black women in STEM work is a gap that we hope this case study will inspire others to further address.

Black Women in the Conventional STEM Fields: What Do the Data Say?

As of 2019, the total percentage of non-Hispanic women (age twenty-five and over) in the US who identify as either Black (a single category) or as multiracial (with Black as one of their several selected racial categories) was 12.9 percent (in 2019, about 96 percent of Black women selected Black as their only racial identification).

According to our definition of conventional STEM, in the year 2019 there were an estimated 8.6 million individuals age twenty-five to sixty-four working full-time and year-round in STEM occupations. An estimated 231,598 of them were women who identified as Black, which was only 2.7 percent of all STEM job holders that year. Averaging across all the years of our sample and focusing on those age twenty-five to sixty-four who are working full-time and year-round reveals that only 3 percent of Black women work in STEM occupations (compared to 11 percent of white men). In addition, after adjusting for standard covariates (education, age, industry, marital status, citizen status, veteran status, and region of the country), we calculate that Black women in STEM occupations have a significant 34 percent wage premium over Black women who do not work in STEM fields. Hence, although the number of Black women working in STEM fields is small overall, the STEM premium for that group is robust.

Within conventional STEM occupations, Black women's median earnings are 75 percent of non-Hispanic white men's, a considerable jump since

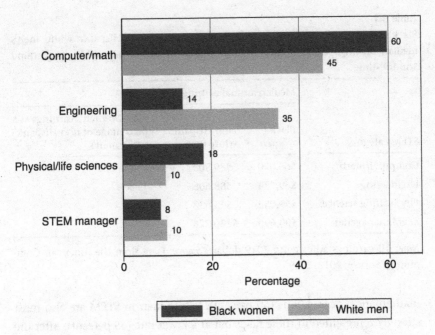

Figure 3.2
Distribution of Black women and non-Hispanic white men across STEM occupations, individuals age 25 to 64 working full-time and year-round. *Source:* Data from the American Community Survey, 2012–2019.

across all occupations, Black women earn only 63 percent of what non-Hispanic white men earn. That said, however, within STEM, Black women's median earnings as a percentage of non-Hispanic white men's median earnings (75 percent) remain less than the ratio of median earnings of all women relative to all men (80 percent). There can be no doubt that STEM occupations provide an economic advantage for Black women relative to other Black women, but this advantage highlights the substantial wage lag under which Black women labor overall.

Having established our parameters, we now dig deeper into the data and compare the distribution of Black women with the distribution of (non-Hispanic) white men in conventional STEM. Figure 3.2 represents how Black women and white men in STEM are distributed across four broad categories of STEM work. As figure 3.2 shows, Black women and white men are distributed across the conventional STEM fields in markedly different ways. Black women in conventional STEM are concentrated in the computing/

Table 3.1

Black women's median earnings as a percentage of non-Hispanic white men's median earnings in STEM occupations, individuals age 25–64 working year-round and full-time

STEM category	Median annual earnings		
	Black women	Non-Hispanic white men	Black women's earnings as a percentage of non-Hispanic white men's
Computer/math	$68,070	$89,903	76%
Engineering	$69,774	$88,606	79%
Physical/life sciences	$59,058	$75,632	78%
STEM managerial	$90,696	$120,226	75%

Note: All earnings adjusted to 2019 dollars. *Source:* Data from the American Community Survey, 2012–2019.

mathematical occupations (60 percent). White men in STEM are also most strongly represented in these fields but at a lower rate (45 percent). After the computer/math fields, Black women are most strongly represented in the physical and life sciences (18 percent), whereas white men in these fields are a relatively low 10 percent. One of the most striking differences in these STEM occupational distribution patterns is in engineering: 35 percent of white men are engineers, whereas only 14 percent of Black women work in these jobs. Conversely, Black women and white men participate at similar rates in the STEM management occupations (8 percent and 10 percent, respectively).

What can be learned from patterns of conventional STEM employment when it comes to median earnings? Table 3.1 indicates that Black women's disadvantages hold across all STEM occupational groupings, regardless of whether they are strongly distributed in an area of conventional STEM work. For example, Black women are obviously disadvantaged by being less represented in engineering, given the relatively high incomes associated with that field: the median earnings of engineers who are white men is $88,606 while the median earnings of Black woman engineers is $69,774, which is 79 percent of white men's earnings. This median wage difference costs Black women in engineering almost $20,000 annually. Even when Black women and white men are similarly distributed in high-paying STEM occupations—for example, in STEM management fields—the same pay ratio emerges (75 percent).

The data on conventional STEM fields tell us that Black women are distributed across groupings of conventional STEM occupations in ways that are different from white men in STEM. When we look at Black women's earnings relative to white men's, however, regardless of the STEM occupational grouping, Black women's earnings consistently fall short of white men's by a little over 20 percentage points in every category. Black women in STEM may fare better than Black women outside of STEM, but they do not do as well as non-Hispanic white men in STEM, regardless of STEM occupation.

Black Women in the STEM-Related Fields: What Do the Data Say?

In 2019, there were an estimated 7.3 million individuals age twenty-five to sixty-four working full-time and year-round in STEM-related jobs, and about 733,950 of them identified as Black women. Over the period of our sample and again focusing on those age twenty-five to sixty-four who work year-round and full-time, we find that only 3.6 percent of non-Hispanic white men work in these occupations. However, about 11 percent of Black women are employed in these jobs (as opposed to 3 percent in conventional STEM). While the STEM premium is a normative and often cited measure of how conventional STEM careers benefit women in any given identity group, the concept of a STEM-related premium is new. When we calculate a STEM-related premium for Black women (which compares earnings in STEM-related occupations to non-STEM occupations while controlling for conventional STEM work), we see that Black women in STEM-related jobs earn 28 percent more than Black women not working in conventional STEM or STEM-related fields. Because our version of a STEM-related premium does not include conventional STEM work, it provides a meaningful snapshot of the significant economic benefits that STEM-related work provides Black women. Figure 3.3 illustrates the distribution of Black women and white men over the six STEM-related occupational groupings.

As is often the case with women in STEM-related work, the nursing professions comprise a significant part of the story for Black women in this economy. Together, vocational and professional nursing work accounts for just short of 60 percent of Black women's participation in STEM-related jobs, with participation in professional nursing making up about two-thirds overall. White men in STEM-related jobs are not strongly distributed in the professional nursing category (14 percent), and they are unlikely to be vocational

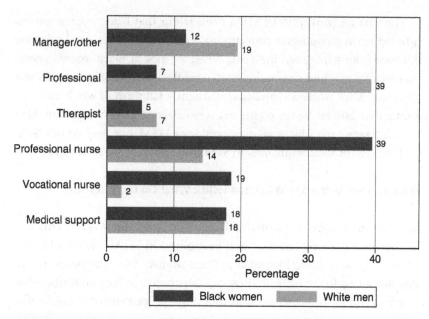

Figure 3.3
Distribution of Black women and non-Hispanic white men across STEM-related occupations, individuals age 25–64 working year-round and full-time. *Source:* Data from the American Community Survey, 2012–2019.

nurses (2 percent). Another area of difference between white men and Black women is STEM-related management, with white men working in these jobs at a higher rate than Black women (19 percent compared to 12 percent). Finally, it is notable that white men are much more likely to be medical professionals than Black women (39 percent compared to 7 percent).

In terms of median incomes (table 3.2), nursing occupations are where Black women's earnings come closest to parity with white men. However, even though well more than half of Black women in STEM-related fields are in some form of nursing work, this group nonetheless experiences significant pay gaps relative to white men: 11 percent in professional nursing and 9 percentage points in vocational nursing. It is sobering to note that the white men who are vocational nurses earn larger median salaries than the Black women who work in that field, despite white men's low distribution in that area (2 percent). The data story of nursing indicates that Black women are systemically and substantially disadvantaged in terms of earnings in the STEM-related fields in which they are most likely to work.

Table 3.2
Black women's median earnings as a percentage of non-Hispanic white men's median earnings in STEM-related occupations, individuals age 25–64 working year-round and full-time

STEM-related category	Median annual earnings		Black women's earnings as a percentage of non-Hispanic white men's
	Black women	Non-Hispanic white men	
Manager/other	$54,023	$86,437	62%
Professional	$95,925	$168,350	57%
Therapist	$61,062	$76,327	80%
Professional nurse	$67,636	$75,761	89%
Vocational nurse	$41,258	$45,457	91%
Medical support	$40,791	$53,635	76%

Note: All earnings adjusted to 2019 dollars. *Source:* Data from the American Community Survey, 2012–2019.

Even more substantial differences in wages appear when we compare Black women and white men across the STEM-related management positions and the high-paying medical professional categories. In the management occupations, Black women make 62 percent of what white men earn. That adds up to a loss in annual median salary of more than $30,000 for Black women in these jobs. In the highest-paying category of medical professional, where white men are distributed much more strongly than Black women (39 percent compared to 7 percent), we see an even uglier earnings picture. Black women earn a mere 57 cents for every dollar earned by white men in these remunerative jobs and experience a relative $70,000 loss of annual median salary. Overall, the data tells a grim story when it comes to what STEM-related work really offers to promote the economic success of Black women.

Stopping at an Intersection: Foreign-Born Black Women in STEM

As is noted at the beginning of this case study, the census category of Black has numerous distinguishing characteristics. Notable among these is that category's often implicit amalgamation of US-born Black populations with all foreign-born Blacks living in the US. While Black can be selected in the census by US-born Black women, it can also be selected by women who are foreign-born and who are likely less directly connected to US-specific contexts that impact the lifelong experience of many US-born Black women. And while a relatively small segment of our sample of Black women in STEM is foreign-born (10 percent in 2019), the presence of foreign-born Black women in the US is growing as the overall population of foreign-born Blacks in the US increases (Anderson and López 2018).

We turn here to the intersection of Blackness with nativity status and the ways in which the data generated by the category Black women in STEM may be intersectionally complicated by the unrecognized variable of foreign-born status. Unless they arrived in the US as children, foreign-born Black women's life experiences are differently impacted by the culturally specific disadvantages and intersectional effects of US racism and sexism. This does not mean that foreign-born women are exempt from forms of racism, sexism, and related systemic disadvantages, including fallout from US colonialist practices. In addition, regardless of their many divergent backgrounds, foreign-born Black women are subject to systemic anti-Black racism as well as possible xenophobia while living and working in the US. But what does it mean if 10 percent of the women who generate the data for Black women working in STEM are not born in the US? What is the data story for the (very heterogeneous) group of Black women hidden within the data on Black women in US STEM occupations?

An estimated 22,966 foreign-born Black women age twenty-five to sixty-four working year-round and full-time worked in conventional STEM fields in 2019. Averaging over all the years of our sample, 31 percent of foreign-born Black women in STEM were born in Latin America, 57 percent were born in Africa, and an additional 7 percent were born in Europe. Overall, foreign-born Black women are distributed very similarly to their US-born counterparts when it comes to STEM occupations (figure 3.4). The percentage of US-born Black women in computer/math fields is slightly higher than the percentage of foreign-born Black women in these same occupations. The converse is true for the physical/life sciences. The likelihood of being in the relatively lucrative engineering fields is about the same for both US-born and foreign-born Black women, and they are also equally likely to work in STEM management.

When we examine STEM median earnings, as shown in table 3.3, some differences emerge: foreign-born Black women have a slightly higher

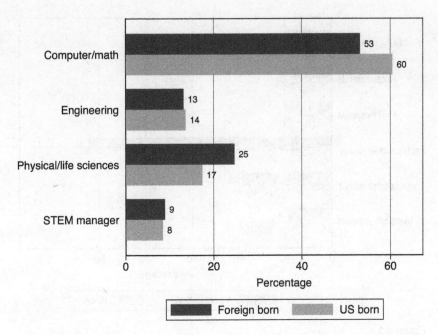

Figure 3.4
Distribution of foreign-born and US-born Black women across STEM occupations, individuals age 25–64 working year-round and full-time. *Source:* Data from the American Community Survey, 2012–2019.

Table 3.3
Foreign-born Black women's median earnings as a percentage of US-born Black women's median earnings in STEM occupations, individuals age 25–64 working year-round and full-time

	Median annual earnings		
STEM category	Foreign-born Black women	US-born Black women	Foreign-born Black women's earnings as a percentage of US-born Black women's
Computer/math	$69,774	$67,636	103%
Engineering	$77,529	$69,603	111%
Physical/life sciences	$59,809	$59,058	101%
STEM manager	$86,437	$90,913	95%

Note: All earnings adjusted to 2019 dollars. *Source:* Data from the American Community Survey, 2012–2019.

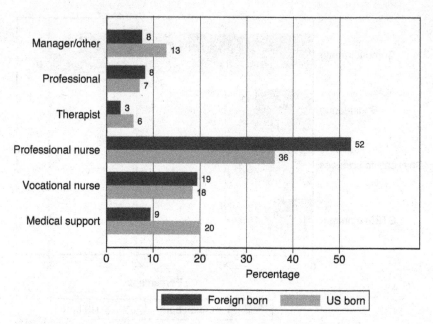

Figure 3.5
Distribution of foreign-born and US-born Black women across STEM-related occupations, individuals age 25–64 working year-round and full-time. *Source:* Data from the American Community Survey, 2012–2019.

median earnings ratio than US-born women in the computer and math fields (about 3 percentage points) and markedly higher earnings in engineering jobs (about 11 percentage points). Median earnings for foreign-born Black women and US-born Black women are about equal in the physical and life sciences, while US-born Black women experience higher median earnings in the high-paying STEM management occupations, where they outearn foreign-born Black women by about 5 percentage points. This is the only conventional STEM area in which the average median salaries of US-born Black women meaningfully exceed those of foreign-born Black women.

While fully 10 percent of women working in the conventional STEM fields were foreign-born and Black, this percentage doubles in the STEM-related fields. A look at the distribution of foreign-born and US-born black women across the STEM-related fields (figure 3.5) reveals several differences between the distributions of these groups and some significant patterns.

More than half of foreign-born Black women in STEM-related fields work as professional nurses (see figure 3.5), whereas only 36 percent of US-born Black women are in the professional nursing occupations. This strong representation of foreign-born workers in the professional nursing field overall may be attributable to the ongoing shortage of registered nurses in the US (England 2015). Figure 3.5 illustrates how, when combined under the umbrella category of Black, the combined percentage of foreign-born Black women plus US-born Black women in the STEM-related fields who are nurses is almost 40 percent. Looking at US and foreign-born Black women separately reveals a meaningful difference between their nursing participation rates that reshapes the overall picture for Black women in STEM-related work.

The disproportionate representation of US-born Black women in the medical-support fields also stands out among these occupational distribution patterns. One in five US-born Black women with STEM-related jobs works in these occupations. Jobs in this category (which include medical technologists and technicians as well as medical records specialists) are among the lowest-paying occupations in STEM-related work. Less than 10 percent of foreign-born Black women in STEM-related fields work in these relatively low-paying professions, and when they do, they experience a 15 percentage point earnings advantage over US-born Black women (table 3.4). This earnings difference calculates to an annual advantage of $6,000 for foreign-born Black women who work in medical support—a significant economic plus for these lower-paying jobs.

Table 3.4 shows that foreign-born Black women have a powerful, consistent economic advantage over US-born Black women in all of the STEM-related fields, with an average earnings advantage of 14 percentage points across all six categories of STEM-related work. Their strong participation in professional nursing work is a particular benefit, as that category is the second-highest-paying category within STEM-related fields. When we look at the most lucrative STEM-related work (medical professionals), we see that for those in STEM-related fields, Black women born abroad are as likely to be medical professionals as their US-born counterparts—8 percent and 7 percent, respectively. However, there are considerable earnings differences: foreign-born Black women who are medical professionals have median earnings of $107,345, giving them a significant advantage of 18 percentage points over their US-born counterparts who have median earnings of

Table 3.4
Foreign-born Black women's median earnings as a percentage of US-born Black women's median earnings in STEM-related occupations, individuals age 25–64 working year-round and full-time

STEM-related category	Median annual earnings		Foreign-born Black women's earnings as a percentage of US-born Black women's
	Foreign-born Black women	US-born Black women	
Manager/other	$64,407	$53,163	121%
Professional	$107,345	$91,310	118%
Therapist	$65,659	$59,825	110%
Professional nurse	$73,822	$65,659	112%
Vocational nurse	$43,690	$40,406	108%
Medical support	$46,415	$40,406	115%

Note: All earnings adjusted to 2019 dollars. *Source:* Data from the American Community Survey, 2012–2019.

$91,310. This translates to an average salary advantage of about $16,000 per year in favor of foreign-born Black women medical professionals. That said, the earnings for both groups remain appallingly low relative to white men. Medical professionals who are white men have median annual earnings of $164,478.

Case Study Highlights

The intersection we examine in this chapter focuses on nativity status.

Conventional STEM Occupations
- Only 3 percent of Black women in our sample work in STEM.
- They are poorly represented in the high-wage fields of engineering and STEM management.
- Black women do not have wage parity with white men in any area of STEM work. They average 75 percent of white men's wages in STEM management, 76 percent in computer/math jobs, 78 percent in the physical/life sciences, and 79 percent in engineering. These patterns are lower than the overall gender earnings ratio of 80 percent.

STEM-Related Occupations

- Eleven percent of Black women are employed in STEM-related jobs.

- Nursing dominates the STEM-related work of Black women, and there is tremendous job segregation in this field relative to white men.

- Pay gaps are substantial for Black women in STEM-related work, and they do not reach parity with white men in any area. Even nursing work (professional and vocational) averages only 90 percent of the wages earned by white men in nursing.

- Black women in high-paying medical professional work earn only 57 percent of white men's wages, and Black women in STEM-related management fare only marginally better at 62 percent.

Stopping at an Intersection: Nativity

- Ten percent of Black women are foreign-born.

- In conventional STEM fields, foreign-born Black women are distributed in ways similar to US-born Black women, but they generally earn more than their US-born counterparts.

- In STEM-related occupations, foreign-born Black women make higher wages than US-born Black women in every category.

- This intersection recalibrates our understanding of Black women and nursing work: in STEM-related occupations, nearly 75 percent of foreign-born Black women work in nursing compared to 56 percent of US-born Black women.

- US-born women are more likely to be in medical support compared to foreign-born Black women. This is the lowest-paying area of all STEM-related fields.

- Foreign-born Black women earn higher wages in all STEM-related categories. This intersectional analysis requires that we rethink the relationship between STEM careers and US-born Black women.

4 American Indian and Alaska Native Women in STEM

Who Is an American Indian/Alaska Native in the United States?

We begin this chapter with some important clarifications about nomenclature. As the category history below illustrates, the term *American Indian* is rooted in centuries of settler colonization, and it flattens and erases the myriad significant differences that exist across different Native communities and cultures. Even so, the term has come to be widely embraced by many Native people in the US. The term *Native American*, although viewed by many as an improvement on *American Indian*, still carries with it the colonial framework of American-ness and is not necessarily preferred by Native people themselves (Grover 2017). The term *Indigenous people*, which generally refers to Native people, also can be used, particularly in global contexts.

In thinking about the issue of language, we generally have chosen to use the terms *Native people* and *Native women* in this chapter. These terms include Native people of both the continental US and Alaska, and they do not impose a direct association with American-ness (and hence do not uncritically invoke settler colonialism). However, whenever we refer to specific data on Native women in STEM, we use the acronym *AI/AN*, which reflects the American Indian/Alaska Native terminology used by the US Census Bureau. The use of AI/AN acknowledges that we are employing Census Bureau data in our quantitative work and serves as a reminder that the Census Bureau continues to collect data under the terms *American Indian/ Alaska Native*. As part of this effort to emphasize transparency around our data and the categories on which it depends, we have also retained the term *American Indian/Alaska Native* for the chapter title and subtitles.

Just as the foundational moment for enumerating the US Black population is embedded in the notorious 1787 three-fifths compromise, the demographic history of Native people in the US is similarly rooted in the US Constitution. In its original form, the Constitution directed that the census be conducted in a manner "excluding Indians not taxed." This stipulation drew a distinction between Native individuals according to their residence, with the result that early versions of the census counted only Native people who lived in white society (that is, civilization) and not on Native lands (Connolly and Jacobs 2020; Jobe 2004). During the first century of the US census, counts of Native people were sporadic and uneven in their administration and outcomes (US Bureau of the Census 2019b). Overall, however, this incoherent system reflected fairly coherent goals—racializing Native people in ways that organized and supported the practices and objectives of settler colonialism. These processes took place in relation to Europeans (whites) and also were part of complex racializing processes associated with Blacks. Early racializing discourses around Native people and Blacks were "situated in relation to each other," and Native identities were continuously (re)defined alongside what it meant to be Black as well as white (Wolfe 2016, 200).

The late nineteenth century saw several significant shifts in the ways Native people were racialized, defined, and enumerated, and demographic processes served as an indispensable tool of settler colonialism. As a result of the Indian Removal Act of 1830 and during the Trail of Tears, Native people were forcibly enumerated by the same government that routinely robbed, displaced, injured, and murdered them. Demography functioned as an additional act of violence and control, and Native people who resisted such efforts were rounded up and enumerated involuntarily (Haveman 2016). The General Allotment Act of 1887 (the Dawes Act) broke up native lands into individual parcels and institutionalized sanguinity regulations to determine eligibility, entering the issue of "blood quantum" into Native identity (the US government did not widely use the factor of blood quantum to manage federally designated tribal identities until the Indian Reorganization Act of 1934) (Spruhan 2006). Around the same time as the Dawes Act, the US Census Bureau shifted its approach to enumerating the Native population, and the 1890 census became the first to include all Native people, regardless of where they lived. The Indian Citizenship Act of 1924 shifted the issue of citizenship by declaring all Native people born in US territories to be US citizens. That change was reflected in the 1930 census, which no longer reported on "Indians in the United States" but "Indians of the United States" (Jobe 2004).

When the census changed to include all Native people in the US, it offered a demographic picture that reflected the outcome of the long-term genocidal process that it had helped to organize and support. Centuries of dehumanization, brutality, forced labor, forced migration, land theft, massacre, introduced disease, and other forms of systematic violence are grimly reflected in the 1890 census, which put the Native population at 248,253 men, women, and children (U.S. Department of the Interior, Census Office 1894, 24). The specific number recorded is less salient than the human and cultural devastation it represents: demographers estimate that between 4,200,000 and 12,250,000 people lived in North America when Europeans first arrived in 1492 (Thornton 1987). Any examination of Native populations must acknowledge the extent to which centuries of racialized atrocities and settler colonialist practices devastated Native people and cultures, leaving a legacy of persistent structural disadvantage for surviving generations. This examination of Native women in STEM occupations is rooted in a deep awareness of this historical context.

Regardless of how the Indian population was defined in the early history of the US census, all counts were based on the assumptions of census enumerators until 1960, when the census introduced racial self-identification and inaugurated the distribution of census forms through the US Postal Service (Connolly and Jacobs 2020). In that year, the Native population jumped an astonishing 52 percent, signaling a watershed moment for data associated with the enumeration of Native people and marking the beginning of an extraordinary growth period in the demographic record (Passel 1996; Thornton 1976). The numbers associated with the Native population have "continued to grow remarkably" over the last several decades, consistently outstripping expectations (Liebler, Bhaskar, and Porter 2016, 508).

The reasons for this impressive change in the data are multiple and complex. Scholars note that while the surge is partially driven by shifts in quantitative demographic factors (such as an overall decrease in mortality and relatively high fertility among Native people), the overall increase is also a function of important developments in the qualitative meanings associated with Native identity itself (Passel 1996). New racial identification patterns have been linked to shifts in the cultural stereotypes associated with Native identities—which in the past half century have changed from widely unfa-vorable to "sympathetic and romanticized"—as well as to the growth of the pan-Indian movement and the progressive adoption of a broader identity called "American Indian" (Eschbach, Supple, and Snipp 1999, 36; Nagel 1996, 140). The data connected to the strong growth of the Native pop-ulation, therefore, are at least in part driven by relatively recent cultural changes in what it means to identify as a Native person.

Shifts in stereotypes plus a more unified umbrella identity concept made it increasingly probable that individuals with Native ancestry might actively identify themselves as American Indian. This upward trend was strength-ened again in 2000, when the census introduced the possibility of identi-fying with more than one race. Although this new option had little effect on the enumeration of other racial groups, it had an "outsized impact" on Native population numbers (Connolly and Jacobs 2020, 205). This impact is partially due to the relatively small size of the overall Native population, but it is also likely that the effect of a multi-race option on Native demo-graphics has been amplified by the possibility that people who identify as American Indian also commonly identify with another race (Norris, Vines, and Hoeffel 2012). In the 2019 American Community Survey (ACS), for example, half of the non-Hispanic American Indian and Native Alaskan population (AI/AN) (about 51 percent) reported being multiracial, with the most likely combination being AI/AN and white. This high rate of mul-tiracial identification is particular to the Native population. Other racial groups counted by the census do not report similarly significant patterns of multiracial identity.

Finally, along with the important effects of racial self-identification, 1960 also marked an expansion in Native categories. In response to Alaska statehood, the 1960 census introduced the categories Aleut and Eskimo, linking the Native peoples of the continental US to the Native peoples of the new state. These racial categories disappeared in the 1970 census and then returned again in 1980 and 1990. In 2000, they were replaced by the more inclusive Alaska Native, the same year the entire Native grouping was renamed American Indian or Alaska Native. That category has remained in use ever since (Pew Research Center 2020).

As the number of Native people enumerated by the US census esca-lated due to changing cultural meanings of Native identification, the new option to select a multiracial identity, and (to a lesser extent) the addition of Alaskan Natives, the census simultaneously began to collect data in another category: in 1970, survey takers who identified as "Indian (Amer.)" were instructed for the first time to also "Print tribe." Hence, even as the category of American Indian found traction as an anchoring concept for some forms of Native organizing, the census began to reflect a more specific aspect of Native identity. This level of data collection has continued uninterrupted since its inception, with the census offering more specificity over time. Censuses from 1990 through 2010 instructed Native people to "Print enrolled or principal tribe," and the 2020 census was the first to accompany survey instructions with a long list of examples.

We note the emergence of the category of tribal identity for numerous reasons. First, it opens up important issues regarding how we talk (and think) about Native communities and cultures. As scholars of indigeneity point out, identity categories for Native people have been typically imposed from outside and usually "served the purpose of the settlers or coloniser" (Madden et al. 2019, 23). *Tribe* itself is not a Native term. The term was applied by Europeans with the objective of diminishing the sovereignty and autonomy of Native nations. As Elizabeth Colson (1986, 6) notes, once it became "inexpedient to recognize the full sovereignty of Native American rivals with whom the English settlements competed for land and political dominion, 'nation' gave way to 'tribe' which carried implications of lesser political status. Tribe thereafter became the term commonly used to distinguish among the populations being incorporated into colonial empires."

Tribe remains the primary term used by the US government to refer to Native communities and cultures. The word remains scattered throughout Native organizations, as well, particularly relative to federally recognized political communities in Native nations (designated as tribal governments). Because the word *tribe* continues to connect the formal processes of US government bureaucracy to Native organizations, it should come as no surprise that the term is used by the US Census Bureau in order to inquire about specific Native identities. A settler colonialist word that is still in use, *tribe* remains formally (and forcibly) connected to Native nations and attached to the census data associated with Native people.

It is in this context that we recognize that the word *tribe* is a term with which we must grapple. In this chapter, we have opted to use the word *tribe* when we are working with or referring to census data or census data-collecting processes. This is essentially a parallel practice to our use of the label AI/AN to describe census data associated with Native people in general. Using the terms *tribe* and *tribal*, however unsavory the words are, renders transparent the specific nomenclature associated with the data we are using. However, whenever possible (that is, when not referring to the census but to Native people or nations more broadly), we refer to Native nations as nations (which is what they are).

Like the exonym *American Indian*, the word *tribe* reflects settler colonialist efforts to reduce Native distinctiveness and power. However, unlike the term *American Indian*, the words *tribe* and *tribal identity* also signal something both authentic and important in the larger context of Native experience. For many Native people, connections to a nation or tribe serve as a primary cultural identity (Connolly et al. 2019), and nation (or tribal) associations reflect belonging in ways that rival or supersede US citizenship (O'Hare 2019). In this context, the census term *tribal identity* additionally highlights differences between formal tribal membership and a Native person's personal identification with a tribe or nation. As noted above, formal enrollment in many tribes has been linked to a genealogical connection (the blood quantum factor) since the 1930s, creating (in theory) measurable parameters for official group membership. Tribal identities as enumerated by the US Census Bureau, however, are not subject to such parameters. Any person who identifies as Native can freely list a tribal affiliation on the census without having to fulfill any requirements for formal tribal enrollment. This marks a difference between official tribal *enrollments* (which are subject to different sets of requirements and managed by Native nations) and self-declared personal tribal *affiliations* as enumerated by the census. Census records of tribal identities will not, therefore, necessarily align with official tribal memberships. Rather, census data aligns with Native peoples' personal identifications.

Tribal identities also call attention to the enormous number and pronounced heterogeneity of Native cultures and nations. There are currently more than 570 federally recognized tribes as well as sixty additional state-recognized tribes, and these include many kinds of social arrangements, including "bands, Rancherias, pueblos, colonies and villages" (Connolly et al. 2019, 71). This enormous variety—of living and family arrangements, forms of self-governance, distributions and kinds of labor, cultural and social systems, spiritual practices, and languages—makes it clear that there is not and has never been a single Indian identity, culture, or way of life.

This testifies to the importance of recognizing tribes insofar as it acknowledges and makes visible some of the many significant differences among Native nations and peoples.

The presence of tribal-level census data also raises an issue that is central to every case study in this book—sample size. While tribal (nation) associations are primary for many Native people, the populations associated with some communities can be extraordinarily small. For example, the 2019 ACS lists small tribes like Comanche (with an estimated 20,100 members), Hopi (16,525 members), and Crow (11,697 members). Cherokee (289,757 members) and Navajo (about 341,702 members) reflect larger populations. And while all Native communities are important, extremely small sample sizes preclude most from generating viable datasets for quantitative examinations of occupational distributions and earnings of Native women. Indeed, the amalgamate category of AI/AN itself, which erases tribal differences yet provides a more robust, usable sample, is itself extremely small. In 2019, the non-Hispanic AI/AN population (including respondents who report an AI/AN identity as a part of multiple racial identities) constituted only 1.3 percent of the US population. Despite recent growth, the AI/AN population remains among the smallest groupings within the racial categories enumerated by the US census.

Finally, when thinking about sample size, it is important to recognize that the population dataset overall for Native people is affected by challenges associated with enumeration (Kesslen 2019). The data indicate that undercounting is an especially pronounced issue for Native people who live in Native homeland areas and that Native people living on federal reservations experience "much higher net undercounts than [Native people] living elsewhere in the country" (O'Hare 2019, 103). We note this factor not only because it highlights a possible instability in Native population data but also because it confirms the salience of reservation life for many Native people, where poverty rates are often high and educational opportunities frequently compromised. As we discuss below, these factors are significant for thinking about the participation of Native women in STEM.

In keeping with our overall model, we examine the data related to AI/AN women's STEM participation by taking into account the salient characteristics of these identities as US census categories at this moment in time. The current census data on AI/AN women have the following distinctive attributes: the data are (1) *self-selected* (the category is chosen by the individual in question, as all US census identity categories have been since 1960), (2) *racialized* (the category historically has been understood as a racial identity as opposed to an ethnic identity, such as Hispanic), (3) *strongly multiracial* (the AI/AN data have the highest percentage of multiracial respondents among all of the major US racial groups), (4) *uniquely heterogeneous* (the data are comprised of many highly variegated identities and nations, or tribes in the census, that often serve as the primary cultural identity group for many Native people), (5) *extremely small in number* (the number is small relative to the larger racial and ethnic US populations of Blacks, Asians, and Hispanics/Latinos), (6) *increasing in size* (numbers are increasing through processes linked to qualitative shifts in cultural patterns of racial self-identification), yet also (7) *undercounted* (this is relative to a critical subgroup of Native people, those living on federally designated reservations).

Because of the sample size limits associated with data collected at the tribal (Native nation) level, our comparisons regarding Native women in STEM will generally employ the less refined but larger AI/AN designation. However, once we have explored the STEM-related patterns for AI/AN women in aggregate, we also take an additional, snapshot look at the data for women in STEM who identify as Cherokee and Navajo, the two largest Native nations enumerated by the census. We move now to a contextualizing overview of Native women in the US labor force, followed by a detailed analysis of occupational and income data related to these women across both conventional STEM and STEM-related jobs. We employ these key data attributes, framed by the larger data story of Native people, to guide us as we intersectionally examine these women's participation and earnings in STEM fields.

American Indian/Alaska Native Women in the US Labor Force

The paid work history of Native people reflects the larger systemic disadvantages to which this group has been historically subject. A recent survey shows that more than three-quarters of AI/AN people believe that Native people in the US experience both institutionalized and individualized forms of unfair treatment based on their race (National Public Radio et al. 2017). This general sense of racialized discrimination and disadvantage is reflected in the ways Native people describe their specific experiences in the US labor force. Although the literature on workplace discrimination and the AI/AN population is frustratingly minimal, a recent survey indicates about one-third of Native people in the US report racial discrimination at work. This includes bias when seeking employment, as well as unfair treatment in terms of equal pay and consideration for promotion while on the job (National Public Radio et al. 2017).

These forms of discrimination have a particular salience given that workforce participation is a marked issue for AI/AN people. Compared to all other racial and ethnic groups tracked by the census, the Native population in the US is characterized by high levels of unemployment (6.6 percent in 2018, the highest in the nation) as well as low levels of labor-market participation (59.6 percent in 2018, the lowest in the nation) (US Bureau of Labor Statistics 2019). While the latter measurement is a concern for any community, it is particularly critical when thinking about Native people relative to economic advancement. Native people experience poverty at extremely high rates. In 2018, the national poverty rate was 25.4 percent for AI/AN people, the highest for all racial/ethnic groups (Muhammed, Tec, and Ramirez 2019). Low levels of workforce participation amplify cycles of poverty, making it more difficult to successfully adjust to changing life circumstances, save money, and build wealth.

Regarding the employment patterns of Native women, we note first that the number of AI/AN women working in the US is small: in 2019, working AI/AN women comprised 1 percent of women in the overall US labor force over the age of fifteen. In that relative context, we see that Native women tend to participate in the labor market at rates lower than white women. Figure 4.1 tracks AI/AN women's labor-force participation relative to white women from 2000 to 2019. We use 2000 as a starting point because it marks the beginning of the multiracial option on the census, a change that substantially increased the numbers associated with the AI/AN population. The year 2000 is when American Indian or Alaska Native was introduced as a uniform umbrella category.

This somewhat lower workforce participation pattern for Native women is shaped by multiple interconnecting variables, many of which are particular to intersectional issues of gender and race. One significant factor for this group is the important role played by Native women—particularly mothers—in many Native communities. Not all Native people live in Native communities, not all women have children, and, as Raymond Foxworth (2016, 6) notes, the "role of Native women in Native communities has always varied from tribe to tribe." However, legacies of settler colonialism

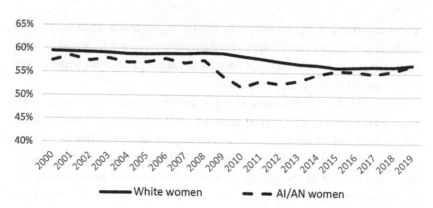

Figure 4.1

US labor-force participation rates: AI/AN women and white women, 2000–2019, age 16 and over. *Source:* US Bureau of Labor Statistics.

have left many Native nations in peril, and the research shows that AI/AN women often play an important, demanding, and unremunerated role as community support persons and protectors of Native cultures (Liddell et al. 2021). In addition, many Native women are mothers, which adds to the burden of unpaid work. The rate of single motherhood is high for Native women: in 2018, 68.2 percent of AI/AN births were to unmarried women (the US average was 39.6 percent) (Martin 2019). Native women also tend to have children at a comparatively young age: in 2018, 8.9 percent of AI/AN births were to mothers less than twenty years old (the US average for that group was 4.8 percent) (Martin 2019).

Patterns around motherhood affect both employability and occupation and also impact Native women's relationship to formal education. Educational attainment is vital for both employment in general and STEM participation, and it is a vexed and challenging issue for Native communities as a whole. In 2019, only 16 percent of Native people reported having a bachelor's degree or higher, compared to 40 percent of whites. Native women fare somewhat better than Native men in terms of bachelor degree completion (17.5 percent compared to 14.5 percent) (US Bureau of the Census 2019a). Educational attainment is clearly an issue for both Native women and men relative to STEM work.

Health and safety are fundamental to human well-being and critical for consistent and successful participation in both educational systems and the labor force. Native communities, however, often fare poorly in these critical areas. Health issues are of concern for Native communities generally, a fact that negatively impacts educational attainment and STEM participation overall (James 2001). These issues are particularly pressing for AI/AN women, who are underserved when it comes to reproductive health and who experience high levels of maternal morbidity and mortality (Gurr 2014). Mental health issues are pronounced for Native women, and their rates of death by suicide are disproportionately high compared to other groups (Curtin and Hedegaard 2019). In the health-related area of physical safety, a 2016 study by the US Department of Justice reported that an extraordinarily high number of Native people report being subject to violence (84 percent of Native women and 81 percent of Native men) (Rosay 2016). Native communities struggle with the disappearance of Native women, and the murder rate for women living on Native land is ten times the national average (Ortiz 2020). In this context, much of this violence is interracial (and not intraracial): perpetrators of violence against Native people (including murder) are unlikely to also be Native (Petrosky et al. 2021). For Native women, incidences of sexual violence are especially high: more than half (56 percent) report surviving sexual violence (Rosay 2016). Overall, health and safety are especially pressing issues for Native communities, and many Native women face elevated challenges in these areas.

Finally, research suggests many issues that negatively and specifically impact AI/AN women's opportunities to participate in STEM work are magnified in the context of life on reservations and in nonurban locations. The rural location of many Native people can negatively affect access to education and health (and other services). For Native people living on reservations and in chronically underserved rural areas, high levels of concentrated poverty, lower employment, geographic isolation, environmental hazards, and lack of transportation alter both life quality and economic opportunity. These issues play a key role in reducing many Native women's opportunities relative to STEM learning and work.

What happens when Native women do participate in the labor market? Given the context we have just provided, it is unsurprising that AI/AN women are disadvantaged when it comes to pay equity. In 2019, Native women age twenty-five and over who are working full-time and year-round in the US experienced a wage gap of a stunning 36 percentage points when compared to working white men. Research on individual nations indicates that even when Native women's tribal affiliations are taken into account, wage gaps between Native women and white men are never less than 30 percent—and in some Native nations, that gap reaches or exceeds 50 percent (Tucker 2019). While the wage-gap factor is a matter of both equity and quality of life, it is also a particularly urgent one for AI/AN women relative to Native families and communities: 58 percent of Native women are single-parent breadwinners (with breadwinner defined as a person earning at least 40 percent of the income in a household with children younger than eighteen) (Institute for Women's Policy Research 2020). This means the majority of Native households depend on Native women's wages. And Native women's wages are severely compromised.

In terms of Native women in STEM fields, much research remains to be done. But while the literature specific to Native women's experience in STEM is emergent, there is a more robust body of literature on Native people in general and STEM participation. Examinations of how Native people experience STEM education emphasize the need for more culturally attentive connections between Native people and STEM learning and engagement. The research on AI/AN people in STEM argues that there is a pronounced disjuncture between conventional learning cultures of STEM and the values and approaches to knowledge common to many Native cultures (Brandt 2008; Howard and Kern 2019; James et al. 1994; McKinley 2007; Waterman and Lindley 2013). Research focused on AI/AN people who work as STEM professionals reinforce these findings, noting the clash between white, Western working cultures of STEM and the values systems associated with many Native communities (Page-Reeves et al. 2017, 2019; Varma and Galindo-Sanchez 2006). Overall, the research on Native people and STEM demonstrates that "the dearth of Indigenous participation in the STEM fields" should be addressed via a more "bicultural paradigm" and an active alignment of STEM education and work with Native "values and kinship structures" (Windchief and Brown 2017, 329). Much more gender-focused, intersectionally sensitive research remains to be done relative to important issues that are specific to Native women and STEM learning and working.

American Indian/Alaska Native Women in the Conventional STEM Fields: What Do the Data Say?

As of 2019, the percentage of non-Hispanic women (age twenty-five and over) in the US who identify as either AI/AN (a single category) or as multiracial (with AI/AN as one of their several selected racial categories) was 1.2 percent. The very few Native women who also identify as Hispanic are included in our sample for chapter 6, Hispanic/Latina Women in STEM. In 2019, about 52 percent of all AI/AN women reported they identified with only one race. According to our definition of conventional STEM, in the year 2019 alone there were an estimated 8.6 million individuals age twenty-five to sixty-four working full-time and year-round in STEM occupations; an estimated 16,958 of them were women who identified being AI/AN, which was fewer than 1 percent of all STEM job holders in 2019. Averaging across all years of our sample and focusing on those age twenty-five to sixty-four working year-round and full-time, only 3.5 percent of AI/AN women work in STEM occupations (compared to 11 percent of non-Hispanic white men). After adjusting for standard covariates (education, age, industry, marital status, citizen status, veteran status, and region of the country), we calculate that AI/AN women in conventional STEM occupations have a 33 percent wage premium over AI/AN women who do not work in STEM jobs.

Within the traditional STEM occupations, AI/AN women's median earnings are 71 percent of non-Hispanic white men's. This is a considerable jump, given that across all occupations, AI/AN women earn only 63 percent of what non-Hispanic white men earn. While Native women's median STEM earnings are fairly robust relative to non-Hispanic white men in STEM (71 percent), they are still less than the median earnings of all women relative to all men (80 percent). STEM occupations offer a strong economic advantage for Native women relative to other Native women, but that advantage highlights the substantial relative wage lag under which Native women labor overall.

Having established our sample parameters, we turn now to the distribution of Native women across conventional STEM occupations and to a deeper examination of their earnings. Figure 4.2 represents how AI/AN women and non-Hispanic white men in STEM are distributed across four broad categories of STEM work.

As figure 4.2 indicates, computer/math-related work dominates Native women's STEM participation. Fully half of AI/AN women working in STEM are employed in computer/math fields, the occupational cluster that also has the highest percentage of STEM workers who are white men (45 percent). Native women are strongly represented in the physical and

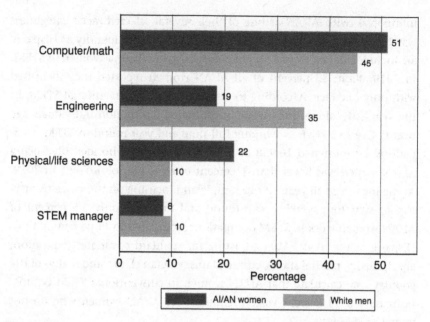

Figure 4.2

Distribution of American Indian/Alaska Native women and non-Hispanic white men across STEM occupations, individuals age 25–64 working year-round and full-time. Because AI/AN people report being multi-race at higher rates than other racial groups, we additionally calculated the STEM participation rates for AI/AN women who reported their racial identity as AI/AN-only. The outcomes were not appreciably different from those shown in figure 4.2 (AI/AN-multi-race). Because of the strong similarities, we have not included AI/AN-only as a separate intersectional point of comparison. *Source:* Data from the American Community Survey, 2012–2019.

life sciences relative to white men (22 percent compared to 10 percent); they are underrepresented in engineering (19 percent compared to 35 percent of white men). Eight percent of AI/AN women in STEM participate in STEM managerial work; about 10 percent of white men participate in these occupations.

When we examine these participation patterns in the context of median annual earnings (table 4.1), we see that AI/AN women are significantly disadvantaged relative to white men across every occupational category in conventional STEM work. In the computer/math fields—where one out of every two Native women in STEM is employed—AI/AN women experience a wage gap of 28 percentage points. In the next-highest area of STEM participation

Table 4.1

American Indian/Alaska Native women's median annual earnings as a percentage of non-Hispanic white men's median annual earnings in STEM occupations, individuals age 25–64 working year-round and full-time

| STEM category | Median annual earnings | | AI/AN women's earnings as a percentage of non-Hispanic white men's |
	AI/AN women	Non-Hispanic white men	
Computer/math	$64,331	$89,903	72%
Engineering	$67,636	$88,606	76%
Physical/life sciences	$56,363	$75,632	75%
STEM managerial	$80,812	$120,226	67%

Note: All earnings adjusted to 2019 dollars. *Source:* Data from the American Community Survey, 2012–2019.

for AI/AN women, the physical and life sciences, Native women experience a wage gap of 25 percentage points. The physical and life sciences are the lowest-paid areas of STEM work for both Native women and white men ($56,363 and $75,632 annual median incomes, respectively). Higher-paid engineering work—in which less than 20 percent of Native women in STEM work—reflects a pay gap that is similar to the physical and life sciences (24 percentage points).

While both Native women and white men participate in STEM managerial occupations at similar rates (9 percent and 10 percent), Native women experience their largest STEM pay gap in this well-paid area of work (33 percentage points). Wages associated with STEM management are the highest among conventional STEM areas. They reflect a stark earnings difference, with Native women earning $80,812 and white men earning $120,226—an almost $40,000 annual difference.

American Indian/Alaska Native Women in the STEM-Related Fields: What Do the Data Say?

In 2019, there were an estimated 7.3 million individuals age twenty-five to sixty-four years working year-round and full-time in STEM-related jobs. An estimated 55,537 were women who reported an AI/AN identity. Over the

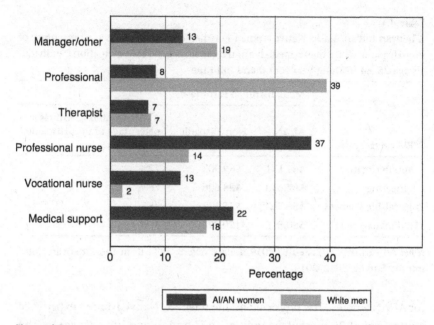

Figure 4.3
Distribution of American Indian/Alaska Native women and non-Hispanic white men across STEM-related occupations, individuals age 25–64 working year-round and full-time. *Source:* Data from the American Community Survey, 2012–2019.

period of our sample focusing on those age twenty-five to sixty-four working full-time and year-round, we find that only 3.6 percent of white men work in these occupations. However, about 10 percent of AI/AN women are employed in such occupations (as opposed to about 3.5 percent in conventional STEM occupations). While the STEM premium is a normative and often cited measure of how conventional STEM careers benefit women in any given group, the concept of a STEM-related premium is new. When we calculate a STEM-related premium for AI/AN women (which compares earnings in STEM-related occupations to non-STEM occupations while controlling for conventional STEM work), we see that AI/AN women in STEM-related jobs earn 29 percent more than Native women not working in conventional STEM or STEM-related fields. This premium is similar to the premium for conventional STEM work (31 percent). Because our version of a STEM-related premium excludes traditional STEM work, it offers a meaningful snapshot of the economic benefits that STEM-related work

Table 4.2

American Indian/Alaska Native women's median annual earnings as a percentage of non-Hispanic white men's median annual earnings in STEM-related occupations, individuals age 25–64 working year-round and full-time

STEM-related category	Annual median earnings		
	AI/AN women	Non-Hispanic white men	AI/AN women's earnings as a percentage of non-Hispanic white men's
Manager/other	$56,363	$86,437	65%
Professional	$93,036	$168,350	55%
Therapist	$55,103	$76,327	72%
Professional nurse	$65,659	$75,761	87%
Vocational nurse	$42,160	$45,457	93%
Medical support	$42,185	$53,635	79%

Note: All earnings adjusted to 2019 dollars. *Source:* Data from the American Community Survey, 2012–2019.

provides Native women. In figure 4.3, we turn to the distribution of Native women and non-Hispanic white men over the six STEM-related occupational groupings.

Nursing dominates the STEM-related work of Native women: half of AI/AN women working in STEM-related occupations are nurses (37 percent professional and 13 percent vocational) compared to only 16 percent of white men. Medical-support work comes in a distant second for Native women (22 percent) and is the only other STEM-related category in which this group participates more than non-Hispanic white men (17 percent). Native women work as medical therapists at about the same rate as white men.

As seen in table 4.2, AI/AN women experience significant pay gaps across all STEM-related fields compared to non-Hispanic white men. For example, in the professional STEM-related occupations, where AI/AN women have their highest median earnings, they earn 55 percent of what white men earn in the lucrative professional occupations. This pay gap of 45 percentage points amounts to $75,315 per year—a gap that is larger than the median earnings of Native women in the other STEM-related categories. Pay gaps are smaller in the other STEM-related occupations but still consequential. For example, Native women experience a pay gap of 35 percentage points in STEM-related managerial work, 28 percentage points when they work as therapists, and 21 percentage points when they work in medical support. The only gaps less than 20 percentage points are in the nursing fields, where Native women who work as vocational nurses earn 93 percent of what white men earn, and in the professional nursing fields, where they earn 87 percent of white men.

Stopping at an Intersection: Native Nation Identities in STEM

Cherokee and Navajo Women

As we note above, tribal identities are primary for many AI/AN people but are obscured within the larger amalgam of the Census Bureau's category of American Indian/Alaska Native. There are multiple reasons why data at the tribal-identity level can be challenging, however. In terms of examining STEM occupations and earnings, small sample sizes alone prevent tribal-level analyses. Given the importance of tribal identities and the rarity with which they are considered, however, we pause here to examine the conventional STEM and STEM-related participation of Native women who affiliate with the two largest tribes, the Cherokee and Navajo nations.

What are the notable characteristics of these data? In all cases, the tribal affiliations reflected in the data are matters of personal identification. Because the census does not ask about enrollment status, the data may or may not reflect a respondent's formal tribal membership. And although we did not intentionally control for race—that is, separate out AI/AN-only women and AI/AN-multiracial women—it may be significant that our data naturally reflects AI/AN-only identity: no woman in our sample who identified as Cherokee or Navajo also identified as multiracial. Finally, small tribal sizes coupled with the low percentage of AI/AN women working in STEM make this analysis more suggestive than analyses that are based on larger samples.

In figure 4.4 we provide information on the STEM occupational distribution, and in table 4.3, the related median annual earnings of Cherokee and Navajo women relative to white men, juxtaposing the data from the two tribal groups.

Figure 4.4 indicates that Cherokee and Navajo women who participate in STEM fields are distributed differently from white men and differently

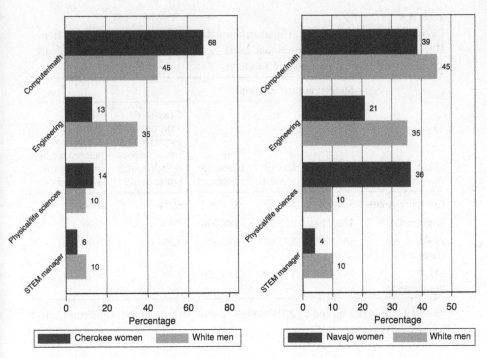

Figure 4.4
Distribution of Cherokee and Navajo women and non-Hispanic white men across STEM occupations, individuals age 25–64 years working year-round and full-time. *Source:* Data from the American Community Survey, 2012–2019.

from each other. More than two-thirds of Cherokee women are in the computer/math fields, and less than 15 percent are in engineering and in the physical/life sciences. Navajo women are much more evenly distributed across STEM work. They are almost evenly split between computer/math occupations (39 percent) and physical/life sciences (36 percent). Women from both Nations lag behind the participation of white men in both the engineering and managerial fields.

In terms of earnings, it is unsurprising that the medium annual salaries for women from both tribes fall significantly below those of white men. That said, general trends indicate that Cherokee women experience smaller pay gaps than Navajo women in STEM (table 4.3). In every STEM category, the pay gap for Navajo women relative to white men exceeds the pay gap experienced by Cherokee women by around 10 percentage points.

Table 4.3
Cherokee and Navajo women's median annual earnings as a percentage of non-Hispanic white men's median annual earnings in STEM occupations, individuals age 25–64 working year-round and full-time

	Median annual earnings			Cherokee women's earnings as a percentage of non-Hispanic white men's	Navajo women's earnings as a percentage of non-Hispanic white men's
STEM category	Cherokee women	Navajo women	Non-Hispanic white men		
Computer/math	$61,887	$53,635	$89,903	69%	60%
Engineering	$70,230	$58,345	$88,606	79%	66%
Physical/life sciences	$61,887	$52,921	$75,632	82%	70%
STEM managerial	$92,683	$60,609	$120,226	77%	50%

Note: All earnings adjusted to 2019 dollars. *Source:* Data from the American Community Survey, 2012–2019.

In figure 4.5 and table 4.4, we show the STEM-related occupational distribution and related median annual earnings of Cherokee and Navajo women relative to white men. In the STEM-related occupations, we see significantly different patterns in the nursing fields. Cherokee women are much more likely to be nurses than Navajo women (53 percent compared to 37 percent, professional and vocational nursing combined). While the majority of Cherokee women in STEM-related jobs are nurses, the most likely STEM-related field of work for Navajo women is medical-support work (44 percent). While women from both nations are distributed more strongly than white men in both nursing and medical-support fields, both Cherokee and Navajo women tend to participate much less than white men in both managerial and professional work. Only 8 percent of Cherokee and 6 percent of Navajo women are in the high-paying professional occupations.

A general look at the median annual earnings of Cherokee and Navajo women in STEM-related fields illustrates that both groups lag behind non-Hispanic white men's earnings in every STEM-related category. As expected, pay gaps with white men are generally smaller in nursing fields. Vocational

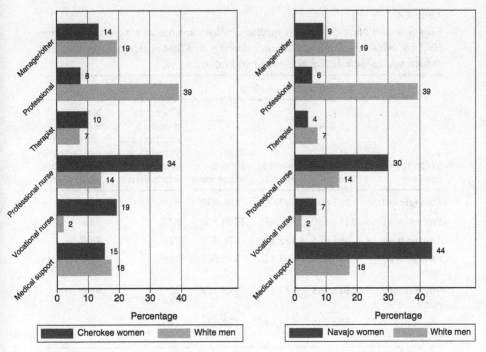

Figure 4.5
Distribution of Cherokee and Navajo women and non-Hispanic white men across STEM-related occupations, individuals age 25–64 working year-round and full-time. *Source:* Data from the American Community Survey, 2012–2019.

nursing, which pays significantly less than professional nursing, has the smaller pay gaps for both tribes. The higher-paying professional categories have large pay gaps—33 percentage points for Cherokee women and 66 percentage points for Navajo women. Perhaps the largest takeaway here, however, is that there are significant differences in STEM-related participation rates and earnings between women from the Cherokee and Navajo nations. This suggests that when it comes to understanding Native women's STEM work and earnings, there are likely important and varied considerations at the tribal levels—considerations that are rarely acknowledged or taken into account by scholars of STEM diversity.

A Note on Native Alaskan Women
One intersectional juncture that we hoped to explore was the STEM participation and earnings of women who identify as Alaska Natives. Like specific

Table 4.4
Cherokee and Navajo women's median annual earnings as a percentage of non-Hispanic white men's median annual earnings in STEM-related occupations, individuals age 25–64 working year-round and full-time

STEM-related category	Median annual earnings			Cherokee women's earnings as a percentage of non-Hispanic white men's	Navajo women's earnings as a percentage of non-Hispanic white men's
	Cherokee women	Navajo women	Non-Hispanic white men		
Manager/other	$52,604	$49,067	$86,437	61%	57%
Professional	$113,460	$57,492	$168,350	67%	34%
Therapist	$54,023	$55,103	$76,327	71%	72%
Professional nurse	$59,426	$59,426	$75,761	78%	78%
Vocational nurse	$41,865	$43,219	$45,457	92%	95%
Medical support	$40,406	$45,836	$53,635	75%	85%

Note: All earnings adjusted to 2019 dollars. *Source:* Data from the American Community Survey, 2012–2019.

tribal identities, the smaller numbers of women who are Alaska Natives tend to disappear into the much larger population of women who identify as American Indian. These numbers are too small to make any meaningful quantitative comparisons—a fact that invites both elevated concern regarding gaps in our knowledge about Native Alaskan women's access to STEM professions as well as the need for robust qualitative data regarding their STEM experiences.

Case Study Highlights

The intersection we examine in this chapter focuses on tribal identity.

Conventional STEM Occupations
- Native women comprise a small part of both the overall US population and the overall STEM labor force.

- Only 3.5 percent of Native women work in conventional STEM jobs.
- Over half of these women participate in computer/math jobs (51 percent); there is low participation in engineering relative to white men.
- Earnings for Native women in conventional STEM work are severely compromised relative to white men; they do not reach parity in any area. Native women earn 67 percent of white men's wages in STEM management work, 72 percent in computer/math fields, 75 percent in physical/life sciences, and 76 percent in engineering professions. These patterns are lower than the overall gender earnings ratio of 80 percent.

STEM-Related Occupations
- Ten percent of AI/AN women work in STEM-related occupations. About 50 percent of AI/AN women are in nursing, and the majority of that group are professional nurses.
- Native women lag severely behind white men in high-paying medical professional work: only 8 percent work in these fields (compared to 39 percent of white men).
- Earnings for Native women in STEM-related work are severely compromised relative to white men; they do not reach parity in any area. Native women make only 55 cents for every dollar earned by white men in the high-paying medical professional fields and only 65 cents in STEM-related management. Vocational nursing boasts the highest ratio (93 percent).

Stopping at an Intersection: Tribal Identity
- Small sample sizes make a comparison of Cherokee and Navajo women in STEM suggestive. Nevertheless, our analysis reveals that these two groups of women have different STEM occupational patterns.
- Cherokee and Navajo women in conventional STEM also have different earnings ratios. Compared to white men, Cherokee women in STEM have stronger earnings than Navajo women.
- Cherokee women are more likely to be vocational nurses, and Navajo women more likely to be in medical support. Both groups come closest to parity with white men in vocational nursing fields and earnings in STEM-related work are low for both groups.

- Divergent patterns between the two groups confirm that tribal identity can be a significant variable for native women in STEM.

Stopping at an Intersection: Native Alaskan Women in STEM

- We had insufficient data to conduct a reliable analysis on Native Alaskan women working in STEM. There is a clear need for focused qualitative research on the intersectional STEM workforce experiences of this distinctive small group.

Who Is Asian/Pacific Islander in the United States?

Asian and Pacific Islander identity is racialized on the US census and characterized by a steady expansion of associated categories over time. This approach to defining and counting a group is unique. The identity category Black, for example, has seen a decrease in associated identities. As of the 2020 census, only two identities—Black and African American—remain attached to that category. And since its appearance on the census in 1980, the ethnic category Hispanic has consistently operated as an umbrella group with the same four options—Mexican, Cuban, Puerto Rican, and Other (with Other allowing for write-in options). The data on Asian people in the US, however, has focused from the outset on people in terms of national origin or identity rather than counting and creating a group called Asians. Instead of using an Asian category, the US census has always offered an array of national origin categories (such as Chinese or Japanese) from which to choose. In fact, on the current American Community Survey (ACS), the word *Asian* appears only in the category Other Asian, providing a generic option for those who do not identify with the other Asian-associated identity groups the census provides.

The data story for Asians in the US begins when the census added Chinese as a category in 1870. This addition can be understood as an important moment in terms of how the census itself actively constructs race and racialized identities. Offered as a new choice in the Color category (other choices were white, Black, mulatto, and Indian), Chinese was categorized by the census survey as a racial option (it was not listed as a possible national, geographical, or ethnic identity). The addition of this immigrant community to the census as a racial group cannot be explained as a response to immigration patterns. During a time of far more substantial immigration from Europe when some European groups (such as the Irish and Jews) were commonly considered to be nonwhite, only Chinese was added to the census in the Color category, and only Chinese immigrants were counted in expressly racialized terms (Mezey 2003).

The project of explicitly racializing Asian people through the census expanded two decades later when Japanese was added as a new category option in 1890 and listed as another Color (that is, racial) option. From 1870 to 1920, Chinese and Japanese remained the sole representatives of Asian populations on the census. In 1920, Filipino, Korean, and Hindu were added to the list of racialized choices. (The Hindu category referred to Southeast Asians, not members of a religious community, and remained in place for three decades.) Around the same time, Asian began to emerge as a cultural identity in the US, as Asian communities banded together in the early 1920s to challenge exclusionary practices via the US Supreme Court (Chen and Buell 2018). The development of this new identity did not affect census survey options, however, which to this day remain uniquely disaggregated for Asian-identified people.

When Hawaii became a state in 1959, Pacific Islander identity began to emerge into the US census, and in 1960 categories for Hawaiian and Part Hawaiian were added to the Asian identity cluster. Since then, there has been an expansion of both Asian and Pacific Islander census categories. These include the addition of Asian groups (such as Asian Indian and Vietnamese in 1980) and also groups native to some Pacific Islands (such as Samoan and Guamanian, also in 1980). The possibility of writing in additional Asian identities is a recent one. It was not until 1990 that US census takers were given the chance to write in other identities under Other Asian or Pacific Islander. Finally, in 2000, the census split Asian and Pacific Islander into two associated racialized clusters, a formula that persists today. In the 2020 census, Asian identity groups were listed in a cluster with a write-in option (Other Asian) at the bottom. Pacific Islander options were listed parallel to the Asian cluster—Native Hawaiian, Samoan, and Chamorro (formerly termed Guamanians, the Chamorro are the indigenous people of the Mariana Islands). Other Pacific Islanders is at the bottom of the second cluster as a write-in option.

Because there is no generic Asian option, there is no simple parallel to the familiar categories white, Black, and American Indian/Alaska Native

(Pew Research Center 2020). Because the data around Asian people is disaggregated on the census and because the total number of people in the US who identify as such is small, it is necessary for us to combine data (that is, merge data from all census groups related to Asian and Pacific Islander) in order to examine the participation of Asian and Pacific Islander women in STEM. That means that the cluster of ACS categories associated with Asians (current options are Chinese, Filipino, Asian-Indian, Vietnamese, Korean, Japanese, and Other Asian) and those associated with Pacific Islanders (current options are Native Hawaiian, Samoan, Chamorro, and Other Pacific Islander) must be combined to form both a group called Asians and a meaningful sample size. Therefore, unless otherwise indicated, this case study uses an amalgamated data set that merges all Asian-associated and Pacific Islander–associated census groups. Except where noted, our use of the term *Asian* will include individuals who identify as Asian and also individuals who identify as Pacific Islander. Because not all Asian-identified people are US citizens, we do not use the term *Asian American* when referring to this group.

We recognize that combining these categories in order to generate a more robust and viable data set erases meaningful national, ethnic, and cultural distinctions, as well as important patterns across variables such as household income, education, and immigrant status. As Linda Trinh Võ (2012, 95) warns, "It is inaccurate to assume Asian American women share some sort of common culture or characteristic when we have such diverse histories and backgrounds." It is therefore important to avoid what Samuel D. Museus and Jon Iftikar describe as the hegemonizing process of "Asianization" (Museus and Iftikar 2013, 23), which makes it "difficult to report on statistics about Asians in STEM without reifying stereotypes" (McGee 2018, 3). Hence, once we have explored the patterns across conventional STEM and STEM-related occupations in aggregate, we also take additional, innovative snapshot looks at (1) patterns in STEM and STEM-related occupations that emerge across associated origin categories among Asian women and (2) STEM and STEM-related occupational data for Pacific Islander women as a distinct group.

How large is the (aggregate) Asian population in the US? Based on the 2019 ACS and counting all non-Hispanic individuals who identify as Asian (including individuals who identify with multiple races), Asians represent about 6.6 percent of the US population. This number is fairly small in comparison to other nonwhite-identified racial groups. The only smaller grouping is American Indian/Alaska Native (including individuals who identified with multiple races) at 1.3 percent. Despite a relatively small overall population size, however, Asian populations comprise a growing part of the future US labor force. Currently, the US Asian population is growing faster than both other nonwhite racial populations and the Hispanic population. Between 2000 and 2019, the US Asian population grew 81 percent (from 10.5 million to 18.9 million) (Budiman and Ruiz 2021). Projections suggest that Asians will become the nation's largest immigrant group around the year 2055 and that they will account for 36 percent of immigrants around that time (Budiman and Ruiz 2021). In addition, these projected trends may be underestimated, given the considerable challenges of polling Asian communities, which are characterized by both a variety of first languages other than English and a well-documented reticence to complete census surveys (Eligon 2020; Gao 2016).

Given the growth of the US Asian population, it should come as no surprise that women who identify as part of that population are also likely to be foreign-born. Data from the 2019 ACS indicate that 75 percent of non-Hispanic Asian women age twenty-five and over are foreign-born, compared with 50 percent of Hispanics, 13 percent of non-Hispanic Blacks, and just 5 percent of non-Hispanic whites. The high number of foreign-born Asian women in the US is rooted in many factors, but one driver is doubtless the passage of the Immigration and Nationality Act of 1965 (the Hart-Cellar Act). The passage of this act nullified the Chinese Exclusion Act of 1882 and the equally exclusive Immigration Act of 1924 (the Johnson-Reed Act), replacing a system that barred Asian immigrants and marking the beginning of a pattern of steady growth in the US Asian immigrant population (Allard 2011). As Grace A. Chen and Jason Y. Buell (2018) note, this later twentieth-century shift in immigration law is linked to an increase in Asian immigration and also to immigration patterns that connect Asian workers with STEM work and other forms of intellectual labor. Seen in this context, the issue of immigrant status is fundamentally relevant for thinking about patterns in STEM occupations and earnings for Asian women working in the US.

In keeping with our overall model, in this case study we examine the data related to Asian/Pacific Islander women's STEM participation by taking into account the specific and salient characteristics of these identities as US census categories at this moment in time. The current census data on Asian/Pacific Islander women have the following distinctive attributes: the data are (1) *self-selected* (the category is chosen by the individual in question, as all US census identity categories have been since 1960), (2) *racialized* (the category is historically understood as a racial identity as opposed to an ethnic identity, such as Hispanic), (3) *representative of a significant number of national, ethnic, and cultural identities that are counted in a uniquely disaggregate manner* (the category includes many disparate groups that are counted individually), (4) *small in number* relative to the larger racial and ethnic US populations of Blacks and Hispanics/Latinos, (5) *increasing in size* (the category is outpacing other racial and ethnic populations), and (6) *more strongly linked to foreign-born status* than any other nonwhite racial category.

Finally, as we construct this framework for our examination of the data associated with Asian women in STEM, we note that the US Asian population is a category that has a particular and unique relationship to STEM occupations. Unlike other nonwhite and non-Hispanic racial and ethnic identity groups, Asian populations are positively associated with STEM work through factors like high STEM job-participation rates, strong overall median STEM earnings, and stereotypes about Asian people's capacity for STEM work or natural interests in STEM fields. These two factors—a numerical overrepresentation of Asians in STEM and the pervasive and often unchallenged cultural stereotypes concerning Asians' ability and interest in STEM—are variables that have shaped the cultural conversation around Asian women in STEM fields. We note these familiar patterns and stereotypes as important factors that influence how (and if) we think about Asian women in STEM.

Overrepresentation is a proportional measure and occurs when the percentage of STEM jobs held by members of a group exceeds the percentage of the overall proportion of the labor force represented by that group. It is instructive that overrepresentation is rarely a variable when it comes to majority identities in STEM occupations. The systemic and historically persistent overrepresentation of men and white people is a basic fact of STEM but not always articulated in STEM participation discussions. Such discussions typically focus on the underrepresentation of certain groups (usually racial and ethnic groups as well as women). Yet the concept of overrepresentation (defined against parity, or proportionally sufficient representation) is a common theme relative to Asians in STEM fields. A strong reliance on this demographic metric has significantly affected the collection of data and shaped our (in)attentiveness to patterns of discrimination or disadvantage for Asians in STEM.

Because it is generally agreed that there are (to use a deeply disconcerting word) "enough" Asians in STEM occupations, the parity approach often sidelines Asians in general and Asian women in particular from the research and data keeping on STEM diversity. Consider, for example, the National Science Foundation (NSF) data associated with STEM diversity published in a 2019 report titled *Women, Minorities, and Persons with Disabilities in Science and Engineering.* Data collected by the NSF are commonly used by scholars and practitioners interested in STEM inclusivity. The NSF data sets, however, frequently separate out Asians because Asians are not proportionally STEM minorities like Black, Hispanic, and Native people. Some NSF data charts that examine issues of STEM inclusivity do not include Asian-identified people at all (National Science Foundation 2019).

Overrepresented Asian women in STEM fields, therefore, flicker in and out of data in uneven ways. In this context, they present a classic example of intersectional erasure, where a racialized identity such as Asian in STEM potentially blocks urgent conversations regarding sexism and xenophobia, especially the specific forms of intersectional, racialized sexism, and xenophobia to which Asian women may be subject. When the experiences of Asian women in STEM are obfuscated, so are their interests and concerns, and so are the unique stereotypes and patterns of racism, sexism, or xenophobia they experience. In some ways, the proportionally measured success of Asians in STEM (in terms of both their presence and STEM earnings) mute larger cultural conversations around both anti-Asian (and often anti-immigrant) bias in general and the more specific barriers and forms of racism, sexism, and xenophobia experienced by Asian women in STEM.

This partial obfuscation raises issues related to pervasive stereotypes about Asians in STEM, stereotypes whose effects are compounded when parity becomes a barrier to Asian-identified people being included in data-driven conversations around STEM diversity. Perceptions of Asian women in STEM are shaped by embedded assumptions around STEM interest and abilities that are associated with Asians in general. For example, the idea that Asian people are naturally gifted in STEM, particularly in the gatekeeping discipline of mathematics, is a familiar stereotype (Aronson et al. 1999; Cvencek et al. 2014; Shah 2019). It is also a destructive stereotype.

While often intended as a compliment, the "Asians are naturally good at STEM" myth can be both burdensome and dehumanizing. It amplifies hierarchized racial differences (such as Asians' perceived racialized status) and associates STEM participation with inherent (and therefore again racialized) factors rather than intelligence, curiosity, or persistence (McGee, Thakore, and LaBlance 2017; Shah 2019).

In addition, as scholars have noted, this racialized approach to Asian STEM success carries a quieter but equally destructive side. The success of the so-called Asian model minority operates as part of a dialectic that also positions Asian-identified people (and the idea of Asianness itself) as a potential threat—an overly successful (overrepresented) group within the US (that is taking more than its fair share of STEM work) as well as an outside threat to US STEM competitiveness (Kawai 2005). Given the relatively high percentage of people (age twenty-five and over) who are identified as non-Hispanic Asian in the US and who are foreign-born (75 percent in 2019), it is easy to see how such stereotypes could smoothly embed both racism and xenophobia into the experiences of many Asian people in US STEM work. Simultaneously, disadvantages likely experienced by this group—for example, biases associated with accented English—remain potentially unseen and unaddressed (Bauman 2013). Within the context of these often-unacknowledged dynamics of sufficient numbers, natural talent, and racialized (often xenophobic) threat, Asian women in STEM must grapple with issues specific to their intersectional position. And these dynamics make it important to examine the actual patterns associated with Asian women's participation in STEM workplaces.

Asian Women in the US Labor Force

We begin our examination of these patterns with a longitudinal look at the overall participation of Asian women in the US labor force. For figure 5.1, we have temporarily made a distinction between Asian-identified women and women who identify as Pacific Islander.

Figure 5.1 begins in 2000, the year that census data collection on various discrete Asian groups becomes most robust, and shows that the US labor-force participation of white women and Asian women has historically been similar. In 2000, the census removed Hawaiian-identified people from the generic Asian grouping, relocating them to the new Pacific Islander

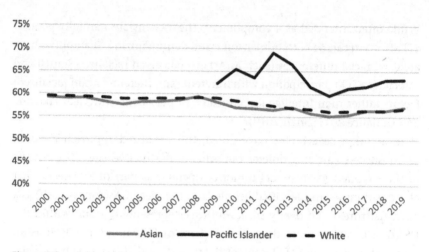

Figure 5.1
US labor force participation rates: Asian, Pacific Islander, and white women, 1980–2019, age 16 and over. *Source:* US Bureau of Labor Statistics.

category. Sample sizes for Pacific Islander women are relatively small (of the 76.8 million women in the workforce in 2019, only 312,000 identified as Pacific Islander), which makes it more difficult to discern trends in their labor-force participation (US Bureau of Labor Statistics 2020b). The snapshot provided by figure 5.1 suggests that Pacific Islander women have markedly higher labor-force participation rates than both Asian (and white) women. This vivid difference in labor-force participation indicates that Pacific Islander women have a labor history of their own that is routinely masked by the data on non-Pacific Islander Asian women. We return to acknowledging these intragroup differences (in figures 5.7 and 5.8 and tables 5.5 and 5.6) when we discuss the STEM participation of Pacific Islander women.

In the context of strong labor force participation over the past decades and in the face of racialized stereotypes about group achievement, it is important to consider the kinds of labor that Asian women in the US actually perform. The strong labor force participation of Asian women (and unless otherwise noted, we include Pacific Islander women in this group going forward) does not mean that Asian women are all working in STEM or that working Asian women are doing similar kinds of work. In fact, the opposite is true: Asian women in the US represent several radically divergent work patterns. Despite the stereotypes, the US population of working

Asian women (which includes a high percentage of immigrant women) is strongly linked to many forms of poorly paid service and manual work. For example, Asian women occupy a disproportionate percentage of low-prestige, low-pay work as laborers, fabricators, and operators (Hesse-Biber and Carter 2005). Historically, a high number of Asian women have engaged in routine, low-pay assembly work, a pattern that is particularly pronounced in the expanding microelectronics industry (Espiritu 2008).

How can we explain Asian women's pronounced presence in low-paying occupations relative to Asian women's strong presence in STEM? Educational patterns are helpful here and shine a light on the seeming conundrum presented by Asian women's considerable presence in both low-paying jobs and high-paying STEM fields. Asian women in the US have a bimodal distribution when it comes to education. Despite embedded stereotypes of uniformly high educational attainment, many Asian women in the US clump strongly toward the lower end of the educational spectrum. For example, 13 percent of this group (age twenty-five and over) have less than a high school education, a percentage that is considerably higher than it is for white, non-Hispanic women (6 percent). The other end of the educational spectrum for Asian women working in the US is strongly in line with stereotypes about Asians' educational achievement: more than half (50 percent) of Asian women have a bachelor's degree or higher. This exceeds the educational attainment of working white, non-Hispanic women (37 percent). And high levels of educational attainment are strongly associated with participation in STEM occupations, regardless of race and ethnicity (Beede et al. 2011). The polarized levels of education reflected in the population of working Asian women indicate that while many Asian women work, the types of work in which they engage are very different—and hence their reasons for entering the paid labor market and their success in it will vary tremendously, as well.

As we turn our attention to specific issues related to STEM fields, we pause to recognize that many Asian women, both US and foreign-born, frequently experience a lack of educational and economic opportunities, struggle with poverty, and engage in dead-end or low-paying work. We must guard against succumbing to glib stereotypes about the high wages of Asian women in the US workforce. The high levels of education attained by a significant proportion of Asian women and their relative success in STEM fields should not blind us to the educational, economic, and occupational challenges faced by many Asian women in the US, particularly immigrant women.

On the positive side of the bimodal educational distribution, the strong representation of Asian women at higher levels of educational attainment helps explain this group's unique wage relationship relative to typically high-earning groups like white men, also making it easier to understand the smaller wage gap between white men and Asian-identified workers in the US. That said, Asian-identified individuals with high levels of educational attainment also experience identity-specific workplace-related challenges. Key among these are issues of leadership and advancement in professional occupations. In this context, professional Asian-identified people frequently encounter what is sometimes termed the *bamboo ceiling*, a system of biases and assumptions that create systemic barriers to their advancement within professional work settings (Hyun 2005; Tso 2018; Yu 2020). Foremost among these biases and assumptions are issues concerning Asians' perceived lack of traditional leadership qualities, drive, and competitiveness. It is debatable whether identifying specific values traditionally associated with many Asian cultures—such as collectivism, avoidance of self-promotion, and respect for age and authority—reflects cultural sensitivity, reinforces sweeping stereotypes, or both. It is not a simple matter to differentiate and navigate between recognizing differences in cultural values and potentially reinforcing damaging stereotypes, and the literature often struggles to work through these tensions (Catalyst 2003a). For the purposes of this case study, however, it is significant that certain values and characteristics are widely perceived as pronounced for Asian-identified people (regardless of country of origin or immigrant status) and as potentially incompatible with successful management within US workplace cultures, including STEM fields. These perceptions about Asian people, which are embedded in gendered and racialized assumptions regarding what constitutes good leadership, can serve as barriers for STEM advancement for Asian professionals in the US.

Within the context of these widely held biases and beliefs, Asian-identified women are doubly disadvantaged. Overall, the general research on women and leadership has shown that *any* woman's possession of traditional leadership attributes—sometimes termed *dominance behaviors*—often conflict with gender-stereotyped expectations for more feminine (that is, cooperative and submissive) behaviors in the workplace (Brescoll and

Uhlmann 2008). Additional research shows that such gender-based expectations and stereotypes around authority are intersectionally shaped and that expectations and perceptions around women's leadership styles are driven by specific combinations of gender and racial identity. Most significant for this particular case study are findings that indicate that regardless of Asian women's behavioral leadership styles (that is, whether or not they display dominant behaviors), Asian women are consistently evaluated as less fit for leadership (Tinkler et al. 2019). Asian women professionals are also often perceived as young and inexperienced, regardless of age (Murti 2017), and they are less likely than women from other racial or ethnic groups to report being proactively mentored in preparation for leadership and management roles in professional occupations (Catalyst 2003a).

The bamboo ceiling seems to hold firm in the specific context of STEM fields. The pattern is borne out by the data in general and also by our examples in this case study, which indicate that despite the much-touted proportional presence of Asian women in STEM fields, this group lags behind when it comes to higher-paying managerial positions (see figure 5.2). While the literature on workplace issues specific to Asian women in STEM is neither well-developed nor robust, it is measurably clear that Asian women are disproportionately absent from STEM managerial roles (Wu and Jing 2011). Perhaps unsurprisingly, the ultimately unhelpful myths of competence that are associated with Asian-identified people in STEM do not appear to cling to Asian women as persistently as they do to Asian men: many Asian women in STEM report being subject to double standards and unfair high expectations (Williams, Multhaups, and Korn 2018). Research indicates that these racialized performance expectations can have particularly damaging effects for Asian people learning and working in STEM (McGee 2018).

In this context, the sufficient overall numbers of Asian-identified people in STEM and the absence of a significant wage gap can short-circuit deeper explorations of the ways in which Asian women are subject to intersectionally specific forms of gender and race stereotyping. These patterns include expectations that their work personas reflect certain stereotypes around Asian femininity such as quietness, passivity, and modesty—qualities that are linked to and complicated by gender as well as adding a new layer of difficulty via widely held perceptions specific to Asians and leadership within the highly competitive and traditionally masculinized cultures of STEM work (Williams, Multhaups, and Korn 2018). Other race- and gender-specific stereotypes may be deployed to police and punish Asian women for racialized gender-role violations (such as failing to be quiet and compliant) or for displaying dominant (traditional leadership) behaviors (for example, the Asian "dragon lady" stereotype) (Lin et al. 2005; Williams, Multhaups, and Korn 2018).

In short, Asian women in STEM labor under the biases that surround women in STEM and women in leadership generally; however, when these gendered and racial stereotypes combine, the forms taken by such bias have an intersectional effect specific to this group. These effects are then masked by the cultural narratives that Asian women disproportionately work in and succeed in STEM. In particular, as Lilian Wu and Wei Jing (2011, 82) note, "The scarcity of Asian women in upper management and leadership positions merits greater attention, more targeted programmatic efforts, and inclusion in the national discussion of the STEM workforce."

Asian Women in the Conventional STEM Fields: What Do the Data Say?

As of 2019, the total percentage of non-Hispanic women (age twenty-five and over) in the US who identify as any of the racial categories associated with Asian identity (a total of ten options comprised of nine specific categories as well as Other Asian) or as multiracial (including any Asian-associated categories) was 6.9 percent. This number includes women who report being associated with any Asian identity group, regardless of whether it is their only reported race (in 2019, about 89 percent of all Asian women reported only one race) or whether they identify as multiracial (so long as one of the races is associated with Asian identity). Asian women who also identify as Hispanic are included in our sample for chapter 6, Hispanic/Latina Women in STEM.

According to our definition of conventional STEM, in the year 2019 alone an estimated 8.6 million individuals age twenty-five to sixty-four were working full-time and year-round in STEM occupations, and an estimated 467,533 of them were women who identified as Asian women, just over 5 percent of all STEM job holders. Averaging across all the years in our sample and focusing on those age twenty-five to sixty-four who work year-round and full-time, we find that an impressive 12 percent of Asian women work in STEM occupations. This percentage is slightly higher than the STEM participation of non-Hispanic white men (11 percent). After adjusting for standard covariates (education, age, industry, marital status, citizen status, veteran status, and region of the country), we calculate that Asian women in STEM occupations have a strong 29 percent wage premium over Asian women who do not work in STEM fields.

Asian women in STEM present a unique case relative to comparisons, particularly when it comes to earnings. While their median earnings are at parity with (and not statistically different from) those of non-Hispanic white men in conventional STEM fields, the average salaries of Asian women in STEM are lower in comparison to Asian men in these fields (88 percent). That said, this case study nonetheless uses non-Hispanic white men as the comparison group for illuminating the STEM participation and earnings of Asian women. There are two reasons for this. First, continued comparison with non-Hispanic white men allows for consistency across all of our case studies. This is important since one of our goals is to offer data that enables intersectional comparisons across groups of women in STEM. Second, despite having less earning power than Asian men overall, non-Hispanic white men remain the most culturally privileged group in the US in terms of both gender and race. Wage gaps are important, but, as we note above, perceived cultural belonging and related bias and stereotypes (such as leadership stereotypes) are particularly important when it comes to thinking about issues that impeded the advancement of Asian women in STEM.

Within the parameters that we have established, figure 5.2 illustrates the overall participation patterns for Asian women and white men in conventional STEM fields. The figure represents how Asian women (and non-Hispanic white men) in STEM are distributed across four broad categories of STEM work.

In the conventional STEM fields, more than three-quarters of Asian women in STEM work in two areas—computer/mathematics (57 percent) and physical/life sciences (21 percent). The participation of Asian women is sharply distinguished from that of white men within the physical and life science occupations: as a percentage of all Asian women in STEM, fully one-fifth work in this area (compared to only 10 percent of white men). White men are more likely to be in engineering: 35 percent are engineers compared to only 16 percent of Asian women. In addition, white men are almost twice as likely to work in STEM management (10 percent compared to 6 percent). As table 5.1 shows, STEM management professions carry the

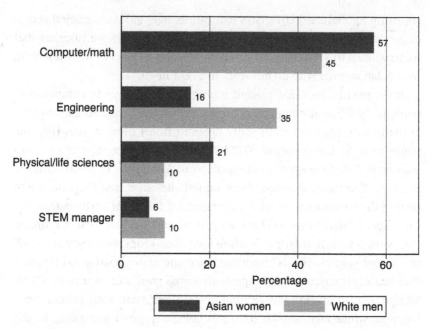

Figure 5.2
Distribution of Asian women and non-Hispanic white men across STEM occupations, individuals age 25–64 working year-round and full-time. *Source:* Data from the American Community Survey, 2012–2019.

Table 5.1
Asian women's median annual earnings as a percentage of non-Hispanic white men's median earnings in STEM occupations, individuals age 25–64 working year-round and full-time

	Median annual earnings		
STEM category	Asian women	Non-Hispanic white men	Asian women's earnings as a percentage of non-Hispanic white men's
Computer/math	$93,390	$89,903	104%
Engineering	$90,183	$88,606	102%
Physical/life sciences	$73,272	$75,632	97%
STEM managerial	$116,007	$120,226	96%

Note: All earnings adjusted to 2019 dollars. *Source:* Data from the American Community Survey, 2012–2019.

highest wages in conventional STEM work. This disparity in the STEM management sector appears to confirm the research that indicates that while Asian women do well in STEM overall, they lag behind at the higher-paying leadership and management levels.

In general, Asian women in conventional STEM fields do remarkably well in terms of median earnings, and, taken as a whole, their salaries are in parity with or exceed the salaries of white men in STEM. There is no indication of a significant pay gap for Asian women in any area of conventional STEM work. As we attend to intersectional characteristics for Asian women (such as immigration status and patterns across dominant identity subgroups), some differences and patterns will emerge that illuminate Asian women's STEM earnings with more nuance.

Asian Women in the STEM-Related Fields: What Do the Data Say?

In 2019, there were an estimated 7.3 million individuals age twenty-five to sixty-four working full-time and year-round in STEM-related jobs. An estimated 505,618 of these individuals identified as Asian women. Over the period of our sample and focusing on those age twenty-five to sixty-four who are working full-time and year-round, we find that only 3.6 percent of white men work in these occupations. However, about 15 percent of Asian women are employed in such occupations (as opposed to about 12 percent in conventional STEM occupations). While the STEM premium is a normative and often cited measure of how conventional STEM careers benefit women in any given identity group, the concept of a STEM-related premium is new. When we calculate a STEM-related premium for Asian women (which compares earnings in STEM-related occupations to non-STEM occupations while controlling for conventional STEM work), we see that Asian women in STEM-related jobs earn 38 percent more than Asian women not working in conventional STEM or STEM-related fields. This premium exceeds the conventional STEM premium (29 percent) for this group. Because our version of a STEM-related premium does not include conventional STEM work, it provides us with a meaningful snapshot of the significant economic benefits that STEM-related work provides Asian women. Figure 5.3 illustrates the distribution of Asian women who work in these fields over the six STEM-related occupational groupings.

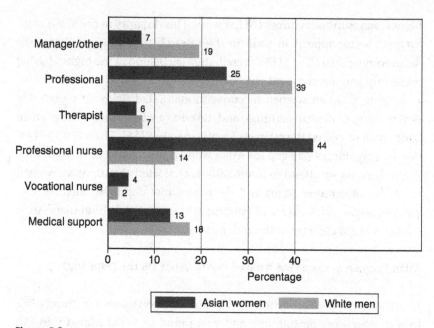

Figure 5.3
Distribution of Asian women and non-Hispanic white men across STEM-related occupations, individuals age 25–64 years working year-round and full-time. *Source:* Data from the American Community Survey, 2012–2019.

There are more pronounced differences between Asian women and non-Hispanic white men when it comes to how those working in the STEM-related fields are distributed. In these occupations, professional nursing is the area of highest participation for Asian women at 44 percent. This level of participation in professional nursing is triple that of white men (14 percent). Asian women who are professional nurses also strongly outpace professional nurses who are white men in terms of median pay (table 5.2), coming in at $1.13 for every dollar earned by white men who work in this field. A similar wage gap that favors Asian women is present for lower-skill vocational nursing occupations as well, although Asian women and white men are far less likely to work in this field (4 percent and 2 percent, respectively).

One in four Asian women in STEM-related fields works in the highest-paying medical professional group. Their robust participation in these occupations helps explain the strong STEM-related premium experienced by

Table 5.2
Asian women's median annual earnings as a percentage of non-Hispanic white men's median annual earnings in STEM-related occupations, individuals age 25–64 working year-round and full-time

STEM-related category	Median annual earnings		Asian women's earnings as a percentage of non-Hispanic white men's
	Asian women	Non-Hispanic white men	
Manager/other	$75,528	$86,437	87%
Professional	$126,484	$168,350	75%
Therapist	$77,529	$76,327	102%
Professional nurse	$85,862	$75,761	113%
Vocational nurse	$49,067	$45,457	108%
Medical support	$52,610	$53,635	98%

Note: All earnings adjusted to 2019 dollars. *Source:* Data from the American Community Survey, 2012–2019.

Asian women. That said, these women still lag behind white men in both participation and earnings: this high-paying job category also represents the largest wage gap, and Asian women in this group earn only seventy-five cents on every dollar earned by white men in those same jobs. STEM-related management is also an area where the distribution of white men and Asian women differs dramatically. White men are almost three times as likely as Asian women to work in STEM-related management (19 percent compared to 7 percent). Asian women's median earnings lag behind in this area, as well, at 87 percent of every dollar earned by white men in STEM-related management.

Stopping at Three Intersections: Nativity Status, Associated Origin Categories, and Pacific Islander Women in STEM

As with all groupings of women in STEM, the data on Asian women is subject to significant cross-cutting variables. Notable among these are nativity status (80 percent of Asian women in STEM identify as foreign-born); an array of different cultural, national, and ethnic identities; and the distinct identity cluster of Pacific Islander. In the sections below, we examine these

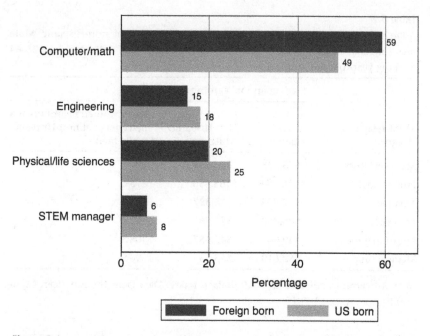

Figure 5.4
Distribution of foreign-born and US-born Asian women across STEM occupations, individuals age 25–64 working year-round and full-time. *Source:* Data from the American Community Survey, 2012–2019.

intersections for Asian women in conventional STEM and STEM-related occupations. In these comparisons, we no longer look at the data on Asian women relative to white men. Rather, we have juxtaposed different groups of Asian women, offering intersectional explorations of how nativity status, associated origin categories, and Pacific Islander identity reveal meaningful differences in the participation and earnings of these intersectional groups.

Nativity Status
Figure 5.4 illustrates the distributions of US-born and foreign-born Asian women across conventional STEM occupations.

As figure 5.4 indicates, the distributions of US-born women in STEM and foreign-born women vary in two distinct areas. Foreign-born Asian women are more strongly represented in the computer and mathematics fields, and US-born Asian women are more likely to work in the physical and life sciences and engineering. US-born Asian women—a group that

Table 5.3

Foreign-born Asian women's median annual earnings as a percentage of US-born Asian women's median annual earnings in STEM-related occupations, individuals age 25–64 working year-round and full-time

STEM-related category	Median annual earnings		Foreign-born Asian women's earnings as a percentage of US-born Asian women's
	Foreign-born Asian women	US-born Asian women	
Computer/math	$95,251	$85,862	111%
Engineering	$92,317	$81,779	113%
Physical/life sciences	$75,141	$68,690	109%
STEM managerial	$121,217	$105,461	115%

Note: All earnings adjusted to 2019 dollars. *Source:* Data from the American Community Survey, 2012–2019.

notably comprises only 20 percent of our sample of Asian women working in STEM—are slightly more likely to be in STEM management. STEM management and leadership positions are the area in which both groups are less strongly distributed.

As table 5.3 shows, foreign-born Asian women outearn US-born Asian women across all conventional STEM categories. This enables us to see that the salaries of foreign-born Asian women in STEM have a buoying effect on the overall median STEM earnings of US-born Asian women. The lower salaries associated with US-born Asian women in STEM are somewhat masked by that effect.

As seen in figure 5.5, the distributions of US-born Asian women and foreign-born Asian women in STEM-related fields are similar, with the exception of marked differences in professional nursing and in medical professional occupations. Almost half (48 percent) of foreign-born Asian women in STEM-related fields are professional nurses compared to about a third (33 percent) of US-born Asian women. A third of US-born Asian women in STEM-related fields are in medical professional occupations, while less than a quarter of foreign-born Asian women in STEM-related fields work in this area. As table 5.4 illustrates, this intersectional look at STEM-related fields reveals a disparity between the earnings of foreign-born Asian women and US-born Asian women that is comparable to conventional STEM jobs.

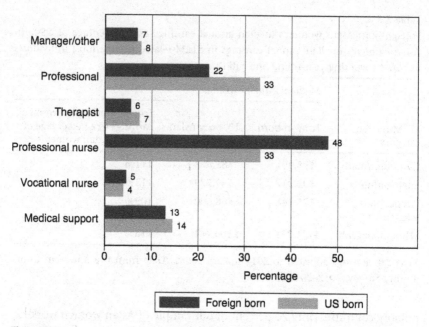

Figure 5.5
Distribution of foreign-born and US-born Asian women across STEM-related occupations, individuals age 25–64 working year-round and full-time. *Source:* Data from the American Community Survey, 2012–2019.

Table 5.4
Foreign-born Asian women's median annual earnings as a percentage of US-born Asian women's median annual earnings in STEM-related occupations, individuals age 25–64 working year-round and full-time

	Median annual earnings		
STEM-related category	Foreign-born Asian women	US-born Asian women	Foreign-born Asian women's earnings as a percentage of US-born Asian women's
Manager/other	$77,529	$70,230	110%
Professional	$129,637	$121,217	107%
Therapist	$80,812	$73,272	110%
Professional nurse	$86,477	$80,037	108%
Vocational nurse	$50,727	$45,091	113%
Medical support	$54,023	$48,621	111%

Note: All earnings adjusted to 2019 dollars. *Source:* Data from the American Community Survey, 2012–2019.

Foreign-born Asian women consistently outearn their US-born counterparts across all the STEM-related occupations. The STEM-related fields, therefore, offer another glimpse of the buoying effect of foreign-born Asian women's earnings on the overall category of Asian women's wages.

Associated Origin Categories

As noted at the beginning of this case study, the category of Asian encompasses a wide array of distinct identities and cultures, such as Japanese, Korean, and Laotian. Although differences among groups are significant, they are rarely taken into account in the literature on STEM diversity. In figure 5.6, we attempt to include them by examining some differences in the STEM occupational distribution across what we term associated origin categories. These specific identities may or may not coincide with one's country of birth (that is, a woman born in the US who identifies as Chinese

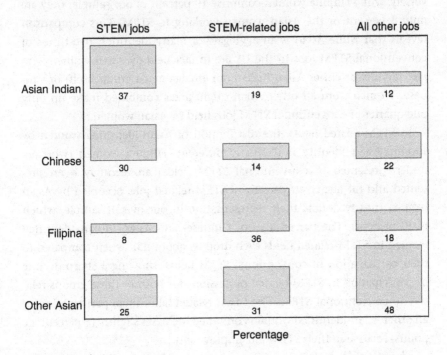

Figure 5.6
Percentage distribution of Asian women by associated origin categories across labor-force sectors, individuals age 25–64 working year-round and full-time. *Source:* Data from the American Community Survey, 2012–2019.

would be a member of the Chinese Asian identity group, as would a woman born in China who also identifies as Chinese). While more specific identities compress significant differences—eliding immigration status, language variations, and so on—they also usefully cut across the US-born and foreign-born divisions we have explored above, offering a look at patterns across ethnic and cultural categories within Asian identity that are rarely explored or even seen.

The dominant three Asian identities in our sample of prime-age full-time women workers are Asian Indian (16 percent), Chinese (22 percent), and Filipina (19 percent). Figure 5.6 shows how Asian women are distributed across three broad sectors of the US workforce—STEM jobs, STEM-related jobs, and all other jobs. Each column of figure 5.6 adds up to 100 percent. For example, 37 percent of Asian women working in STEM identify as Asian Indian. This exceeds their representation in our sample (16 percent). Conversely, while Filipina women comprise 19 percent of our sample, they are only 8 percent of the Asian women working in STEM. This comparison reveals that while Asian is an aggregate of many identities, two-thirds of conventional STEM jobs in the US are in fact held by Asian women who also identify as either Asian Indian (an amalgamated group itself) or Chinese. Women from all other Asian origin areas combined make up only one-quarter of conventional STEM jobs held by Asian women.

In STEM-related fields, the distribution of Asian-identified women by specific Asian identity is distinctly different. Filipina women (who are underrepresented in conventional STEM fields) are strongly overrepresented and fill nearly 40 percent of STEM-related jobs occupied by Asian women (nearly double their representation in our overall sample, which is 20 percent). The percentages of Chinese- and Asian Indian–identified women in STEM-related fields each drop by about half when compared to their participation in conventional STEM fields, showing a sharp decline in participation in STEM-related professions for both of these groups relative to conventional STEM. The STEM-related labor-force participation of all other Asian-identified women combined increases slightly (6 percentage points) relative to their STEM job employment.

Overall, this exploration of trends in specific Asian identities shows that generic use of the undifferentiated category Asian women screens significant differences around patterns—and experiences—in conventional STEM and STEM-related field participation. The dominance of Chinese- and

Asian Indian–identified women in STEM indicates that widely held beliefs around the overrepresentation of Asian women in STEM are not patterns that equally include all Asian women. Our point here is not that US STEM fields have "too many" Asian women from any particular ethnic, national, or cultural group. Rather, our data show that a closer look at these distributions brings up important issues related to opportunities and success for all Asian women relative to STEM work. This look at specific Asian identities overturns the argument that issues of sufficient representation of Asian women in STEM are not germane and opens new questions about how to promote the success of all women—including all Asian women—in STEM.

Pacific Islander Women and STEM: Making a Small STEM Population Visible

Pacific Islander Americans are descendants from the indigenous peoples of Oceania. Sometimes also referred to as Oceanians, people in this group encompass many diverse cultures. The 2020 census offers three Pacific Islander identities—Native Hawaiian, Samoan, and Chamorro—as well as the Other Asian write-in area for this group (Tongan, Fijian, and Marshallese are cited as examples). This segment of the US population is very small and is usually collapsed into the data related to Asians (a general approach we have also employed). The standard practice of merging Pacific Islander women with Asian women reveals the unstable nature of identity categories: the association of Pacific Islanders with the Asian category is purely a census-based decision. As indigenous people, Pacific Islanders could arguably be counted with Native people and included in the American Indian/Alaska Native category.

Pacific Islander women have historically participated in the labor force at higher rates than other Asian women (see figure 5.1). This marked difference and our interest in looking at differences masked by standard data have led us to look closely at Pacific Islander women in STEM. In the analyses below, we return to using white men as a comparison group in order to create a parallel version to the charts and tables that pertain to all Asian women.

When we focus on the subset of Asian women who identify as Pacific Islander, we see that 12 percent of them participate in STEM jobs. These

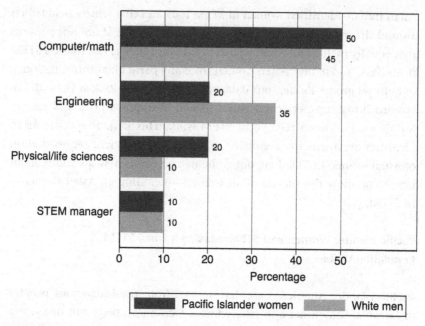

Figure 5.7
Distribution of Pacific Islander women and white men across STEM occupations, individuals age 25–64 working year-round and full-time. *Source:* Data from the American Community Survey, 2012–2019.

women enjoy a strong 35 percent STEM premium relative to Pacific Islander women who do not work in STEM jobs. If we look at the earnings of Pacific Islander women in the general workforce, we see that women from this group earn a mere 67 percent of what white men earn (as noted earlier, in aggregate Asian women are in earnings parity with white men). In conventional STEM occupations, that percentage increases to 85 percent. This represents a substantial lag behind white men but also reflects a smaller wage gap and a substantive improvement in terms of earning power.

As seen in figure 5.7, Pacific Islander women are distributed across STEM work in notable ways, particularly relative to STEM managerial jobs. Both 10 percent of Pacific Islander women and 10 percent of white men working in STEM report being STEM managers. As table 5.5 shows, these jobs have the highest median income among conventional STEM fields. However, Pacific Islander women in STEM management also experience their largest

Table 5.5
Pacific Islander women's median annual earnings as a percentage of non-Hispanic white men's median annual earnings in STEM occupations, individuals age 25–64 working year-round and full-time

STEM category	Median annual earnings		Pacific Islander women's earnings as a percentage of non-Hispanic white men's
	Pacific Islander women	Non-Hispanic white men	
Computer/math	$75,761	$89,903	84%
Engineering	$79,095	$88,606	89%
Physical/life sciences	$69,774	$75,632	92%
STEM managerial	$94,915	$120,226	79%

Note: All earnings adjusted to 2019 dollars. *Source:* Data from the American Community Survey, 2012–2019.

STEM-field pay gap relative to white men (21 percentage points). Pacific Islander women work in engineering occupations less than white men (20 percent report being engineers compared to 35 percent of white men). This is more than Asian women as an aggregate group (16 percent; see table 5.2). Pacific Islander women also experience a solid pay gap in those fields (11 percentage points).

Our look at Pacific Islander women is an excellent example of the value of intersectional analysis. Throughout this case study, our data for Asian women in STEM has consistently included Pacific Islander women—and, as we have shown, the picture for Asian women has looked positive in terms of income parity. However, when we look at Pacific Islander women in STEM, different equity issues emerge. Participation in STEM management, which is a marked issue for Asian women overall, drops away. And income parity issues, which we saw as a minimal concern for Asian women overall, emerge with troubling strength.

The distribution of Pacific Islander women in STEM-related fields is radically different from the distribution of non-Hispanic white men in these fields (figure 5.8). Professional nursing dominates, accounting for 40 percent of Pacific Islander women's STEM-related work, and this group also has a strong presence in medical-support jobs (22 percent). Although few

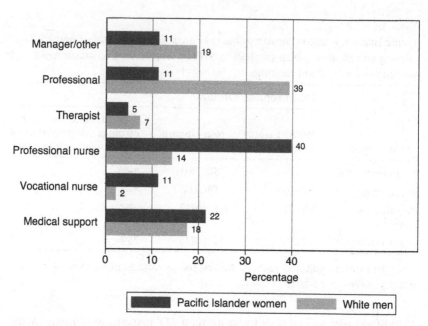

Figure 5.8
Distribution of Pacific Islander women and white men across STEM-related occupations, individuals age 25–64 working year-round and full-time. *Source:* Data from the American Community Survey, 2012–2019.

Pacific Islander women work in medical therapy occupations (5 percent as compared to white men's 7 percent), they are otherwise fairly evenly distributed across the remaining STEM-related fields: vocational nursing, STEM-related management, and medical professional work all make up about 11 percent of their work.

With the exception of the nursing occupations, Pacific Islander women in STEM-related fields experience some pay gaps that are invisible within the aggregate data for all Asian women (see table 5.1). As table 5.6 makes clear, their largest earnings gap (30 percentage points) is in the STEM-related management category, closely followed by medical professionals (24 percentage points). Pacific Islander women do well in other categories, however, and their annual average earnings exceed the average salaries of white men in professional nursing and therapist work. (In vocational nursing, salary differences between these two groups are not statistically different.)

Table 5.6
Pacific Islander women's median annual earnings as a percentage of non-Hispanic white men's median annual earnings in STEM-related occupations, individuals age 25–64 working year-round and full-time

STEM-related category	Median annual earnings		Pacific Islander women's earnings as a percentage of non-Hispanic white men's
	Pacific Islander women	Non-Hispanic white men	
Manager/other	$60,609	$86,437	70%
Professional	$127,382	$168,350	76%
Therapist	$80,509	$76,327	105%
Professional nurse	$81,960	$75,761	108%
Vocational nurse	$45,457	$45,457	100%
Medical support	$45,796	$53,635	85%

Note: All earnings adjusted to 2019 dollars. *Source:* Data from the American Community Survey, 2012–2019.

Case Study Highlights

The intersections we examine in this chapter focus on nativity status, associated origin categories, and Pacific Islander women in STEM.

Conventional STEM Occupations
- Asian women participate in STEM work at a high rate (12 percent), slightly surpassing that of white men (11 percent).
- Engineering stands out as an area of low participation. Only 16 percent of Asian women in STEM are engineers, compared to 35 percent of white men.
- More than three-quarters of Asian women in STEM work in computer/math (57 percent) and physical/life sciences (21 percent).
- The earnings of Asian women in STEM are largely at parity with white men's earnings.

STEM-Related Occupations
- Fifteen percent of Asian women work in STEM-related jobs.
- A quarter of Asian women in these jobs work in the high-paying professional category.

- About half of Asian women are nurses; most of those women work as professional nurses.

- Despite strong participation in medical professional occupations, Asian women's earnings are only 75 percent of those of white men. There is an earnings gap of 13 percentage points in managerial work.

- Remaining categories reflect wages that are equal to or greater than those of white men (Asian women's professional nursing earnings are 113 percent of white men).

Stopping at an Intersection: Nativity Status

- Eighty percent of our sample of Asian women is foreign-born.

- The conventional STEM distribution of foreign-born and US-born Asian women is generally similar overall.

- Earnings strongly favor foreign-born women in conventional STEM. They outearn US-born Asian women in every conventional STEM category.

- In STEM-related work, earnings strongly favor foreign-born Asian women over US-born Asian women. US-born Asian women are more likely to be medical professionals, and foreign-born Asian women are more likely to be professional nurses.

Stopping at an Intersection: Associated Origin Categories

- The three dominant origin categories associated with Asian women in conventional STEM work are Asian Indian (16 percent), Chinese (22 percent), and Filipina (19 percent).

- Asian Indian women are strongly represented in conventional STEM jobs. Filipina women are underrepresented in conventional STEM and but strongly represented in STEM-related work.

Stopping at an Intersection: Pacific Islander Identity

- Pacific Islander women's overall percentage distribution across conventional STEM work is similar to all Asian women.

- In stark contrast to Asian women overall, Pacific Islander women experience meaningful pay gaps across conventional STEM work—16 percentage points in math/computing, 11 percentage points in engineering, 8 percentage points in physical/life sciences, and 21 percentage points in STEM managerial.

- In STEM-related jobs, the overall distribution of Pacific Islander women is similar to that of all Asian women.
- In STEM-related work, Pacific Islander women lag behind white men in management (30 percentage points), medical professional (24 percentage points), and medical support (15 percentage points). Wages for this group are equal to or slightly greater than those of white men in the nursing and therapist categories.

Who Is Hispanic/Latina in the United States?

Racial identity has been a foundational interest of the US census since its inception. The terms *Hispanic* and *Latino*, however, are linked to a census category that is both relatively new and understood to be unrelated to race. If you identify as Hispanic or Latino on the US census, you have not identified as white, Black, or a member of any racial group. You have instead selected a recently devised, multifaceted ethnic category that signals a connection to a large and disparate cluster of countries, cultures, and places of origin.

The ethnonyms of Hispanic and Latino are both relatively new and unique as census categories. Although the census listed the category Mexican as a race for one year (in 1930, as a response to an influx in immigration from Mexico around the time of the Mexican Revolution), interest in counting Hispanic/Latino populations is a relatively recent phenomenon (Nobles 2000). The move to an ethnicity question begins with the 1970 census, the first questionnaire to feature a (nonracialized) question about a respondent's origins and descent. The options—Mexican, Puerto Rican, Cuban, Central/South American, Other Spanish, and None—make it clear that this question is directed toward groups we would now identify as Hispanic/Latino. The word *Hispanic* itself first appears in 1980 (Spanish/Hispanic Origin or Descent); the question offers broader identities associated with Mexican identity/heritage, changes Other Spanish to Spanish/Hispanic, and no longer names Central/South American as an option. In 1990, the census began to provide space for respondents to write in a response if they were not represented in the choices provided. In 2000, Latino was added ("Is this person Spanish/Hispanic/Latino?"). The 2010 and 2020 censuses both asked, "Is this person of Hispanic, Latino, or Spanish origin?" (Pew Research Center 2020).

In thinking about Hispanic/Latina-identified women in STEM occupations, it is important to understand that the categories of Hispanic and Latina are not only new to the census but also often (although not always) understood as different in their meanings. Hispanic is commonly understood to indicate a person residing in the US who is descended from Spanish-speaking populations, while Latino is widely understood to indicate a person residing in the US who is from or has descended from people from Latin America. These definitions are contested, however, and people who identify as Hispanic/Latino have complex and multifaceted relationships to these identity labels (Rinderle and Montoya 2008). Indeed, there is so much debate about their relative meanings that the Hispanic/Latino naming dispute is a subject of critical inquiry, and scholars argue about the production, use, and effects of these terms (Acuña 2003; Mora 2014). Some argue against use of these terms altogether. In short, Hispanic/Latino origin is a politicized category through which we can readily see the inherent instability of social identities as they are produced and debated (Davila 2000; Hernández 2019).

When considering the terminology issues attached to this category, it is important to recognize that the US census uses these categories interchangeably, eliding possible distinctions between them. The 2020 census simply defines Hispanic or Latino as "a person of Cuban, Mexican, Puerto Rican, South or Central American, or other Spanish culture or origin regardless of race." This means that when the census asks about ethnicity, the question merges a broad cluster of varied ethnic identities that are often defined differently (and often understood as distinct). At the same time, diversity among Hispanic/Latino ethnic groupings is also on the rise, and census data reflect a "significant increase" in the number of national-origin categories cited by the US Hispanic/Latino population over the last forty years (Schmidt et al. 2009, 25). The census further complicates its conflation of so many identities and cultural contexts by adding the category Spanish origin. Spanish origin can be interpreted in many ways but is commonly understood to indicate people living in the US who are from Spain or descended from Spanish people, which adds people of European origin to the undifferentiated mix. Given these parameters, data associated with Hispanic/Latina women essentially offers two very different possible pictures—a single, broad grouping that includes all women who identify as Hispanic/Latina and a large number of subgroups associated with about twenty countries or regions.

The census's untroubled amalgamation of the terms *Hispanic*, *Latino*, and *Spanish* is the inverse of the approach taken by scholars and activists who seek to add subtlety and distinctiveness to these categories or even to deconstruct them entirely. In this case study, we employ the hybrid term *Hispanic/Latina* because we wish to avoid the impossible task of evaluating the suitability of these conflicted terms. We use the term *Hispanic/Latino* when referring to both women and men, but, because of our focus on individuals who identify as women, we use the word *Latina* whenever possible. Because the term *Latinx* is not clear in its point of reference (it can be seen as gender inclusive but also as a way to refuse or deconstruct gender categories) and has also been subject to a decidedly mixed reception by Hispanic/Latino communities, we do not use that term in this case study (McWhorter 2019; Peñaloza 2020). We use the single term *Hispanic* only when labeling graphs and tables because that term directly reflects the way the American Community Survey (ACS) labels its data.

Although the parameters of this identity category may be contested, Hispanic/Latino has historically been the only ethnicity of interest to US government demographers and the only ethnic identity that has been accorded its own separate (nonracial) census question. When it comes to ethnicity, the census asks only about Hispanic/Latino/Spanish heritage and then divides survey takers into two root populations. A response of no exits survey takers from the question and moves them forward; a response of yes directs respondents to select from several specific ethnic origin categories (such as Mexican, Puerto Rican, or Cuban) or to write in the name of other countries or regions.

Until the 2020 census, any interest in ethnicity was entirely focused on Hispanic/Latino people. The very recent (and somewhat controversial) introduction of write-in spaces under the racial categories of both white and Black may ultimately complicate an already complex data picture around ethnicity (Conde 2020). In the 2020 census, people who identified as white or Black were provided with text boxes and the following instructions: "Print, for example, German, Irish, English, Italian, Lebanese, Egyptian, etc." These unprecedented instructions tilt a question focused on racial identity toward the collection of information that could easily be understood as pertaining to ethnic identity. It remains to be seen if and how the collection of ethnic data within a racial category will impact our understanding of ethnic and racial census categories and related data—and if it will impact the ACS's focus on Hispanic/Latino as the only ethnic identity of interest. At least for now, the explicit collection of nonracialized ethnic data remains solely connected to Hispanic/Latino-identified people.

The distinction between race and ethnicity is particularly important for our intersectional investigation of women in STEM because people who identify as Hispanic/Latino on the census can and do identify as any race. In 2019, 67 percent of Hispanic respondents who were women age twenty-five and over reported white as their sole racial identity, and about 26 percent identified their race as Other. The category Other indicates they identified racially as neither white nor the three other racial categorizations that the census offers (Black, Asian/Pacific Islander, and American Indian/Alaska Native). Many Hispanic/Latino people identify as white. A significant number of Hispanic/Latino people also report a wide variety of nations and regions as representative of their racial identities under the racial category Other (and do not identify as white, Black, Asian, or Native American). These trends indicate that Hispanic/Latino-identified people have a complex relationship to racial identity.

Over the last several decades, the US Hispanic/Latino population has increased significantly. From 1970 to 2019, the Hispanic/Latino population grew from 9.6 million persons to 60.6 million persons, a long surge in growth that is beginning to slow in pace (Noe-Bustamante, Lopez, and Krogstad 2020). As of 2019, the total percentage of people in the US who identify as Hispanic/Latino was 18 percent. The makeup of the Hispanic/Latino population has also changed over time, including a rise in identifying with the category Other Latino rather than the specific countries of origin traditionally offered by the US census (Guzmán and McConnell 2002). While the category of Hispanic/Latino has not necessarily become any more stable in terms of its content, the strong increase in the number of individuals identifying as Hispanic/Latino testifies to the importance of attending to the labor story associated with this significant group.

Finally, immigration/foreign-born status is an important variable for the Hispanic/Latina population. In 2019, 50 percent of Hispanic women age twenty-five and over living in the US self-identified as foreign-born. This high percentage indicates that immigrant status is of amplified significance for Hispanic/Latina women and likely to shape opportunities and experiences of bias. Cultural, linguistic, social, and other differences may combine with anti-immigration bias to trigger the various forms of systemic injustice that emerge from ethnocentrism, racism, and xenophobia—or any combination of the three.

As we examine the numbers related to Hispanic/Latina women in STEM, we recognize the current census data on Hispanic/Latina women have the following distinctive attributes: the data are (1) *self-selected* (like all US census responses, the category is chosen by the individual in question), (2) *focused on ethnicity* (Hispanic/Latina identity is the only freestanding category explicitly designated as an ethnicity by the census), (3) *flattened across a significant number of ethnic identities* (despite a steady increase in national-origin diversity, the category of Hispanic/Latina merges a substantial variety of regional/national origins and ethnic identities), (4) *racialized in highly diverse ways* (Hispanic/Latina ethnic identity is strongly linked to white identity but also connected to many other racial identities, including both standard census racial categories and racial identities that are not named by the census), (5) *growing substantially over the last half century* (the US Hispanic population has increased sixfold since the 1970s) (Noe-Bustamante, Lopez, and Krogstad 2020), (6) *strongly linked to immigrant status* (while immigrant status is not necessarily connected to American citizenship, Hispanic/Latina women have an outsized likelihood of being foreign-born).

We move now to a contextualizing overview of Hispanic/Latina women in the US labor force, followed by a detailed analysis of occupational and income data related to these women across both conventional STEM and STEM-related jobs.

Hispanic/Latina Women in the US Labor Force

Like all women of color, Hispanic/Latina women in the US labor force are impacted by the experience of bias and the effects of negative stereotypes that cut across both gender and race or ethnicity. Hispanic/Latina women face both overt and covert discrimination at work, regardless of their occupational fields. Research on Hispanic/Latina women working in the US demonstrates that forms of gender, racial, or ethnic bias intersectionally shape their work experiences (Chavez 2011; Gutiérrez y Muhs et al. 2012; Hesse-Biber and Carter 2005; McKinsey & Company and

LeanIn.org 2021). The research suggests that the (real or perceived) factor of immigrant status—particularly the factor of second-language accents—broadly and significantly affects the reality of Hispanic/Latino people's working lives and careers, negatively impacting key success factors such as hireability and perceived leadership potential (Ballesteros 2015; Hosoda, Nguyen, and Stone-Romero 2012). Overall, Hispanic/Latina women in the labor force intensely experience intertwined, intersectional systemic disadvantages across multiple fronts. Sexism, racism, ethnocentrism, and xenophobia often interact in multiple intersectional combinations, powerfully affecting the opportunities and experiences of working Hispanic/Latina women.

The labor-force participation of Hispanic/Latina women is distinguished by a large number of ethnic and cultural differences that affect the extent to which we can generalize about this group's participation in the US labor force (Bucknor 2016; Catanzarite and Trimble 2008). Within the context of that important caveat, overall trends illustrate that while Hispanic/Latina women have historically worked slightly less than white women, the long-standing gap has recently closed. Figure 6.1 begins with the first usage of the term *Hispanic* in the 1980 census. In 2019, working Hispanic/Latinas

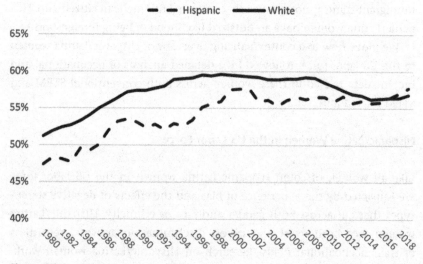

Figure 6.1
US labor-force participation rates: Hispanic and white women, 1980–2019, age 16 and over. *Source:* US Bureau of Labor Statistics.

comprised 18 percent of women (age sixteen and over) in the overall US labor force.

A number of factors have likely influenced long-term trends around Latinas and paid work, including low human capital as well as marriage- and family-related patterns (Kahn and Whittington 1996). Historically, Hispanic/Latina culture has been shaped by both strongly demarcated gender roles and traditional family structures. As Damary Bonilla-Rodriguez (2016, 340) notes in her study of Latinas in the workplace, "an important aspect of Latino culture involves following traditions and beliefs . . . including those related to gender roles." The relative persistence of traditional gender roles in Hispanic/Latino communities (such as the man/breadwinner role and the woman/caretaker role) may influence who is most likely to participate in the paid labor market and how they do so, especially relative to full-time work. Traditional gender roles dictate that Hispanic/Latina women are often perceived as responsible for the private role of caretaker, which involves unpaid labor such as housework, cooking, and childcare. And while such traditions can descend into stereotyping and are neither absolute nor uniformly salient for all Hispanic/Latino groups and communities, they are likely to operate as variables in overall labor trends.

Compounding the effects of an historically traditional gendered division of labor in many Hispanic/Latina cultures is the importance of maintaining familial ties and the significant effect of family connections and obligations on this group. Traditional gender roles are combined with a culture that strongly values sustaining and nurturing broad family connections. While family should also be understood as a critical place of support, in the context of the (often already gendered) demands of family responsibilities, family size has been a factor in at least two ways for Hispanic/Latina women. First, Latinas have historically had more children than most other groups, and the birth rate for Hispanic/Latino populations in the US has exceeded those of non-Hispanics for many decades. Only recently has the trend begun to decline (Noe-Bustamante, Lopez, and Krogstad 2019). Second, family size and related obligations can be understood in terms of the scope of practical and emotional labor and in terms of number of children. Research on Hispanic/Latina women in the workplace indicates that "family life extends beyond the nuclear family," suggesting that familial obligations may be more broadly defined for Hispanic/Latina women than for women in many other groups (Catalyst 2003b, 12; Gutierrez Rinchiera

2020). This potentially amplifies multidimensional unpaid work obligations for Latinas who are engaged in unpaid family-related caretaking roles.

Like all women of color, Hispanic/Latina women in the US work disproportionately in low-paying, low-skill jobs (National Women's Law Center 2014). In 2014, the most common industry in which Hispanic/Latino women worked was restaurants and other food services (10.4 percent), while the most common occupation for this group was maid/housekeeping cleaner (6.4 percent) (Bucknor 2016). These trends in paid labor indicate that the Hispanic/Latina population is systemically underserved in terms of employment opportunities and also in preparation for paid employment. Overall, Hispanic workers have a lower level of educational attainment than other nonwhite racial and ethnic groups. Data from the 2019 ACS indicate that members of the Hispanic/Latino population over age twenty-five are half as likely to hold a college degree as non-Hispanic whites. The disconnect between Hispanic/Latino workers and educational opportunity is no doubt a factor in the persistence of low-wage work for this community and certainly impacts their STEM field participation.

Finally, the Hispanic/Latino immigrant population, like many US immigrant communities, is subject to many specific forms of exploitation. This raises the additional possibility of invisible or inaccurate data around immigrant Hispanic/Latina women (particularly undocumented women) who often work informally (and for low pay) as private domestic workers, childcare providers, and so on (Romero 2016). In other words, it is possible that the number of working Hispanic/Latina women is actually greater than established workforce participation data indicate.

Beyond generic women-of-color approaches, little research has centered on the occupational experiences of Latinas in the STEM workforce. The available scholarship that exists tends to be focused on Latinas in academic STEM faculty jobs. This research shows that Hispanic women in academic STEM encounter many forms of bias, including bias particular to their intersectional position as Latinas (Cantú 2012). They report the negative assumptions about competence and discounting of accomplishments that is typical of women of color in STEM, frequent encounters with anti-immigrant stereotypes, and associations with domestic and caretaking work (such as being misrecognized as housekeeping or secretarial staff) (Williams, Phillips, and Hall 2014). Notably, the transition gap from STEM training to STEM work is a gendered one for Hispanic populations. When it comes to transitioning from school to STEM occupations, Latinas are significantly less likely than Latino men to enter the STEM workforce (Excelencia in Education 2015). As more Latinas enter the workforce and STEM jobs are touted as offering promises of higher incomes, it is more important than ever to understand the experiences of Latinas in the STEM professions.

Hispanic/Latina Women in Conventional STEM Fields: What Do the Data Say?

As of 2019, the total percentage of women (age twenty-five and over) in the US who identified as Hispanic was 15.1 percent. According to our definition of conventional STEM, in the year 2019 alone there were an estimated 8.6 million individuals age twenty-five to sixty-four working full-time and year-round in STEM occupations. An estimated 186,862 of them were women who identified as Hispanic/Latina, which was about 2 percent of all STEM job holders. Averaging over all the years of our sample and focusing on those age twenty-five to sixty-four working full-time and year-round reveals that only 2.2 percent of Hispanic/Latina women work in STEM occupations (compared to 11 percent of non-Hispanic white men). After adjusting for standard covariates (education, age, industry, marital status, citizen status, veteran status, and region of the country), we calculate that the Hispanic/Latina women who work in STEM occupations have a significant wage premium of 34 percent over Hispanic/Latina women who do not work in STEM fields.

Within the STEM occupations, Hispanic/Latina women's median earnings are 72 percent of non-Hispanic white men's, a considerable jump since across all occupations Hispanic/Latina women earn only 54 percent of what white men earn. While Hispanic/Latina women's median STEM earnings are robust (72 percent of non-Hispanic white men's), however, they are still less than the ratio of the median earnings of all women relative to all men (80 percent). There can be no doubt that STEM occupations provide a strong economic advantage for Hispanic/Latina women relative to other Hispanic/Latina women, although that advantage also highlights the substantial relative wage lag under which this group labors overall.

Having established our parameters, we now dig deeper into the data and examine the distribution of Hispanic/Latina women across conventional STEM occupations. Figure 6.2 represents how Hispanic women and

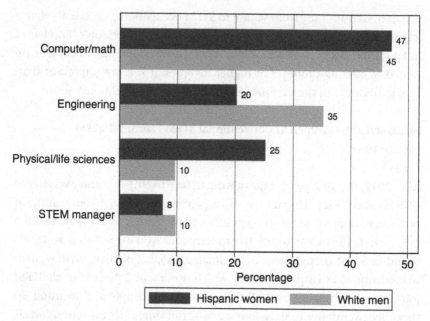

Figure 6.2
Distribution of Hispanic women and non-Hispanic white men across STEM occupations, individuals age 25–64 working year-round and full-time. *Source:* Data from the American Community Survey, 2012–2019.

non-Hispanic white men in STEM are distributed across four broad categories of STEM work.

As figure 6.2 shows, both Hispanic/Latina women and non-Hispanic white men working in STEM are most strongly represented in the computer/math fields (47 percent and 45 percent, respectively). However, when it comes to the physical/life sciences, a quarter of Hispanic/Latina women in STEM work in these areas while only 10 percent of white men do. Hispanic/Latina women are far less likely to be engineers than white men: within the STEM professions, 35 percent of white men are engineers, but only 20 percent of Hispanic/Latina women are in these fields.

What can be learned from these different patterns of STEM employment, particularly when it comes to earnings? If Hispanic/Latina women in STEM earn 72 percent of what non-Hispanic white men in STEM earn, judging from these distributions it would seem likely that this group is especially disadvantaged by a lower representation in engineering, given the relatively high incomes in that field. In addition, Hispanic/Latina women who are

Table 6.1
Hispanic women's median annual earnings as a percentage of non-Hispanic white
men's median annual earnings in STEM occupations, individuals age 25–64 working
year-round and full-time

STEM occupation	Median annual earnings		Hispanic women's earnings as a percentage of non-Hispanic white men's
	Hispanic women	Non-Hispanic white men	
Computer/math	$65,423	$89,903	73%
Engineering	$67,044	$88,606	76%
Physical/life sciences	$59,058	$75,632	78%
STEM managerial	$87,883	$120,226	73%

Note: All earnings adjusted to 2019 dollars. *Source:* Data from the American Community Survey, 2012–2019.

engineers experience a pay gap of 24 percentage points relative to white
men in those fields as seen in table 6.1. It is also worth noting that Hispanic/
Latina women's markedly strong representation in the physical/life sciences
(25 percent) places one in four Hispanic/Latina women in the STEM category
that features the lowest median wages in STEM (for both Hispanic/Latina
women and white men). In this lower-paying STEM occupational category,
the wage gap (22 percentage points) brings Hispanic/Latina women closest
to the median earnings of white men. Overall, the gap between Hispanic/
Latina women's and white men's median earnings is relatively similar for
each of the four STEM occupational categories. It is readily apparent that
STEM work does not guarantee earnings parity with white men for Hispanic
women but instead reflects a consistent and substantial wage gap.

Hispanic/Latina Women in the STEM-Related Fields: What Do the Data Say?

In 2019, there were an estimated 7.3 million individuals age twenty-five to
sixty-four working full-time and year-round in STEM-related jobs, and an
estimated 476,960 of these individuals were Hispanic/Latina women. Over
the period of our sample and focusing on those age twenty-five to sixty-four
who work year-round and full-time, we find that only 3.6 percent of non-
Hispanic white men work in these occupations. However, about 6.5 percent

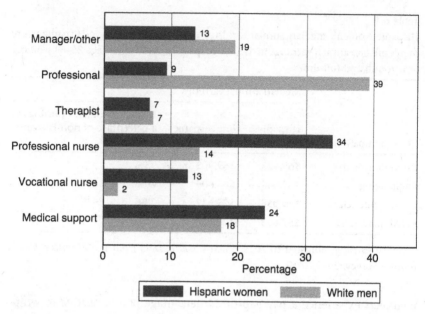

Figure 6.3
Distribution of Hispanic women and non-Hispanic white men across STEM-related occupations, individuals age 25–64 working year-round and full-time. *Source:* Data from the American Community Survey, 2012–2019.

of Hispanic/Latina women are employed in such occupations (as opposed to about 2.2 percent in conventional STEM). While the STEM premium is a normative and often cited measure of how conventional STEM careers benefit women in any given identity group, the concept of a STEM-related premium is new. When we calculate a STEM-related premium for Hispanic/Latina women (which compares earnings in STEM-related occupations to non-STEM occupations while controlling for conventional STEM work), we see that Hispanic/Latina women in STEM-related jobs earn 29 percent more than Hispanic/Latina women not working in conventional STEM or STEM-related fields. This premium is somewhat less than the conventional STEM premium (34 percent) for this group. Because our version of a STEM-related premium does not include conventional STEM work, it provides us with a meaningful snapshot of the significant economic benefits that STEM-related work provides Hispanic/Latina women. Figure 6.3 illustrates the distribution of Hispanic/Latina women and non-Hispanic white men over the six STEM-related occupational groupings.

Table 6.2
Hispanic women's median annual earnings as a percentage of non-Hispanic white men's median annual earnings in STEM-related occupations, individuals age 25–64 working year-round and full-time

STEM-related category	Median annual earnings		Hispanic women's earnings as a percentage of non-Hispanic white men's
	Hispanic women	Non-Hispanic white men	
Manager/other	$52,730	$86,437	61%
Professional	$90,183	$168,350	54%
Therapist	$60,609	$76,327	79%
Professional nurse	$67,044	$75,761	88%
Vocational nurse	$41,258	$45,457	91%
Medical support	$40,791	$53,635	76%

Note: All earnings adjusted to 2019 dollars. *Source:* Data from the American Community Survey, 2012–2019.

When we examine the work of Hispanic/Latina women relative to non-Hispanic white men in STEM-related fields, we see a strong level of variation across the occupational patterns in each category. Almost half of all Hispanic/Latina women in STEM-related work are in the (combined) nursing professions (47 percent). Compared to white men, Hispanic/Latina women are distributed strongly in both areas of nursing: 34 percent of Hispanic women in STEM-related work are professional nurses, and only 14 percent of white men are in these professions; 13 percent of Hispanic/Latina women are vocational nurses, compared to only 2 percent of white men in STEM-related fields. Differences in average median wages show Hispanic/Latina women nonetheless remain at an earnings disadvantage: Hispanic/Latina women earn 88 percent of what white men earn in the higher-paying field of professional nursing, and Hispanic/Latina vocational nurses earn 91 percent of what vocational nurses who are white men earn (table 6.2). Although Hispanic/Latina women are distributed far more strongly in the nursing fields, on average these women still earn less than white men in the nursing occupations.

In terms of the high-paying STEM-related field of medical professionals, 39 percent of white men in STEM-related jobs occupy this field (a total comparatively similar to the total number of Hispanic/Latina women in the combined nursing fields, which is 47 percent). The median income for medical professionals who are white men is $168,350. Only 9 percent of Hispanic women in the STEM-related fields are medical professionals, and that group has a much smaller median income of $90,183. This difference means that, on average, Hispanic/Latina women medical professionals earn only 54 percent of what white male medical professionals earn. This is the most substantial gap between Hispanic women and white men within the STEM-related occupation subcategories. Notably, there is also a strong wage gap in the STEM-related managerial fields, where Hispanic/Latina women experience a pay gap of 39 percentage points relative to white men in these occupations. Finally, almost one in four Hispanic/Latina women working in the STEM-related fields labors in medical-support jobs; along with vocational nursing, these jobs are the lowest-paying in the STEM-related groupings.

Stopping at Three Intersections: Race, Nativity Status, and Associated Origin Categories of Hispanic/Latina Women in STEM

As we have noted, the category of Hispanic/Latina is difficult to define and subject to significant cross-cutting variables, particularly race, foreign-born status (45 percent of Hispanic/Latina women in our sample identify as foreign-born), and a wide variety of cultural and ethnic identities. In this section, we intersectionally examine these three key categorical instabilities for Hispanic/Latina women in the STEM and STEM-related occupations. In the comparisons that follow, we no longer compare Hispanic/Latina women to non-Hispanic white men. Rather, we juxtapose different groups of Hispanic/Latina women, examining the question of whether variables such as race, nativity status, and variation in associated origin reveal different patterns within STEM participation and earnings.

Racial Identity

In 2019, the majority (67 percent) of ACS respondents age twenty-five and over who identified as Hispanic/Latino also racially identified as white. Technically, that places most of the US Hispanic population in the historically most privileged racial group. But the idea that the majority of US Hispanics/Latinos might routinely benefit from white privilege is swiftly confounded by both common sense and the research on the forms of bias and discrimination routinely experienced by this group. Our first intersectional investigation of Hispanic/Latina women in STEM therefore pauses at the intersection of Hispanic/Latino ethnicity and race.

In our sample of Hispanic/Latina women in STEM, 71 percent of this group identified as white, 5 percent identified with a single standard nonwhite census racial category (that is, Black, Asian/Pacific Islander, or American Indian/Alaska Native), another 5 percent identified with two or more of the standard racial categories, and 18 percent of Hispanic/Latina women identified as neither white nor as a member of a standard nonwhite census racial category. This means almost 20 percent of Hispanic/Latina women in STEM fields report a wide range of nonwhite racial identifications outside of the racial categories offered by the census.

Despite the significance of race as a primary indicator of systemic disadvantage and the common perception that white identity automatically carries the social and economic benefits of white privilege, our data analysis shows that self-identification as white has no significant effect on the occupational distribution of Hispanic/Latina women in STEM fields (figure 6.4).

Similarly, self-identification as white is not strongly relevant for the earnings of Hispanic women in these occupations. As shown in table 6.3, wage differences between Hispanic/Latina women in STEM who identify as white and Hispanic/Latina women in STEM who identify as women of color are mostly negligible. (In the computer/math occupations, the differences between these two groups are not statistically different.) The one exception to this is the highest-paying set of jobs in conventional STEM— the STEM managerial occupations. Although both groups work in this area at about the same rate (8 percent), white-identified Hispanic/Latina women in STEM managerial jobs enjoy a substantial earnings advantage over their nonwhite counterparts, with the latter earning only eighty-three cents for every dollar earned by a Hispanic/Latina woman who identifies as white.

In our sample of Hispanic/Latina women in STEM-related occupations, 70 percent of this group identifies as white, a percentage similar to that of Hispanic/Latina women in the conventional STEM fields. However, of those who identify as a race other than white, 10 percent report Black as their race while nearly 70 percent identify as neither white nor as a member of a standard nonwhite census racial category (defined here as women who identify as Black, Native American/Alaska Native, Asian/Pacific Islander),

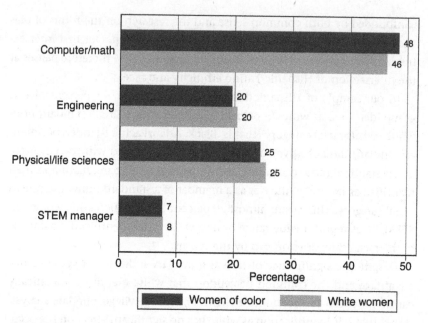

Figure 6.4
Distribution of Hispanic women across STEM occupations by race, individuals age 25–64 working year-round and full-time. *Source:* Data from the American Community Survey, 2012–2019.

Table 6.3
Median annual earnings of Hispanic women of color as a percentage of white Hispanic women's median annual earnings in STEM occupations, individuals age 25–64 working year-round and full-time

	Median annual earnings		
STEM category	Hispanic women of color	White Hispanic women	Hispanic women of color's earnings as a percentage of white Hispanic women's
Computer/math	$65,423	$65,423	100%
Engineering	$65,423	$67,680	97%
Physical/life sciences	$56,948	$60,609	94%
STEM managerial	$75,141	$90,913	83%

Note: All earnings adjusted to 2019 dollars. *Source:* Data from the American Community Survey, 2012–2019.

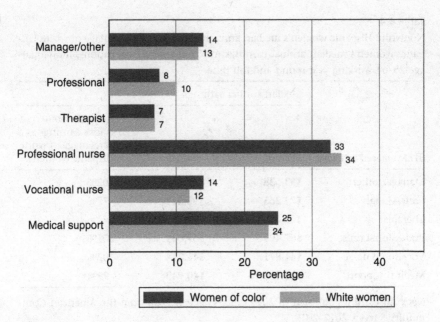

Figure 6.5
Distribution of Hispanic women across STEM-related occupations by race, individuals age 25–64 working year-round and full-time. *Source:* Data from the American Community Survey, 2012–2019.

while 15 percent report that they identify with two or more of the major race groupings.

In the STEM-related fields, we see a similar pattern between the distribution of white and Hispanic women of color, and there is very little variation (less than 2 percentage points) between the distribution patterns of these two groups across the occupational distributions (figure 6.5).

In terms of earnings, as seen in table 6.4, the only significant wage gap (greater than 5 percentage points) between white-identifying Hispanic/Latina women and Hispanic women of color in the STEM-related fields is in the medical professional occupations. The median earnings of white Hispanic/Latina medical professionals is $96,611, and the median earning of Hispanic/Latina medical professionals of color is $74,265, indicating that these women earn only 77 percent of what their white Hispanic counterparts earn. There are no substantial wage gaps in the other STEM-related categories.

Table 6.4
Nonwhite Hispanic women's median annual earnings as a percentage of white Hispanic women's median annual earnings in STEM-related occupations, individuals age 25–64 working year-round and full-time

STEM-related category	Median annual earnings		Hispanic women of color's earnings as a percentage of white Hispanic women's
	Hispanic women of color	White Hispanic women	
Manager/other	$53,538	$52,599	102%
Professional	$74,265	$96,611	77%
Therapist	$59,426	$61,187	97%
Professional nurse	$67,495	$67,044	101%
Vocational nurse	$41,871	$41,214	102%
Medical support	$40,406	$40,949	99%

Note: All earnings adjusted to 2019 dollars. *Source:* Data from the American Community Survey, 2012–2019.

Nativity Status

When we examine Hispanic/Latina women's STEM occupations relative to nativity status, we see that US-born Hispanic/Latina women in STEM are much more likely to be involved in the computer/math fields than their foreign-born counterparts (50 percent compared to 41 percent) (figure 6.6).

Foreign-born Hispanic/Latina women are significantly more likely to be engineers than their US-born counterparts (24 percent compared to 18 percent) and somewhat more likely to work in the physical/life sciences (28 percent compared to 24 percent).

In terms of earnings, foreign-born Hispanic/Latina women enjoy a slight advantage over their US-born counterparts when it comes to the computer/math occupations (the largest occupational category for both of these groups of Hispanic/Latina women) (table 6.5). However, foreign-born Hispanic/Latina women make only 87 percent of what their US-born counterparts make in the physical and life sciences. Median wages are nearly identical for Hispanic women who are engineers, regardless of origin; the same is true for the STEM managerial occupations.

In terms of participation in the STEM-related professions, there are also few significant disparities between US- and foreign-born Hispanic women

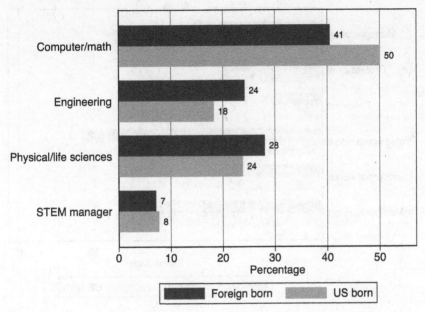

Figure 6.6
Distribution of foreign-born and US-born Hispanic women across STEM occupations, individuals age 25–64 working year-round and full-time. *Source:* Data from the American Community Survey, 2012–2019.

Table 6.5
Foreign-born Hispanic women's median annual earnings as a percentage of US-born Hispanic women's median annual earnings in STEM-related occupations, individuals age 25–64 working year-round and full-time

STEM-related category	Median annual earnings		Foreign-born Hispanic women's earnings as a percentage of US-born Hispanic women's
	Foreign-born Hispanic women	US-born Hispanic women	
Computer/math	$68,549	$64,649	106%
Engineering	$65,423	$68,549	95%
Physical/life sciences	$53,672	$61,887	87%
STEM manager	$89,736	$86,872	103%

Note: All earnings adjusted to 2019 dollars. *Source:* Data from the American Community Survey, 2012–2019.

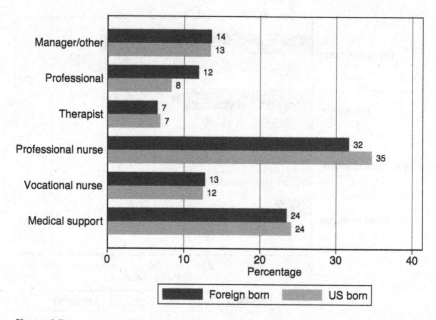

Figure 6.7
Distribution of foreign-born and US-born Hispanic women across STEM-related occupations, individuals age 25–64 working year-round and full-time. *Source:* Data from the American Community Survey, 2012–2019.

Table 6.6
Foreign-born Hispanic women's median annual earnings as a percentage of US-born Hispanic women's median annual earnings in STEM-related occupations, individuals age 25–64 working year-round and full-time

STEM-related category	Median annual earnings		Foreign-born Hispanic women's earnings as a percentage of US-born Hispanic women's
	Foreign-born Hispanic women	US-born Hispanic women	
Manager/other	$50,948	$53,672	95%
Professional	$80,812	$94,915	85%
Therapist	$59,971	$60,916	98%
Professional nurse	$66,454	$67,495	98%
Vocational nurse	$39,196	$42,088	93%
Medical support	$42,138	$40,406	104%

Note: All earnings adjusted to 2019 dollars. *Source:* Data from the American Community Survey, 2012–2019.

in terms of occupation (figure 6.7). Only the medical professional category reveals a meaningful difference, with 12 percent of foreign-born Hispanic women employed in that category compared to 8 percent of US-born Hispanic women.

When we examine this particular occupational category in terms of earnings, we see that the median earnings of US-born Hispanic women who are medical professionals are significantly higher than the median earnings of foreign-born Hispanic women in those occupations ($94,915 compared to $80,812 or a pay gap of 15 percentage points) (table 6.6). Foreign-born Hispanic women in the relatively low-paying medical-support fields have a slight earnings advantage over their US-born counterparts.

Associated Origin Categories

When a Hispanic/Latina woman completes the census, she is invited to identify her Hispanic, Latino, or Spanish origin. Three of her options are specific: "Yes, Mexican, Mexican Amer, Chicano," "Yes, Puerto Rican," and "Yes, Cuban." According to data from the 2019 ACS, these groups have the largest populations within the Hispanic/Latino category. Her fourth option is a generic grouping that asks for a write-in description: "Yes, another Hispanic, Latino, or Spanish origin—Print, for example, Salvadoran, Dominican, Colombian, Guatemalan, Spaniard, Ecuadorian, etc." Although all of these options name countries, they do not reflect where an individual was born, nor do they indicate citizenship. We term these more granular groupings associated origin categories because they represent a cluster of possibilities—literal birthplace, ethnic heritage, close cultural connection, or some (or all) of the above. In 2019, Hispanic/Latino census respondents identified with more than twenty such categories.

In our final intersectional examination of Hispanic/Latina women, we turn briefly to the question of associated origin categories to provide a new kind of snapshot of the general participation patterns of various origin subgroups of Hispanic/Latina women in STEM. The dominant three specific Hispanic identities in our sample are Mexican (58 percent), Puerto Rican (10 percent), and Cuban (4 percent), while the other 27 percent are all other Hispanic/Latina identities. Our purpose is to acknowledge—if only at

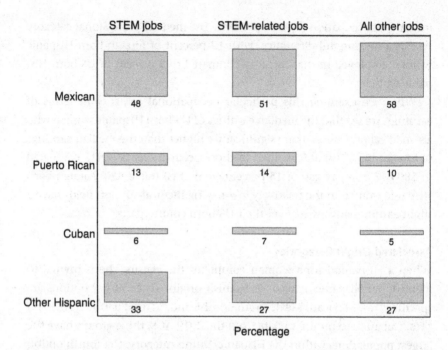

Figure 6.8
Distribution of Hispanic women by associated origin categories across labor-force sectors, individuals age 25–64 working year-round and full-time. *Source:* Data from the American Community Survey, 2012–2019.

a broad level across labor-force sectors—any significant participation differences within the Hispanic/Latina populations working in STEM. Figure 6.8 shows how Hispanic/Latina women of various origins are distributed across three broad US workforce sectors—STEM jobs, STEM-related jobs, and all other jobs. The columns add up to 100 percent—for example, of all Hispanic/Latina women who work in STEM, 48 percent are of Mexican origin, 13 percent are of Puerto Rican origin, 6 percent identify as Cuban, and the rest, 33 percent, are from other origins.

This snapshot of Hispanic/Latina women from the major associated origin groups shows that those associated with the Mexican, Mexican American, Chicana group are underrepresented in both conventional STEM (48 percent) and STEM-related occupations (51 percent) relative to that group's proportion of our sample (58 percent of the Hispanic/Latina women represented in our sample are of Mexican origin). Because the Mexican category is by far the dominant associated origin group for Hispanic/Latina women in STEM, this disparity is noteworthy. Compared to their representation in the overall population of women in our sample, Hispanic/Latina women of Cuban origin are strongly represented in STEM (Cuban women are 4 percent of our sample but 6 percent of the STEM workforce). Women from the Other Hispanic group—which includes many origins, cultures, and ethnicities—are slightly better represented in conventional STEM jobs when compared to their STEM-related and non-STEM workforce participation. Their STEM representation is greater than their presence in our overall sample.

Case Study Highlights

The intersections we examined in this chapter focused on racial identity, nativity status, and associated origin categories.

Conventional STEM Occupations
- Only 2.2 percent of Hispanic/Latina women participate in conventional STEM. They comprise a small percentage of the total US STEM workforce.
- Their STEM participation is dominated by the computer/math (47 percent) and physical/life sciences (25 percent) fields.
- Earnings for Hispanic/Latina women in conventional STEM work are severely compromised relative to white men; they do not reach parity in any area. They earn 73 percent of white men's wages in both STEM management and computer/math fields, 76 percent in engineering professions, and 78 percent in physical/life sciences. These patterns are lower than the overall gender earnings ratio of 80 percent.

STEM-Related Occupations
- About 6.5 percent of Hispanic/Latina women work in STEM-related occupations.
- Their work in these areas is strongly dominated by the two nursing areas and the medical-support fields: 71 percent of all Hispanic/Latina women in STEM-related occupations are in one of these three occupational clusters.

- Only 9 percent of Hispanic/Latina women in STEM-related jobs work in high-paying medical professions.
- Earnings for Hispanic/Latina women in STEM-related work are overall severely compromised relative to white men; they do not reach parity in any area. They make only fifty-four cents for every dollar earned by white men in the medical professional fields and only sixty-one cents in STEM-related management jobs.
- Hispanic/Latina women make 91 percent of white men's salaries in vocational nursing.

Stopping at an Intersection: Racial Identity
- Racial identity comparisons (white Hispanic women compared to Hispanic women of color) reveal little difference in distributions across conventional STEM fields. The only sizable pay gap emerges for foreign-born Hispanic women in STEM managerial occupations (83 percent of white Hispanic women's earnings).
- There are also few differences in the STEM-related work distribution. Pay ratios are at or close to parity. The exception is the high-paying medical professional jobs where Hispanic women of color earn only 77 percent of what white Hispanic women earn.

Stopping at an Intersection: Nativity Status
- US-born Hispanic/Latina women are more likely to be in computer/math and less likely to be engineers than foreign-born Hispanic/Latina women. Earnings between these groups are fairly close except for physical/life sciences, where foreign-born Hispanic women earn only 87 percent of US-born Hispanic women's earnings.
- In the STEM-related fields, occupational distributions are similar. The most significant difference in earnings occurs in the medical professional category, where foreign-born Hispanic women make only 85 percent of US-born women's earnings.

Stopping at an Intersection: Associated Origin Categories
- The dominant three specific Hispanic/Latina origin categories in our sample are Mexican (58 percent), Puerto Rican (10 percent), and Cuban

(4 percent). The remaining 27 percent of Hispanic/Latina women are associated with an array of other origin categories.

- Compared to their presence in the overall population, Hispanic/Latina women of Mexican origin are underrepresented in conventional STEM. Those identifying with a Puerto Rican or Cuban origin are more strongly represented in conventional STEM than in the overall population.

7 Foreign-Born Women in STEM

Understanding the Category "Foreign-Born"

In an ideal world, our analysis of the STEM occupational distributions and earnings of women not born in the US would not be so tightly welded to the term *foreign-born*. In the US census, foreign-born stands as a straightforward, measurable category that simply indicates an individual was born outside of the US or its territories and did not have a parent or parents who were US citizens. But as a label, foreign-born has an othering effect, and its emphasis on foreignness is inaccurate, as well. Many people not born in the US may not identify as foreign: they may consider the US to be their home, identify as Americans, and hold US citizenship. Emphasizing foreignness in ways that do not match an individual's self-perceptions can easily be seen—and felt—as marginalizing.

However, while it is not a desirable term, there are several reasons we have grudgingly capitulated to the term *foreign-born* in this case study. Ironically, central among these is that the term is broadly inclusive: membership in this group does not depend on one's country of origin, means of entry to the US, length of stay, legal status, or citizenship. The term *immigrant*—which has a more inclusive feel to it and is often used synonymously with the term *foreign-born*—is inaccurate relative to our data because, under most definitions, immigration technically implies permanent residency. Hence, while all immigrant women are by definition foreign-born, not all foreign-born women are necessarily immigrants. And although this may at first seem like an exercise in semantics, the issue of permanent residency is important for thinking about patterns in STEM work. For example, as we discuss below, the H-1B visa—which plays an outsized role in bringing global STEM talent to the US—is technically a temporary work visa.

Our use of the term *foreign-born* to describe our data also helps illuminate another important aspect about this group: even if we wished to, we cannot clearly differentiate among internal subgroups such as naturalized US citizens, US permanent residents, temporary workers, refugees, or asylum seekers. There is a scarcity of data regarding how any foreign-born worker enters the US labor market, and we are unable to track visa types (which can be family-related, student, or employer-sponsored) or changes in status classifications across time (for example, a transition from temporary visa status to permanent residence). Hence, although it is more generic than we wish, our definition of *foreign-born* does not address these distinctions.

Regardless of whether we use the term *foreign-born* (which we use when referencing specific data) or *immigrant* (which we sometimes use as a generic term for people who come to the US from abroad), we recognize that the global movement of people and labor is a crossroads of politics, policies, economics, human rights, race, and gender and that the topic is deeply fraught. Having unpacked our terminology and the logic behind it, we offer three additional conceptual parameters for this case study.

First, issues and patterns pertaining to foreign-born women who work in the contemporary US STEM labor force are deeply embedded in the larger dynamics of global migration and linked to the international flow of people, workforce (non)opportunities, and global poverty and wealth. Those dynamics are connected to additional factors we can only gesture toward here—including centuries of colonization and residual colonial practices, the spiraling effects of climate change, the shifting roles of nation-states in a modern global economy, and long-standing imbalances of both power and resources between the global south and north. However, as is the case with all of our intersectional work here, our analyses of foreign-born women are limited to examining occupational distributions and earnings within the US STEM labor force. Although the scope of our work makes it impossible to directly address larger intertwined global dynamics, we acknowledge that they are in play.

Second, we recognize that the experiences of foreign-born people in the US workforce are and have always been at least partially shaped by political and cultural dynamics that resonate around social identities and power. Historically, nativism and xenophobia in the US have taken and continue to take myriad forms and focus on many different groups (including Asians, Catholics, Jews, Mexicans, and Muslims, for example). These forces are always in play, even though the target groups in question change over time,

including the exclusion of Chinese people, anti-Catholicism, and an obses-
sion with constructing a border wall between the US and Mexico. These
dynamics include structural forms of advantage, as well, such as prefer-
ential treatment for Europeans or for immigrants understood to be white.
Social identities, and not just national ones, matter when thinking about
foreign-born workers in the US.

Third, we recognize that the only people truly native to the North American continent are people from Native nations. While the global flow of
workers to the US is part of the larger project of US nation-building and is
also inherently linked to the global competitiveness of the US economy,
both US nation-building and the global economy are also ultimately based
on multiple forms of colonialism. We acknowledge the ways in which both
the US and global economies are rooted in settler colonialism and in empire,
and it is in this context that we have chosen to avoid the terms *native* and
non-native when describing US-born and foreign-born women workers.

As we turn toward our examination of foreign-born women workers in
the US STEM labor force, we recognize that the current public discourse
around foreign-born workers is in many ways already closely attached to
STEM fields and shaped by two prominent, often intertwined narratives.
First among these is the concept of the US STEM shortage. In the introduction, we examine the close connections between the STEM shortage narrative and arguments for supporting diversity in STEM. The actual existence
of a STEM shortage is, in fact, highly contextual and debatable (Teitelbaum
2014; Xue and Larson 2015). Nonetheless, many STEM diversity efforts
lean strongly on the claim that a failure to tap into all forms of American talent (including US-born women and people of color) has diminished
competitiveness and harmed the US economy as a whole. Such arguments
promote STEM diversity initiatives by claiming they expand the American
STEM talent pool and support US economic competitiveness on the global
scale. Ironically, this argument does not recognize the roles that both the
US economy and global capitalism already play in widely and systemically
exploiting and harming women and people of color (especially women of
color) on the global scale.

In the context of this case study, however, common use of the STEM
shortage narrative to promote STEM diversity takes on an additional disturbing dimension: it powerfully—if quietly—erases the many foreign-
born women, including women of color, who currently work in US STEM
fields. Within the STEM shortage diversity narrative, foreign-born women

in STEM (including foreign-born women of color) do not belong to the untapped, underrepresented US populations understood to be in need of support, nor are they typically used to represent the advantages of a diverse workplace. Rather, if we follow the STEM shortage narrative to its logical end, foreign-born women represent members of a problematic population that a more diverse US talent base will replace as this normative vision of domestic diversity is achieved.

The second (and related) dominant narrative centers on immigration policy and the H-1B visa program. Since the beginning of the program in 1990, H-1B visas have been designated for individuals who have skills involving the "theoretical and practical application of a body of highly specialized knowledge" and who hold the equivalent of a bachelor's degree (US Citizenship and Immigration Services 2021). These visas are formally designated as nonimmigrant and are usually limited to a total of six years. However, H-1B visas are exceptions in that they are the only dual-intent visas issued by the US, meaning the holder of this temporary visa can also legally apply for permanent residency. H-1B visas are therefore unique in their potential to permanently alter the US workforce. Given that STEM workers typically have high levels of educational achievement and possess specific professional skills, the H-1B visa program stands as ground zero for a visible national debate about the place of foreign-born workers in the US STEM economy (Torres 2017).

Unsurprisingly, the H-1B debate overlaps strongly with conflicting opinions around the STEM shortage and diversity. Opponents of a strong H-1B program (such as labor unions) frequently deploy a pro-diversity approach in order to argue for a reduction in H-1B visas, arguing that "the current H-1B visa program limits career opportunities for [US-born] women, African Americans, and Latinos" (AFL-CIO 2020). The intersectional erasure of foreign-born women is powerfully apparent in this context, as there is an implicit understanding that *women* means only women who are US-born (or US citizens). Advocates for women in STEM fields often (and somewhat ironically) claim there is an "overdependence on the H-1B visa program to the detriment of other sources such as women" (Branson 2018, 156). This thinking persists even though the 2019 American Community Survey (ACS) (women age twenty-five to sixty-four working full-time and year-round) shows that women comprise about 25 percent of the foreign-born STEM workforce and that the vast majority of that group (nearly 80 percent) are women of color (including Hispanic women).

On the other hand, employer-based organizations and other lobbyists deploy the STEM shortage to argue that a strong H-1B program is the linchpin of STEM innovation and critical for national interests. For example, when the election of Donald Trump indicated an imminent scaling back of the H-1B program, industry reaction featured references to the STEM shortage and dire warnings for the US economy, particularly the tech sector (Wingfield and Isaac 2017). Immigrant-focused groups such as the American Immigration Council (2020a) pointed to shortfalls in the STEM labor force, arguing that foreign-born workers fill a "critical need in the U.S. labor market—particularly in the Science, Technology, Engineering, and Math (STEM) fields."

There is no correct answer to the debates that circulate around foreign-born workers in STEM. The STEM shortage issue depends on what STEM field is measured, who measures it, and how and when it is measured (Xue and Larson 2015). And research has shown that the H-1B program's effects on the US economy (including variables such as foreign-born and US-born workers' wages, employment rates, production, prices, impact on STEM field type, and areas of innovation) flow in many directions (Bound, Khanna, and Morales 2017). What interests us here, however, is not the truth about the STEM shortage or the impact of H-1B visas on the STEM economy. Rather, our goal is to highlight the enormous cultural dominance of these debates alongside the invisibility and general silence regarding the experiences of foreign-born workers—especially foreign-born women workers—in STEM. Narratives of the STEM shortage and diversity as economic advantage are everywhere, and debates about the H-1B program reverberate from major media outlets to academic research to presidential campaigns (Thompson 2017). But nowhere in these powerful, looping narratives about foreign-born STEM talent can we discern any real interest in the issues confronting foreign-born women. Instead, while this population's skills and abilities are clearly desirable and their presence in the STEM workforce is considerable, they appear (if they appear at all) largely in narratives that are not their own and usually when such narratives prove useful to the interests of others. One primary goal of this case study, then, is to contribute to a conversation that focuses on the actual experiences of this group of racially, ethnically, and culturally diverse women in STEM.

Finally, alongside the powerful discursive and conceptual patterns that shape contemporary debates specific to foreign-born workers in STEM, our data are also framed by more familiar perspectives on US immigration (defined here simply as people coming to the US from abroad). Overall, the foreign-born population is significant: in 2019, about 14 percent of the US population reported being foreign-born. The US has the largest total population of immigrants in the world (about forty million people), accounts for about 20 percent of the world's immigrants, and is the destination of about one million new immigrants every year (Budiman 2020). While the foreign-born population in the US is relatively large, more than sixty other countries have more immigrants per capita than the US does (United Nations 2019). And although the US immigrant population is diverse (nearly every country in the world is represented in any given year), more than half of the current immigrant population comes from two locations—Asia (broadly defined and including Southeast Asia) and the nation of Mexico (28 percent and 25 percent, respectively, in 2018) (Budiman 2020). This makes the US immigrant population less varied overall than, for example, the immigrant populations of the UK or Canada (Connor and Lopez 2016).

In keeping with our overall model, in this case study we examine the data related to foreign-born women's STEM participation by acknowledging the specific and salient characteristics of this identity as a US census category at this moment in time. The current census data on foreign-born women have the following distinctive attributes: the data are (1) *technically easy to define* (the category foreign-born is easily measurable and indicates an individual was born outside the US or its territories and is not the child of a US citizen), (2) *extremely diverse in terms of immigration status subgroups* (foreign-born individuals can hold a variety of different visas and classifications), (3) *potentially shifting across immigration status subgroups in ways that cannot be traced in this dataset* (for example, a foreign-born worker may be classified as a temporary worker one year and a permanent US resident the next), (4) *diverse across racial, ethnic, and other highly salient forms of social identity and likely not to be white* (nearly 80 percent of US foreign-born women workers in STEM, age twenty-five to sixty-four working full-time, are women of color, (5) *significant in size* (foreign-born women in STEM were about 14 percent of the US population in 2019), and (6) *projected to continue to grow in coming decades* (Cohn 2015).

Foreign-Born Women in the US Labor Force

We begin our examination of the occupational distribution and earnings of foreign-born women in STEM with a look at US labor-force participation

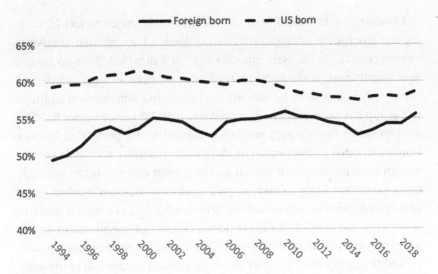

Figure 7.1
US labor-force participation rates: Foreign-born and US-born women, 1994–2019, age 16 and over. *Source:* Sarah Flood, Miriam King, Renae Rodgers, Steven Ruggles, and J. Robert Warren, "Annual Social and Economic Supplement," *Current Population Survey: Version 8.0*, Integrated Public Use Microdata Series (Minneapolis, MN: IPUMS, 2020).

for this group. Figure 7.1 illustrates the labor-force participation rates of foreign-born and US-born women beginning in 1994, the first year nativity information was collected by the Current Population Survey.

As a whole, foreign-born women consistently participate in the labor force at a lower rate than US-born women. This pattern is a distinctly gendered one, as the labor-force participation rate of foreign-born men has regularly surpassed that of US-born men since 2000 (Nunn, O'Donnell, and Shambaugh 2018).

Given the pronounced heterogeneity of foreign-born women as a group, there are many different subgroup-specific factors that contribute to this pattern. However, there are likely some overarching variables in play. Means of entry, for example, may affect the work participation of foreign-born women. In 2019, foreign-born women authorized to reside in the US were more likely than foreign-born men to come to the US through family-based admissions options (via family-based preference categories or as an immediate relative of a US citizen) and less likely than foreign-born men to arrive via employment-based visas (US Department of Homeland Security 2020).

Marriage and childbirth patterns are also likely major factors in shaping the labor-force participation rates of foreign-born women relative to women born in the US. Data from the 2019 ACS show foreign-born women were much more likely to be married than US-born women (62 percent compared to 52 percent for women age twenty-five and over). In addition, this group has substantially higher fertility than US-born women: in 2019, 5.7 percent of foreign-born women compared to 4.8 percent of US-born women reported giving birth. This difference in fertility is notable because foreign-born mothers (age sixteen and over with children under age eighteen) are far less likely to take on paid work than US-born mothers—60.4 percent compared to 70.3 percent in 2019. Greater levels of unpaid domestic and family care work (including childcare) are probably explanatory factors when it comes to foreign-born women's lower paid workforce participation.

Additional variables that may keep foreign-born women out of the workforce include the work-related challenges associated with being undocumented. Although the undocumented population is difficult to count and not all undocumented people engage in paid labor, it is estimated that about one in four US immigrants is undocumented (American Immigration Council 2020b; Budiman 2020). Missing data on undocumented foreign-born women could affect our understanding of foreign-born women's overall work participation. English proficiency is also a factor that affects this group. ACS data show that English proficiency correlates strongly with work participation: foreign-born women (age sixteen and over) with limited English proficiency are almost 20 percentage points less likely to engage in paid labor than foreign-born women who report being English proficient.

When we examine the situation for working foreign-born women, educational attainment is a particularly noteworthy variable. In 2019, about 19 percent of foreign-born workers who are women (age twenty-five and over) had not completed high school. This is nearly five times greater than the percentage of women US-born workers who do not have a high school degree (about 4 percent). However, women foreign-born workers and women US-born workers (again age twenty-five and over) have similar high school graduation rates (about 21 percent for each group in 2019), and these groups earn bachelor's or more advanced degrees at similar rates as well (about 38 percent for foreign-born workers and 42 percent for US-born workers).

Given the fairly bimodal distribution of education for foreign-born workers, particularly the large number who have not graduated from high school, it is unsurprising that foreign-born workers are more likely to work in lower-paying service occupations than US-born workers and less likely to be employed in professional and management work. In 2019, the vast majority of foreign-born women (age twenty-five and over) working in the US worked as maids and housekeeping cleaners. Otherwise, this group worked mostly as personal care aides, janitors and building cleaners, cashiers, nurses, and cooks. While these jobs fill important economic niches and social needs, the situation for foreign-born women reflects a reality that is often shaped by lower-paying work and poverty: in 2019, nearly one out of five immigrant women workers earned federal poverty-level wages ($12,490 per year or less). This is a significantly higher percentage than the 12.3 percent US poverty rate as a whole. An additional 7.6 percent earned annual wages that were above poverty level but not more than $25,000. Only 4.8 percent of foreign-born women working in the US earned more than $150,000 per year in 2019.

We have provided this snapshot of the general situation for foreign-born women who work in the US because it is critical for gaining a holistic perspective on the situation for foreign-born women in STEM. Highly educated, highly likely to be authorized to work, and engaged in occupations that are associated with strong wages, foreign-born women STEM workers reflect an employment reality that stands in stark contrast to the lived experiences of the majority of foreign-born women who work in the US. Their labor story is not representative of the larger group. Rather, it is exceptional. This contrast matters because the work and wage patterns associated with foreign-born women in STEM should not be allowed to mask or misrepresent the many challenges and disadvantages more generally experienced by foreign-born women working in the US.

Finally, despite the many disparities that characterize their labor experiences, one marked commonality does extend across this diverse group—a lack of research on foreign-born women's experience of workplace discrimination. Technically, Title VII of the Civil Rights Act of 1964 protects all US workers from discrimination based on real or perceived national origin. And the foreign-born category includes women from a wide range of racial and ethnic identities—including Asian women, Hispanic women, Black women, and white women—who are (despite legal protections) subject to forms of bias (such as sexism and racism) that are widely recognized as salient and commonly studied. But research on unfair workplace treatment of foreign-born workers *because they are foreign-born (or perceived as such)* is sparse. Members of this group are understood to be "under-studied" (Dietz 2010, 104) and to "arguably have received less attention" from scholars of employment discrimination (Bradley-Geist and Schmidtke 2018, 159). They are routinely described as the "invisible men and women of diversity research" (Bell, Kwesiga, and Berry 2010) and the "forgotten minority" (Binggeli, Dietz, and Krings 2013).

The occasional deep dives that have been made into this issue (see especially Dietz 2010 and Bradley-Geist and Shmidtke 2018) reveal a spectrum of factors regarding unfair workplace treatment of foreign-born workers that are wide-ranging and in need of further exploration. Overall, the research on workplace diversity focuses on master categories such as gender and race and rarely addresses issues relative to foreign-born women as a group. In a replication of the intersectional erasure apparent in arguments about STEM shortage and diversity, matters related to the workplace experiences of foreign-born women are folded into other identities and other diversity issues until they largely disappear. There is no single truth to the experiences of immigrants in the labor market, and studies need to take many factors (including race and gender) into account. Issues also need to be modulated by variables, such as changes in the salience of certain identities, shifting stereotypes around those identities, current national attitudes around immigration, and so on. But as of now, the research falls woefully short in terms of attending to the workplace experiences of foreign-born women. This holds true for STEM fields as well. While the national conversation focuses obsessively on the presence of foreign-born workers in STEM, it does not show equal interest in their workplace experiences.

Foreign-Born Women in the Conventional STEM Fields: What Do the Data Say?

As of 2019, the total percentage of women age twenty-five and older in the US who identify as foreign-born was 18 percent. According to our definition of conventional STEM, in the year 2019 alone an estimated 8.6 million individuals age twenty-five to sixty-four worked full-time and year-round in STEM occupations, and an estimated 545,954 of them were women who identified as foreign-born, which was just about 6 percent of all STEM job holders. Averaging across all the years of our sample and focusing on those age twenty-five to sixty-four who work year-round and full-time reveals that 6.4 percent of foreign-born women work in STEM occupations (compared to 11 percent of non-Hispanic white men). After adjusting for standard covariates (education, age, industry, marital status, citizen status, veteran status, and region of the country), we calculate that foreign-born women in STEM occupations have a significant 34 percent wage premium over foreign-born women who do not work in STEM fields. Hence, the STEM premium for foreign-born women is robust.

Within conventional STEM occupations, foreign-born women's median earnings are 96 percent of non-Hispanic white men's, a powerful jump since across all occupations foreign-born women earn only 62 percent of what non-Hispanic white men earn. There can be no doubt that STEM occupations provide a strong economic advantage for foreign-born women relative to other foreign-born women, and that advantage starkly highlights the substantial wage lag under which many foreign-born women labor overall.

Having established our parameters, we now dig deeper into the data and compare the distribution of foreign-born women with the distribution of non-Hispanic white men across conventional STEM occupations. Figure 7.2 represents how foreign-born women and white men in STEM are distributed across four broad categories of STEM work.

Figure 7.2 indicates that well over half of foreign-born women who work in STEM work in the computer/math fields, a participation rate that is 9 percentage points higher than that of white men. An even bigger difference is seen in the physical and life sciences, where the participation rate of foreign-born women is over twice that of white men (23 percent compared to 10 percent). These gaps emerge because of white men's high participation in engineering (35 percent) compared to that of foreign-born women (17 percent). Foreign-born women also participate in STEM management at a lower rate than white men (7 percent compared to 10 percent).

Although there are significant differences in how non-Hispanic white men and foreign-born women are distributed across STEM fields, their earnings are remarkably similar (table 7.1). Foreign-born women and white men are essentially at parity with respect to earnings in the computer/math fields and the engineering fields, and only relatively small differences emerge in the physical and life sciences (a pay gap of 8 percentage points). The pay gap of 7 percentage points in STEM management does, however, translate to a comparative annual average loss of $9,000 for foreign-born women in these jobs.

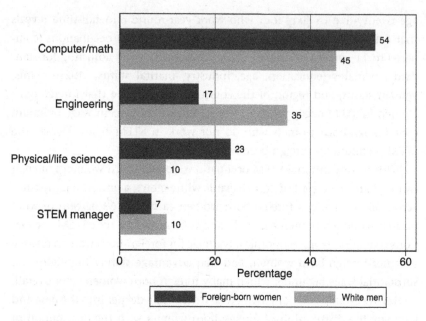

Figure 7.2
Distribution of foreign-born women and non-Hispanic white men across STEM occupations, individuals age 25–64 working year-round and full-time. *Source:* Data from the American Community Survey, 2012–2019.

Table 7.1
Foreign-born women's median annual earnings as a percentage of non-Hispanic white men's median annual earnings in STEM occupations, individuals age 25–64 working year-round and full-time

	Median annual earnings		
STEM category	Foreign-born women	Non-Hispanic white men	Foreign-born women's earnings as a percentage of non-Hispanic white men's
Computer/math	$91,243	$89,903	101%
Engineering	$85,876	$88,606	97%
Physical/life sciences	$69,784	$75,632	92%
STEM managerial	$111,219	$120,226	93%

Note: All earnings adjusted to 2019 dollars. *Source:* Data from the American Community Survey, 2012–2019.

Foreign-Born Women in the STEM-Related Fields: What Do the Data Say?

In 2019, an estimated 7.3 million individuals age twenty-five to sixty-four were working full-time and year-round in STEM-related jobs, and an estimated 764,135 of them were foreign-born women. Over the period of our sample and focusing on those age twenty-five to sixty-four who work full-time and year-round, we find that only 3.6 percent of white men work in these occupations. However, about 10.3 percent of foreign-born women are employed in such occupations (as opposed to 6.4 percent in conventional STEM). While the STEM premium is a normative and often cited measure of how conventional STEM careers benefit women in any given identity group, the concept of a STEM-related premium is a new one. When we calculate a STEM-related premium for foreign-born women (which compares earnings in STEM-related occupations to non-STEM occupations while controlling for conventional STEM work), we see that foreign-born women in STEM-related jobs earn a substantial 39 percent more than foreign-born women not working in conventional STEM or STEM-related fields. Because our version of a STEM-related premium does not include conventional STEM work, it provides a meaningful snapshot of the significant economic benefits that STEM-related work provides foreign-born women. Figure 7.3 illustrates the distribution of foreign-born women and white men over the six STEM-related occupational groupings.

Figure 7.3 makes clear that foreign-born women working in the STEM-related fields are distributed quite differently than white men: over half are nurses (either professional or vocational), while only 16 percent of white men are nurses. White men are far more likely to be professionals or work in STEM-related managerial fields. These differences translate into some rather significant pay gaps (table 7.2).

Foreign-born women in high-paying medical professional jobs face a wage gap of 27 percentage points compared to white men. This translates to a comparative average annual salary loss of $45,000. The pay gap is only slightly smaller in the STEM-related management area (24 percentage points or about $20,000 per year). In contrast, foreign-born women who are professional nurses outearn white men in those same jobs by 7 percentage points. Pay gaps in the other areas, while favoring white men, are relatively small.

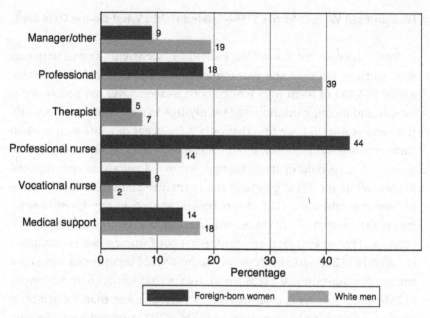

Figure 7.3
Distribution of foreign-born women and non-Hispanic white men across STEM-related occupations, individuals age 25–64 working year-round and full-time. *Source:* Data from the American Community Survey, 2012–2019.

Table 7.2
Foreign-born women's median annual earnings as a percentage of non-Hispanic white men's median annual earnings in STEM-related occupations, individuals age 25–64 working year-round and full-time

	Median annual earnings		
STEM-related category	Foreign-born women	Non-Hispanic white men	Foreign-born women's earnings as a percentage of non-Hispanic white men's
Manager/other	$65,423	$86,437	76%
Professional	$122,940	$168,350	73%
Therapist	$73,822	$76,327	97%
Professional nurse	$80,812	$75,761	107%
Vocational nurse	$44,303	$45,457	97%
Medical support	$49,510	$53,635	92%

Note: All earnings adjusted to 2019 dollars. *Source:* Data from the American Community Survey, 2012–2019.

Stopping at Four Intersections: Gender, Race, Citizenship, and Origin Categories of Foreign-Born Women in STEM

Foreign-born status, like all aspects of identity, is shaped by other attributes. Based on our examination of foreign-born status as a social identity, we have identified four key intersections that further illuminate how foreign-born status and STEM work intersect. Below, we examine STEM occupational distributions and earnings across four intersections—gendered nativity status, race and ethnicity, citizenship (US and non-US), and origin categories. In doing so, we no longer exclusively use non-Hispanic white men as a comparison group but also juxtapose different groups of women.

Gendered Nativity Status: US-Born Women and Foreign-Born Women

Comparisons between US-born and foreign-born individuals in STEM are fairly common, but comparisons between US-born women and foreign-born women in STEM are not. In this instance, we no longer use non-Hispanic white men as a comparison group, but we juxtapose these two different groups of women. We make this latter comparison in figure 7.4. The distribution of these groups of women is slightly different in the computer/math and STEM management occupations; percentages are similar in engineering and the physical/life sciences.

Similar distributions, however, do not translate into similar earnings. In all four of the conventional STEM occupational clusters, foreign-born women in STEM outearn their US-born counterparts (table 7.3). The difference is particularly striking in the computer/math occupations, where foreign-born women outearn US-born women by a full 25 percentage points (an almost $18,000 annual difference).

In figure 7.5, we turn to the distribution of US-born and foreign-born women across the six STEM-related fields. Nursing (both professional and vocational) is where both of these groups of women are most strongly represented. The largest difference between foreign-born women and US-born women is the gap of 7 percentage points in the professional fields.

Table 7.4 reveals that foreign-born women have an earnings advantage over US-born women in every field except STEM-related management, where the median earnings of the two groups are not statistically different. The earnings advantage of foreign-born women in STEM-related work ranges from 7 percentage points to 18 percentage points (in professional nursing).

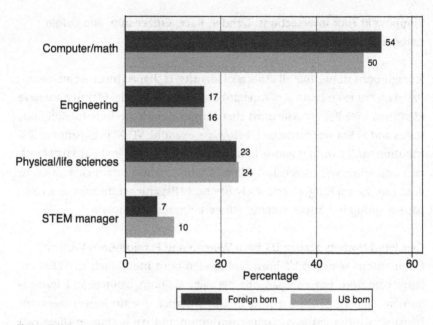

Figure 7.4
Distribution of foreign-born women and US-born women across STEM occupations, individuals age 25–64 working year-round and full-time. *Source:* Data from the American Community Survey, 2012–2019.

Table 7.3
Foreign-born women's median annual earnings as a percentage of US-born women's median annual earnings in STEM occupations, individuals age 25–64 working year-round and full-time

	Median annual earnings		
STEM category	Foreign-born women	US-born women	Foreign-born women's earnings as a percentage of US-born women's
Computer/math	$91,243	$73,272	125%
Engineering	$85,876	$74,751	115%
Physical/life sciences	$69,784	$64,331	108%
STEM managerial	$111,219	$98,134	113%

Note: All earnings adjusted to 2019 dollars. *Source:* Data from the American Community Survey, 2012–2019.

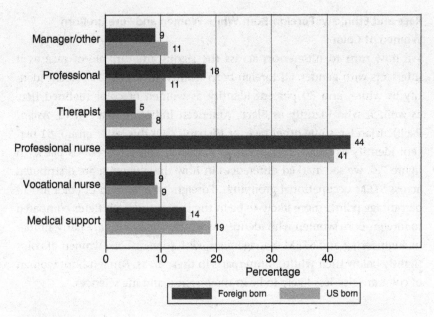

Figure 7.5
Distribution of foreign-born women and US-born women across STEM-related occupations, individuals age 25–64 working year-round and full-time. *Source:* Data from the American Community Survey, 2012–2019.

Table 7.4
Foreign-born women's median annual earnings as a percentage of US-born women's median annual earnings in STEM-related occupations, individuals age 25–64 working year-round and full-time

| STEM category | Median annual earnings | | Foreign-born women's earnings as a percentage of US-born women's |
	Foreign-born women	US-born women	
Manager/other	$65,423	$65,386	100%
Professional	$122,940	$108,047	114%
Therapist	$73,822	$65,659	112%
Professional nurse	$80,812	$68,549	118%
Vocational nurse	$44,303	$41,258	107%
Medical support	$49,510	$43,219	115%

Note: All earnings adjusted to 2019 dollars. *Source:* Data from the American Community Survey, 2012–2019.

Race and Ethnicity: Foreign-Born White Women and Foreign-Born Women of Color

We now turn to differences across the significant variable of race as it intersects with gender. Of foreign-born women in STEM, 20 percent identify as white, and 80 percent identify as women of color (defined here as women who identify as Black, American Indian/Alaska Native, Asian/Pacific Islander, some other race, or Hispanic). Of this latter group, 81 percent identify as Asian, 13 percent as Hispanic, and 5 percent as Black. In figure 7.6, we see marked differences in how these women are distributed across STEM occupational groupings. Foreign-born women of color are 14 percentage points more likely to be in the computer/math fields compared to foreign-born women who identify as white. The groups are fairly similar in engineering and STEM management, with foreign-born women of color slightly below their white counterparts in these areas. Foreign-born women of color are also less likely to be in the physical and life sciences.

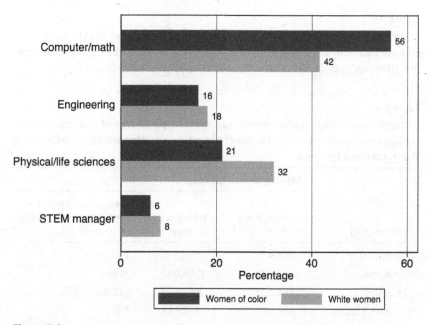

Figure 7.6
Distribution of foreign-born women across STEM occupations by race/ethnicity, individuals age 25–64 working year-round and full-time. *Source:* Data from the American Community Survey, 2012–2019.

Table 7.5
Foreign-born women's median annual earnings by race/ethnicity in STEM occupations, individuals age 25–64 working year-round and full-time

STEM category	Median annual earnings		
	Nonwhite foreign-born women	Non-Hispanic white foreign-born women	Foreign-born women of color's earnings as a percentage of non-Hispanic white foreign-born women's
Computer/math	$91,800	$90,183	102%
Engineering	$87,231	$83,067	105%
Physical/life sciences	$68,701	$71,992	95%
STEM managerial	$111,116	$112,368	99%

Note: All earnings adjusted to 2019 dollars. *Source:* Data from the American Community Survey, 2012–2019.

The distributional differences shown in figure 7.6 do not translate into large earnings differentials. As seen in table 7.5, foreign-born women of color have a slight earnings advantage in the computer/math fields despite a lower distribution there. White foreign-born women have a slight earnings advantage in the physical and life sciences, an area where they are less well represented. Foreign-born women of color outearn foreign-born white women by 5 percent in engineering, and the two groups are roughly the same in the STEM managerial fields.

Turning to the foreign-born women in STEM-related occupations, as with the STEM occupations, 20 percent identify as white, and 80 percent identify as women of color (defined here as women who identify as Black, American Indian/Alaska Native, Asian/Pacific Islander, some other race, or Hispanic). Of this latter group, the racial breakdown is different from those in STEM jobs in that while the majority (60 percent) identify as Asian, sizable percentages report a Hispanic identity (19 percent), and another 20 percent identify Black, making nonwhite foreign-born women in the STEM-related occupations a more diverse group than their STEM counterparts. Figure 7.7 displays the distribution of these two groups over the STEM-related occupations, where nursing occupations sharply divide participation patterns. Well over half (56 percent) of foreign-born women of color are nurses (professional or vocational) compared to 42 percent of

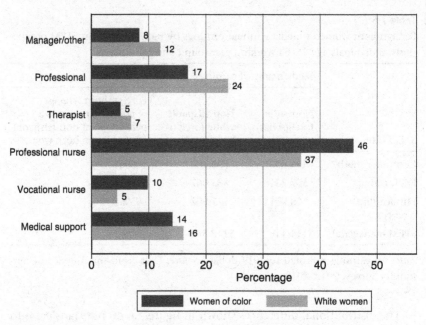

Figure 7.7
Distribution of foreign-born women across STEM-related occupations by race/ethnicity, individuals age 25–64 working year-round and full-time. *Source:* Data from the American Community Survey, 2012–2019.

foreign-born women who identify as white. In turn, foreign-born women who identify as white are more represented than foreign-born women of color in every other STEM-related occupational cluster.

In table 7.6, we see that when it comes to the intersectional point of race, stronger rates of participation in a STEM-related field do not predict wages across any groups. Foreign-born white women are distributed most strongly in the professional nursing fields (46 percent) but experience a pay gap of 4 percentage points. Women of color are more likely to be STEM-related managers (12 percent compared to 8 percent), but they experience a pay gap of 11 percentage points in these fields relative to white women. Perhaps the most significant finding we can take from table 7.6 is that the professional medical fields—where often significant pay gaps are common between groups we compare—show no real differences between the salaries of these two groups. The median earnings of therapists are not statistically different.

Table 7.6

Foreign-born women's median annual earnings by race/ethnicity in STEM-related occupations, individuals age 25–64 working year-round and full-time

STEM-related category	Median annual earnings		
	Foreign-born women of color	Non-Hispanic white foreign-born women	Nonwhite foreign-born women's earnings as a percentage of non-Hispanic white foreign-born women's
Manager/other	$64,407	$71,965	89%
Professional	$122,124	$123,775	99%
Therapist	$73,822	$73,822	100%
Professional nurse	$80,812	$77,529	104%
Vocational nurse	$43,964	$46,402	95%
Medical support	$48,621	$52,338	93%

Note: All earnings adjusted to 2019 dollars. *Source:* Data from the American Community Survey, 2012–2019.

Citizenship

In figure 7.8, we focus on the distribution of foreign-born women in STEM by US citizenship status. As noted at the beginning of this case study, we are unable to track alterations in the citizenship status of foreign-born women, so such fluctuations within our data are not detectable. In addition, it is reasonable to assume that citizenship may in many cases be linked to the length of time an individual has spent in the US—and hence to seniority and possibly higher pay. Citizenship, therefore, is a fairly unstable measure.

Foreign-born women who are citizens are 4 percentage points more likely to be engineers and 3 percentage points more likely to be STEM managers. The reverse is true for noncitizen women, who are more likely to be in the computer/math fields (56 percent compared to 52 percent) and the physical and life sciences (25 percent compared to 22 percent).

The most notable overall pattern associated with earnings for these two groups is that foreign-born women who are citizens have stronger earnings than noncitizen women, regardless of the STEM occupational cluster (table 7.7). The difference is least significant in engineering, where foreign-born noncitizen women earn ninety-four cents for every dollar a foreign-born citizen woman in this field earns. However, quite sizable pay gaps emerge in favor of citizens in the areas of physical and life sciences (a pay gap of

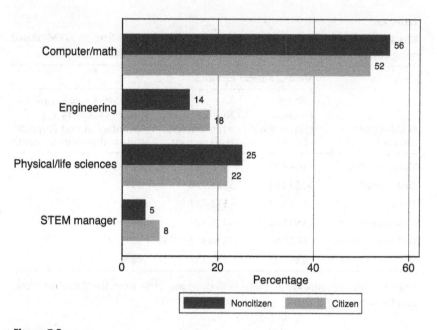

Figure 7.8
Distribution of foreign-born women by citizenship status across STEM occupations, individuals age 25–64 working year-round and full-time. *Source:* Data from the American Community Survey, 2012–2019.

Table 7.7
Foreign-born women's median annual earnings by citizenship status in STEM occupations, individuals age 25–64 working year-round and full-time

STEM category	Median annual earnings		
	Foreign-born women who are not citizens	Foreign-born women who are citizens	Foreign-born noncitizen women's earnings as a percentage of foreign-born citizen women's
Computer/math	$87,673	$94,915	92%
Engineering	$83,067	$87,927	94%
Physical/life sciences	$60,609	$79,095	77%
STEM managerial	$101,978	$118,080	86%

Note: All earnings adjusted to 2019 dollars. *Source:* Data from the American Community Survey, 2012–2019.

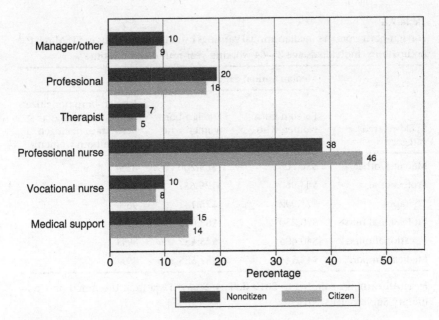

Figure 7.9
Distribution of foreign-born women by citizenship status across STEM-related occupations, individuals age 25–64 working year-round and full-time. *Source:* Data from the American Community Survey, 2012–2019.

33 percentage points) and STEM management (a pay gap of 14 percentage points). Although citizenship may be a proxy for length of time in the US, it is clearly valuable in terms of earnings.

We next turn our attention to the STEM-related fields, focusing again on how foreign-born women are distributed across STEM-related jobs by citizen status (figure 7.9).

Within the category of foreign-born women, citizens are more likely to be professional nurses (46 percent) than are noncitizens (38 percent). For the remaining job clusters, noncitizen women are slightly more represented.

STEM-related work reflects a pattern that is similar to the one found in the conventional STEM fields: in every area of work, noncitizen women earn lower annual salaries on average than women who are citizens (table 7.8). While the two groups have nearly identical median pay when they work as therapists, the remaining pay gaps are significant. Despite nearly equal representation in management and the professional fields, noncitizens

Table 7.8

Foreign-born women's median annual earnings by citizenship status in STEM-related occupations, individuals age 25–64 working year-round and full-time

STEM-related category	Median annual earnings		
	Foreign-born women who are not citizens	Foreign-born women who are citizens	Foreign-born noncitizen women's earnings as a percentage of citizen foreign-born women's
Manager/other	$56,700	$69,700	81%
Professional	$83,960	$129,657	65%
Therapist	$71,992	$75,141	96%
Professional nurse	$70,230	$83,067	85%
Vocational nurse	$40,406	$45,457	89%
Medical support	$43,543	$51,525	85%

Note: All earnings adjusted to 2019 dollars. *Source:* Data from the American Community Survey, 2012–2019.

experience large pay gaps in both areas: a difference of 19 percentage points in management translates to an average comparative loss of $13,000. An impressive pay gap of 35 percentage points in the medical professional area translates to an average loss of more than $45,500 annually for noncitizen foreign-born women.

Associated Origin Categories

One characteristic of the group foreign-born women is both consistent and significant—the high level of variation (cultural, linguistic, racial, ethnic) that characterizes this group. The strong heterogeneity of foreign-born women means it is useful to look at the area from which these women arrive to the US.

In our sample of full-time prime-age foreign-born women, one-half (49 percent) were born in Latin America, and one-third (33 percent) in Asia. Ten percent are from Europe, 5 percent are from Africa, and 2 percent were born in other areas of the world. In figure 7.10, we show how these women are distributed across STEM work, STEM-related work, and other kinds of jobs. Each column of figure 7.10 adds up to 100 percent. For example, looking at the STEM jobs column, we see that 68 percent of foreign-born women working in STEM are from Asia, 3 percent are from Africa, and so on.

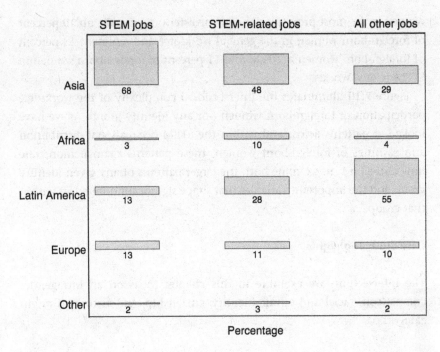

	STEM jobs	STEM-related jobs	All other jobs
Asia	68	48	29
Africa	3	10	4
Latin America	13	28	55
Europe	13	11	10
Other	2	3	2

Percentage

Figure 7.10
Percent distribution of foreign-born women by associated origin category across labor-force sectors, individuals age 25–64 working year-round and full-time. *Source:* Data from the American Community Survey, 2012–2019.

Looking across all three of these columns, it is clear that, in the context of their origin category, larger workforce patterns for foreign-born women can be very different from their more specific patterns in STEM employment. For example, women from Asia are represented much more strongly in STEM (68 percent) and STEM-related work (48 percent) than they are in the labor force in general (33 percent). The opposite is true for women from Latin America: they comprise 49 percent of foreign-born women in the labor force in general but only 13 percent of foreign-born women in STEM and 28 percent of foreign-born women in STEM-related work.

Patterns for women from Africa show a strong concentration in STEM-related occupations, where they make up 10 percent of foreign-born women in those areas. African women comprise 4 percent of the foreign-born women in the general workforce, however, and only 3 percent of the foreign-born women in conventional STEM. The role of European-born women is the most proportional and consistent: they make up 10 percent of foreign-born women in the general workforce and represent 13 percent of foreign-born women in STEM and 11 percent of foreign-born women in STEM-related work.

Figure 7.10 illuminates the intersectional complexity of the workforce participation of foreign-born women—or any identity group. As we have looked at patterns across and within the STEM occupational distribution and earnings of foreign-born women, these patterns again demonstrate how critical it is to examine both the larger patterns of any given identity group and the important variables that shape significant differences within that group.

Case Study Highlights

The intersections we examine in this chapter focus on an intragender comparison, racial and ethnic identity, citizenship, and associated origin categories.

Conventional STEM Occupations
- About 6.4 percent of foreign-born women work in conventional STEM occupations.
- Within conventional STEM work, this group is heavily represented in computing/math (54 percent) and the physical/life sciences (23 percent). Only 17 percent are engineers.
- Pay ratios between foreign-born women and white men are not strongly divergent. Foreign-born women's earnings are consistently above 93 percent (STEM managerial), and they are at parity with white men in the computer/math fields.

STEM-Related Occupations
- About 10.3 percent of foreign-born women work in STEM-related jobs.
- Two-thirds of foreign-born women in STEM-related work are in either nursing (professional and vocational) or medical support.
- Foreign-born women earn 107 percent of what white men earn in professional nursing and are close to parity in therapist, vocational nursing, and medical-support work.

- Eighteen percent of foreign-born women work in the medical professional category (compared to 39 percent of white men) but experience significant pay gaps both in this area (27 percentage points) and high-paying STEM-related management occupations (24 percentage points).

Stopping at an Intersection: An Intragender Comparison
- The occupational distribution patterns for foreign-born and US-born women are similar.
- Foreign-born women outearn US-born women in all categories in conventional STEM. Disparities are sometimes strong (for example, in computing/math work, US-born women experience a 25 percent pay gap relative to foreign-born women).
- In the STEM-related fields, foreign-born women are more likely to be professionals and less likely to be therapists/medical support. Foreign-born women solidly out-earn US-born women in all STEM-related jobs except management (where earnings are at parity).

Stopping at an Intersection: Racial and Ethnic Identity
- Foreign-born women of color are more likely to be in computing/math, and white foreign-born women are more likely to be in physical/life sciences. These patterns do not translate into any meaningful earnings differences.
- In STEM-related work, foreign-born women of color and white foreign-born are both likely to be nurses. However, white foreign-born women are far more likely to be professional nurses, and foreign-born women of color more likely to be vocational nurses.
- White foreign-born women are more likely to work in higher-paying medical professional jobs and as management. The only meaningful earnings difference between these groups is in STEM-related management, where foreign-born women of color earn only 89 percent of what white foreign-born women earn.

Stopping at an Intersection: Citizenship
- In conventional STEM work, foreign-born women who are US citizens are distributed similarly to foreign-born women who are not. US citizens are somewhat more strongly represented in STEM management.

- Foreign-born women who are US citizens outearn foreign-born women who are not across all areas of conventional STEM. Notable earnings gaps for noncitizen foreign-born women in STEM are in the physical/life sciences (23 percent), as well as the high-paying STEM management fields (14 percent).
- The distribution of these groups in STEM-related work is not overly dissimilar. Foreign-born women who are citizens are more likely to be professional nurses while foreign-born women who are not citizens are more likely to be vocational nurses.
- Across all areas of STEM-related work, foreign-born women who are US citizens outearn foreign-born women who are not. Earnings gaps are especially large for medical professionals, where foreign-born noncitizen women earn only 65 percent of what their citizen counterparts earn.

Stopping at an Intersection: Associated Origin Categories

- Foreign-born women working in STEM are a heterogeneous group whose origins are unevenly distributed across the globe: half are from Latin America, one-third are from Asia, one-tenth are from Europe, and one-twentieth are from Africa.
- Relative to the larger sample of foreign-born women in conventional STEM, foreign-born women from Asia are significantly overrepresented. Foreign-born women from Europe are slightly overrepresented.
- Foreign-born women from Latin America are significantly underrepresented both in conventional STEM and STEM-related occupations.

8 Women with Disabilities in STEM

Who Has a Disability in the US?

Being a person with a disability is a complex identity that is welded to concepts that are central to this book—opportunity, bias, and systemic disadvantage. The significance of the category is matched by its complexity: to ask what the term *disability* means is to invoke (intertwined) political, economic, legal, medical, and social factors whose richness and dimensionality far exceed what this case study can summarize. The literature on the history of disability in the US reveals not only entrenched ableism but also the extent to which the idea of disability has transformed over the last century (Albrecht, Seelman, and Bury 2003; Francis and Silvers 2016; Grue 2016; Stiker [1999] 2019). And like many social-identity categories, disability cuts both ways: it is a social project that is always under construction and is also increasingly understood as an identity group and a focal point for building communities, seeking rights and protections, and promoting positive social change.

Disability and being a person with a disability are subject to an especially broad spectrum of definitions. On one hand, disability is a relatively straightforward demographic attribute: it is a characteristic with which any person may freely and broadly identify, much like race, ethnicity, or gender. Understood this way, any individual's identification as a person with a disability can be based solely on their understanding of that term relative to their own situation. On the other hand, the category of disability is subject to a seemingly countless number of official parameters from the Americans with Disabilities Act (ADA), the US Centers for Disease Control, and the World Health Organization (US Centers for Disease Control and Prevention 2021a; US Department of Justice 2021; World Health Organization 2021).

The US Census Department straightforwardly admits that while many agencies refer to and measure populations with disabilities, "because of the differences in definitions, an individual may be considered to have a disability under one set of criteria but not by another" (Brault 2012, 1). Disability, for example, can encompass a wide range of human experience, including mobility, sensory processing, neuroatypicality, and mental health. As sociologist of disability Jan Grue (2016, 958) summarizes: "If there is a single, easy way to define disability, it has yet to be found."

We begin by noting one important and high-stakes conundrum around disability and identity: formal recognition of an identity as a person who has a disability is not always possible for an individual who may personally identify as having a disability. Official definitions of disability can be precise and can vary substantially among legal, medical, and other agencies. One individual can be caught between many institutions (such as public schools, insurance companies, and the Social Security Administration), and, while anyone can identify as having a disability, qualifying as a person with a disability is another matter. The matter of qualification is also a consequential one, as institutional structures control important services, programs, and benefits that affect the well-being of many people with disabilities. No matter how we understand the attribute of disability, in the twenty-first century in the US, many people with disabilities live in the crossfire of highly politicized and often conflicting definitions of disability that powerfully impact the quality of their lives.

Along with the consequential differences between private and public definitions of disability, the population with disabilities fluctuates in many other significant ways. A disability can be permanent or temporary. Disability can be lifelong or brief. Some people are born with a disability, and others acquire one. And a disability can be acquired by anyone and at any time, making the category significantly different from, for example, foreign-born status or American Indian/Alaska Native identity. Finally, the condition of having a disability is both universally possible and common. While the estimates vary from agency to agency, in 2018 the US Census Department estimated that more than one in ten people (12.6 percent or 40.6 million) in the US were living with a disability (US Bureau of the Census 2020a). The frequency of disability as a demographic attribute makes people with disabilities one of the largest minority categories in the US (US Centers for Disease Control and Prevention 2021b).

Given the potential differences between definitions and the high number of changing variables that cut across the population with disabilities, counting people with disabilities is a challenging undertaking. These challenges are amplified by contemporary debates regarding how (and if) to consider disability an identity at all. In "Counting Disability," Glenn Fujiura and Violet Rutkowski-Kmitta (2001, 69) distinguish between "a disability studies perspective and statistics on disability." A disability-studies perspective recognizes the chameleon-like nature of disability. In this model, disability is not an identity but rather a set of contextualized attributes that "belong to a continuum of human capability and function" (Grue 2016, 962). This perspective differs substantially from the more definitionally fixed model that has strengthened since passage of the ADA in 1990. This model encourages people with disabilities to identify as such, creating a relatively stable population demographic and producing normative statistics on disability. As useful and comfortable as these statistics may be, however, conventional data based on a population with disabilities is just one way of conceptualizing disability.

The US Census Department stands out as a major source of data around disability. This history goes back to the 1880 decennial census, which uses the word *disability* but deploys categories that are very different from those we use today. The census's interest in disability has been uneven over time, but historically the most consistent characteristic has been a focus on whether an individual is able to engage in paid labor. However, as is the case with other attributes, the census's interest in the idea of disability as identity has broadened over time as meanings attached to being a person with a disability have transformed with the social movements of the 1960s and 1970s and the emergence of a civil rights perspective. By 1980, the census questionnaire expanded from work-related questions to include one about public transportation use. By 1990, questions had come to include independent living and self-care.

In framing this case study and creating a data story for women with disabilities in STEM fields, we have limited ourselves to a discussion of disability as defined by the annual American Community Survey (ACS). Although identical questions around gender, race, and ethnicity continued to be posed by both the ACS questionnaire and the decennial census, disability-related questions no longer appear on the general census. The migration of disability from the decennial census to only the ACS is a product of census survey history. As the long form of the decennial census became increasingly cumbersome at the end of the twentieth century, the ACS was developed as a way to ensure "continuous measurement of the U.S. population and to reduce the scope, cost, and complexity of the decennial census" (US Bureau of the Census 2021). The 2000 general census was the last census to ask disability-related questions, and the ACS, which went into full production in 2005, essentially took over the disability attribute at that time. While it is not the only survey to ask about disability, the ACS is arguably the most consistent and widely used and has asked the same disability-related questions since 2008. Other surveys that ask about disability (the Current Population Survey, for example) cannot provide such a consistent and large data set.

On the surface, the ACS considers disability status a matter of self-identification. People who complete the ACS can identify as having a disability or not, in their own context and according to their own self-assessment. This approach appears to be shaped solely by whether a person identifies as (that is, considers themselves) a person with disabilities—a not uncomplicated process that does not necessarily always reflect if a person is living with a disability (Forber-Pratt et al. 2017). In working with this ACS data, therefore, we have in principle adopted a group-based approach in which disability functions as a self-identified attribute that comprises a population.

While this approach seemingly frees us from sifting through conflicting versions of what counts as a disability, there is nonetheless a passive level of definitional pressure in the ACS. This takes the form of disability types, six clearly defined categories that the ACS provides to anyone who indicates they have a disability:

1. Is this person deaf, or does he/she have serious difficulty hearing?
2. Is this person blind, or does he/she have serious difficulty seeing, even when wearing glasses?
3. Because of a physical, mental, or emotional condition, does this person have serious difficulty concentrating, remembering, or making decisions? (5 years old or older)
4. Does this person have serious difficulty walking or climbing stairs? (5 years old or older)
5. Does this person have difficulty dressing or bathing? (5 years old or older)

6. Because of a physical, mental, or emotional condition, does this person have difficulty doing errands alone such as visiting a doctor's office or shopping? (15 years old or older) (US Bureau of the Census 2020b).

Each disability type is specific to areas of functionality, and there is no Other category that allows for additional or differing perspectives. Therefore, while anyone who takes the ACS may identify as a person with disabilities, the six disability types give a specific shape to disability. No form of authority interferes with anyone claiming the disability attribute, but there are a set of back-door categories that define how an identity of having a disability is articulated.

We note this as a way of demonstrating that although the ACS gives respondents latitude in choosing their identities, it is not innocent of specific parameters. The identities of ACS respondents are protected, and there are no stakes (resources or rights) involved in claiming an identity as a person with disabilities on the ACS. But ACS disability data are still shaped by an institutional hand. For example, not being able to see well "even when wearing glasses" is part of having a visual disability, but hearing aids are not mentioned when it comes to hearing disabilities. "Difficulty dressing or bathing" independently is a category of disability, but difficulty preparing food or feeding oneself is not. Our point here is not that ACS categories are wrong but that they are categories in the first place. Even if respondents self-identify as having a disability, the survey draws the parameters of disability experience. And those decisions have very much shaped the data we use here.

Finally, we return to the challenges of counting but now in a more familiar vein. Even with a particular data set selected and with a full recognition of the advantages and limitations of that data, there is still the issue of who takes (or can take) any survey. The US Census Bureau considers people with disabilities hard to count—a formal categorization that indicates a demographic is likely to be undercounted (US Bureau of the Census 2018). Challenges to the enumeration of people with disabilities include issues of accessibility stemming from forms of systemic inequality. Accessibility problems are especially pronounced when it comes to technology, a problem that will only increase as influential surveys such as the 2020 decennial census go digital. Studies suggest that compared to people without disabilities, individuals with disabilities are less likely to go online, own internet-capable technology, or feel confident regarding technology use (Anderson and Perrin 2017). These difficulties are further compounded by the fact that people with disabilities are disproportionately represented among other hard-to-count groups (such as people of color, especially within American Indian/Alaska Native and Black populations) and among people who are experiencing homelessness or poverty (Bialik 2017).

In what follows, we examine the data related to the STEM participation of women with disabilities by taking into account the specific and salient characteristics of having a disability as an ACS category at this moment in time. The current ACS disability data on women with disabilities have the following distinctive attributes: the data are (1) *self-selected* (they are chosen as a category by the individual in question), (2) *structured by specific subcategories* (they are structured by six separate disability types without the inclusion of a generic Other or fill-in option), (3) large in number and *representative of more than one in ten people living in the United States*, (4) measuring a population likely to *intersect with multiple vulnerable populations* (this includes populations of people of color and socioeconomically disadvantaged people), and (5) *highly changeable* over the lifespan and potentially inclusive of any person during their lifetime.

We move now to a brief contextualizing overview of women with disabilities in the US labor force, followed by a detailed analysis of occupational and income data related to women with disabilities across conventional STEM and STEM-related work. In our analysis, we use the particular characteristics of ACS disability data to guide us as we intersectionally examine the participation and earnings in STEM fields of women with disabilities.

Women with Disabilities in the US Labor Force

Figure 8.1 uses ACS data to provide a snapshot of the overall labor-force participation of women with disabilities. The figure begins in 2008, the year in which the ACS adopted its current disability-related questions. In order to best illustrate the impact that having a disability might have on workplace participation, we have compared women who are living with a disability to women who do not have a disability.

Figure 8.1 illustrates the enormous difference that disability makes when it comes to women's engagement in paid work. Because of the high level of diversity across disabilities, we recognize that addressing labor-force issues

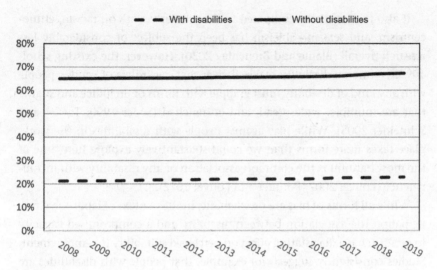

Figure 8.1
US labor-force participation rates: Women with and without disabilities age 16 and over. *Source:* Data from the American Community Survey, 2008–2019.

faced by women with disabilities is possible only in broad ways. Given the profound labor-force participation disparities between women with and without disabilities, it is imperative to at least sketch out some of the core issues that shape the trends around paid work participation and disability.

Labor-force participation issues are closely related to the matter of qualifying as a person with a disability. Much of the research on the labor-force participation of people with disabilities has centered on whether the main social insurance program for individuals with disabilities, the Social Security Disability Insurance (SSDI) program, is a work disincentive. Individuals who apply for SSDI benefits may have to stop working for a period of several months—even if they are able to work—in order to access those needed benefits. If benefits are denied, they may return to the workforce. Depending on how long the application process takes, however, their disability may have worsened, or they may have lost some work capacity due to a deterioration of skills. If they are granted benefits, benefits cease if they earn more than certain monthly limits. A robust scholarly literature has demonstrated that the SSDI program negatively affects the workforce participation patterns of some individuals with disabilities, depending on the severity of their disability (Maestas, Mullen, and Strand, 2013).

It also matters that—compared to the scholarly work on racism, ethno-centrism, and sexism—ableism has been the subject of considerably less research overall (Blaine and Brenchley 2020). However, the existing schol-arly literature on disability makes it clear that, regardless of gender, people with any kind of disability must grapple with forms of prejudice and stigma that are multiple, widespread, and entrenched (Söder 1990; Towler and Schneider 2005). While bias against people with disabilities in the work-place takes more forms than we could substantively explore here, one of the most harmful is the common association of any disability with incom-petence (Louvet 2007; Rohmer and Louvet 2012).

While all forms of bias are problematic, in the context of labor-force par-ticipation the association between disability and a compromised capacity to perform has a devastating effect on perceived suitability for employment. Studies consistently suggest, for example, that people with disabilities are less likely to get job interviews than similarly qualified individuals without disabilities (Ameri et al. 2018; Ravaud, Madiot, and Ville 1992). Compro-mised access to interviews combined with pervasive cultural stereotypes about low productivity and poor performance unfairly reduce the path-ways to paid work for people with disabilities. These constricted entryways unjustly deprive many people with disabilities of critical economic and per-sonal development opportunities that they wish to access. A study by the Kessler Foundation (2015) shows that the majority of working-age people with disabilities want to work.

People with disabilities who do enter the labor force—as well as people who acquire a disability during their time in the labor force—are not only confronted with persistent bias but may also encounter issues pertaining to access and appropriate accommodation. In 1990, the ADA signaled a shift away from a focus on the limitations of people with disabilities and a reori-entation toward eliminating discrimination against people with disabili-ties in all forms of public life. Although subsequent iterations of the ADA have unfortunately narrowed the definition of having a disability, the ADA still emphasizes the legal obligation of most US employers to provide rea-sonable accommodation for qualified individuals with disabilities (Francis and Silvers 2016). The effect of this legislation on the workplace has been profound, and the literature makes clear that reasonable accommodations are consistently associated with positive work-related outcomes across the spectrum of disability types (Houtenville et al. 2013). Nonetheless, despite the requirements of the law and the positive outcomes associated with the ADA, access issues continue to create substantial employment obstacles for people with disabilities. Despite the ADA, many people with disabilities routinely experience problems related to access or failures of accommodation in the workplace that negatively affect their ability to work (Anand and Sevak 2017; Hill, Maestas, and Mullen 2016).

Disability is also an intersectional issue. The overlay of disability with gender is significant for working women with disabilities, and an intersectional perspective reveals the harmful effects experienced by members of this group as they seek to participate and succeed in the workplace. At the global scale, the employment situation for women with disabilities is especially grim: they are far more likely to "experience unequal hiring and promotion standards, unequal pay for equal work and occupations with low pay" than both people without disabilities and men with disabilities (Lindstrom, Hirano, and Ingram 2020, 388). US women with disabilities who work experience profound economic disadvantages. According to the 2019 ACS, working-age women (age sixteen and over) with disabilities have an average labor-force participation rate of 23 percent, and only half (46 percent) of working women with disabilities in the labor force work full-time and year-round. Women with disabilities comprise only 2.1 percent of the full-time workforce. In terms of earnings, this group experiences severe pay gaps: working women with disabilities earn only sixty-seven cents to every dollar earned by men without disabilities, seventy-six cents to every dollar earned by men with disabilities, and eighty-three cents to every dollar earned by women without disabilities. This employment reality is marked by a poverty rate of 22 percent, which is more than double the overall US poverty rate.

The intersectional effects of being both a woman and having a disability are economically devastating. Perhaps unsurprisingly, a closer look reveals that the combined disadvantage of gender and disability results in specific forms of employment-related prejudice harsher than those experienced by men with disabilities. For example, research indicates that women job applicants with disabilities are subject to stronger forms of bias than men with disabilities and also judged to be less competent than that group (Louvet 2007). Disability type has also been shown to make a difference in how women with disabilities are perceived. Women with physical disabilities are subject to less negative judgment than women with intellectual disabilities, while bias against men with disabilities remains constant across disability type (Coleman, Brunell, and Haugen 2015). The literature further suggests that women with disabilities who work in fields that are strongly identified with men—arguably most STEM fields—may also experience more bias and receive fewer accommodations (Breward 2020). In short, women with disabilities are subject to a host of "substantively distinct" and pernicious forms of disadvantage that affect both their access to employment and their experiences in the paid labor force (Bend and Priola 2018; Lindstrom, Hirano, and Ingram 2020, 395; Traustadóttir 2006). Despite the evidence, "Neither disability policies designed to ensure employment of people with disabilities nor policies aimed at gender equity in employment have recognized the specific employment barriers experienced by women with disabilities" (US Department of Labor n.d.). The issues that affect working women with disabilities are supported by data and well documented, but when it comes to policy development and other interventions, working women with disabilities fall all too neatly and silently through the intersectional cracks.

How does STEM work fit into these larger trends? Even though the literature on working women with disabilities is expanding, the literature on women with disabilities working in STEM occupations is extremely small. Like the research that examines systemic bias relative to historically marginalized groups in STEM, the majority of scholarship on people with disabilities in STEM focuses on STEM education—a critical area of inquiry given the well-documented ableism that permeates academia (Bargerhuff, Cowan, and Kirch 2010; Brown and Leigh 2020; Dolmage 2017). At first glance, participation data related to STEM education seems hopeful, suggesting undergraduates with disabilities participate in STEM majors at about the same rate as those without disabilities. The NSF reports that "28% of undergraduates with one or more disabilities were enrolled in [a] STEM field, about the same proportion as undergraduates without disabilities" (National Science Foundation 2019). But a closer look at the participation data reveals that the category of disability can also mask critical interactions with gender, race, and ethnicity—attributes that we already know are associated with underrepresentation in STEM. Few researchers have attended to women STEM students with disabilities, but those who have tangentially done so report that "students with disabilities face issues of gender equity in STEM education and occupations similar to those faced by members of the general population" (Burgstahler and Chang 2009, 38). And although the numbers of undergraduate students with disabilities participating in STEM look promising on the surface, recent research confirms that "[women] and minority SWDs [students with disabilities]" are "underrepresented substantially in STEM fields" (Lee 2020, 16).

Given the frequent intersectional erasure of women with disabilities in STEM education literature, it should not be surprising that a tremendous amount of work remains to be done in terms of rendering visible the lived experiences of women with disabilities who are working in STEM. Some research is underway, although a great deal of it is nonintersectional and focused on people with disabilities in general (as opposed to women or people from underrepresented groups with disabilities). In 2014, an information-gathering event cohosted by the US Department of Labor's Office of Disability Employment Policy (ODEP) and the National Council on Disability (NCD) found that stereotypes, a lack of mentors, and employers' lack of knowledge about the ADA were common barriers to the success of people with disabilities who worked (or planned to work) in STEM (Wilkie 2014).

It seems clear that gender does matter for thinking about disability and STEM work. An in-depth qualitative study of the experiences of women with disabilities working in STEM suggests that gender is of such significance that at least some women with disabilities in STEM jobs perceive gender bias to be a more pronounced obstacle than ableism (Coleman 2017). Op-ed essays by and about women with disabilities who are aspiring STEM professionals suggest that gender bias is compounded by disability status and that disability disclosure, while necessary to access needed accommodations, can be met with negative reactions and increase the burden for women with disabilities working in STEM (Shanahan 2016, 2017). An intersectionally sensitive study at the Science History Institute's Oral History Center posits that the experiences of scientists with disabilities are "best understood with [the] idea of intersectionality in mind" (Martucci 2017). This study and others like it may produce additional qualitative materials that could help illuminate issues facing women with disabilities who have worked and are working in STEM.

Finally, along with the frequently missing intersectional variables of gender and race/ethnicity, one critical element for thinking about disability in the context of STEM is the variety of ways that disability can appear across the lifespan. As the National Science Foundation suggests, the fact that anyone can have or acquire a disability may make a substantial difference in the relationship between disabilities and STEM work: "Disabilities acquired at birth or at an early age may influence decisions to pursue S&E [science and engineering] studies; those acquired at later ages may influence opportunities to continue or seek employment" (National Science Foundation 2017). It is therefore unwise to draw conclusions about the impact of disability on STEM work participation without at least some attention to this variable.

Women with Disabilities in Conventional STEM Fields: What Do the Data Say?

As of 2019, the total percentage of women (age twenty-five and over) in the US who identified themselves as having a disability was 17.2 percent. According to our definition of conventional STEM, in the year 2019 alone there were an estimated 8.6 million individuals age twenty-five to sixty-four working full-time and year-round in STEM occupations. An estimated 74,355 of them were women who identified as having a disability, which was less than 1 percent of all STEM job holders in 2019. Averaging across all the years of our sample and again focusing on those age twenty-five to sixty-four who work full-time and year-round, we find that only 3.3 percent of women with disabilities work in STEM occupations (compared to 11 percent of white men). Additionally, after adjusting for standard covariates (education, age, industry, marital status, citizen status, veteran status, and region of the country), we calculate that women with disabilities in conventional STEM occupations have a robust 35 percent wage premium over women with disabilities who do not work in STEM fields.

Within the traditional STEM occupations, the median earnings of women with disabilities are 75 percent of non-Hispanic white men's in STEM jobs, a significant jump since across all occupations women with disabilities earn only 61 percent of what non-Hispanic white men earn. That said, however, the median STEM earnings of women with disabilities as a percentage of non-Hispanic white men (75 percent) remains less than the ratio of the median earnings of all women relative to all men (80 percent). Thus, while STEM occupations provide a strong economic advantage (a 35 percent premium) for women with disabilities relative to other working women with disabilities, this advantage highlights the substantial relative wage lag under which women with disabilities labor overall.

We turn now to an exploration of the distribution and earnings of women with disabilities across conventional STEM and STEM-related occupations followed by additional comparisons within specific identity intersections. As a way of contextualizing these comparisons, we first consider the factor of disability type. This allows us to see if the STEM participation of women with disabilities (an aggregate group) might vary internally according to the various kinds of disabilities reported. To avoid double counting women, we limited our examination of disability type in conventional STEM occupations to women who reported only one disability (81 percent of the group). Our results showed that this group's participation in STEM fields does not vary strongly by disability type and that conventional STEM participation patterns stay relatively constant across this factor. In the STEM-related fields, the exact same percentage (81 percent) of women with disabilities report only one disability. In the STEM-related fields, the distribution varies only slightly with a single disability type: women who identify as having a disability in the area of self-care are slightly more likely to work in STEM-related fields.

This quick examination of disability type indicates that the participation of women with disabilities in STEM work is largely independent of the kind of disability they have. This finding is significant because it confirms that our participation and earnings analyses do not mask significant STEM participation variations across kinds of disability. We can, therefore, state with confidence that what follows applies to an aggregate group that is (for the most part) evenly distributed across the six disability types used by the ACS. Figure 8.2 represents how women with disabilities and white men in STEM are distributed across four broad categories of STEM work.

As figure 8.2 shows, both women with disabilities and non-Hispanic white men are most strongly represented in the computer/math fields (56 percent and 45 percent, respectively), and women with disabilities are twice as likely to work in the physical/life sciences as white men (20 percent compared to 10 percent). Engineering fields show the most significant participation differences between these two groups, with white men in STEM more than twice as likely to be engineers than women with disabilities. White men are somewhat more likely to work in STEM managerial fields (10 percent compared to 8 percent).

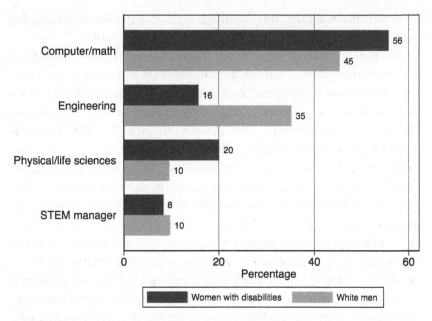

Figure 8.2
Distribution of women with disabilities and non-Hispanic white men across STEM occupations, individuals age 25–64 working year-round and full-time. *Source:* Data from the American Community Survey, 2012–2019.

The earnings information in table 8.1 enables us to connect important economic outcomes to the participation patterns in figure 8.2. Across all STEM categories, women with disabilities in STEM fields experience significant pay gaps relative to white men. The gaps are lowest where women with disabilities are most strongly represented—the physical/life sciences (a pay gap of 22 percentage points in the category with the lowest average salaries for both groups) and computer/math (a pay gap of 24 percentage points). In both engineering work and in STEM management, where white men proportionally exceed women with disabilities, women with disabilities experience a pay gap of 28 percentage points. This earnings difference is particularly substantial in terms of STEM management work, which has the highest overall average salaries for both groups: a pay gap of 28 percentage points in STEM management translates to an average loss of more than $33,000 annually for women with disabilities who work in those fields.

Table 8.1
Median annual earnings of women with disabilities as a percentage of median annual earnings of non-Hispanic white men in STEM occupations, individuals age 25–64 working year-round and full-time

STEM category	Median annual earnings		Women with disabilities' earnings as a percentage of non-Hispanic white men's
	Women with disabilities	Non-Hispanic white men	
Computer/math	$68,549	$89,903	76%
Engineering	$63,950	$88,606	72%
Physical/life sciences	$59,058	$75,632	78%
STEM managerial	$86,437	$120,226	72%

Note: All earnings adjusted to 2019 dollars. *Source:* Data from the American Community Survey, 2012–2019.

Women with Disabilities in the STEM-Related Fields: What Do the Data Say?

Using our definition of STEM-related fields in 2019, there were an estimated 7.3 million individuals age twenty-five to sixty-four working year-round and full-time in STEM-related jobs, and 198,463 of them self-reported as women with disabilities. Over the period of our sample and focusing on those age twenty-five to sixty-four who work year-round and full-time, we find that only 3.6 percent of non-Hispanic white men work in these occupations. However, about 9.4 percent of women with disabilities work in STEM-related jobs (as opposed to about 3.3 percent in conventional STEM occupations). While the STEM premium is a normative and often cited measure of how conventional STEM careers benefit women in any given group, the concept of a STEM-related premium is new. When we calculate a STEM-related premium for women with disabilities (which compares earnings in STEM-related occupations to non-STEM occupations while controlling for conventional STEM work), we see that women with disabilities in STEM-related jobs earn a substantial 31 percent more than women with disabilities not working in conventional STEM or STEM-related fields. Because our version of a STEM-related premium does not include traditional STEM work, it provides us with a meaningful snapshot

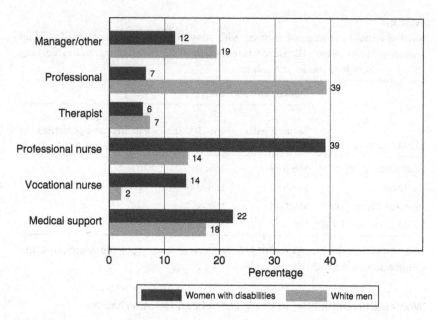

Figure 8.3
Distribution of women with disabilities and non-Hispanic white men across STEM-related occupations, individuals age 25–64 working year-round and full-time. *Source:* Data from the American Community Survey, 2012–2019.

of the significant economic benefits that STEM-related work provides women with disabilities.

Within the STEM-related fields (figure 8.3), women with disabilities and white men tend to do very different kinds of work. Only in the relatively small therapist cluster are they present in similar percentages. Otherwise, distribution patterns split between the nursing professions (in which women with disabilities outstrip white men) and medical professional work (which white men dominate). A woman with disabilities working in the STEM-related fields is twice as likely to be a professional nurse and seven times more likely to be a vocational nurse than a white man. A white man is more than five times more likely to work as a medical professional than a woman with disabilities. White men also outpace women with disabilities in terms of participation in STEM management fields—19 percent to 12 percent.

As in conventional STEM work, the average median salaries of women with disabilities lag behind the parallel salaries of non-Hispanic white men

Table 8.2
Median annual earnings of women with disabilities as a percentage of median annual earnings of non-Hispanic white men in STEM-related occupations, individuals age 25–64 working year-round and full-time

STEM-related category	Median annual earnings		Women with disabilities' earnings as a percentage of non-Hispanic white men's
	Women with disabilities	Non-Hispanic white men	
Manager/other	$60,113	$86,437	70%
Professional	$88,599	$168,350	53%
Therapist	$62,667	$76,327	82%
Professional nurse	$68,669	$75,761	91%
Vocational nurse	$39,718	$45,457	87%
Medical support	$40,791	$53,635	76%

Note: All earnings adjusted to 2019 dollars. *Source:* Data from the American Community Survey, 2012–2019.

in every occupational grouping (table 8.2). The resultant pay gaps generally align with participation trends. In the nursing professions, where women with disabilities are strongly represented, the pay gaps are smallest—and professional nursing salaries are the second-highest for women with disabilities in STEM-related fields. Pay gaps expand dramatically in the STEM-related areas of work that are both dominated by men and high-paying. Women with disabilities make 30 percentage points less in relatively high-paying STEM management work and experience an enormous pay gap of 47 percentage points in the highest-paying category of medical professional. Our data show the median earnings of a white man who is a medical professional are almost $80,000 more a year than a woman with disabilities in those fields.

Stopping at Three Intersections: Gender, Race/Ethnicity, and Disability Type

As with all aspects of identity, the experience of having a disability shapes and is shaped by other attributes. We have identified disability status and gender (women who identify as having a disability and women who do not), race/ethnicity, and general disability type (physical versus cognitive

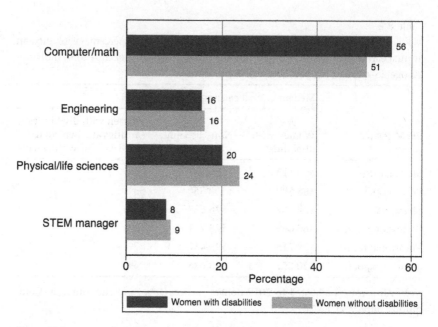

Figure 8.4
Distribution of women with and without disabilities across STEM occupations, individuals age 25–64 working year-round and full-time. *Source:* Data from the American Community Survey, 2012–2019.

disability) as intersectional points that can shed new light on the participation and earnings of women with disabilities who work in STEM. In the next section of this case study, we examine these three intersections. In doing so, we no longer exclusively use non-Hispanic white men as a comparison group but also juxtapose different groups of women.

Women with and without Disabilities

Figure 8.4 illustrates the distributions of women with and without disabilities across conventional STEM occupations. Overall, the distribution patterns are similar. These two groups participate in engineering and STEM management work at nearly identical rates; they differ by a mere 4 percentage points in computer/math fields (with the advantage going to women with disabilities) and physical/life sciences (with the advantage going to women without disabilities).

In table 8.3, however, critical differences emerge between these groups. On average, women with disabilities make less than their counterparts

Table 8.3
Median annual earnings of women with disabilities as a percentage of median annual earnings of women without disabilities in STEM occupations, individuals age 25–64 working year-round and full-time

STEM category	Median annual earnings		
	Women with disabilities	Women without disabilities	Women with disabilities' earnings as a percentage of women without disabilities'
Computer/math	$68,549	$78,390	87%
Engineering	$63,950	$77,359	83%
Physical/life sciences	$59,058	$65,423	90%
STEM managerial	$86,437	$101,014	86%

Note: All earnings adjusted to 2019 dollars. *Source:* Data from the American Community Survey, 2012–2019.

without disabilities in every occupational category in conventional STEM. The pay gaps experienced by women with disabilities range from 10 percentage points in the physical/life sciences (which has the lowest average income of all STEM categories for these groups) to 17 percentage points in engineering. Notably, while both groups are similarly distributed in the highest-paying STEM category of STEM management, a substantial pay gap of 14 percentage points exists in those occupations. Women without disabilities in STEM management outearn women with disabilities by a substantial $14,500 per year.

The STEM-related occupations reflect slightly more variation in the distribution between these two groups of women (figure 8.5). Women with disabilities are more likely to work in the vocational nursing and medical-support fields. Women without disabilities are more likely to work as professional nurses and as therapists and are significantly more likely to be medical professionals. Both groups participate at similar rates in STEM-related management.

Unlike the conventional STEM occupations, in STEM-related occupations differences in average salaries between women with and without disabilities are not stark (table 8.4). That said, while both groups earn less than white men across STEM-related work, women with disabilities still earn less than women without disabilities across every STEM-related job cluster. Average salary differences show that most pay gaps are less than 10

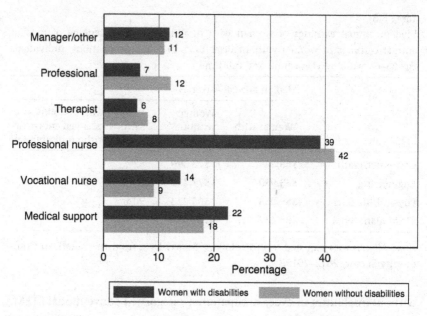

Figure 8.5
Distribution of women with and without disabilities across STEM-related occupations, individuals age 25–64 working year-round and full-time. *Source:* Data from the American Community Survey, 2012–2019.

Table 8.4
Median annual earnings of women with disabilities as a percentage of median annual earnings of women without disabilities in STEM-related occupations, individuals age 25–64 working year-round and full-time

STEM-related category	Median annual earnings		Women with disabilities' earnings as a percentage of women without disabilities'
	Women with disabilities	Women without disabilities	
Manager/other	$60,113	$65,423	92%
Professional	$88,599	$110,757	80%
Therapist	$62,667	$66,454	94%
Professional nurse	$68,669	$70,230	98%
Vocational nurse	$39,718	$41,598	95%
Medical support	$40,791	$44,011	93%

Note: All earnings adjusted to 2019 dollars. *Source:* Data from the American Community Survey, 2012–2019.

percentage points, with essentially no difference in the area of professional nursing. The highest-paying STEM-related category, professional medical work, is an outlier: women with disabilities experience a significant pay gap of 20 percentage points in the medical professions relative to women without disabilities. This results in a substantial average loss of about $22,000 annually for women with disabilities.

Race and Ethnicity: White Women and Women of Color with Disabilities

Of women with disabilities in STEM, 70 percent identify as white, and 30 percent identify as women of color (defined here as women who identify as Black, American Indian/Alaska Native, Asian/Pacific Islander, some other race, or Hispanic). Of this latter group, 45 percent identify as Black, while about 25 percent report either Asian or Hispanic. In terms of occupational distribution (figure 8.6), white women with disabilities in the STEM fields are represented slightly more in engineering and the physical/life sciences,

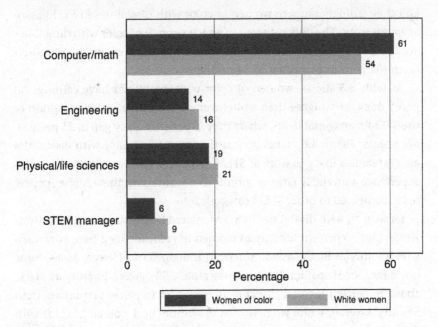

Figure 8.6
Distribution of women with disabilities by race/ethnicity across STEM occupations, individuals age 25–64 working year-round and full-time. *Source:* Data from the American Community Survey, 2012–2019.

Table 8.5

Median annual earnings of women with disabilities by race/ethnicity in STEM occupations, individuals age 25–64 working year-round and full-time

STEM category	Median annual earnings		
	Women of color with disabilities	Non-Hispanic white women with disabilities	Women of color with disabilities' earnings as a percentage of non-Hispanic white women with disabilities'
Computer/math	$69,784	$67,636	103%
Engineering	$63,276	$64,407	98%
Physical/life sciences	$63,243	$57,265	110%
STEM managerial	$69,150	$87,883	79%

Note: All earnings adjusted to 2019 dollars. *Source:* Data from the American Community Survey, 2012–2019.

and they strongly outpace women of color with disabilities in STEM management work. The only category in which women of color with disabilities are more strongly represented than their white counterparts is computer/math (61 percent compared to 54 percent).

As table 8.5 shows, women of color with disabilities have earnings on parity or slightly higher than white women, with the notable exception of the STEM managerial fields, where they experience a pay gap of 21 percentage points. Figure 8.6 makes it clear that women of color with disabilities are also far less likely to work as STEM managers. Here we see that they also experience a uniquely large economic disadvantage in these higher-paying fields compared to other STEM categories.

Of women with disabilities in STEM-related fields, 70 percent identify as white, and 30 percent identify as women of color (defined here as women who identify as Black, Asian, American Indian/Alaska Native, Asian, some other race, or Hispanic). Of this latter group, 50 percent identify as Black, about 26 percent report a Hispanic identity, and 16 percent report an Asian identity. Overall, white women with disabilities and women of color with disabilities are distributed across STEM-related work in similar ways (figure 8.7). Some disparities jump out in nursing work: women of color with disabilities are less likely to be professional nurses than white women with disabilities (35 percent compared to 41 percent) and more likely to work

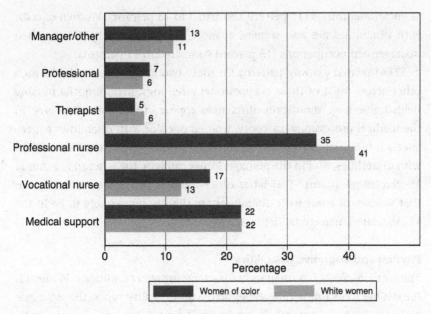

Figure 8.7
Distribution of women with disabilities by race/ethnicity across STEM-related occupations, individuals age 25–64 working year-round and full-time. *Source:* Data from the American Community Survey, 2012–2019.

Table 8.6
Median annual earnings of women with disabilities by race/ethnicity in STEM-related occupations, individuals age 25–64 working year-round and full-time

STEM-related category	Median annual earnings		Women of color with disabilities' earnings as a percentage of non-Hispanic white women with disabilities'
	Women of color with disabilities	Non-Hispanic white women with disabilities	
Manager/other	$52,056	$64,255	81%
Professional	$75,632	$91,929	82%
Therapist	$64,828	$61,587	105%
Professional nurse	$69,774	$68,549	102%
Vocational nurse	$40,075	$39,711	101%
Medical support	$42,426	$40,345	105%

Note: All earnings adjusted to 2019 dollars. *Source:* Data from the American Community Survey, 2012–2019.

as vocational nurses (17 percent compared to 13 percent). Women of color with disabilities are also somewhat more likely to work in STEM-related management occupations (13 percent compared to 11 percent).

STEM-related earning patterns for these two groups are similar to each other across most of these occupational groupings, including the nursing fields (table 8.6). Significant differences appear in two areas, however. In the medical professional category, women of color with disabilities experience a substantial pay gap of 18 percentage points relative to white women with disabilities, and in the manager/other category the pay gap is a similar 19 percentage points. This latter observation is perhaps surprising given that women of color with disabilities are slightly more likely to be in the STEM-related managerial fields (see figure 8.7).

Physical and Cognitive Disabilities

The word *disability* is a small term for a large array of conditions. While it is impossible to examine differences across all disability types, the aggregate category disability potentially masks significant differences among people with disabilities. For this intersectional look at women with disabilities in STEM, we have divided the heterogeneous category of disability into two general groupings—physical disabilities and cognitive disabilities. Physical disabilities include issues such as visual, auditory, and motor impairments, while cognitive disabilities refer to conditions such as autism, dyslexia, dyscalculia, memory loss, or disorders of mental health. While distinctions between groupings are rudimentary—and an individual may have both physical and cognitive disabilities—a look at the differences between them helps illustrate how disability type matters. In the data that follow, we compare women in STEM who report either a physical or a cognitive disability (figure 8.8).

When it comes to distribution across conventional STEM work, there are few remarkable differences in the STEM job category distributions between women with physical and cognitive disabilities. Participation in computer/ math fields and the physical/life sciences is essentially identical, and the distinctions that do exist are not large. Women with physical disabilities participate in engineering slightly less (3 percentage points) and in STEM management slightly more (2 percentage points) than women with cognitive disabilities.

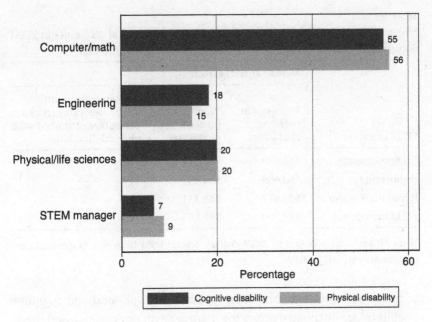

Figure 8.8
Distribution of women with physical disabilities and women with cognitive disabilities across STEM occupations, individuals age 25–64 working year-round and full-time. *Source:* Data from the American Community Survey, 2012–2019.

Near-equivalency in participation patterns between these groups does not carry over to earnings. While all women with disabilities who work in STEM fields earn less on average than white men, women with physical disabilities outearn women with cognitive disabilities in every STEM occupational category (table 8.7). The pay gaps between these groups of women range from 6 percentage points in engineering, 9 percentage points in computer/math fields, 15 percentage points in the physical/life sciences, and 21 percentage points in STEM management work. STEM management is the highest-paying category of STEM, and women with cognitive disabilities are not only slightly less likely to work in these fields but make on average less than $18,000 annually than women with physical disabilities who engage in this same work. Overall, the median earnings of women with physical disabilities are similar to the median earnings of all women with disabilities (see table 8.1), but the same is not true for women with cognitive disabilities.

Table 8.7

Median annual earnings of women with cognitive and physical disabilities in STEM occupations, individuals age 25–64 working year-round and full-time

STEM category	Median annual earnings		
	Women with cognitive disabilities	Women with physical disabilities	Women with cognitive disabilities' earnings as a percentage of women with physical disabilities'
Computer/math	$63,639	$69,774	91%
Engineering	$60,609	$64,407	94%
Physical/life sciences	$53,672	$63,131	85%
STEM managerial	$69,700	$87,883	79%

Note: All earnings adjusted to 2019 dollars. *Source:* Data from the American Community Survey, 2012–2019.

In the STEM-related occupations, women with physical and cognitive disabilities are distributed across the management, professional, and therapist categories at the same rates (figure 8.9). Significant differences appear in other fields: women with physical disabilities are 7 percentage points more likely to work in professional nursing than women with cognitive disabilities, while women with cognitive disabilities are more likely to work in vocational nursing (by 3 percentage points) and the medical-support fields (by 6 percentage points).

As with the conventional STEM fields, when compared to women with physical disabilities, women with cognitive disabilities are subject to additional and substantial earnings disadvantages across every STEM-related occupational category. Pay gaps between these two groups of women are most pronounced in the occupational categories where they are most similarly distributed. When compared to women with physical disabilities, women with cognitive disabilities make (on average) 14 percentage points less in the management fields, earn 18 percentage points less as therapists, and experience a pay gap of 35 percentage points in the medical professional fields. In the case of this last category, which is the highest-paying for all groupings compared in table 8.8, the pay gap is substantial. Women with cognitive disabilities experience powerful earnings gaps relative to women with physical disabilities in most areas, regardless of how they are distributed across the occupational groups.

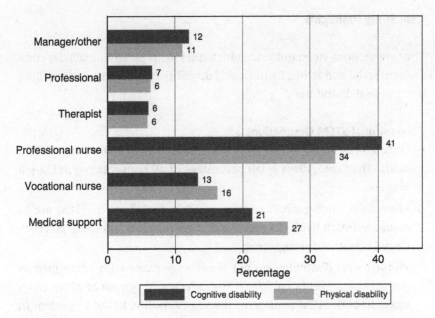

Figure 8.9
Distribution of women with cognitive disabilities and women with physical disabilities across STEM-related occupations, individuals age 25–64 working year-round and full-time. *Source:* Data from the American Community Survey, 2012–2019.

Table 8.8
Median annual earnings of women with cognitive and physical disabilities as a percentage median annual earnings of white men in STEM-related occupations, individuals age 25–64 working year-round and full-time

STEM-related category	Median annual earnings		Women with cognitive disabilities' earnings as a percentage of women with physical disabilities'
	Women with cognitive disabilities	Women with physical disabilities	
Manager/other	$54,519	$63,243	86%
Professional	$63,276	$97,243	65%
Therapist	$53,635	$65,346	82%
Professional nurse	$64,239	$69,774	92%
Vocational nurse	$36,100	$40,497	89%
Medical support	$36,912	$42,426	87%

Note: All earnings adjusted to 2019 dollars. *Source:* Data from the American Community Survey, 2012–2019.

Case Study Highlights

The intersections we examine in this chapter focus on an intragender comparison, racial and ethnic identity, and disability type (cognitive disabilities and physical disabilities).

Conventional STEM Occupations

- Only 3.3 percent of women with disabilities work in conventional STEM fields. They comprise a small percentage of all conventional STEM job holders.
- More than three-quarters of women with disabilities in STEM are in computer/math fields (56 percent) or physical/life sciences (20 percent). Only 16 percent are engineers.
- Women with disabilities do not reach wage parity with white men in any area of conventional STEM. They average 72 percent of white men's wages in both STEM management and engineering fields, 76 percent in computer/math, and 78 percent in the physical/life sciences. These patterns are lower than the overall gender earnings ratio of 80 percent.

STEM-Related Occupations

- About 9.4 percent of women with disabilities work in STEM-related fields, almost three times as many as in conventional STEM jobs.
- In the STEM-related fields, three-quarters of women with disabilities are in nursing work (39 percent professional and 14 percent vocational) or medical support (22 percent). Only 7 percent work in the high-paying medical professional occupations.
- Earnings for women with disabilities in STEM-related work are compromised relative to white men; they do not reach parity in any area. They make fifty-three cents for every dollar earned by white men in medical professional fields, and the resulting $80,000 annual earnings gap exceeds the salaries of women with disabilities in every other category but professional itself.
- STEM-related earnings for this group are strongest in nursing. Women with disabilities make about 90 percent of what white men earn in professional nursing and come close to that in vocational.

Stopping at an Intersection: An Intragender Comparison

- Women with disabilities and women without disabilities are similarly distributed across the conventional STEM fields.
- Women without disabilities outearn their counterparts with disabilities in every category of conventional STEM. Pay gaps range from a minimum 10 percentage points (physical/life sciences) to 17 percentage points (engineering).
- Women with disabilities and women without disabilities are also generally distributed in similar ways across the STEM-related fields. The exceptions are that women with disabilities are more likely to be vocational nurses, and women without disabilities are more likely to be medical professionals.
- While pay gaps are smaller in STEM-related work than in conventional STEM, women without disabilities still outearn women with disabilities in every category. In the high-paying medical professional jobs, the pay gap is a significant 20 percentage points.

Stopping at an Intersection: Racial and Ethnic Identity

- A comparison of white women with disabilities and women of color with disabilities reveals some differences in conventional STEM distribution. White women with disabilities are more likely to be in STEM managerial work, and this is also the area with the largest pay gap (21 percentage points in favor of white women with disabilities).
- Women of color with disabilities out-earn white women with disabilities in the physical and life sciences by 10 percentage points. In the other STEM fields, pay is close to parity between the two groups.
- In STEM-related fields, women of color and white women with disabilities are similarly distributed, with nursing being dominant for both. White women are more likely to be professional nurses, while women of color are more likely to be vocational nurses.
- There is earnings parity between these groups in most STEM-related areas. However, pay gaps favoring white women with disabilities emerge in management (19 percentage points) and the medical professional occupations (18 percentage points).

Stopping at an Intersection: Disability Type (Cognitive and Physical Disabilities)

- Women with physical disabilities and women with cognitive disabilities are overall similarly distributed in conventional STEM work. Women with physical disabilities are slightly less likely to be engineers (and more likely to be in management).

- Earnings gaps favor women with physical disabilities over women with cognitive disabilities in every area of STEM work. Pay gaps are smaller in engineering (6 percentage points) and computer/math (9 percentage points) and larger for physical/life sciences (15 percentage points) and STEM-related management (21 percentage points).

- In the STEM-related occupations, nursing and medical-support work dominate for both of these groups.

- Earnings ratios favor women with physical disabilities over women with cognitive disabilities in every area of STEM-related work. Earnings ratios range between 82 percent and 92 percent overall, with medical professions as an outlier: women with cognitive disabilities in these jobs make 65 percent of what their counterparts with physical disabilities make.

9 Lesbians, Bisexual Women, Trans Women, and Gender-Nonbinary Individuals in STEM

LGBTQ+: Some Working Definitions

Like the phrase *women of color*, the acronym *LGBTQ+* (lesbian, gay, bisexual, transgender, and Queer) links identities whose experiences are shaped by comparable but not identical forms of oppression. Just as white supremacy and ethnocentrism structure various forms of racism and ethnic bias, the identity group LGBTQ+ is framed by regimes of gender and sexual normalcy, specifically, compulsory heterosexuality and enforced cisgenderedness. LGBTQ+ people routinely face active exclusion and stigma, including entrenched associations with social deviance, illness, and crime; weak or entirely absent legal protections; and many normalized forms of social marginalization, political targeting, and outright violence.

Although LGBTQ+ is a useful acronym, the four groups we address in this chapter—lesbians, bisexual women, trans women, and gender-nonbinary people in STEM—differ from each other in significant ways. Lesbian and bisexual woman are sexual identity categories: lesbians are people who identify as women and who have a primary affective and/or sexual attraction to women, and bisexual women experience affective and/or sexual attraction to both women and men. The categories of lesbian and bisexual woman reinforce the idea that the gender of one's object choice defines one's sexual identity and also rely on the gender identity of the subject herself. A person must identify as a woman to be a lesbian or a bisexual woman. Importantly, these terms refer to social identities, not behaviors. For example, some women who have sex with other women do not identify as lesbians, and some women who identify as bisexual may not engage in intimate behavior with anyone.

The category of trans woman references gender identity and is not associated with any specific sexual identity. Trans women are typically described as women who were assigned male at birth, and that is the definition we ascribe to here. Some women who were assigned male at birth may identify as women and not as trans women. Because trans women are women, this case study operates on the premise that identifying as a trans woman is the choice of the individual involved and should not be a descriptive label imposed from the outside. Trans women may claim—or decline to claim—any sexual identity (such as straight, lesbian, or bisexual).

Gender nonbinary is an umbrella term for individuals who do not identify within the conventional gender binary. Sometimes also called gender nonconforming, this is a heterogeneous group of people who may (for example) identify as entirely outside of the gender binary, as having two or more genders, and/or as having a fluctuating relationship with gender. Unlike trans women, gender-nonbinary people do not identify as women in the sense of having a fixed gender identity, and our inclusion of this diverse group is in no way intended to suggest they do. Rather, our goal is to highlight the important challenge to cisgender privilege represented by gender-nonbinary people. Although limited in scope, our inclusion of gender-nonbinary individuals recognizes the power of cisgender privilege and the stranglehold the gender binary has on our thinking about gender, identity, and (especially quantitative) data.

Finally, we do not focus separately on Queer as an identity group, even though this chapter often uses the acronym LGBTQ+. Long deployed as a derogatory term for LGBT people, the word *Queer* was repurposed in the 1990s to indicate a radical break with stable, identity-focused, civil rights–based models for change. This version resists definition, rejects stable categories of gender and sexual identity, and disrupts the systems of power through which some identities are validated and others are stigmatized. In other words, "Queerness can never define an identity; it can only ever disturb one" (Edelman 2004, 17). In this sense, Queer highlights the limits of fixed sexual and gender-identity categories and dovetails with our own critical approach to data and categorization (Ruberg and Ruelos 2020).

In common usage today, however, Queer is slightly less contrarian. It typically functions as shorthand for LGBT people and often—especially when combined with a plus sign—indicates any identity that is not heteronormative and/or cisgendered. Queer therefore simultaneously invokes a number of different groups (including ones that we examine separately here, such as lesbians and bisexual women) and additionally suggests a capacious recognition of gender and sexual identities (such as asexual, pansexual, genderqueer, and so on). Our use of Q+ throughout this chapter, therefore, is not meant to indicate any specific identity group as much as it is a broader commitment to acknowledging every way of being that moves outside of and against hegemonic heteronormative cisgenderedness.

Lesbians, Bisexual Women, Trans Women, and Gender-Nonbinary People

While there can be no doubt that all forms of sexual desire and all relations with (and against) gender identity have always existed, the production of specific social identities around certain desires and particular relationships to gender is a cultural and historical process. Like many other identity categories (being Hispanic, for example, or having a disability), the sexual and gender identities currently in circulation have emerged and morphed in response to changing dynamics of power, politics, and institutions (Foucault 1978; Seidman 2010). This is true of identities now so firmly established that they appear to be self-evident (such as heterosexual and homosexual), as well as more contemporary identities such as trans and gender nonbinary. The fact that new sexual and gender identities have proliferated since the late twentieth century does not make these identities inherently more constructed (or less real) than other identity groups (Cover 2018). It simply means they are dynamically in flux—and expanding—at this historical juncture.

We begin this examination of lesbians, bisexual women, trans women, and gender-nonbinary people in STEM with a look at these different groups' historical relations to identity and visibility. The two most established identity groups—lesbians and bisexual women—are framed by the idea of homosexuality, a category formed by later nineteenth-century discursive and institutional frameworks of pathology and crime. Homosexuality was originally as much a diagnosis as an identity, and links between same-sex desire and illness have proved to be extremely durable. The association has hardened via both cultural beliefs (homosexuality is a sickness) and institutions (the APA listed homosexuality as a mental illness until 1973). Homosexuality has also been historically linked to illegality, and the state has long worked to manage homosexual behavior via the law. Sodomy laws associated with same-sex desire are perhaps the most recognizable version of the state's investment in suppressing consensual sexual expression between adults. In the US, such laws were in place until 2003. The legal persecution of people who identify as LGB or who engage in same-sex sexual activity is reflected in countless historical examples (Bronski 2011). Overall, the history of homosexuality in the US reflects both deeply rooted cultural stigma and multiple layers of formalized persecution.

Perpetual threats to their well-being and safety have meant that many gay, lesbian, and bisexual individuals have stayed closeted in order to protect their jobs, partners, friends, families, and lives. But with the rise of the multiple civil rights movements of the 1960s and 1970s, new patterns developed around homosexual identity and visibility. Deeply influenced by the second-wave feminist movement, the later twentieth-century push for LGB rights marked a turn toward a rights-focused, group-based model for identity and the politics of coming out. Coming out originally indicated a person's entrance into homosexual communities, but as the modern gay and lesbian movement got underway, it came to be understood as an important personal and public process of identity-claiming (Chauncey 1994). This model was strengthened in the 1980s and 1990s by the devastating impact of the AIDS crisis on vulnerable populations, particularly sexual minorities. The rallying cry of AIDS activism, "Silence = Death," encapsulated a new understanding that lesbian, gay, and bisexual people must be seen and heard in order to survive. Since then, coming out has taken its place as a defining aspect of modern gay, lesbian, and bisexual life. The decision to claim (or not claim) one's membership in the larger LGB group is now understood to be a cornerstone of LGB experience.

Compared to homosexuality, trans and gender nonbinary are more recent categories. Awareness of these identities has increased rapidly over the past few decades as each has slowly evolved into a recognizable group. Throughout history, however, there have always been gender-variant individuals who have moved away from their assigned gender toward another gender or an indeterminate space (Feinberg 1996; Snorton 2017; Stryker 2017; Stryker and Whittle 2006). In this context, trans and gender-nonbinary individuals have only recently become established as specific kinds of people. This shift has moved trans and gender-nonbinary people toward minority-group status while also producing the boundaries that grouphood entails (Halberstam 2017; Valentine 2007). Trans and gender-nonbinary people are slowly but surely being linked to the characteristics of systemically disadvantaged identity groups in a liberal state, including cultural recognizability, perceived collective interests, and shared subject positions from which to mobilize for change. However, group identities also carry disadvantages because they generate a reliance on the very systems (such as medicine and the law) that have engineered forms of oppression (Spade 2012) and produce new regimes of normalcy that are accompanied by internal and external demands for coherence. In the case of gender-variant populations, Austin Johnson (2016) has labeled this phenomena *transnormativity*.

Despite their emergence into increasingly recognizable, specific identities, trans people and gender-nonbinary individuals remain embedded in the patterns of marginalization, disadvantage, and violence that have long constrained and harmed gender-variant people. Historically, the medical establishment has engaged in pathologizing methods of diagnosis and cure. Medical discourses also continue to shape and exacerbate the struggles of trans people. Gender dysphoria remains a diagnosis in the American Psychiatric Association's *Diagnostic and Statistical Manual of Mental Disorders*, fifth edition (DSM V), and many trans people must rely on pathologized self-narratives in order to access gender-affirming medical care (such as access to therapy, hormones, or surgery) (Spade 2006). Legal restrictions have included passing laws against impersonation of the opposite sex and cross-dressing, disadvantaging trans people in terms of employment, marriage, the military, and so on (Beemyn 2014; Enke 2012). Recent research confirms entrenched patterns in which trans people continue to be routinely targeted and abused by the law and by law enforcement (Burns 2020; James et al. 2016; Serpe and Nadal 2017).

Lesbians, bisexual women, trans women, and gender-nonbinary people are modern identity categories—that is, they only recently have been understood as specific groups. In different ways and to varying degrees, intertwined medical and legal systems have defined all these groups against normalcy, health, and public safety by positioning them as abnormal, sick, and threats to public welfare. In response, these groups have come together to fight against the systems that have produced and defined them. Over the past twenty years, the unstinting efforts of LGBTQ+ activists and their allies have altered the US medical and legal landscape. In 1973, homosexuality was removed from the DSM, and, while gender dysphoria remains a pathology, it is an improvement on its predecessor, gender-identity disorder. On the legal side, sodomy laws were struck down as unconstitutional by the US Supreme Court in 2003 (*Lawrence v. Texas*), same-sex marriage was legalized in 2015 (*Obergefell v. Hodges*), and federal workplace protections for LGBT people were included under Title VII of the Civil Rights Act of 1964 in 2020 (*Bostock v. Clayton County, Georgia*).

These medical and legal milestones are enormous, and they matter. But they have not undone the fraught nature of LGBTQ+ visibility or the dangers of LGBTQ+ life. Progress in the US has been followed by anti-LGBTQ+ hate, and the backlash against the expansion of medical and legal protections for LGBTQ+ people has become increasingly ferocious and widespread. Since 2018, more than 670 anti-LGBTQ bills have been filed in US state legislatures (Lavietes and Ramos 2022). Proposed legislation includes a wide range of attempts to constrict visibility and rights, including education-based censorship (such as Florida's infamous "Don't say gay" legislation in 2022) and religious refusal bills. A high proportion of these bills target the vulnerable trans and nonbinary populations. In 2022, more than 150 bills aimed at undercutting trans rights and well-being were introduced across the US (Branigin and Kirkpatrick 2022). Such measures attempt (among other things) to restrict bathroom access, ban sports participation, forbid use of correct pronouns and names, and curtail or ban access to gender-affirming care.

In the context of this legislative onslaught, violence against trans and gender-variant people is epidemic and escalating. Trans and gender-nonbinary individuals in the US are four times more likely to experience violent crime than cisgendered people (Flores et al. 2021). Such violence is often fatal: 2021 was the deadliest year on record for trans and gender-nonbinary people in the US with at least 59 people killed; the vast majority of these individuals were people of color (Human Rights Campaign 2021). In addition, between legalized discrimination and outright murder lies the murky land of structurally invisible forms of violence. Trans and gender-nonbinary people are frequently threatened by violence or narrowly escape it, they avoid reporting violence for fear of retaliation, and the violence reported by these populations is not properly recorded or taken seriously by law enforcement (Thoreson 2021).

Because LGBTQ+ people must actively manage their self-presentation and identities, they often make life decisions based on the understanding that they will inevitably encounter bias—or worse. In 2020, more than half of LGBTQ+ people (54 percent) reported hiding a relationship to avoid discrimination, while more than a third (35 percent) made their decisions about where to work based on their LGBTQ+ status (Mahowald, Gruberg, and Halpin 2020). Trans people report discrimination, including workplace discrimination, at higher rates than other LGBTQ+ groups (Mahowald, Gruberg, and Halpin 2020). Entrenched cisgendered heteronormativity and a culture of embedded and explicit threat make visibility a vexed, often life-threatening issue for LGBTQ+ people.

Queer Data

Our brief look at LGBTQ+ identities as a set of historically produced categories provides the necessary framework for thinking about the complex and conflicted question of LGBTQ+ data. Until recently, formalized attempts at seeing LGBTQ+ people have generally aimed at eliminating them, not enumerating them. So it should come as no surprise that LGBTQ+ demographics are both recent in origin and controversial in nature. In the late 1940s and early 1950s, Alfred Kinsey's famous sexological studies showed that homosexuality (or, at least, same-sex desire) is a common part of human experience (Kinsey et al. 1948). While not conventionally demographic, Kinsey's work helped frame an enduring cultural interest in identifying a hidden yet present homosexual population. With the rise and spread of LGBTQ+ civil rights movements in the 1960s and 1970s and the associated turn toward the politics of coming out, the presence of a gay and lesbian population became even more culturally resonant as minority group status solidified (Singer and Deschamps 2017). These historical factors have helped make generic overall population measurement the main focus of demographic research on LGBTQ+ people. As a result, the question "What percentage of the US population is gay or lesbian or (more recently) LGBTQ+?" has long dominated both scholarly work and the discourse around Queer demography (Gates 2011; Gates and Ost 2004; Laumann et al. 2000).

More detailed data have slowly begun to be generated as various groups now associated with LGBTQ+ identities have increased in visibility over time. For example, we can predict there will be (and there are) more data associated with lesbians than trans women because the social category of lesbian has been around considerably longer than the social category of trans woman. As new categories emerge, new demographic work follows. TransPop, a pioneering national effort to collect health data on trans people, exemplifies such an effort; other data-producing studies on nonbinary people are appearing, as well (TransPop 2021; Wilson and Meyer 2021). The steady movement toward LGBTQ+ identity politics has bolstered LGBTQ+ demographics, which in turn has generated scholarship on the production of "better" data on LGBTQ+ populations, especially relative to newer groups (like nonbinary people). Researchers now routinely engage with issues regarding best practices for collecting data on gender-diverse populations (Broussard, Warner, and Pope 2018; Doan 2016; GenIUSS Group 2014; Magliozzi, Saperstein, and Westbrook 2016). Recent work shows that this interest has extended to the demographics of gender-variant populations in STEM (Casper, Atadero, and Fuselier 2022).

Despite these efforts, however, the value of collecting data around LGBTQ+ identities remains a fraught question. Even if gathering some kinds of demographic data associated with LGBTQ+ people is now possible, it is important to ask if such data—and the perils associated with collecting and deploying them—are truly desirable. On one hand, some critics see the persistent refusal to collect data on LGBTQ+ people as an example of intentional erasure and a form of violence. For example, neither the decennial census nor the American Community Survey (ACS) has ever asked about sexual orientation or gender identity, and many LGBTQ+ advocates have interpreted this as a hostile refusal to better understand and address the urgent needs of vulnerable groups. In 2017, a draft of the 2020 census was released with sexual and gender-identity status questions, and many LGBTQ+ advocates protested when those questions were removed (O'Hara 2017; Tashman 2018). In 2017, the Trump administration removed existing sexual orientation measures from two Department of Health and Human Services surveys aimed at assessing older populations, blocking the collection of data associated with challenges affecting older Queer people (Gates 2017). This process, sometimes labeled straightwashing, has been condemned as harmful to LGBTQ+ individuals because it perpetuates the symbolic erasure of such individuals while also blocking information that could drive effective public policy on their behalf (Naylor 2020; Velte 2020). The COVID-19 crisis provided a compelling instance of the dangers of missing data. During the pandemic, issues particular to LGBTQ+ health could not be assessed and addressed partly because "the collection of sexual orientation and gender-identity data is scattershot at best" (Kramer 2021). And in the context of STEM inclusivity, scholars have also begun more consistently to note and condemn the absence of LGBTQ+ related data, arguing that data collection centered on diverse STEM populations has widely ignored LGBTQ+ individuals and that the failure to collect such data has done real harm (Burnett et al. 2022; Freeman 2021).

But there is a powerful tension between claims that data collection on the LGBTQ+ community will advance the well-being of these populations and opposing positions that argue such data are the gateway to elevated state control. First, critics of group-based data collection note that this practice solidifies and naturalizes LGBTQ+ categories, which (like all identity groups) are entirely constructed. The reification of LGBTQ+ identities through data collection embeds those stabilized groupings into the larger systems that have produced them, locking Queer people into established debates, shoehorning them into a preset array of identities, and delegitimizing Queers who do not fit.

Second, in a world where both the state and global capitalism rely on massive, intertwined systems of big data, loss of privacy and hostile forms of surveillance go hand in hand with pervasive and often predictive data-centered knowledge infrastructures. US history readily demonstrates that the collection of identity-based (usually racialized) data—nonwhite immigrant populations, Muslim populations post-9/11, and Black Lives Matter activists, for example—can be an engine of invasive social control. As our earlier discussion of Queer lives and visibility issues notes, persistent and often structurally legitimized forms of threat already make it risky for Queer individuals to disclose their sexual and/or gender-variant identities. The threats inherent in data collection are elevated for Queer people, whose existence teeters on the brink of being perceived as inherently deviant and as public threats. The capture of LGBTQ+ data can mean damaging exposure, elevated threat, loss of privacy, misrepresentations of lived experience, unwanted or negative interactions with policing and health-care systems, and increased future vulnerability. Such data will inevitably be racialized, as well. Overall, many LGBTQ+ people are rightly suspicious of category-based data's potential to establish regimes of definitional control and surveillance—particularly in a time of retrenchment in which legislative actions seeking to control LGBTQ+ populations are expanding and informal systems of violence are escalating.

As we look at lesbians, bisexual women, trans women, and gender-nonbinary individuals in STEM, we must be mindful of these tensions around the collection of Queer data. We recognize that data can be a means of harm and restriction as well as a means of recognition and expansion of well-being. Hence, as we proceed with our look at LGBTQ+ data, we frame our work within three generic contextualizing factors—all of which illuminate LGBTQ+ demographics but also productively point to the inherent instability of LGBTQ+ categories and LGBTQ+ data itself.

First, decades of longitudinal tracking of LGBTQ+ population size has produced one fairly solid consensus: while the size of the LGBTQ+ population in the US is debatable, it is growing. In the General Social Survey, for example, the number of adults identifying as LGB doubled from 2.7 percent in 2008 to 5.4 percent in 2016 (Gates 2017). The Gallup Poll, which began asking respondents about LGBT identity in 2012, reflects steadily climbing rates, as well—from 3.5 percent in 2012 to 5.6 percent in 2020 (Jones 2021). This growth is likely explained by profound changes in the social meanings of being LGBTQ+ as well as increased visibility overall (Impelli 2021). And because the shift to minority group status—and associated growth in visibility—has taken place over time, there is also a generational pattern within the LGBTQ+ population: the younger the age group, the higher the percentage of LGBTQ+-identified people in it (Jones 2021). These trends remind us that new LGBTQ+ data is not a truth but rather historically produced by social and political forces.

Second, sexual and gender identities are not stable and do not necessarily hold still over the lifespan, especially for LGBTQ+ people. Compulsory heterosexuality ensures most individuals are labeled heterosexual at the start of their lives, and gender identity is usually socially imposed before birth. With heteronormativity and cisgenderedness dominating as the forced default settings for human identity, arriving at and embracing a lesbian, bisexual, trans, or gender-nonbinary identity can be a lifelong, challenging process. Unsurprisingly, research suggests that people in the Queer population experience their identities at a level of indeterminacy much greater than what is implied by seemingly static categories like LGBT (Ruberg and Ruelos 2020). LGBTQ+ data are further destabilized when we recognize that sexual identities and gender identities remain in motion (both as personal identities and as social categories) across time.

Third, although there is expanding interest in the demographics associated with LGBTQ+ people, the data collected so far have been narrow in scope—that is, limited in both survey size and type. As demographic work on LGBTQ+ population size began to accelerate at the end of the twentieth century, smaller surveys (such as the General Social Survey and the National Survey of Family Growth) have usually asked about sexual practices—but no surveys with large samples and detailed questions have emerged (Baumle and Dreon 2019). Opportunities to examine LGBTQ+ issues quantitatively, such as STEM occupational patterns and earnings, remain very scarce.

As with all of the case studies in this book, the Census Bureau plays a role, but that role is limited. Despite the federal government's refusal to add sexual and gender-identity measures, US Census Bureau data is nonetheless strongly associated with the occupations and earnings of lesbians. This trend emerged from the Bureau's 1990 attempt to understand the population of unmarried, cohabiting couples using a question regarding unmarried partners. That question opened the possibility of identifying partnered respondents as gay or lesbian by identifying households where two adults identified as both the same sex and being in a domestic partnership. The resulting data "opened doors for demographic research" on gay and lesbian populations (Baumle and Dreon 2019, 282). Since then, researchers have often used ACS data to represent partnered gays and lesbians, a trend that has dominated the LGBTQ+ data landscape and enabled research on STEM work and earnings via familiar occupational codes and income questions backed up by an enormous sample. Despite the usefulness of these data, however, serious limitations are attached to them. One of these is that ACS data reflect only partnered lesbians and exclude the population of *un*partnered lesbians, yet are often used to make inferences about lesbians overall. In addition, any woman partnered with another woman may potentially be a bisexual woman and not a lesbian. The data we use, therefore, do not account for a large group of lesbians (unpartnered lesbians) and additionally reflect both an overcount of partnered lesbians and a disturbing erasure of (same-sex partnered) bisexual women.

Along with the ACS, there is a second source that allows us to gain a glimpse of STEM occupational patterns and earnings for both lesbians and bisexual women. The National Health Interview Survey (NHIS) is a small, face-to-face survey of about 87,500 adults and children in about 35,000 households per year. Since 2013, the survey has asked adult respondents about their sexual identity (for example, if they are straight, gay/lesbian, bisexual, or something else) (Sansone and Carpenter 2020): we use data

Table 9.1

Overview of relevant characteristics for American Community Survey (ACS) and National Health Interview Survey (NHIS) data collection on LGBTQ+ women in STEM

	American Community Survey (ACS)	National Health Interview Survey (NHIS)
Survey type	General survey	Health survey
Sample type and average size	National survey with 3 million individuals per year	National Survey with 87,500 individuals per year
Workforce status	Allows us to distinguish between full-time and part-time work	Does not allow us to distinguish between full-time and part-time work
Occupational codes	Census Occupational Code Lists	Informed by Census Occupational Code Lists (less detailed for confidentiality)
LGBTQ+ groupings available	Partnered lesbians only (bisexual women partnered with women are wrongly assumed to be lesbians in this sample)	Individual lesbians and bisexual women only
Sample years	2012–2019	2013–2018

from the Integrated Public Use Microdata Series (IPUMS) as cited in Blewett et al. (2022). The survey does not include any questions about gender identity. The NHIS also asks about occupation but uses broad occupational codes due to the sensitive nature of the information collected and the need to protect respondent confidentiality. NHIS occupation codes are similar to those used by the ACS but not identical.

Table 9.1 offers an overview of the data-collection processes and characteristics of the two surveys we use in this case study.

As table 9.1 indicates, neither the ACS nor the NHIS provides any data regarding transgender or gender-nonbinary populations, which means we cannot directly include either group in our data-driven analyses of STEM occupations and wages. However, even though we are unable to explore the specific STEM work patterns and earnings of these groups, we remain committed to the inclusion of trans women and gender-nonbinary populations wherever possible in this chapter and have included these groups in our discussions of the (STEM) workforce experiences of LGBTQ+ people, below.

Lesbians, Bisexual Women, Trans Women, and Gender-Nonbinary Individuals in the US Labor Force

The experiences of LBT women and gender-nonbinary people in the US labor force have been shaped by several factors. Arguably, the most significant among these is the long-standing absence of federal-level protections against workplace discrimination. In the past, some states (and localities) put LGBTQ+-specific protections in place, but many did not. In 2018, 48 percent of US states did not have any employment protections in place for people who were (perceived as) LGBTQ+ (Movement Advancement Project, American Civil Liberties Union, and Lambda Legal 2018). In 2020, the US Supreme Court ruled that Title VII of the Civil Rights Act of 1964 protects gay and transgender workers from employment discrimination, effectively ending variations at the state level.

The ACS and NHIS data we use below precede this 2020 decision, as does most of the research literature, and it is not possible to predict how the decision will affect the experiences of LGBTQ+ people in the workplace. However, as both history and scholarship show all too clearly, entrenched forms of systemic bias experienced by groups are not eliminated by the presence (or absence) of laws. Every case study in this book demonstrates that legal protections do not eliminate the stubborn and pervasive presence of racism, ethnocentrism, sexism, and ableism (for example) in the workplace. As recent backlashes against LGBTQ+ rights and protections indicate, homophobia, bisexual erasure, transphobia, and cisgender binarism continue to have destructive impacts—and are on the upswing in the US.

What does the economic landscape look like for LGBTQ+ people in the US? As a whole, this community experiences poverty at relatively high rates, despite the "widely accepted narrative that the LGBT population is more affluent and powerful than the rest of the population" (Velte 2020, 70). In 2019, about 22 percent of the US LGBT population lived in poverty, with transgender people and cisgender bisexual women experiencing poverty at the highest rates (29 percent for both groups) (Badgett, Choi, and Wilson 2019). Because LGBTQ+ people have historically been "stigmatized, discriminated against, and harassed in all areas of life," workplace discrimination against LGBT people has long been both culturally normative and institutionally acceptable (Pichler and Ruggs 2018, 177). About a fifth (20 percent) of LGBTQ+ people report being discriminated against when applying for work; a similar proportion (22 percent) report discrimination in terms of equal pay and/or promotion (National Public Radio et al. 2018). LGBTQ+ people of color report workplace discrimination at significantly higher rates than white LGBTQ+ people (32 percent compared to 13 percent) (National Public Radio et al. 2018). Informal work environments can be hostile for LGBTQ+ people: jokes about this group are normative, as are microaggressions (Nadal et al. 2016). About half (46 percent) of LGBTQ+ workers report being closeted in their workplace (Fidas and Cooper n.d.).

While workplace discrimination is common for each of the groups we examine in this case study, their experiences in the labor market and workplace vary. Because lesbian women are typically included in studies with gay men, their experiences of workplace discrimination are generically well-documented but rarely specific relative to gender. They strongly reflect the general patterns noted above (Lubensky et al. 2004; Pichler and Ruggs 2018). Of note is the supposed earnings advantage for lesbians (shaped by ACS data and thus focusing solely on partnered lesbians—some of whom, as we note above, may in fact be bisexual women) (Baumle and Poston 2011; Peplau and Fingerhut 2004). That advantage has been put into question by recent work (also focused on women who are likely to be partnered lesbians) that suggests lesbian workers (particularly younger lesbians) may in fact be at an earnings disadvantage relative to partnered heterosexual women (Martell 2019).

Despite the fact that the majority of LGBTQ+ people in the US identify as bisexual, the experience of bisexual women is strongly marked by bisexual invisibility (Jones 2021). Bisexual invisibility is the outcome of a society fixated on the heterosexual/homosexual dyad: one excellent example is the common assumption that anyone in a same-sex partnership is gay or lesbian and not bisexual. Bisexual people are less frequently recognized as a sexual minority group, and they also experience biphobia from both the heterosexual and the gay/lesbian communities (Yoshino 2016). The literature on bisexuality in the workplace suggests that the majority of bisexual workers have experienced discrimination in terms of hiring, pay, and/or promotion, as well as a workplace climate that is both overtly and covertly hostile (Tweedy and Yescavage 2014). The literature on bisexual people in the workplace does not generally distinguish between the experiences of bisexual men and bisexual women. However, in keeping with overall patterns for the LGBTQ+ community, research does indicate that bisexual people of color report higher levels of discrimination than white bisexuals (Tweedy and Yescavage 2014). Bisexual workers are subject to pernicious forms of bias such as hypersexualization due to stereotypes that bisexuals are sexually promiscuous (Burneson 2017). In addition, because bisexuality does not fit comfortably into the straight/gay binary, employers are less effective (and less interested) in crafting workplace protections for this group (Popova 2018). Given the negative experiences of many bisexuals in the workplace and a lack of bisexual-specific protections, bisexuals self-disclose in the workplace less frequently than gay and lesbian employees (Arena and Jones 2017). This vicious cycle of self-protection reinforces the problem of invisibility, furthering patterns of workplace indifference and discrimination.

Like sexual identity, gender performance and (perceived) gender identity is a strong predictor of workplace climate and experience. As a whole, members of the LGBTQ+ community are generally more likely to be gender policed at work than non-LGBTQ+ people. A recent Human Rights Campaign survey indicates one in five LGBTQ workers report that coworkers explicitly or implicitly suggest that their self-presentation should be more gender conforming, compared to one in twenty-four workers who are non-LGBTQ (Fidas and Cooper n.d.).

Given this high level of workplace pressure around gender conformity, it is not surprising that both trans women and gender-nonbinary people routinely experience significant levels of cultural bias, social marginalization, and structural discrimination in the labor market and the workplace. In 2015, the US Transgender Survey reported that more than a quarter (27 percent) of trans people who held or applied for a job reported being fired, not hired, or denied a promotion because of their gender identity or gender expression (James et al. 2016). Along with gender policing and overt forms of discrimination, transgender people experience a pronounced absence of both social support and trans-inclusive policies and report a high level of anticipatory stress around how they—and/or any changes in their gender identity or presentation—will be received in the workplace (Mizock et al. 2018). Many of the issues faced by trans and nonbinary people in the workplace are different and additional to those experienced by LGB people, including conflicts over restroom access, inadequate health benefits, and improper use of names and pronouns (Pichler and Ruggs 2018). Many workplaces lag severely in terms of both climate sensitivity and practical policy when it comes to naming and addressing trans-specific issues (Sheridan 2016).

The process of gender-affirming transitions can also present an important work-related challenge for some trans people. Although the literature focused on transgender people in the labor force rarely addresses distinctions between trans women and trans men at work, the research that does exist suggests that (for trans workers who identify with the gender binary) transitions can bring substantial, gender-driven changes in both wages and status. Estimates suggest that trans women who transition at work see a wage decrease of about 30 percent while trans men experience a slight wage increase (Schilt and Wiswall 2008). These gender hierarchies are also reflected in workplace cultures: coming out as a trans woman produces less favorable reactions among coworkers than coming out as a trans man, and trans women who transition at work experience a decline in authority not similarly experienced by trans men (Law et al. 2011).

How do STEM fields fit into the larger patterns of LGBT labor-market experiences? Much like LGBT-related data, the research on LGBT people in STEM is not as established as it is for some other underrepresented groups. A literature in this area is emerging, however, although it often focuses on the generic grouping LGBTQ+ and rarely addresses the specific experiences of lesbians, bisexual women, trans women, or gender nonbinary people.

Consistent with broader LGBTQ+ history, invisibility emerges as the most pronounced issue confronting LGBTQ+ workers in US STEM fields. While coming out in any workplace can be difficult, LGBTQ+ visibility in STEM jobs can be particularly challenging because of a deeply rooted mythology that STEM work is (and should remain) fundamentally detached from personal matters (Mattheis, De Arellano, and Yoder 2020). In this context, LGBT identities are often wrongly cast as private characteristics and not significant social factors that influence the STEM workplace (Smith 2014). Because LGBTQ+ invisibility is in line with the long-established maxim that successful STEM work is unrelated to a STEM worker's personal circumstances, being out as LGBTQ+ may be perceived as violating STEM "norms of impersonality" (Freeman 2020, 145) as well as being incongruous with STEM excellence and a failure to be "professional and rigorous" (Cech and Waidzunas 2011; Sinton et al. 2021). A normative belief that working in STEM and being out as LGBTQ+ are incompatible both with each other and with excellence has been documented in both academic STEM work and the broader world of STEM employment (Bilimoria and Stewart 2009; Mattheis, De Arellano, and Yoder 2020).

The high-stakes nature of LGBTQ+ visibility in STEM workplaces has multiple negative consequences, particularly around belonging in STEM. The strongly cisgender, heteronormative cultures of STEM compound the challenges associated with the critical process of forming and maintaining a STEM identity, resulting in particularly complex negotiations of self for LGBTQ+ STEM professionals (Mattheis, De Arellano, and Yoder 2020). For women and people (women) of color, coming out as LGBTQ+ compounds gender- and race-based challenges related to STEM identity formation. Given the powerful association of STEM with cisgender norms and heteronormativity, it is not surprising that LGBTQ+ people working in STEM fields often experience feelings of social isolation, interpersonal discomfort, and stress associated with misrepresenting one's self: all of these patterns have been linked to lower well-being and job satisfaction (Yoder and Mattheis 2016). Recent research indicates that nondisclosure of Queer identity has a negative effect on LGBTQ+ scientists' publishing productivity (Nelson, Mattheis, and Yoder 2022). Feelings of social marginalization can also negatively affect the establishment of supportive mentoring relationships and professional networking, two critical processes for STEM professionals (Atherton et al. 2016; Cech and Waidzunas 2021).

Recent research has further illuminated how being a LGBTQ+ professional in STEM is associated with other systemic disadvantages. LGBTQ+ STEM professionals have reported that they experience fewer opportunities to develop career-building skills, less access to work-related resources than non-LGBTQ+ identified peers, and more professional devaluation (such as being treated as less skilled by their non-LGBTQ+ colleagues) (Cech and Waidzunas 2021). Research further suggests that, relative to non-LGBTQ+ coworkers, LGBTQ+ STEM workers experience higher levels of work-related health issues (insomnia, stress, and depressive symptoms) and more frequently consider leaving STEM professions (Cech and Waidzunas 2021).

A better understanding of LGBTQ+ STEM employment experiences is closely tied to the question of data. Both the National Science Foundation and the National Institutes of Health collect data on gender, race and ethnicity, and disability, but neither organization includes sexual orientation or gender identity in their diversity-tracking efforts. Despite the dangers of data collection we have already discussed, this fact does restrict the research on LGBTQ+ people in STEM and impacts the lives of LGBTQ+ individuals working in STEM. Ironically, the failure to include LGBTQ+ STEM populations in data collection means this group can be shut out of support initiatives directed at underrepresented groups, adding measurable professional disadvantage to personal erasure (Haley 2020).

Much of the key literature on LGBTQ+ STEM workplaces relies on data collected by the researchers themselves (Cech and Waidzunas 2021 and Yoder and Mattheis 2016, for example). Other scholars have taken an approach that is similar to ours, using ACS data (inferring lesbian identity from its same-sex couple measurement, despite the erasure of bisexual women with same-sex partners) alongside data from the NHIS (which directly asks about sexual orientation) (Badgett, Carpenter, and Sansone 2021; Freeman 2020; Sansone and Carpenter 2020). Despite the urgent need to more directly include trans women and gender nonbinary people in STEM inclusivity discussions—a call that we vigorously repeat here—that need has largely remained unmet (Haley 2020; Restar and Operario 2019).

Lesbians, Trans Women, and Gender-Nonbinary Individuals in Conventional STEM Fields: What Do the Data Say?

Data Set 1: American Community Survey

The advantages of the ACS as a data source are considerable—a sample size of three million respondents per year, detailed income questions, and precise occupational codes (see chapter 2 for a discussion of the ACS). The ACS does not directly assess sexual orientation or gender identity, however. What the ACS does provide is limited to cases where the householder (usually the individual who owns the home or whose name is on the lease) indicates they live with an unmarried partner (or, since 2013, a spouse or partner) of the same sex. The data associated with this group can be used to draw inferences about members of same-sex couples.

So little data on the LGBTQ+ community has historically been available that ACS data on same-sex partners has dominated the demographic research on gays and lesbians for decades. While we also use these data, we want to repeat our earlier claim that this approach is compromised. First, it focuses only on one segment of a population (the partnered segment), which means it is possible our sample is "missing over half of the . . . lesbian population" (Morello 2013). In addition, this measure will overcount

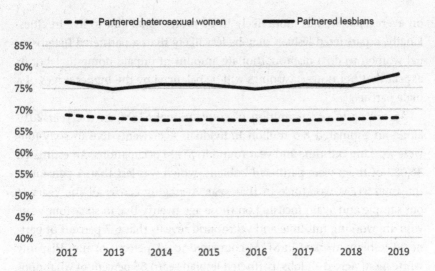

Figure 9.1

US labor-force participation rates: Partnered lesbians and partnered heterosexual women, 2012–2019, age 16 and over. *Source:* Data from the American Community Survey.

lesbians because bisexual women who are in same-sex partnerships will be wrongly included (and wrongly erased as bisexuals). Finally, the use of a relationship question to ascertain lesbian identity introduces more error via the possible misreporting of sex (Baumle and Dreon 2019). With these substantial limitations in mind, we turn to figure 9.1, which depicts the labor-force participation rates of partnered lesbians and heterosexual women.

The labor-force participation of partnered lesbians is consistently higher than that of partnered heterosexual women. This difference is not surprising, given that the economic advantages experienced by many men in the workplace lead to many partnered heterosexual women leaving the workforce or adjusting to part-time work in order to retain a higher family income while accommodating the increase in unpaid domestic labor associated with cohabitation. The powerful cultural factors of traditional gender roles can affect partnered heterosexual women as well, framing and driving many decisions. Same-sex couples also have fewer children than different-sex couples, which may affect needs for the unpaid labor associated with child care. For partnered lesbians, many factors are in place that support high levels of workplace participation: this group is better educated on average, as well as more likely to be professional and to live in cities. Finally, a partnered lesbian may be less likely than a partnered heterosexual women to do a disproportionate amount of unpaid domestic labor or expect that her (lower) earnings will be balanced by the higher wages of a male partner.

According to our definition of conventional STEM, in the year 2019 alone an estimated 8.6 million individuals age twenty-five to sixty-four were working full-time and year-round in STEM occupations. An estimated 36,083 of them were partnered lesbians, which was less than 1 percent of the total STEM workforce in that year. Averaging across all the years of our sample and again focusing on those age twenty-five to sixty-four years who are working full-time and year-round reveals that 6.7 percent of partnered lesbians worked in STEM compared to 11 percent of non-Hispanic white men. Across all jobs, partnered lesbians earn 86 percent of what non-Hispanic white men earn—which rises to 90 percent when we focus on STEM jobs. Both of these are higher than the overall wage ratio of 80 percent of all women when compared to all men. After adjusting for standard covariates (education, age, industry, marital status, citizen status, veteran status, and region of the country), the STEM premium for partnered lesbians is 23 percent, indicating STEM jobs boost these women's earnings compared to their counterparts not working in STEM.

Figure 9.2 represents how partnered lesbians and non-Hispanic white men in STEM are distributed across four broad categories of STEM work. Almost half (48 percent) of partnered lesbians in conventional STEM occupations work in computer/math fields, which is only slightly more than the percentage of non-Hispanic white men (45 percent). Almost a quarter of partnered lesbians (24 percent) work in the physical/life sciences, but only about 10 percent of white men work in those fields. More than a third of white men in STEM are in engineering, but only 16 percent of partnered lesbians are in these jobs. Partnered lesbians in STEM participate in the STEM management fields at a rate slightly higher than white men (12 percent compared to 10 percent).

Median earnings for partnered lesbians in STEM occupations are consistently strong relative to non-Hispanic white men's earnings (table 9.2). The pay gaps for partnered lesbians across STEM occupational clusters range from 8 to 10 percentage points. That said, even smaller gaps are meaningful. For example, the proportion of partnered lesbians in STEM management

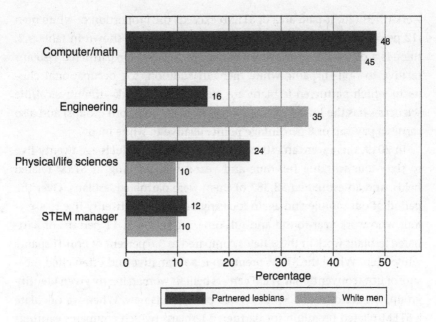

Figure 9.2
Distribution of partnered lesbians and non-Hispanic white men across STEM occupations, individuals age 25–64 working year-round and full-time. *Source:* Data from the American Community Survey, 2012–2019.

Table 9.2
Partnered lesbians' median annual earnings as a percentage of non-Hispanic white men's median annual earnings in STEM occupations, individuals age 25–64 working year-round and full-time

STEM occupation	Median annual earnings		Partnered lesbians' earnings as a percentage of non-Hispanic white men's
	Partnered lesbians	Non-Hispanic white men	
Computer/math	$82,516	$89,903	92%
Engineering	$80,509	$88,606	91%
Physical/life sciences	$69,774	$75,632	92%
STEM managerial	$108,047	$120,226	90%

Note: All earnings adjusted to 2019 dollars. *Source:* Data from the American Community Survey, 2012–2019.

work (the highest-paid area of STEM) exceeds the proportion of white men (12 percent compared to 10 percent). Nonetheless, as shown in table 9.2, there is a difference in median earnings of $12,000 for partnered lesbians relative to non-Hispanic white men. In addition, the occupational cluster in which partnered lesbians are most likely to work—the physical/life sciences—has the lowest average wages in STEM (for both groups) and also carries a pay gap of 8 percentage points relative to white men.

In 2019, there were an estimated 7.3 million individuals age twenty-five to sixty-four working full-time and year-round working in STEM-related fields, and an estimated 58,387 of them were partnered lesbians. Over the period of our sample and again focusing on those age twenty-five to sixty-four who work year-round and full-time, we find that 11 percent of partnered lesbians work in these fields compared to 3.6 percent of non-Hispanic white men. While the STEM premium is a normative and often cited measure of how conventional STEM careers benefit women in any given identity group, the concept of a STEM-related premium is new. When we calculate a STEM-related premium for partnered lesbians (which compares earnings in STEM-related occupations to non-STEM occupations while controlling for conventional STEM work), we see that this group earns a substantial 26 percent more than their counterparts working in conventional STEM or STEM-related fields.

The STEM-related distribution of partnered lesbians and non-Hispanic white men (figure 9.3) reflects familiar gendered patterns: 43 percent of partnered lesbians who work in STEM-related jobs are nurses (either professional or vocational), while only 16 percent of white men in STEM-related fields are in these jobs. Partnered lesbians and white men are similarly represented in the medical-support fields (17 percent compared to 18 percent), while partnered lesbians are less likely than white men to work in STEM-related management (15 percent compared to 19 percent). There is a marked difference in the medical professional fields, where only 15 percent of partnered lesbians work (compared to 39 percent of white men).

Pay gaps for STEM-related earnings run in two directions. In the nursing fields, there is earnings parity in professional nursing, and partnered lesbians' earnings surpass those of non-Hispanic white men in vocational nursing by a full 7 percentage points (table 9.3). Pay gaps that run in the other direction are fairly similar to those in conventional STEM: white men earn more than partnered lesbians in the medical-support fields (10 percentage

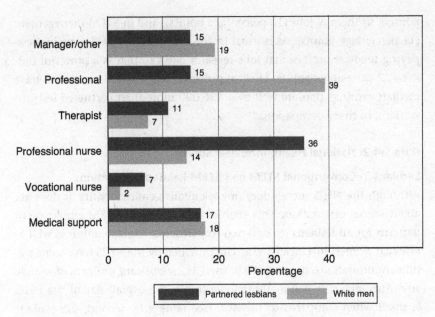

Figure 9.3
Distribution of partnered lesbians and non-Hispanic white men across STEM-related occupations, individuals age 25–64 working year-round and full-time. *Source:* Data from the American Community Survey, 2012–2019.

Table 9.3
Partnered lesbians' median annual earnings as a percentage of non-Hispanic white men's median annual earnings in STEM-related occupations, individuals age 25–64 working year-round and full-time

STEM-related category	Median annual earnings		Partnered lesbians' earnings as a percentage of non-Hispanic white men's
	Partnered lesbians	Non-Hispanic white men	
Manager/other	$77,359	$86,437	89%
Professional	$131,826	$168,350	78%
Therapist	$68,549	$76,327	90%
Professional nurse	$75,141	$75,761	99%
Vocational nurse	$48,621	$45,457	107%
Medical support	$48,473	$53,635	90%

Note: All earnings adjusted to 2019 dollars. *Source:* Data from the American Community Survey, 2012–2019.

points), in therapy jobs (10 percentage points), and in STEM-management (11 percentage points). As is usual in the STEM-related fields, the highest-paying medical professional jobs reveal a pay gap that is a powerful out-lier—22 percentage points. Medical professionals who are white men have median earnings that are well over $36,000 more than partnered lesbians working in those occupations.

Data Set 2: National Health Interview Survey

Lesbians in Conventional STEM and STEM-Related Occupations

Although the NHIS survey does not ask about gender identity, it does ask about sexual orientation. This enables us to examine STEM employment patterns for all lesbians (as opposed to partnered lesbians only), as well as bisexual women specifically. The data provided by the NHIS have some significant limitations, however. First, there is a significant problem of sample size. Although it is nationally representative, the overall size of the NHIS is small when compared to the ACS (see table 9.1). Second, this issue is compounded because the identities we examine here are gender-specific (they apply to women only) and also carry sufficient social stigma to discourage respondents from disclosing to an interviewer in person. Third, our exclusive focus on STEM occupations—a relatively small segment of the US workforce—reduces the sample even further. Finally, due to a change in survey wording and the timeframe in which sexual orientation related questions were asked, our sample is for only six years (2013–2018). With these factors in place, it is not surprising that NIHS data does not always have sufficient data to fill out the picture for these women in STEM, and entire occupational categories can come up empty.

The NHIS poses additional challenges when it comes to occupational codes for STEM and STEM-related jobs. These are similar but not the same as those used by the ACS. NHIS codes are also based on the Census Bureau's Occupational Code Lists, but they are aggregated to a higher level to provide confidentiality (see appendix A for occupations associated with NHIS STEM/STEM-related groupings). This makes job clusters less precise (for example, there is not a STEM management cluster) and also opens the possibility that some NHIS STEM occupations may not also be classified as STEM in the ACS (and vice versa).

NHIS data also does not allow us to differentiate between full- and part-time workers. The variable of part-time employment has a powerful effect on labor-related data, especially for women, who are more likely to work part-time than men. Therefore, while the NHIS allows us a glimpse of how lesbians (both partnered and unpartnered) fare in STEM work, there is a substantial trade-off: we do not know the extent to which the earnings outcomes we present are affected by our inability to distinguish between full- and part-time workers.

Because of a significantly smaller sample size, lower reporting due to identity stigma, fewer years of data, and relatively low participation in STEM, sample sizes for lesbians and bisexual women are small. Because of these convergent factors, the results we present using the NHIS data set are more suggestive than our other analyses that are based on larger samples. That said, we feel strongly that even a general representation of lesbians and bisexual women in STEM contributes something to the larger project of better understanding these groups' participation and earnings in STEM and STEM-related work.

When it comes to labor-force participation rates, a general comparison of lesbians and bisexual women with heterosexual women shows that lesbians and bisexual women consistently participate more in the US labor force (figure 9.4). This pattern is similar to figure 9.1, which indicates that

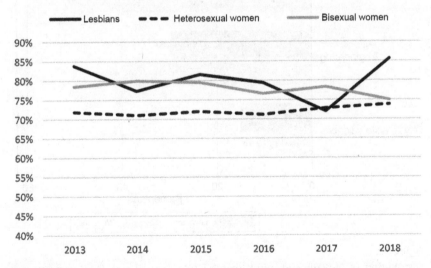

Figure 9.4
US labor-force participation rates: Lesbians and heterosexual women, 2014–2018, age 18 and over. *Source:* Data from the National Health Interview Survey.

partnered lesbians participate more in the labor force than partnered heterosexual women.

Using the 2018 NHIS, we find an estimated 11.5 million individuals age twenty-five to sixty-four working in STEM occupations, of whom 27,781 are lesbians. Over the years of our sample (2013–2018), 3.9 percent of lesbians report working in STEM jobs compared to 10.3 percent of non-Hispanic white men. After adjusting for standard covariates (education, age, industry, marital status, citizen status, veteran status, and region of the country), the STEM premium for lesbians is a robust 40 percent. Across all jobs, lesbians earn 60 percent of what non-Hispanic white men earn, although the median earnings ratio rises to 64 percent when focused on STEM occupations.

Figure 9.5 represents how lesbians and non-Hispanic white men in STEM are distributed across three broad categories of STEM work. In this case, the occupational distribution and earnings of lesbians in STEM are shaped by

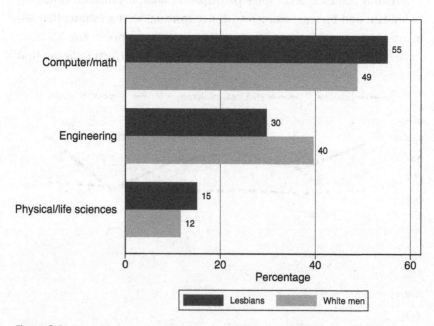

Figure 9.5
Distribution of lesbians and non-Hispanic white men across STEM occupations, working individuals age 25–64. *Source:* Data from the National Health Interview Survey, 2013–2018.

the particular configurations of NHIS occupational codes and the inclusion of both full- and part-time STEM workers.

Figure 9.5 suggests STEM participation patterns that are generally similar to the ACS. Lesbians in STEM are most strongly distributed in computer/ math fields, as are white men. Lesbians are less likely to be engineers than white men (30 percent compared to 40 percent), although NHIS data suggests that all lesbians might be distributed in engineering at a higher percentage than partnered lesbians (the ACS indicates 16 percent of partnered lesbians in STEM are engineers). The physical/life sciences data suggests (as was also indicated by ACS data for partnered lesbians) all lesbians may be more likely to work in this area than white men.

Due to the presence of part-time and full-time workers in our NHIS sample, it is difficult to compare the NHIS earnings data with that of the ACS. A snapshot look at median earnings by STEM occupation group in table 9.4 indicates there are likely substantial differences between the median earnings of lesbians and white men in STEM. Of the substantial pay gaps we see here, the data indicate engineering has the smallest earnings difference between these groups.

In 2018, an estimated 15 million individuals age twenty-five to sixty-four were working in STEM-related jobs, and about 92,259 of them identified as lesbians. Over the period of our sample (2013–2018) and again focusing on workers age twenty-five to sixty-four, we find that only 3.2 percent of non-Hispanic white men work in these occupations compared

Table 9.4
Lesbians' median annual earnings as a percentage of non-Hispanic white men's median annual earnings in STEM occupations, individuals age 25–64

| STEM category | Median annual earnings | | Lesbians' earnings as a percentage of non-Hispanic white men's |
	Lesbians	Non-Hispanic white men	
Computer/math	$51,221	$83,700	61%
Engineering	$68,946	$79,553	87%
Physical/life sciences	$51,221	$75,454	68%

Note: All earnings adjusted to 2018 dollars. *Source:* Data from the National Health Interview Survey, 2013–2018.

to 10.6 percent of lesbians. When we calculate a STEM-related premium for lesbians (which compares earnings in STEM-related occupations to non-STEM occupations while controlling for conventional STEM work), we see that lesbians in STEM-related jobs earn 21 percent more than lesbians not working in conventional STEM or STEM-related fields.

Within the compressed STEM-related occupational groupings that the NHIS allows, our data are most reliable for the professional and medical-support occupations. Because no lesbians in our sample report being therapists and because the nursing occupations are particularly affected by part-time/full-time work status differentials, we have omitted these clusters from our more granular examination of earnings. (These groups remain part of the data reported for our larger sample, however.)

NHIS data on the professional and medical-support occupations show patterns that are somewhat similar to the ACS data. Lesbians and white men are distributed fairly similarly in the medical-support fields (figure 9.6). Lesbians are less likely than white men to work in medical professional occupations and far more likely to work as nurses.

Table 9.5 offers a snapshot look at STEM-related earnings for these groups. NHIS data on the professional and medical-support occupations suggest pay gaps of 28 and 23 percentage points (respectively), in favor of white men in these fields. Unfortunately, we cannot report data on nursing salaries due to the combined effects of a high level of divergence across different types of nursing work and our inability to distinguish between full-time and part-time work. While much less precise than we would wish it to be, the NHIS data indicates likely pay gaps for lesbians who work in STEM-related occupations.

Bisexual Women in Conventional STEM and STEM-Related Occupations

Using the 2018 NHIS survey, we find an estimated 11.5 million individuals age twenty-five to sixty-four working in STEM occupations, of whom 25,862 identify as bisexual women. Over the years of our sample (2013–2018), 5.7 percent of bisexual women report working in STEM jobs compared to 10.3 percent of non-Hispanic white men. After adjusting for standard covariates (education, age, industry, marital status, citizen status, veteran status, and region of the country), the STEM premium for bisexual women is a robust 44 percent. Across all jobs, bisexual women earn 37 percent of what

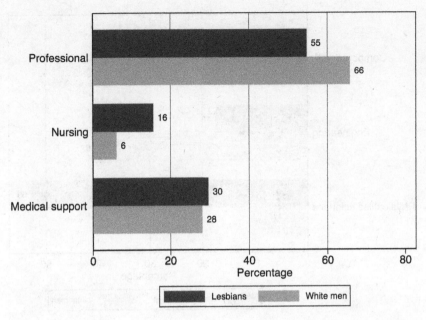

Figure 9.6
Distribution of lesbians and non-Hispanic white men across STEM-related occupations, working individuals age 25–64. *Source:* Data from the National Health Interview Survey, 2013–2018.

Table 9.5
Lesbians' median annual earnings as a percentage of non-Hispanic white men's median annual earnings in STEM-related occupations, individuals age 25–64

STEM-related category	Median annual earnings		Lesbians' earnings as a percentage of non-Hispanic white men's
	Lesbians	Non-Hispanic white men	
Professional	$67,805	$94,162	72%
Nursing	N/A	N/A	N/A
Medical support	$32,337	$41,850	77%

Note: All earnings adjusted to 2018 dollars. *Source:* Data from the National Health Interview Survey, 2013–2018.

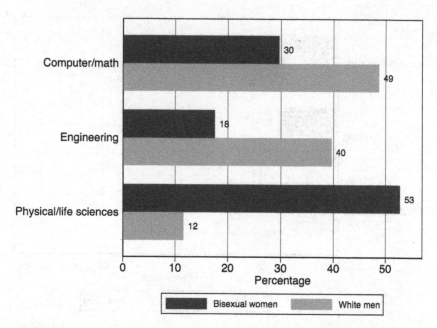

Figure 9.7
Distribution of bisexual women and non-Hispanic white men across STEM occupations, working individuals age 25–64. *Source:* Data from the National Health Interview Survey, 2013–2018.

non-Hispanic white men earn. This median earnings ratio rises to 65 percent when focused on STEM occupations. The fact that NHIS data includes women working part-time may help explain these low earnings ratios.

Figure 9.7 shows the STEM occupational distribution of bisexual women compared to non-Hispanic white men. Particularly small sample sizes make the data for engineering suggestive. Nevertheless, we see that bisexual women are less likely to be engineers and far more likely to work in the physical and life sciences.

Table 9.6 shows the median earnings by STEM occupation cluster for bisexual women and non-Hispanic white men. Sizeable pay gaps exist in all fields, with the highest being for engineering, where bisexual women earn 54 percent of what white men earn (a pay gap of 46 percentage points). Earnings ratios are higher in computer/math and physical/life sciences but do not reach 70 percent.

Table 9.6

Bisexual women's median annual earnings as a percentage of non-white men's median annual earnings in STEM occupations, individuals age 25–64

STEM category	Median annual earnings		
	Bisexual women	Non-Hispanic white men	Bisexual women's earnings as a percentage of non-Hispanic white men's
Computer/math	$56,343	$83,700	67%
Engineering	$43,116	$79,553	54%
Physical/life sciences	$49,584	$75,454	66%

Note: All earnings adjusted to 2018 dollars. *Source:* Data from the National Health Interview Survey, 2013–2018.

An estimated 129,623 bisexual women report STEM-related occupations. Over our sample period, we find that only 3.2 percent of non-Hispanic white men work in a STEM-related job, while 11 percent of women who self-identify as bisexual report a STEM-related job. The STEM-related premium for these women—excluding the high-paying conventional STEM occupations from the comparison—is 3 percent. While this is in stark contrast to that of lesbians in the NHIS, it highlights both the difficulty of working with small sample sizes and hints that the non-STEM/STEM-related work that bisexual women do may be different than that of lesbians.

Figure 9.8 depicts the occupational distribution of bisexual women and non-Hispanic white men who work in STEM-related fields. When compared to white men, bisexual women are far more likely to be nurses and far less likely to work in the professional fields. While a sizable percentage of both groups are engaged in the medical-support fields, bisexual women are still 9 percentage points more likely to be in these fields than white men. Table 9.7 shows that bisexual women's earnings lag far behind those of non-Hispanic white men, though once again we cannot report the earnings for nurses. In the medical professional cluster, bisexual women lag behind the earnings of white men with a median earnings ratio of 65 percent. The earnings ratio is particularly low at 37 percent in the medical-support area.

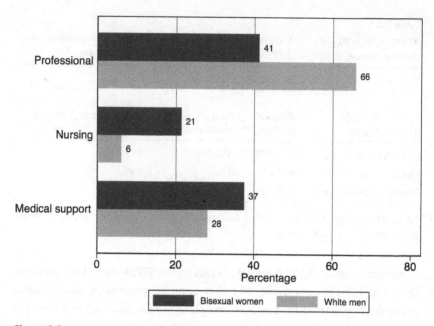

Figure 9.8
Distribution of bisexual women and non-Hispanic white men across STEM occupations, working individuals age 25–64. *Source:* Data from the National Health Interview Survey, 2013–2018.

Table 9.7
Bisexual women's median annual earnings as a percentage of non-Hispanic white men's median annual earnings in STEM-related occupations, individuals age 25–64

STEM-related category	Median annual earnings		Bisexual women's earnings as a percentage of non-Hispanic white men's
	Bisexual women	Non-Hispanic white men	
Professional	$60,906	$94,162	65%
Nursing	N/A	N/A	N/A
Medical support	$15,336	$41,850	37%

Note: All earnings adjusted to 2018 dollars. *Source:* Data from the National Health Interview Survey, 2013–2018.

A Note on Trans Women and Gender Nonbinary Individuals

The research shows that trans women and gender nonbinary individuals are routinely subject to enormous systemic disadvantages in the workplace—including the STEM workplace. For a number of reasons, it is impossible to quantitatively track STEM occupational patterns or earnings for these groups. Gender identity is rarely included in surveys, and, even if such data were to be collected, the sample sizes for trans women and gender-nonbinary individuals in STEM are likely to be small. In addition, as we have discussed above, collecting quantitative data on these vulnerable groups may be an unhelpful or even dangerous practice. Although we cannot provide a parallel analysis of the occupational distribution and earnings of these groups in STEM, it seems clear that the research on quantitative data must (1) continue to recognize and push back against the established dominance of the gender binary and (2) more actively attend to issues faced by trans women and gender nonbinary individuals in STEM occupations.

Case Study Highlights

We have identified notable outcomes and summarized results from both the American Community Survey (ACS) and the National Health Interview Survey (NHIS).

The American Community Survey: Partnered Lesbians

Partnered Lesbians in Conventional STEM Occupations

- About 6.7 percent of partnered lesbians work in conventional STEM occupations.
- In conventional STEM, partnered lesbians are less likely than non-Hispanic white men to be in engineering (16 percent compared to 35 percent) and more likely to be in physical/life sciences (24 percent compared to 10 percent).
- Pay gaps between these groups are small. Partnered lesbians lag behind in terms of wages, but all pay ratios are above 90 percent.

Partnered Lesbians in STEM-Related Occupations

- Eleven percent of partnered lesbians work in STEM-related occupations.

- A large percentage of partnered lesbians (43 percent) work in nursing, compared to only 16 percent of non-Hispanic white men. They are far less likely to be medical professionals (15 percent compared to 39 percent of white men).

- Pay gaps between partnered lesbians and non-Hispanic white men are modest in the STEM-related fields, and lesbians outearn white men in vocational nursing (7 percentage points) and are at parity in professional nursing. Professional occupations are the exception and lesbians experience a pay gap of 22 percentage points.

National Health Interview Survey: Lesbians and Bisexual Women

The small sample size of the NHIS—combined with the small number of women who both work in STEM and also identify as a lesbian or bisexual woman—make our analyses suggestive.

Lesbians in Conventional STEM Occupations

- About 3.9 percent of lesbians work in conventional STEM occupations.

- Within a compressed set of occupational categories for conventional STEM, 30 percent of lesbians are engineers compared to 40 percent of non-Hispanic white men.

- Significant earnings gaps between lesbians and non-Hispanic white men in STEM appear for all areas, with the smallest wage gap in the engineering fields.

Lesbians in STEM-Related Occupations

- Nearly 11 percent of lesbians work in STEM-related occupations.

- In STEM-related work, lesbians (similar to non-Hispanic white men) are strongly represented in the professional occupations.

- Lesbians are not at earnings parity with non-Hispanic white men. They experience an earnings ratio of 72 percent in professional work and 77 percent in medical-support occupations.

Bisexual Women in Conventional STEM Occupations

- About 5.7 percent of bisexual women work in conventional STEM occupations.

- Over 50 percent of bisexual women in conventional STEM are in the physical/life sciences. There are few in engineering (18 percent compared to 40 percent of non-Hispanic white men).
- Pay gaps for bisexual women in STEM are high—over 30 percentage points in all occupational clusters.

Bisexual Women in STEM-Related Occupations
- Eleven percent of bisexual women report a STEM-related occupation.
- Bisexual women are most likely to be in medical-support and nursing fields. Their pattern of STEM-related employment is similar to the pattern for lesbian women in STEM-related work (NHIS).
- Bisexual women have a wage gap of 35 percentage points in the medical professional occupations compared to non-Hispanic white men.

10 Mothers in STEM

Motherhood as Identity

Motherhood is a fundamentally gendered term that refers to people who identify as women who give birth to or adopt children. Identifying as a woman is central to the definition: trans men who give birth or adopt, for example, are fathers or parents, not mothers (Margaria 2020). Motherhood also has a long history as a bedrock feminist issue. It plays an outsized role in matters of gender, sexuality, agency, autonomy, and the organization of economic, cultural, and social life (Kawash 2011; Kinser 2010; Rich 1976). In short, motherhood matters.

Because of its enormous effects on the lives of the women who experience it, the principle of voluntary motherhood (that is, pregnancy and/or motherhood by choice) has been a focus of feminist thought and action since the nineteenth century (Ross and Solinger 2017). Nonetheless, many factors associated with motherhood by choice—such as access to sex education, birth control, and reproductive health services—remain highly controversial in the US. Continual struggles to expand or constrict reproductive rights and freedoms provide visceral public illustrations of what feminists have long understood: the questions of who becomes a mother, and when and why, lie directly at the intersections of gender and power.

In 2022, the US Supreme Court overturned *Roe v. Wade*, the landmark 1973 decision that recognized abortion as a constitutionally protected right. The *Dobbs v. Jackson Women's Health Organization* decision has upended the landscape of reproductive rights and reproductive health in the US. In overturning the right to abortion, the Supreme Court's ruling moved abortion-related issues back to the state level, creating a wildly uneven and unstable mix of both guaranteed rights and draconian restrictions and essentially rewriting the relationship between women and voluntary motherhood in the US. In the coming decades, this fundamental shift in the legal landscape of abortion access will doubtless have far-reaching, negative impacts on many women's relationships to personal autonomy, health, educational attainment, and paid work. All of these factors matter for human thriving—and all of them powerfully shape women's participation in STEM work, as well.

If the personal and political stakes around motherhood in the US are fraught, vast, and complex, it may at first appear that simply asking "Who is a mother?" might be more straightforward. But such is not the case. Along with being attached to womanhood and spliced to fundamental issues of personal and civic agency, the hypernaturalized category of mother is a legal category that is managed by multiple institutions. In the case of adoption, for example, only the courts can make nonbiological motherhood official or award permanent custody of a child. In cases of child abuse or neglect, only the courts can take children from their biological or adoptive mothers. Systemic forms of injustice such as racism, classism, and heteronormativity intersect with the work of the state, further shaping who is recognized as a mother. Research shows, for example, that child welfare interventions are more prevalent for families of color (particularly Black families) and that socioeconomically disadvantaged families are also disproportionately targeted for interventions in parenting (Edwards et al. 2021; Roberts 2002). And although same-sex adoption has been legal in all US states since 2017, obstacles to legal recognition as a mother persistently arise for lesbian women who parent nonbiological children (Warbelow, Avant, and Kutney 2020). In addition, mothers of record are not always the women who are primary caretakers of a child: a woman who is a child's permanent caretaker (such as a grandmother or family friend) and regularly fills that child's material and emotional needs may not necessarily be formally recognized as that child's mother. Similarly, some women who give birth to a child (surrogate mothers, for example) may not be involved in raising that child. Hence, like all identity categories, motherhood is managed by institutions and ideologies, shaped by intersections with other identities, and surprisingly unstable.

Because standard census products (like the ACS) make it difficult to determine who is a mother in a multigenerational or multifamily household, we have chosen to employ the Current Population Survey (CPS) for this case study (we use the publicly available data extracts from the Center for Economic and Policy Research, 2020).* The CPS is jointly organized by the Census Bureau and the Department of Labor and is often used to determine the labor-force participation and earnings of mothers (e.g., US Bureau of Labor Statistics 2020a). Because CPS survey data is based on a particular week in the year, we have limited our sample to mothers who report working thirty-five or more hours in that week. This also means that in this case study we present weekly earnings for women who work thirty-five or more hours per week instead of annual earnings. Because the CPS allows us to identify mothers only if their child (biological, step, or adopted) is under age eighteen and lives in the same household, we are unlikely to identify mothers whose children are grown or no longer live at home.

As with all of our examinations of women in STEM occupations, our data on mothers is shaped by the broadly salient characteristics of this group in a twenty-first-century US context. Perhaps the most significant fact about motherhood is that this identity is claimed by the majority of women in the US. In 2018, 85 percent of women between age forty to fifty had given birth. This large percentage does not take into account the important population of women who are mothers by adoption, and it is noteworthy that data on adopted children has historically been omitted from information-gathering processes. Traditional demographics based on biological reproduction (such as number of births) often obscure adoptions. The US Census, for example, did not begin collecting adoption-related data until the year 2000. It is important, therefore, to acknowledge that mothers by adoption are mothers—and that it is estimated that about 2 percent of American families have adopted children (Adoption Network n.d.).

Given their large number, mothers are an extraordinarily diverse group whose experiences are intersectionally shaped by race, ethnicity, socioeconomic class, sexuality, and many other aspects of identity. Although this category is both enormous and heterogeneous, we can observe a few distinguishing characteristics of mothers in the US. First, after some years of

---

*In order to identify which women in a household have children, the Center for Economic and Policy Research uses a variable created by the National Bureau of Economic Research that measures the number of a woman's own children under age eighteen in the primary family in the household.

steady and marked decline, the completed fertility rate has risen from an average 1.86 children per woman in 2006 to just over two in 2018 (Barroso 2021). US mothers are also having children later in life, and in 2019 the mean age at which women became mothers was twenty-seven years (Martin et al. 2021) compared with twenty-five years in 2000 (Martin et al. 2002). Over the past few decades, childbearing has also steadily increased among women with higher levels of educational attainment, a particularly resonant fact for women working in STEM occupations (Livingston 2018b). The COVID-19 pandemic flattened the birth rate, however: in 2020, the number of US births was the lowest since 1973 (Howard 2021). This downward trend was spread evenly among women from all age groups between age fifteen and forty-four (Hamilton, Martin, and Osterman 2021). It is impossible to predict the long-term effects of COVID-19, but some at least short-term impact on the US birth rate seems likely.

Motherhood in the US is also distinguished by its relation to larger family structures, especially the relatively high likelihood of mothers raising children alone. In 2019, according to the CPS, about one in four women was raising children without a partner or spouse in the home (22.7 percent). This number far outstrips the overall number of solo fathers in the US, which is about 8.2 percent. Such marked differences suggest that many women and men have divergent experiences in terms of child-rearing. Mothers disproportionately grapple with the demands of single parenthood, which involves both the economic costs of child-rearing as well as the time and effort involved in the performance of unpaid childcare. Perhaps unsurprisingly, households headed by single mothers are twice as likely to fall below the poverty threshold as those headed by single fathers (Eickmeyer 2017).

Another salient characteristic of motherhood—regardless of who experiences it and under what conditions it takes place—is its relationship to time. Motherhood is unique in that it can be acquired (at the earliest) only in the teenage years and (unlike many of the other identities covered in this book) is not a characteristic determined at birth. In addition, most children move in an arc from complete dependency to independent adulthood, and the work of caring for a newborn infant differs greatly from parenting a teenager or being the mother of another adult. While the emotional and psychological power of a mother-child relationship may last a lifetime, the dependency of children typically decreases, and the practical demands of motherhood usually diminish over the lifespan. This fact makes the age of children a significant factor in the material experience of motherhood.

In what follows, we examine the data related to mother's STEM participation by taking into account the salient characteristics of motherhood as a CPS category at this moment in time: motherhood is (1) *not a matter of self-identification* but calculated relative to children in the household, (2) *gender-specific* in that only people who identify as women are considered mothers, (3) a *large category that is representative of the majority of adult women* living in the US, (4) a *heterogeneous* group that is modulated by many other identity categories, (5) more likely to be *performed solo* than fatherhood, (6) more likely to be *associated with poverty*, and (7) a time-based role that is both *acquired as a teenager or adult* and (normally) *less demanding* as children become independent adults.

Mothers in the US Labor Force

The demands of motherhood change relative to the dependence of children, and figure 10.1 shows the labor-force participation of two groups—mothers whose youngest child is under age eighteen and mothers whose youngest child is under age six. The figure begins in 1975, a date that allows

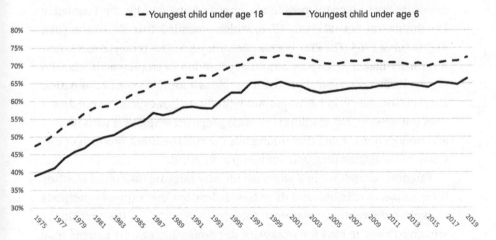

Figure 10.1
US labor-force participation rates: Labor-force participation of women (age 16 and over) by age of youngest child in the household, 1975–2019. *Source:* US Bureau of Labor Statistics, Women's Bureau.

us to show the considerable changes in mothers' labor-force participation over the last half century.

As figure 10.1 illustrates, from 1975 to 2019 the overall labor-force participation rates of both groups of mothers have substantially increased over time. In the context of this general uptick, important factors such as race and class have long shaped work-related patterns for women overall. For example, as we discuss in chapter 3, elevated economic pressures associated with systemic anti-Black racism have meant that Black women's labor-force participation has historically exceeded that of white women (see figure 3.1); therefore, the trends in mothers' workforce participation shown in figure 10.1 mask potentially significant intersections between motherhood and racial/ethnic identity, class status, and so on.

While working mothers are now a routine part of US workplaces, the experiences of working mothers in the US are characterized by persistent and entrenched challenges. These include the problem of workplace discrimination (such as forms of bias and prejudice attached to working mothers), as well as the enormously complex and long-standing social problem of work-life reconciliation (which includes issues such as imbalances in paid work and care work, lack of family leave, and the scarcity and cost of childcare).

When it comes to workplace discrimination against mothers, pregnancy (and not motherhood) has the most direct protections. Workplace discrimination against pregnant people is expressly forbidden by the Pregnancy Discrimination Act (PDA) of 1978, which amended Title VII of the Civil Rights Act of 1964. The PDA is a milestone in workplace protections because it formally makes pregnancy a normal condition of employment, classifying discrimination against pregnant people as a form of sex discrimination (Siegel 2018). The PDA has important limitations, however. Most notably, it does not require that employers provide pregnant employees with needed accommodations, a fact that undergirds the still-persistent problem of discrimination against pregnant workers (Eaton 2019).

Parenthood itself is not a protected identity category (like racial identity, for example, or religion), and there is no federal law that expressly prohibits workplace discrimination against parents. Depending on the specifics of any given case, redress for workplace discrimination against parents may be sought through various channels such as Title VII, the Americans with Disabilities Act of 1990, the Equal Pay Act of 1963, the Family and Medical Leave Act of 1993, and so on. In addition, there are an increasing number of specific protections from family responsibility discrimination. To date, 195 local and state jurisdictions in the US have addressed discrimination against parents via legislation that outlaws inequitable treatment based on family care responsibilities, including parental responsibilities (Calvert 2020). It is estimated these protections extend to 30 percent of US workers, leaving about two-thirds of US workers on their own to develop strategies for redress via other legal and procedural avenues (Calvert 2020).

There can be no doubt that mothers are routinely subject to various forms of workplace disadvantage as mothers (Goldstein 2018), commonly known as the motherhood penalty. Over the last two decades, research has traced the many ways in which mothers generally fare less well in the labor market. The motherhood penalty is often linked to a disadvantage associated with paid wages. Researchers have tracked meaningful and persistent gaps between the salaries of mothers and women without children, as well as gaps among mothers who are different types of earners (Anderson, Binder, and Krause 2003; Budig and England 2001; Budig and Hodges 2010; Glauber 2018; Jee, Misra, and Murray-Close 2019). Unsurprisingly, the motherhood penalty has been shown to be associated with time away from the labor force associated with having children (Staff and Mortimer 2012) and to differ according to age (younger mothers are typically affected more) (Kahn, García-Manglano, and Bianchi 2014). The COVID-19 pandemic has provided further evidence that "the motherhood wage penalty still exists," suggesting mothers (and nonparents) have been more affected by pandemic layoffs than fathers (Dias, Chance, and Buchanan 2020; Pepping and Maniam 2020, 120).

The motherhood penalty is also driven by cultural beliefs about mothers as workers. Bias and stereotypic thinking about mothers can affect their workforce experiences. These forms of bias include being perceived as less competent, less dependable and committed, and less authoritative and can result in a lower likelihood of being hired as well as other forms of discrimination (Bernard, Paik, and Correll 2008; Correll, Bernard, and Paik 2007). In addition, working mothers can be undermined by common motherhood myths, unfounded but culturally resonant beliefs that associate women with childcare abilities and domestic skills while dissociating them from paid work (Verniers and Vala 2018). All of this helps build what researchers have termed the maternal wall, an apt image for the impediments faced by mothers in the US workforce (Crosby, Williams, and Biernat 2004).

Many factors structure the maternal wall but none is more familiar, fundamental, and intractable than struggles associated with work-life imbalance and reconciliation. At the highest level of analysis, working mothers in the US are embedded in a system that minimally enables their persistence and success in the paid labor force. Most industrialized nations provide some paid family leave, invest in available, affordable childcare and child well-being, and secure the rights of mothers and fathers to thrive in the workplace without being penalized for becoming or being parents. This is not so in the United States. Working parents in the US have minimal family leave protections, limited or sporadic access to scarce and often prohibitively expensive childcare, and uneven protections from discrimination once they return to work. In the US, a working mother may or may not have paid leave, she may or may not be able to find or afford childcare that allows her to continue to work, and she may or may not be protected from workplace discrimination as a parent.

The absence of uniformly available paid family leave makes the US a global outlier: the US ranks last in a comparison of paid parental leave across forty-one nations in the European Union and the Organization for Economic Cooperation and Development (Ro 2019). Protected family leave did not exist in the US until the passage of the Family and Medical Leave Act (FMLA) in 1993. Essentially unchanged for over a quarter of a century, FMLA is broad in scope and weak in effect: it guarantees twelve weeks of unpaid, protected leave for eligible workers who have a new child or a seriously ill family member or who become seriously ill themselves (US Department of Labor 2021). Multiple eligibility requirements constrict the FMLA's impact: only 56 percent of US employees are estimated to qualify for benefits (Brown et al. 2020). This curtails the helpfulness of a policy already severely limited by the fact that many workers (even eligible ones) cannot afford unpaid leave. Family leave is thus often determined by workers' personal situations (such as personal wealth, protections associated with their city, state, or employer, and so on).

The adverse effects of this situation on mothers are many. Only 43 percent of employees in single-parent households can access FMLA benefits, while 63 percent of employees in dual-parent households can do so (Brown et al. 2020). As we have shown, mothers are far more likely than fathers to parent alone, which makes them less likely to access FMLA. In addition, women and men use FMLA at different rates, including for the birth or adoption of a child, and evidence shows that women both need leave and take leave at higher rates than men (Herr, Roy, and Klerman 2020). The amount of time taken for a birth or adoption shows a marked gender difference: women take about three times more FMLA leave than men (fifty-four business days compared to eighteen business days) (Herr, Roy, and Klerman 2020). In addition, women's use of workplace options such as leave and flexible time are perceived differently. The literature shows that women are more likely to experience flexibility stigma (negative outcomes associated with the legitimate use of such options) (Burkus 2017; Munsch 2016; Williams, Blair-Loy, and Berdahl 2013). Whether it is lost income, interrupted or truncated career paths, or gendered bias based on their choices, mothers are singularly disadvantaged when it comes to family leave.

Leave-taking is closely linked to unpaid care work, which has long been seen as another core piece of the maternal wall. Women typically perform more family-related care work than men, and the burden of unpaid care work associated with parenting is generally greater for mothers than fathers. Research indicates that when opposite-sex partners have children, working mothers take on more unpaid childcare-related work (Hochschild and Machung 2012; Yavorsky, Dush, and Schoppe-Sullivan 2015). When opposite-sex couples parent together, the strong majorities of both women (78 percent) and men (62 percent) agree that the woman partner or spouse does more work in terms of managing children's schedules and activities (Barroso and Horowitz 2021). Mothering, therefore, is likely to involve a heavier unpaid labor burden for women than fatherhood does for men, putting women at a practical disadvantage in terms of time and energy devoted to children (and not to paid work).

The heavy burden of unpaid care on working mothers is magnified by a lack of affordable childcare. According to the Bureau of Labor Statistics, the cost of childcare in the US has more than doubled in the last two decades (US Bureau of Labor Statistics 2020a). Many working families find the high price of quality childcare to be out of reach, and quality childcare is often inaccessible (Gould and Cooke 2015). The United States does not invest in childcare. Among OECD nations, the US ranks last in terms of how much governments spend on childcare for toddlers: the OECD average is $14,436 per child, and the US spends $500 per child (Miller 2021a). The necessity of taking on unpaid childcare has been identified as a major factor in women's decision making relative to the US labor market and is strongly linked to women's tendency to take on part-time paid work (a factor that can lead to both lower earnings over time and truncated career paths) or to leave the workforce entirely (Goldin et al. 2017; Kubota 2018; Schochet 2019). While parenting responsibilities affect all parents, women are more likely to adjust their careers and make compromises in paid work when family care issues arise (Horowitz 2019; Parker 2015).

The COVID-19 pandemic has made clear working mothers' fraught relation to childcare while also worsening the situation. Early scholarship suggests that working mothers experienced a larger childcare burden than fathers during the pandemic and that the COVID-19 crisis is now "associated with a reduction in working hours and an increased probability of transitioning out of employment for working mothers" (Zamarro and Prados 2021, 2011). The exodus of mothers from the workforce due to COVID-19 and its aftermath is likely to negatively impact many working mothers for years to come (Miller 2021b).

Cultural narratives often focus on the "choices" of working mothers: will these women "opt out" or "lean in"? (Belkin 2003; Sandberg 2013). But obstacles faced by working mothers are structural, and personal decisions can manage social issues only at the individual level (Orgad 2019; Stone 2007; Williams 2010). These choices are driven by unseen and unacknowledged systemic forces creating a pernicious loop. In order to have and raise children, women often choose to stay home, take time away from work, or take flexible, lower-paid, part-time work. This reinforces specific employment patterns, contributing to sex segregation by job and lower wages for mothers. Choosing gendered occupations associated with women—teaching, nursing, secretarial jobs—enables mothers to do more unpaid care. All the while, this cycle of gendered paid and unpaid labor supports a myth that mothers want to stay home to raise children and hence choose to do so, reinforcing the cultural belief that care is a gendered quality.

The participation of women in STEM occupations intersects with the many challenges faced by mothers in the US labor force. The cultural narrative around the potential tug of war between career and unpaid family care work is well-known to young women and functions as a documented variable in their career decision making (Friedman and Weissbrod 2005). Young women (more than young men) show anticipatory concerns about balancing career and family care work and typically see these issues as ones that they must solve on their own (Gerson 2009). When it comes to STEM occupations, worries about working motherhood can surface before women make career choices or have children. Concerns about work-life conflicts within STEM have been shown to focus on care work, and the belief that STEM careers are not family friendly can have a chilling effect on many younger women's STEM ambitions (Tan-Wilson and Stamp 2015; Weisgram and Diekman 2017). Research has shown that for women preparing for STEM careers (such as PhD students and postdoctoral students) their pathway is compromised by the looming issue of potential motherhood, which threatens women's legitimacy in STEM, supports parenthood-repudiating behaviors, and generates gender-specific burdens of fear and anxiety (De Welde and Laursen 2011; Thébaud and Taylor 2021).

These anxieties are grounded in reality. When women do join the STEM workforce, they are twice as likely as men to report making substantial compromises in their STEM careers to accommodate motherhood (Wyss and Tai 2010). Studies of women in STEM industry jobs indicate that the demands of STEM occupations are often extreme and the pressure to accommodate arduous work with family care responsibilities can have negative consequences for women, including attrition from STEM (Servon and Visser 2011). Academic STEM careers suggest a similar picture. Like high-achieving STEM industry workers, academic STEM is often embedded in the myth of the devoted ideal worker, a fact that raises the issue of flexibility stigma (Cech and Blair-Loy 2014) and makes work-life reconciliation extremely challenging for both women and men (Lincoln and Ecklund 2016).

Motherhood and family-work conflicts in general are thus enormous factors currently shaping the US STEM workforce. An eight-year longitudinal sample of STEM professionals showed that after their first child, 43 percent of new mothers leave full-time STEM work (that is, they work part-time, work elsewhere, or leave the labor force), while 23 percent of new fathers do so (Cech and Blair-Loy 2019). These significant gender differences are consistent "irrespective of variation by discipline, race, and other demographic factors" (Cech and Blair-Loy 2019, 4182). These numbers surpass the attrition rates of childless STEM workers and illustrate that in the US full-time STEM occupations are often incompatible with parenthood in general and that the negative effects impact women in STEM far more than men.

The many challenges associated with working motherhood in the US (in both STEM and the workforce generally) will ultimately be amplified by the restrictions on women's reproductive autonomy associated with the 2022 Supreme Court decision in *Dobbs v. Jackson Women's Health Organization*. Loss of control over reproductive decisions influences women's educational attainment and career planning, and destabilizes their ability to participate in the workforce. *Dobbs* will affect more than patterns of actual childbearing. It will reshape many women's sense of security and expectations about the future, constraining their overall economic options and also potentially harming the economic well-being of future generations (Jones and Bernstein 2019). These far-reaching negative effects will be especially elevated for women of color, especially Black women, who generally seek abortions more frequently than white women, who are more likely to have problem pregnancies, and who are less likely to have health insurance (Slaughter and Jones 2022).

Given the well-documented challenges of being a mother in a STEM workforce protected by *Roe v. Wade* (1973), there is broad anticipation that the recent (and uneven) removal of that uniform protection will increase the obstacles associated with women working in STEM fields (e.g., Van der Meulen et al. 2022). Professional organizations that support women in STEM occupations echo this concern. For example, the Association of Women in Science (2022) issued a statement condemning the *Dobbs* decision, noting it will "have an adverse impact on women in the STEM professions." The Society of Women Engineers (2022) has responded similarly, noting that "removing access to health care (and privacy in health-care decisions) will disproportionately affect women, especially women of color and individuals with limited finances, in achieving their full potential in careers as engineers and leaders." There is little doubt that the *Dobbs* decision will exacerbate the difficulties associated with women both engaging and remaining in STEM work.

Finally, as we move toward the data on mothers in STEM occupations, it is important to recognize the pertinent links between (gendered) care work and US age demographics. There are now more older people in the US than at any time in history, the fastest-growing age demographic is eighty-five and over, and by 2030 one in five people in the US will be over age sixty-five (Poo 2015). More than one in ten US parents is already providing care for another adult (Livingston 2018a). Affordable, reliable quality elder care is as rare as childcare, and the need for such care is far less predictable. Patterns around unpaid care work hold true relative to elder care: women do most of it, and the strains of this growing social burden will amplify current challenges associated with this kind of labor (Gedye and the Washington Monthly 2019). The negative impacts of the demands of elder care on women (especially mothers) in STEM are already in motion, and they are understudied (Jean, Payne, and Thompson 2015; Servon and Visser 2011). The expanding nature of family care work will become ever more important for future research on STEM inclusivity and work-life issues.

Mothers in the Conventional Stem Fields: What Do the Data Say?

In 2019, 76 percent of women age twenty-five and over reported being mothers. According to our definition of conventional STEM and using data from the CPS, in 2019 alone there were an estimated 9.2 million individuals age twenty-five to sixty-four working full-time in STEM occupations (this is a higher total than that reported by the ACS, most likely because CPS data does not distinguish between year-round and non-year-round workers and is based on a weekly snapshot). An estimated 802,481 of them were women who identified as mothers, which was 8.7 percent of all STEM job holders that year. Averaging across all the years of our sample and focusing on those working full-time age twenty-five to sixty-four reveals that only 4 percent of mothers work in STEM occupations (compared to 10.9 percent of non-Hispanic white men). In addition, after adjusting for standard covariates (education, age, industry, marital status, citizen status, veteran status, and region of the country), we calculate that mothers in STEM occupations have a 19 percent wage premium over mothers who do not work in STEM fields. Hence, although the number of mothers working in STEM fields is small overall, there is a considerable STEM premium for that group.

Within conventional STEM occupations, mothers' median earnings are 87 percent of non-Hispanic white men's. These median earnings are strong, given that across all occupations mothers earn only 76 percent of what non-Hispanic white men earn. Indeed, within STEM, mothers' median earnings as a percentage of non-Hispanic white men's median earnings (87 percent) are significantly higher than the ratio of median earnings of all women relative to all men (81 percent, using the CPS).

Having established our parameters, we now dig deeper into the data. Figure 10.2 represents how mothers and non-Hispanic white men in STEM are distributed across four broad categories of STEM work. Just over half

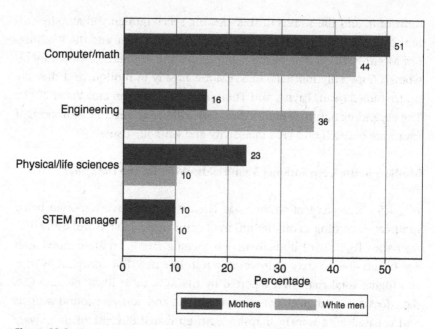

Figure 10.2
Distribution of mothers and non-Hispanic white men across STEM occupations, individuals age 25–64 working full-time. *Source:* Data from the Current Population Survey, 2012–2019.

(51 percent) of the mothers in conventional STEM are in the computing/ mathematical occupations. White men in STEM are also most strongly represented in these fields but at a lower rate (44 percent). After the computer/ math fields, mothers are most strongly represented in the physical and life sciences (23 percent), whereas white men in these fields are a relatively low 10 percent. One of the most striking differences in these STEM occupational distribution patterns is in engineering: 36 percent of white men are engineers, whereas only 16 percent of mothers report working as engineers. Conversely, mothers and white men participate at similar rates in the STEM management occupations (10 percent respectively).

There are some striking differences in how mothers and non-Hispanic white men distribute themselves across the conventional STEM jobs, and there are some meaningful earnings differentials, as well. Table 10.1 indicates that mothers earn only 87 percent of what non-Hispanic white men earn in the computing/mathematics fields despite their strong representation there. Although this is above the pay ratio for all women relative to

Table 10.1
Median weekly earnings of mothers as a percentage of non-Hispanic white men's median weekly earnings in STEM occupations, individuals age 25–64 working full-time

	Median weekly earnings		
STEM category	Mothers	Non-Hispanic white men	Mothers' earnings as a percentage of non-Hispanic white men's
Computer/math	$1,440	$1,665	87%
Engineering	$1,462	$1,635	89%
Physical/life sciences	$1,346	$1,468	92%
STEM managerial	$1,871	$2,054	91%

Note: All earnings adjusted to 2019 dollars. *Source:* Data from the Current Population Survey, 2012–2019.

men (84 percent), it is a deficit of $225 per week for mothers in this field compared to white men. Assuming a fifty-week work year, this adds up to a consequential $11,250 annually. A similar pay gap exists for mothers who are engineers. They earn 89 percent of what white men who are engineers earn. In the physical/life sciences as well as the STEM managerial jobs, mothers earn around 90 percent of what white men earn. These gender earnings gaps may seem modest, but they add up over time.

Mothers in the STEM-Related Fields: What Do the Data Say?

In 2019, an estimated 8.1 million individuals age twenty-five to sixty-four were working full-time in STEM-related jobs (this is a higher total than that reported by the ACS, most likely because CPS data does not distinguish between year-round and non-year-round workers and is based on a weekly snapshot). An estimated 2.3 million were mothers. Over the period of our sample focusing on those age twenty-five to sixty-four who work full-time, we find that only 3.5 percent of non-Hispanic white men work in these occupations. However, about 12.1 percent of mothers are employed in these jobs (as opposed to 4 percent in conventional STEM). While the STEM premium is a normative and often cited measure of how conventional STEM careers benefit women in any given identity group, the concept of a STEM-related premium is a new one. When we calculate a STEM-related premium

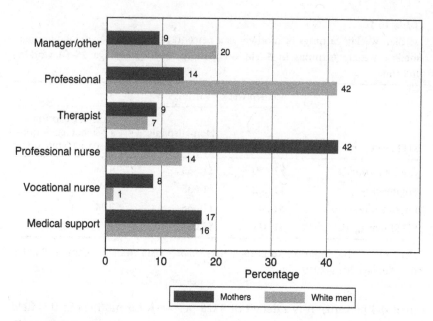

Figure 10.3

Distribution of mothers and non-Hispanic white men across STEM-related occupations, individuals age 25–64 working full-time. *Source:* Data from Current Population Survey, 2012–2019.

for mothers (which compares earnings in STEM-related occupations to non-STEM occupations while controlling for conventional STEM work), we see that mothers in STEM-related jobs earn 28 percent more than mothers not working in conventional STEM or STEM-related fields. Because our version of a STEM-related premium does not include conventional STEM work, it provides a meaningful snapshot of the significant economic benefits that STEM-related work provides mothers. Figure 10.3 illustrates the distribution of mothers and white men over the six STEM-related occupational groupings.

As is often the case with women in STEM-related work, the nursing professions comprise a significant part of the story for mothers. Together, vocational nursing and professional nursing account for half of mothers' participation in STEM-related jobs, with participation in professional nursing making up most of this. White men in STEM-related jobs are not strongly represented in the professional nursing category (14 percent) and are unlikely to be vocational nurses (only 1 percent). White men are more strongly represented in

Table 10.2
Median weekly earnings of mothers as a percentage of non-Hispanic white men's median weekly earnings in STEM-related occupations, individuals age 25–64 working full-time

| STEM-related category | Median weekly earnings | | Mothers' earnings as a percentage of non-Hispanic white men's |
	Mothers	Non-Hispanic white men	
Manager/other	$1,250	$1,622	77%
Professional	$1,871	$2,271	82%
Therapist	$1,212	$1,407	86%
Professional nurse	$1,228	$1,389	88%
Vocational nurse	$790	$978	81%
Medical support	$834	$1,070	78%

Note: All earnings adjusted to 2019 dollars. *Source:* Data from the Current Population Survey, 2012–2019.

the professional occupations (42 percent compared to 14 percent) and in STEM management positions (20 percent compared to 9 percent).

Table 10.2 shows how these participation distributions play out in terms of earnings differentials. The highest-paying occupations in the STEM-related fields are the professional occupations and the managerial occupations, and in these two fields, mothers experience some of their largest pay gaps compared to non-Hispanic white men. In the management occupations, mothers experience a pay gap of 23 percentage points compared to white men, which narrows only slightly (close to 18 percent) for professional jobs. The situation is better for professional nurses, where mothers are strongly represented and earn 88 percent of what white men in this field earn. Mothers working in medical support earn only 78 percent of what white men earn. Even in vocational nursing, where there are very few white men, the mothers in this field experience a pay gap of 19 percentage points.

Stopping at Two Intersections: Marital Status and Race/Ethnicity

In a group as heterogeneous as mothers, many different intersectional explorations are possible. Based on the general characteristics of the data for women who are mothers, we have selected two areas of focus for a closer

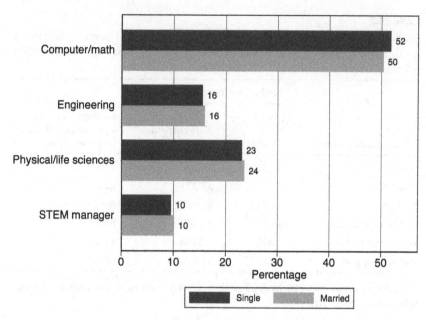

Figure 10.4
Distribution of mothers by marital status across STEM occupations, individuals age 25–64 working full-time. *Source:* Data from the Current Population Survey, 2012–2019.

look at mothers in STEM fields—marital status and race/ethnicity. Marital status is especially important because of the strong economic differences that already divide single mothers and married mothers within the general population. And, given the broad array of racial/ethnic differences and the overall reliability of race/ethnicity as a significant factor for STEM work, we have opted to explore the combined effects of gender and race/ethnicity for this group.

Marital Status
Most of the mothers working in STEM are married (81 percent). In figure 10.4, we show the distribution of mothers by marital status over our four main STEM categories. The distributions are similar and resemble those of all mothers (see figure 10.2).

However, when we look at the earnings of mothers by marital status, differences emerge. Single mothers, particularly those in the engineering fields, fare poorly relative to married mothers (table 10.3), earning only 74

Table 10.3
Median weekly earnings of mothers by marital status weekly earnings in STEM occupations, individuals age 25–64 working full-time

STEM category	Median weekly earnings		
	Single mothers	Married mothers	Single mothers' earnings as a percentage of married mothers'
Computer/math	$1,233	$1,481	83%
Engineering	$1,120	$1,518	74%
Physical/life sciences	$1,166	$1,372	85%
STEM managerial	$1,931	$1,859	104%

Note: All earnings adjusted to 2019 dollars. *Source:* Data from the Current Population Survey, 2012–2019.

percent of what the latter earn, amounting to a difference of nearly $400 per week. Earnings ratios are not much better in the computer/math and the physical/life sciences fields, where married mothers outearn their single counterparts by at least 15 percentage points. These are meaningful gaps. Single mothers slightly outearn married mothers in the STEM managerial fields, an area where both groups participate equally. This is the area where both groups see their highest median earnings.

Similarly to mothers in STEM, most mothers working in STEM-related fields are married (77 percent). In this case, however, there are some important differences in how single and married mothers are distributed. This is particularly pronounced in the professional category, where married mothers are more likely to participate than single mothers (16 percent compared to 6 percent). Another notable difference is in the vocational nursing field, which attracts more single mothers (14 percent) than married mothers (7 percent). Both groups are strongly represented in the professional nursing fields. Single mothers are also strongly represented in the medical-support fields (figure 10.5).

Table 10.4 makes clear that these participation differences translate into meaningful earnings differences. Single mothers in the professional fields earn only 68 percent of what married mothers earn. Earnings are also low for single mothers compared to married mothers in the manager/other category but are relatively equal in the nursing professions. Not only are single mothers less likely to be in the higher-paying STEM-related occupations,

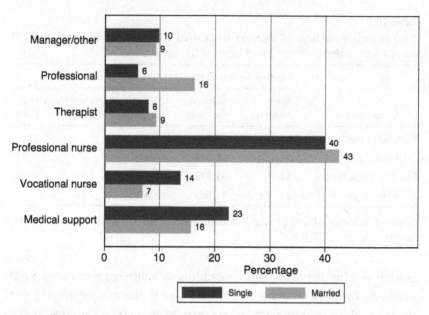

Figure 10.5
Distribution of mothers by marital status across STEM-related occupations, individuals age 25–64 working full-time. *Source:* Data from Current Population Survey, 2012–2019.

Table 10.4
Median weekly earnings of mothers by marital status in STEM-related occupations, individuals age 25–64 working full-time

	Median weekly earnings		
STEM-related category	Single mothers	Married mothers	Single mothers' earnings as a percentage of married mothers'
Manager/other	$1,000	$1,342	75%
Professional	$1,334	$1,958	68%
Therapist	$1,137	$1,231	92%
Professional nurse	$1,183	$1,242	95%
Vocational nurse	$769	$805	95%
Medical support	$755	$873	87%

Note: All earnings adjusted to 2019 dollars. *Source:* Data from the Current Population Survey, 2012–2019.

but, when they are there, the earnings gaps are significant. And single mothers are strongly represented in the two lowest-paying STEM-related occupations of medical support and vocational nurse.

Race and Ethnicity: White Mothers and Mothers of Color

Of mothers working in STEM, 56 percent identify as white, and 42 percent identify as women of color (defined as women who identify as Black, American Indian/Alaska Native, Asian/Pacific Islander, some other race, or Hispanic). Over half (58 percent) of the mothers of color report an Asian identity.

Figure 10.6 depicts the distribution of mothers by their racial/ethnic identification across the four traditional STEM groupings. Mothers of color dominate in the computer/math fields (59 percent compared to 44 percent), while white mothers are 10 percentage points more likely to be in life sciences fields and 4 percentage points (50 percent) more likely to be in STEM management. Table 10.5 reveals how these differences in participation translate into earnings gaps.

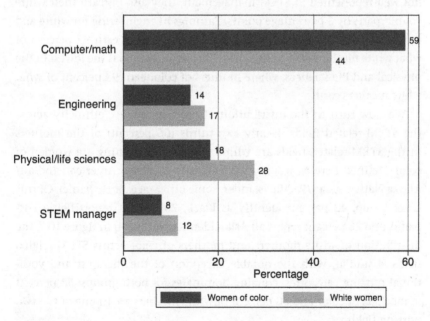

Figure 10.6
Distribution of mothers by race/ethnicity across STEM occupations, individuals age 25–64 working full-time. *Source:* Data from the Current Population Survey, 2012–2019.

Table 10.5

Median weekly earnings of mothers by race/ethnicity in STEM occupations, individuals age 25–64 working full-time

	Median weekly earnings		
STEM category	Mothers of color	Non-Hispanic white mothers	Mothers of color's earnings as a percentage of non-Hispanic white mothers'
Computer/math	$1,518	$1,349	113%
Engineering	$1,449	$1,492	97%
Physical/life sciences	$1,273	$1,370	93%
STEM managerial	$1,946	$1,859	105%

Note: All earnings adjusted to 2019 dollars. *Source:* Data from the Current Population Survey, 2012–2019.

Mothers of color in computer/math fields earn 113 percent of what white mothers in STEM earn. Despite the fact that mothers of color are not well-represented in STEM management, they also outearn their white counterparts by 5 percentage points. Earnings in engineering for white and mothers of color are close to parity: mothers of color earn 97 percent of what white mothers earn in this field. The earnings ratio is the lowest in the physical and life sciences, where mothers of color earn 93 percent of what white mothers earn.

We now turn to the distribution of mothers by race/ethnicity across the STEM-related fields. Nearly two-thirds (66 percent) of the mothers in the STEM-related fields are white, while the remaining are women of color (defined here as women who identify as Black, American Indian/Alaska Native, Asian/Pacific Islander, some other race, or Hispanic). Of this latter group, 42 percent identify as Black, 26 percent report being Hispanic, and 28 percent report an Asian identity. As shown in figure 10.7, the distribution of white mothers and mothers of color across STEM-related fields is similar, with the notable exception of the therapist and vocational nursing categories. Nursing dominates for both groups: 52 percent of mothers of color and 50 percent of white mothers are in one of the two nursing fields.

Table 10.6 depicts how these distributions play out in terms of earnings. Despite their relatively equal participation in the STEM-related managerial

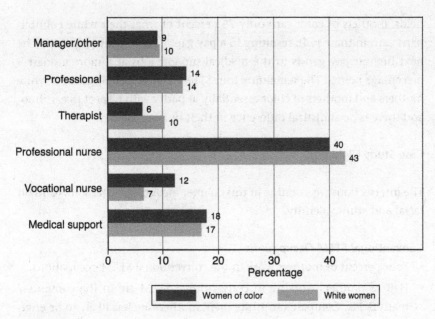

Figure 10.7
Distribution of mothers by race/ethnicity across STEM-related occupations, individuals age 25–64 working full-time. *Source:* Data from Current Population Survey, 2012–2019.

Table 10.6
Median weekly earnings of mothers by race/ethnicity in STEM-related occupations, individuals age 25–64 working full-time

STEM-related category	Median weekly earnings		Mothers of color's earnings as a percentage of non-Hispanic white mothers'
	Mothers of color	Non-Hispanic white mothers	
Manager/other	$1,043	$1,341	78%
Professional	$1,830	$1,894	97%
Therapist	$1,189	$1,231	97%
Professional nurse	$1,229	$1,227	100%
Vocational nurse	$790	$791	100%
Medical support	$783	$861	91%

Note: All earnings adjusted to 2019 dollars. *Source:* Data from the Current Population Survey, 2012–2019.

fields, mothers of color earn only 78 percent of what their white counter-parts earn in these jobs, resulting in a pay gap of 22 percentage points. The next highest pay gap is in the medical-support jobs at a more modest 9 percentage points. The remaining four STEM-related groupings show white mothers and mothers of color essentially at parity with respect to earnings, and there is no statistical difference in their nursing salaries.

Case Study Highlights

The intersections we examine in this chapter focus on marital status and on racial and ethnic identity.

Conventional STEM Occupations
- Four percent of mothers work in the conventional STEM occupations.
- Half of mothers working in conventional STEM are in the computer/ math fields. Compared to white men, mothers are less likely to be engi-neers (16 percent compared to 36 percent) and more likely to be in the physical/life sciences (23 percent compared to 10 percent).
- Mothers' STEM earnings are close to but not in parity with white men's. The pay gap hovers around 10 percentage points. The biggest earnings gap (13 percentage points) is in computer/math, the occupational area where the majority of mothers are clustered.

STEM-Related Occupations
- About 12.1 percent of mothers report working in the STEM-related fields.
- Fifty percent of mothers in STEM-related work are nurses (professional plus vocational).
- Mothers are poorly represented in STEM-related management fields, where they also experience their most substantial earnings gap (23 per-centage points).
- Fourteen percent of mothers are in high-paying medical professional jobs (compared to 42 percent of white men), and in those jobs they make 82 percent of white men's wages.
- Earnings for mothers in STEM-related work lag behind white men's and do not reach parity in any area. Overall, median earnings ratios are larger than the wage gaps in conventional STEM work.

Stopping at an Intersection: Marital Status

- Eighty-one percent of mothers working in conventional STEM occupations are married.
- Married and single mothers are distributed across the STEM occupations in strikingly similar ways.
- Pay gaps in conventional STEM are sizable and favor married mothers. They earn more than single mothers by 17 percentage points in computer/math, 26 points in engineering, and 15 points in the physical/life sciences. The exception is STEM management: single mothers earn 104 percent of what married mothers earn.
- In STEM-related work, single mothers are more likely to be vocational nurses or work in medical support. Married mothers are more likely to be medical professionals (16 percent compared to 6 percent).
- Earnings are close to parity in both types of nursing and therapy work, but married mothers enjoy a sizable earnings advantage in both the higher-paying medical professional area (32 percentage points) and in management (25 percentage points).

Stopping at an Intersection: Racial and Ethnic Identity

- Fifty-eight percent of mothers in STEM identify as white, and 42 percent identify as women of color. Of the women of color, more than half (58 percent) report an Asian identity.
- Women of color who are mothers are strongly represented in computer/math (almost 60 percent, compared to white mothers at 44 percent).
- White mothers are more strongly represented than mothers of color in both the engineering fields and the physical/life sciences.
- Wages are generally close between these groups, with some favoring mothers of color and others favoring white mothers.
- The STEM-related distributions of these groups are nearly identical except for therapists, which favors white women, and vocational nursing, which favors women of color. Earnings are also similar across most of the categories. The notable exception is the category of management, where the earnings ratio is 78 percent in favor of white mothers.

11 Realities and Possibilities: Rethinking the Economics of Women in STEM Work

> It is not enough to be sensitive to difference; we must ask what difference the difference makes. Instead of saying, how can we include women of color, women with disabilities, etc., we must ask what our analysis and organizing practice would look like if we centered them in it. By following a politics of re-centering rather than inclusion, we often find that we see the issue differently, not just for the group in question, but everyone.
>
> —Andrea Smith, "Without Bureaucracy, Beyond Inclusion: Re-centering Feminism" (2006)

Disparate Measures traces the shifting evolutions of various identity categories and contextualizes them within the current US STEM workplace. It offers an array of intersectional data about what kinds of work women in STEM do and what they earn when they do it, expanding our knowledge about women in STEM and also raising myriad questions about equity in STEM careers. But what does this wealth of information and economic data add up to? And how does it advance our thinking about STEM diversity and our ability to make productive and transformative change?

Although it is an appealing idea, we cannot offer a single solution for the inequities connected to STEM work. The patterns of sex segregation and wage differences demonstrated by our case studies reflect vexing issues that have long plagued both workers and scholars. In addition, the problems faced by women in US workplaces—sexism, racism, ethnocentrism, ableism, xenophobia, homophobia, transphobia, and bias against mothers—are enormous and multifaceted. And as both intersectionality theory and our own data analyses show, these matters are intertwined. If we are serious about equity in STEM, it is clear no to-do list will diversify STEM fields, shift stilted occupational distributions across conventional STEM and STEM-related work, and close often appallingly large wage gaps.

But if straightforward answers are not easy to find, there can be no doubt that a sea change in current cultural narratives around women and STEM work is long overdue, as is a reconsideration of approaches to STEM diversity that may serve corporate interests and the US economy well but women far less so. In this chapter, we offer seven recommendations for beginning such a reconsideration. These recommendations are not a toolkit or a collection of action steps. They are interconnected conceptual reorientations based on findings that have emerged from our data-driven, intersectional economic analysis. Our hope is that they will serve as both challenges and entry points from which we can better identify patterns of inequity and begin to disrupt the erasures, silences, and stalemates that hinder progress.

1.   Face STEM Work Realities: Climate, Wages, and the Reproduction of Social Hierarchies

In chapter 1, we offered a close look at the cultural narratives that circulate around the US economy and STEM diversity. We unpacked the ways in which diversity in STEM has become a magic wand that will supposedly resolve a host of problems—the STEM shortage, US economic struggles relative to STEM innovation and productivity, and stubborn forms of socioeconomic stratification. This equation has shaped decades of effort and financial investment on the part of businesses, nonprofits, higher education, and the federal government, all aimed at producing not only more STEM workers but more diverse STEM workers.

But what happens when STEM work is done by people who have been historically less likely to be in those fields? Their experiences in STEM are often very different from and considerably less positive than those of majority populations. Powerful problems lurk beneath the shiny surface of STEM careers. For example, STEM workers who identify as women or as Black report that their work lives are steeped in bias and negative work-life issues. A significant 2018 study by the Pew Research Center shows that women in STEM occupations report being subject to particularly high levels of sexual harassment and discrimination and that they widely consider their gender as an impediment to their careers (Funk and Parker 2018). In that same report, 62 percent of Blacks who work in STEM report racial discrimination in the workplace, compared to 50 percent of Black workers in non-STEM jobs, and 42 percent of Hispanics in STEM report similar experiences of bias (Funk and Parker 2018).

These patterns of discrimination and a negative work climate in the STEM workplace have been corroborated by many organizations. In 2020, the conservative American Enterprise Institute reported that women are more likely than men to regret getting a STEM degree and that "40 percent of STEM degree holders say women face more obstacles in STEM than they do in other fields. (Among [women] respondents, this number rises to over 50 percent.)" (Orrell and Cox 2020, 1). It also reported that 30 percent of people with STEM degrees say Blacks in STEM "face more obstacles in STEM than they do in other industries (more than 40 percent of nonwhite respondents say the same)" (Orrell and Cox 2020, 1). About a third (31 percent) of STEM degree holders agree Blacks "face more obstacles in the STEM field[s] than they do in other industries, and 29 percent say Hispanic Americans do" (Orrell and Cox 2020, 13).

These data offer much to be concerned about regarding sexism and racism in STEM, particularly because the research shows that while gender- and race-based discrimination can be found in any occupation, STEM workplaces are especially problematic. However, these quite typical STEM workplace diversity reports are also instructive in some unintended ways. First, both demonstrate the sharp intersectional erasure that (silently) structures standard STEM diversity data. Women and Blacks, for example, are typically treated as separate groups, and Black women fall through the statistical cracks. These intersectional silences mean that women from disadvantaged groups disappear as human subjects, while crucial information about the asymmetrical flow of power within STEM work is lost. Second, these reports reflect deep (albeit separated) interests in gender and race but no real interests in other identities associated with systemic disadvantage. The Pew Report, for example, is focused on women and men and includes race and ethnicity but does not include disability, LGBTQ status, and foreign-born status, nor do those categories appear in much of the data on bias in STEM work, unless the research is focused on those other identities.

Finally, while both of these reports engage somewhat with the question of occupational distribution in STEM (such as the areas of STEM where bias is most pronounced for women), they completely ignore the issue of wages and pay gaps. This ringing silence is normative for most STEM diversity

Table 11.1

Median weekly earnings of women as a percentage of non-Hispanic white men's median weekly earnings in STEM by intersectional identity group, individuals age 25–64 working full-time and year-round

Intersectional identity group	Median weekly earnings: Women as a percentage of non-Hispanic white men
Black women	75%
American Indian/Alaska Native women	71%
Asian/Pacific Islander women	100%
Hispanic women/Latinas	72%
Foreign-born women	96%
Women with disabilities	75%
Partnered lesbians (includes partnered bisexual women)	90%
Mothers	87%

Note: All earnings adjusted to 2019 dollars. *Source:* Data from the American Community Survey or the Current Population Survey, 2012–2019.

data. Although economic advancement is frequently cited as the fundamental reason that women from disadvantaged groups should engage in STEM work, questions of earnings and pay equity are rarely broached.

As *Disparate Measures* shows in ample detail, this last characteristic is part of a larger pattern of omission. Table 11.1 illustrates (in an abbreviated way) diverse women's STEM earnings and shows that, relative to non-Hispanic white men in STEM, wage gaps exist across a large array of intersectional groups. In many cases, women's STEM earnings fall below the overall US labor-force gender earnings ratio of 80 percent.

These general patterns offer red flags that should command increased attention, perhaps most urgently because they suggest that diverse women's STEM earnings often follow many contours of social stratification rather than disrupt them. Table 11.1 suggests that STEM work does not always shift patterns of economic disadvantage. Instead, in many cases it reproduces those patterns in the context of (generally stronger) STEM occupation wages.

In this context, *we recommend a turning away from the distracting myth that STEM careers resolve patterns of social stratification and serve as unproblematic forms of economic advantage for diverse women*. We must begin to address the complex mesh of opportunities and inequities that comprise the reality of STEM work, a process that requires relinquishing some comfortable myths of STEM. Rather than relying solely on the familiar mantra of "How can various groups of women get in?," we must also ask another sobering and equally difficult question: "What are these groups getting into?"

2. Reconsider Standard Metrics: Proportional Representation and the STEM Premium

Normative data on STEM field diversity are rarely intersectional. Instead, they often focus on gender and race as separate categories and are largely unconcerned with the pay inequities experienced by many women. What, then, does STEM data usually measure? And how do our habits of measurement implicitly shape the way we think about equity and diversity in STEM?

Our work on women in STEM strongly suggests that the metrics that characterize STEM diversity work are in need of a closer examination. Among these is the concept of *proportional representation*. Anyone familiar with STEM diversity research will recognize the ubiquitous framing statement that certain groups—usually women or people of color—are underrepresented in STEM. Indeed, underrepresentation functions as the premier justification for investing time and money in the matter of STEM diversity. Its importance in STEM inclusivity work is hard to overestimate.

There are good reasons why the concept of underrepresentation has long served as a STEM equity barometer. First and foremost, proportional representation does matter. Underrepresentation can signal important factors such as constricted opportunities, limited access, hostile educational and workplace climates, and other discrimination patterns. Research shows members of numerically underrepresented groups can experience feelings of tokenism in the workplace and performance stress due to exaggerated visibility and social isolation as outsiders (Kanter 2008). Proportional representation data are a compelling way to demonstrate systemic disadvantage: they are easy to understand, simple to depict, and (because they are quantitative measures) seem inherently objective. No wonder the concept carries such persuasive authority.

This approach to diversity does, however, have unrecognized constraints. Proportional representation can be deployed for only certain kinds of identities, such as the kinds of populations we think we capture via quantitative data. It appears to work for gender (problematically reinforcing the gender binary) and for race/ethnicity (because race/ethnicity is so commonly reported). It does not translate to many other identities, however. For example, straightforward demographic measures do not mesh well with rapidly shifting populations such as people with disabilities or with many smaller intersectional groupings.

The LGBTQ+ population provides a good illustration of this issue. Despite the now well-documented presence of homophobia and transphobia in STEM, we cannot accurately claim that Queer people are underrepresented in these fields. Because sexual and gender identities are rarely included in standard surveys, there is no baseline measure for Queer populations. It is also problematic to simply argue that this group should be enumerated. As we note in detail in chapter 9, visibility is a deeply confounding issue for Queer people, especially trans and gender-nonbinary people, who are often erased but also incentivized to control information about their sexual and/ or gender identities. Such factors complicate data collection, problematizing a well-meaning but potentially dangerous push for "better numbers" on the LGBTQ+ population. In short, it is hard to argue we need more Queer people in STEM. In principle, that certainly may be the case, but there is no way to know if LGBTQ+ individuals are proportionally present, and it may well be unwise to try and find out. Unfortunately, however, because of our heavy reliance on proportional representation arguments, this means that LGBTQ+ communities are often excluded from standard rationales for STEM diversity.

These matters are important because of the outsized role representational parity has come to play in STEM diversity work. In many ways, the concept has shifted from a metric to an actual outcome. Almost any corporate or higher education diversity statement will likely suggest that proportional representation is as much a goal as a measurement and has become as much a way to solve the problem of systemic disadvantage as to signal its presence. But while proportional representation may indeed have positive impacts, it is not a guarantee that bias, discrimination, or wage gaps will disappear. In fact, attrition can be masked if members of a certain group are regularly leaving an organization and being replaced by new members of that same group, a "revolving-door" scenario where the people themselves change but the group numbers stay the same. And as noted above, some groups simply cannot be (and perhaps should not be) represented in countable terms. Proportional representation matters but only as a limited diagnostic tool for some groups in some ways. It is not a solution to bias and inequity in STEM.

Another key metric that needs reconsideration is the *STEM premium*. As we explain in chapter 3, the STEM premium typically compares the earnings of women who work in STEM to those of women who do not work in STEM, and it often functions as the fulcrum for the claim that STEM careers economically advantage women. The STEM premium leads to statements such as (to quote a recent representative article in *Forbes*) "we need more women in STEM jobs to grow the economy and women in STEM jobs have greater job security and higher pay than those in non-STEM jobs" (Michelson 2021). The STEM premium has value as a measure and is one way to help us understand the economic power of STEM jobs. But the STEM premium also actively (and too conveniently) obscures many of the important issues we raise repeatedly in this book. In the context of women's frequent economic disadvantage relative to white men in STEM, the STEM premium serves as a data point that can distract us from seeing inequities within STEM occupations. Intersectional analyses show that economic inequality is woven into the fabric of STEM and that STEM wage gaps should be part of our thinking about (missed) economic opportunities. But the discursive dominance of the STEM premium distracts from that work because it depicts STEM as a clear advantage for women.

There is another layer to this issue, as well. Because it compares women to other women, the STEM premium is a measure of supposed advantage for women that actually relies on women's wider systemic economic disadvantage. It is the comparatively low overall wages of women working in the US labor force that make the STEM premium an exciting and positive measure. The premium normalizes women's generally low wages, turning attention away from that enormous problem and leaving it uninterrogated and intact. Women's STEM wage success stories—which, as we have shown, are more complex and compromised than they first seem—become part of a dynamic that masks gender-based exploitation by silencing larger conversations around women's broader working patterns and overall lower wages.

The economic realities and myths around women in STEM cannot be properly seen and interrogated until we rethink our measures of success. *We recommend a reconsideration of the metrics around STEM diversity, with an emphasis on moving away from the fetishization of both proportional representation and the STEM premium as ways to (mis)measure the economic advantages of STEM for diverse women.*

3. Women of Color in STEM: Taking a More Nuanced Approach to Critical Difference(s)

Rather than seeing identities as self-evident and static, *Disparate Measures* supports intersectional economic analysis by situating identity categories as flexible and quantitative data as contingent. In this context of categorical plasticity, we suggest diverse women working in STEM will be better served if identity groupings—including intersectional ones—are deployed in more nuanced and nimble ways. And first among the categories that require urgent attention and concentrated effort is the grouping women of color.

The aggregate term *women of color* has been in use for many years. It generates samples large enough to engage in data-based research and serves as a focal point around which to create policy and change. Women of color in STEM (and outside of it) have often made and continue to make savvy political use of this broader category. Small population size and patterns of intersectional erasure have made it critical for women of color to develop coalitions and professional networks to build support and solidarity within the entrenched dynamics of white supremacy. Research confirms that such coalitions among women of color have, at least in academic STEM jobs, emerged as effective drivers for change (Armstrong and Jovanovic 2017).

A women-of-color approach highlights often ignored intersectional data and intersectional experiences and can foster needed community in the face of systemic racism. However, as our intersectional case studies show, categories associated with intersections of gender and race/ethnicity in STEM work often diverge in meaningful ways. Racial/ethnic identity categories have very different histories, and those histories uniquely shape human experience and data. There are crucial distinctions across the forms of bias and discrimination experienced by different groups of women of color in STEM, and racially diverse women working in STEM often have dissimilar economic outcomes. For example, Black, American Indian/Alaska Native, Asian, and Hispanic/Latina women in STEM experience different overall pay gaps relative to white men, sort differently across STEM occupational groupings, and participate in the labor force at different rates. It is in this context that we join with others who argue for the increasing importance of disaggregating race/ethnicity data when possible (Sharpe 2019). As our analyses indicate, a level of greater precision is critical for effectively understanding and addressing racism and ethnocentrism in STEM work.

Our work further suggests it is also productive to think intersectionally within various race/ethnicity identity categories because these categories themselves run the risk of becoming monolithic. If we wish to understand the economics of diverse women in STEM in a more sophisticated way—and the data show that such work is critical for many women of color—we must see the differences within differences, particularly in the context of race and ethnicity. *Disparate Measures* models this kind of next-level thinking. In chapter 3, for example, we note the strong presence (10 percent) of foreign-born Black women within the overall population of Black women in STEM and examine differences between these groups. Our work on women with disabilities (chapter 8) examines disability type (cognitive compared to physical), a meaningful distinction that is rarely made. Our look at foreign-born women in STEM through the lens of US citizenship in chapter 7 is particularly illuminating. If we want to find ways to support diverse women in STEM, especially women of color, this level of analysis must be part of the effort to see the most vulnerable groups.

More nuance is badly needed, and our work shows it is possible to use carefully contextualized quantitative data for these kinds of intersectional explorations. That said, deeper intersectional comparisons such as these also mean we must learn not only to calculate in an intersectional way but also to think intersectionally. Noting differences within seemingly stable identity categories for women of color (and other groups) reveals asymmetrical systemic workings of power that help us better understand—and ultimately address—issues related to diverse women in STEM. That said, a commitment to better understand the dynamics of disadvantage and power within any gender/race grouping requires a conscious awareness that the purpose is not to rank forms of disadvantage. We must heed Audre Lorde's admonition that there is not—and should not be—a "hierarchy of oppressions" and Ange-Marie Hancock's warning not to participate in the "oppression olympics" (Hancock 2011; Lorde 1983). Avoiding such errors is a central tenet of intersectionality.

So, for example, when we examine the differences between the STEM work patterns and earnings of foreign-born Black women and US-born Black women (chapter 3), our goal is not to imply that foreign-born Black women have an easier experience than US-born Black women, nor do we suggest their working lives are less compromised by anti-Black racism. Our point is that their STEM work experience is likely to be different. Foreign-born Black women's relationships to educational and vocational opportunities are usually rooted in legacies other than the entrenched social, cultural, and economic inheritances of US anti-Black racism. How they come to STEM and their intersectional experiences of racism and sexism in the STEM workplace may not only be profound and vast, but also profoundly and vastly different. These differences must be recognized not simply because they are there but because they are meaningful and they can also help us better see and understand the situations of US-born Black women, as well.

Finally, as challenging as this is, those engaged in STEM diversity work must recognize that categories change. A nimbler approach to categories will allow us to recognize and better adjust to a reality that every case study in this book makes readily apparent: identities refuse to hold still—even seemingly self-evident categories like gender and race. An easy example of this is the sharp rise in the number of people in the US who identify as multiracial, a category that saw an increase of 276 percent between the 2010 and 2020 censuses (Jones et al. 2021). The emergence of new groups associated with gender and sexuality—gender nonbinary, asexual, Queer—makes this clear, as well (Cover 2018).

With these factors in mind, our case studies on women of color in STEM lead us to a cluster of four recommendations: First, *economic issues associated with women of color working in STEM are still absolutely urgent.* Despite the cultural narratives that tout the advantages of STEM work for women of color, this group is disadvantaged overall compared to white men. We must begin to take seriously how different combinations of sexism and racism are persistently reflected in STEM participation and STEM earnings. Second, *more intracategory nuance is needed as we consider women of color in STEM work.* When we work to understand power and privilege in STEM, we must allow identities to be complicated—not because such complications are interesting but because they illuminate issues faced by the most vulnerable groups. Third, as we orchestrate intersectional analyses, *leaders and policymakers must not engage in work that hierarchizes oppression or uses intersectional comparisons to rank groups.* Finally, organizations and institutions that want to stay on the cutting edge of STEM diversity work should be attuned to history: identities evolve, and categories morph. *To make both data and policy more timely and effective, we recommend keeping abreast of category shifts and adjusting for emergent groups, rather than relying on familiar groupings.*

4. Unpacking STEM: Attend to the Subfields of Conventional STEM Work

Attention to the subcategories that comprise STEM work is critical for building a future in which economic equity for women in STEM is a possibility. Located between the sweeping category of STEM and a vast array of many individual occupations, STEM subfields allow us a productive viewpoint from which to examine the critical (and complicated) relationship between diverse women and the kinds of STEM work in which they engage. Throughout *Disparate Measures*, we have examined how intersectional groups of women are proportionally distributed across four clusters of STEM occupations—physical/life sciences, computer/math, engineering, and STEM management (following Langdon et al. 2011)—and have (usually) compared these groups with the distribution of non-Hispanic white men. What these comparisons reveal is instructive.

First, *subgrouping comparisons undercuts the notion that if women in STEM fields experience negative pay differences, it is because they work in lower-paying areas of STEM.* The reality is more complicated. Women in STEM (proportionally) gravitate toward the physical/life sciences more strongly than white men do—a fact corroborated by every intersectional case study in this book. And of the four STEM occupational clusters, the physical/life sciences also tend to have lower wages. Despite women's relatively strong proportional representation in these fields, however, white men in the physical/life sciences nonetheless outearn women in every one of the key intersectional groups we examine, including Asian women and foreign-born women (who often do well relative to white men). Strong interest does not mean wage parity.

Wages in computer/math jobs are substantial, and both diverse women and white men are likely to work in these occupations. Despite strong relative participation, earnings gaps are often severe. For example, Black women in STEM are likely to work in this cluster (60 percent), and white men are also strongly represented (45 percent) (see figure 3.2). Yet Black women's annual median earnings are 76 percent of what white men earn in these fields (see table 3.1). About 51 percent of Native women in STEM work in computer/math (see figure 4.2), but they earn 72 percent of what white men earn (see table 4.1). Half of the mothers working in STEM are in computer/math, and they experience a pay gap of 13 percentage points compared to white men. Even when participation levels are high for both intersectional groups of women and for white men and wages are strong overall, women often face severe relative disadvantages.

This analysis is important because it forces us to recognize that *economic inequity is built into every area of STEM work*. That means we can no longer take refuge in the idea that (diverse) women choose to work in the wrong STEM fields. It also sets an important context for the wage realities of engineering and STEM management. Engineering is typically considered a high-paying field, although *white men's median wages in computer/math now slightly exceed their median wages in engineering*. What also stands out about engineering is the consistently low proportional representation of diverse women: in all of the case studies in this book, women's proportional representation in engineering is outstripped by white men's. Women are consistently missing (compromised) opportunities in these fields. Wage gaps vary across groups but are often substantial, suggesting that while women may make more as engineers than in some other STEM fields, their median salaries are almost always lower than those of white men in engineering.

The largely ignored area of STEM management deserves focused attention, particularly because of the ways in which it signals that *there are key links between leadership roles and economic power in STEM work*. STEM management work earns the best wages in STEM work, and the median annual pay for white men is $120,226. This is a relatively small cluster of occupations, with one in ten white men in STEM working in these jobs. Many groups of women match or come close to that level of participation, however: 10 percent of mothers and 8 percent of Black women, American Indian/Alaska Native women, Hispanic/Latina women, and women with disabilities work in STEM management. Partnered lesbians actually exceed the proportion of white men (12 percent are STEM managers). The overlapping categories of Asian women and foreign-born women in STEM (about a third of foreign-born women in our sample are Asian) are exceptions. Only 6 percent of Asian women are STEM managers, even though they are represented strongly in STEM overall. This suggests that despite stereotypes that Asian and foreign-born women are advantaged in STEM, biases regarding Asian women's capacity for leadership (see chapter 6) may affect their advancement into these well remunerated careers.

Given the relatively strong participation of many groups of diverse women, wage differences in STEM management are stunning. With the exception of mothers and foreign-born women, STEM management has the largest pay gap for every group of women we examine. A pay gap of 25 percentage points relative to white men costs Black women in STEM management $29,530 in median salary annually, a pay gap of 28 percentage points costs women with disabilities $33,789, and a pay gap of 33 percentage points costs American Indian/Alaska Native women $39,414. Even partnered lesbians, who are proportionally represented in these jobs at a rate higher than white men (12 percent compared to 10 percent) experience a wage gap of 10 percentage points ($12,179). STEM leadership is an area of marked economic disadvantage for many groups of women.

This quick look at the distribution differences and wage inequalities in STEM management points toward the future comparisons that this book hopes to inspire. Intersectional research on economic (in)equities in STEM work must grapple with closer investigations that help better explain the disturbing wage differences we see within STEM fields. For example, it is likely that much remains to be learned by looking at patterns of wage variations for subfields that are often melded together (such as the physical/life sciences or in computer/math work). The dynamics of horizontal segregation—the phenomenon in which different groups in the same general occupation perform different types of (differently paid) work—should be more deeply examined intersectionally, as well. While *Disparate Measures* provides an economic analysis and comparative baseline across broad subgroups in conventional STEM, delving deeper into intersectional economic subgroup dynamics will be a key next step for understanding factors that are driving the larger patterns we see.

Subgroups themselves are dynamic because human circumstances, technology, and market demands constantly reshape them, and this makes it important to attend to their evolving nature, as well. Given an ever-increasing reliance on technology, for example, it seems reasonable to expect job growth to continue in associated areas (Fayer, Lacey, and Watson 2017). Indeed, the surge in computer-related jobs may be recalibrating the economics of computer/math fields (recall that the median earnings of white men in computing/math are now higher than in engineering).

Unpredictable global events also shift the economics of STEM subgroupings: for example, the US Bureau of Labor Statistics predicts an upswing in life sciences work because of the COVID-19 pandemic (Torpey 2021).

Overall, our data indicate that we must learn to think more consistently and conduct research in terms of STEM subfields. As a recent National Science Board report suggests, the broad term *STEM* is limited in what it can tell us, given the variety of jobs involved (National Science Board 2015). In this context, *we recommend a stronger focus on the STEM work clusters and a more consistent recognition that, regardless of subfield, diverse women are consistently economically disadvantaged in all STEM work*. It is an error to attribute all forms of economic inequality in STEM to women's work choices, and we must resist the cultural habit of holding up hot STEM job areas as if they are neutral in their wages and their climates. In addition, *we further recommend increased attentiveness to high-paying STEM jobs centered on leadership and management*. Our work on STEM subfields signals meaningful links between leadership roles and marked economic inequality for diverse women in STEM work.

5. Unpacking STEM-Related: Attend to the Subfields of STEM-Related Work

STEM-related jobs usually refer to health care–related occupations and are only sporadically included in the research on STEM. Requisite levels of education and expertise vary greatly across these jobs, and associated activities can be very different. Nonetheless, *Disparate Measures* includes this heterogeneous occupational set because these jobs are a significant, rapidly growing segment of the STEM-associated labor force and are also significant for women: in 2019, more than 70 percent of STEM-related jobs were held by women. Further, while women dominate STEM-related work, women's median earnings in STEM-related jobs are only 75 percent of men's STEM-related earnings. This means that gender-based wage inequities are entrenched at many levels in a set of occupations often touted as offering strong economic opportunities for women.

The patterns in participation and earnings that we see across our many intersectional economic comparisons suggest it is useful to look at the six clusters of STEM-related work in four groupings—health-care support, nursing, management, and medical professional work. Given the variety of jobs that fall under the STEM-related category, grouping them in this manner lets us dial down the challenges of extreme heterogeneity. Admittedly, however, even when we scale up to the four clusters below, we are limited to broad generalizations.

Health-care support work (medical-support and medical-therapist occupations) are comparatively lower-paying jobs that require lower educational attainment and engagement with STEM content. Overall, there are (loosely) similar patterns of participation for intersectional groups of women and for white men, reflecting the fact that some STEM-related jobs do offer significant work possibilities to women without four-year degrees and open opportunities for women from groups that have historically faced obstacles to educational attainment. These jobs do not create equal economic opportunities, however. With the exception of Asian and foreign-born women, pay gaps between diverse women and white men run from solid to substantial (often greater than the gender pay gap of 20 percentage points that characterizes the overall US labor force). Black, American Indian/Alaska Native, Hispanic, and women with disabilities are especially disadvantaged. So while these jobs are fairly accessible, this STEM-related career cluster offers diverse women and white men very different economic opportunities.

Nursing occupations are exceptional. Across all our analyses, they stand out as unique in terms of the strength of diverse women's participation and earnings. Because of differences in education as well as wages, our analyses have consistently disaggregated nursing into professional and vocational nurses. Overall, the high-demand and growing nursing sector is a powerful economic avenue for many intersectional groups of women. Across our case studies, *women in STEM-related jobs are more likely to work in a nursing field than in any other STEM-related job*. Black women have the highest overall proportional representation in nursing fields (58 percent), and partnered lesbians have the lowest (a still-substantial 43 percent). Only 16 percent of non-Hispanic white men in STEM-related occupations are nurses. While earnings differ across subfields, professional nursing boasts strong salaries, and the median average salary for women overall exceeds $70,000. Despite this good news, however, gendered earnings patterns are disappointingly consistent: despite relatively weak participation in nursing work, white men outearn every intersectional group of women we look at except Asian and foreign-born women.

STEM-related management fields are an eclectic group, but they reinforce the concerning patterns around women, wages, and leadership that we saw in conventional STEM occupations. Nineteen percent of white men are in these jobs, and their median wages are strong at $86,437 annually. Women from every intersectional group participate at lower rates (the overall participation of women is 11 percent), and all of these groups experience pay gaps, sometimes at elevated levels. Black, American Indian/Alaska Native, and Hispanic women experience pay gaps of 38 percentage points, 35 percentage points, and 39 percentage points, respectively. Asian women and foreign-born women's pay gaps are 13 percentage points and 24 percentage points. When we look at diverse women in STEM-related jobs, leadership-related work again emerges as a vital issue.

Our final cluster, *medical professional work*, includes jobs that require significant education/training and often reflect high levels of responsibility for care: physicians, dentists, veterinarians, and so on are in this group. As one would expect, wages in this group are the highest across the STEM-related job clusters and represent the greatest economic opportunities. They also vividly highlight—as well-remunerated jobs too often do—the most severe inequalities. In terms of participation, 39 percent of white men in STEM-related fields are in this category; all groups of women participate at much lower rates. Only 7 percent of Black women, 8 percent of American Indian/Alaska Native women, and 9 percent of Hispanic women are in these fields. This pattern is echoed across other groups. When diverse women do work in this area, the wage differences are staggering and feature enormous pay gaps such as 43 percentage points (Black women), 45 percentage points (American Indian/Alaska Native women), 46 percentage points (Hispanic women), and 47 percentage points (women with disabilities). Women from groups with traditionally strong STEM earnings come in with large pay gaps, as well—25 percentage points (Asian women) and 27 percentage points (foreign-born women). The economic experience of high-paying medical professional work is very different for women and men.

As we note above in recommendation 4, more specific economic examinations of job clusters will help us to better understand and explain the wage patterns we see. It is in this context that we note the significance of occupational segregation within STEM-related fields. More pronounced than in the conventional STEM fields, occupational segregation in STEM-related work suggests women may find niches in full-time jobs that still afford them sufficient flexibility to balance gender-specific roles (such as caretakers) with their professional aspirations (Goldin 2014). As physicians, for example, women may pursue family medicine rather than surgery in order to maintain control of their time. Some STEM-related roles are also strongly linked to gendered occupational stereotypes (such as nursing for women), a fact that can affect career decisions as well as patterns of participation and earnings (Ridgeway 2011). Diving more deeply into these kinds of issues is far beyond the scope of this book, but such explorations comprise a critical next step for research on the economics of STEM-related work.

Our recommendations in this area start with a call for more intentional and integrated focus on the economics of women and STEM-related work, particularly relative to diverse women. *We recommend that advanced medical care work—professional nurses and medical professionals—should be more frequently folded into the broader work on conventional STEM.* It is likely that they—and other health-care jobs—have fallen through the cracks partially because STEM diversity research has focused on higher-education settings (which are not organized relative to health care). Inclusion of these key occupational areas will shed much needed attention on sharply gendered/racialized participation trends and wage gaps. In addition, *we recommend further research on specific STEM-related job clusters and more focused research on internal sex segregation patterns, especially within the higher-paying fields.* Extreme variations combined with sharp economic inequities create an unseen but critical employment landscape that must become part of STEM diversity conversations.

6. Embrace Interdisciplinarity: Intersectional Economic Analysis as a Model

Although *Disparate Measures* is primarily focused on critiquing cultural narratives about the economic promises of STEM, our work also demonstrates the value of the fresh perspectives that are generated by creative interdisciplinary approaches. Such interdisciplinary approaches can contribute to the effort to move past the conceptual stalemates in which STEM diversity is mired.

One way to understand the type of reframing we suggest here is to consider the familiar epistemological structures that have guided the research on systemic inequality generally and STEM diversity specifically. The study of individual bias, for example, has transformed our perceptions of human behavior. Grounded primarily in the discipline of psychology, concepts like implicit bias, stereotype threat, and microaggressions have become indispensable for understanding the dynamics of discrimination and inequity. Meanwhile, fields like sociology illuminate how the state, the law, socioeconomic class, the family, and other formal and informal institutions shape rights, opportunities, resources, and status. Newer fields such as organizational studies similarly lean toward complex systems approaches and away from individual behaviors, holding that there "is no such thing as an individual actor, absent the relationships he or she is embedded within" (Tomaskovic-Devey and Avent-Holt 2019, 4). And economists who accept unjust forms of social power as a key economic variable (and not all do) address matters of social inequality and STEM in relation to labor and the marketplace.

All these disciplines recognize (at least to some degree) that individuals and systems interact and mutually constitute each other within chicken-and-egg dynamics of privilege and disadvantage. And our descriptions of these enormous, heterogeneous intellectual fields are admittedly overgeneralized. But we mention them to make the point that research on diversity (STEM and otherwise) has become somewhat conceptually siloed. This is why working strategically for change now usually means bundling various approaches. What training sessions will help reduce bias and improve workplace climates? How can specific cultures of STEM work be shifted away from white, masculinized, cis/hetero, ableist norms? What policy adjustments will remove structural obstacles and inequities within (STEM) organizations? These familiar questions have tremendous value, and asking them is necessary and laudable. After all, combining insights and approaches is part of successful problem solving. But, given the stubborn intractability of workplace inequities in STEM, evidence suggests we have reached some limits.

We recommend a boundary-breaking shake-up in the epistemological landscape of STEM diversity work that centers on the productively destabilizing influence of intersectional thought. New cross-cutting conceptual approaches could help push forward original thinking while still taking into account the varied and valuable current research on bias and discrimination, racialized/gendered cultures of STEM, organizational policy, and so on. *Disparate Measures* makes a fair example of such a project by using the concepts of quantitative data and intersectionality as dual lenses through which to illuminate the fortunes of diverse women across the US STEM workforce. This intersectional approach defamiliarizes conventional identities, reframes them within the considerable research on workplace bias, troubles the neutrality and authority of identity-based quantitative data, and effectively deploys such data. This kind of project is interdisciplinary at its core—and it can go where no disciplinary approach to identity or data can go alone.

Yet as intellectually liberating as it may be, it is worth noting that these reframings also represent a place of precarity—a fact that intersectional theorists know well. As Sumi Cho, Kimberlé Williams Crenshaw, and Leslie McCall (2013, 793) note, "Pressure to locate a project firmly within a conventional field when part of the project is directed precisely at that field's conceptual limitations replicates on an academic level the same constraints that confronted plaintiffs who challenged the categorical apparatus in antidiscrimination law." In other words, just as the US legal system has struggled with the intersectional claim that a single-identity approach fails to represent the oppressions and experiences of vulnerable groups, traditional academic disciplines often struggle to value projects that expose and move past conventional disciplinary constraints. However, such risks should neither reduce our commitment to questioning conceptual habits nor limit us from thinking across disciplines and outside the STEM diversity box.

7. Break the STEM Bubble: STEM Careers in a Neoliberal Marketplace

The most powerful frameworks are so naturalized we barely see them, so deeply ingrained we can easily forget they are there. Our final recommendation requires a willingness to take a close look at such a framework—the twenty-first-century neoliberal marketplace of which US STEM careers are a part. *We recommend that as we think about the future of STEM work, we consider the broader characteristics of the economic system in which that work is embedded—including that system's inherently gendered, racialized, and classed aspects.* STEM careers do not exist in a bubble, and it is an analytical and political failure to think and act as if they do.

The educational landscape is the first place to turn when it comes to larger systems linked to STEM. Support for STEM diversity is tightly knitted to education via both K-12 schools and the academy. The number of

STEM-focused K-12 programs has risen steadily over the last two decades, and academia has generated a substantial body of research in this area. Such scholarship is used to foster broader student engagement, fight stereotype threat and implicit bias, nurture growth mindsets and persistence, make STEM identities imaginable for groups traditionally unassociated with STEM, and examine bias within STEM content itself. Higher-education efforts emphasize the hiring, retention, and thriving of diverse STEM faculty who will teach coming generations, and there is a sophisticated, valuable literature on conceptualizing and enacting meaningful change in the academy (see especially Laursen and Austin 2020 and McGee 2021).

Educational institutions have become naturalized as the ground zero of STEM diversity efforts. Yet while they play a critical role in driving both knowledge and change, a closer look at the centrality of education in STEM diversity work suggests that some familiar economic logics are in play. Within these logics, it is understood that educational institutions will produce talented individuals trained in STEM and that those individuals are needed to protect and expand the US economy's global dominance. While educators foster STEM participation and diversity for many purposes, the state (the National Academy of the Sciences and the National Science Foundation are excellent examples) invests in education-oriented STEM diversity work for a remarkably consistent and explicit reason—to ensure the production of more workers who will fill STEM jobs, become STEM innovators, and strengthen US economic competitiveness. Grace A. Chen and Jason Y. Buell (2018, 611) identify this approach as a "producerist ideology" within which attention and resources are distributed relative to historically disadvantaged groups according to "their potential for contribution to national interests."

Because the research shows that diverse teams drive excellence, innovation, and profits, diversity has become a particularly valued attribute in the production of STEM workers (Eswaran 2019; Hunt et al. 2018; Sheppard 2018). Happily (or so the logic goes), STEM jobs will reward diverse workers with higher pay and sometimes citizenship, outcomes that will ease long-standing patterns of social stratification. Overall, at this level of analysis, "STEM diversity" can be described as a nationalist, market-driven project that deploys education to create diverse human capital in order to ensure US economic competitiveness while assuming that increased social equality will be a natural market side-effect.

The focus on broadening participation in STEM via education helps solve the riddle of why academic STEM jobs so thoroughly dominate the research on diversity and equity in STEM occupations. A thriving, diverse STEM faculty plays a critical role in producing new STEM workers, but most STEM jobs are not in academia, meaning the research on diversity in STEM occupations is largely divorced from the greater US STEM workforce. The research often addresses gaps between STEM education and the STEM workplace (many women with STEM backgrounds never enter the STEM workforce) (Sassler et al. 2017) as well as STEM work attrition (women leave STEM jobs at disproportionate rates) (Harris 2019). But overall, because academia is expected to drive STEM markets by producing new STEM workers, funded research on STEM occupations has focused on a fairly narrow group of academic STEM jobs. The literature on diversity and equity in the entire US STEM workforce is comparatively superficial and sparse.

Disparate Measures was in large part written to address that superficiality and sparseness and to provide a strong basis for further work. As part of that ongoing work, it will be crucial to reach past educational frameworks more regularly and take the larger dynamics of US corporate capitalism into account. It is in this context that we offer two (admittedly sweeping) recognitions we believe are needed for creating equity in STEM work.

1. Neoliberal Corporate Capitalism Does Not and Will Not Drive Social Equality.

US capitalism is founded on and embedded in systemic racial/ethnic exploitation and the unpaid labor of women. From slavery and the exploitation of immigrants to other forms of systemic white supremacy and from the formal exclusion of women from paid labor to today's deeply gendered access structures, modern capitalism has been and remains dependent on certain constellations of (paid and unpaid) work that establish, adjust to, and reinforce the fault lines of social strata both domestically and globally (Acker 1990, 2013). As *Disparate Measures* shows, when it comes to the fortunes of diverse women in STEM, their participation and wage patterns often echo these strata. The parallels are not a coincidence. Rather, they suggest that even though educational institutions work hard to promote STEM diversity and equity, STEM workers (including academics) enter a labor force where fundamentally entrenched, hierarchized dynamics of race, gender, and other social hierarchies are fully in play.

One powerful engine that sustains and drives these stubborn, histori-cized labor-force hierarchies is the myth of meritocracy. The belief that indi-vidual ability and hard work drive individual economic outcomes within a neutral market has been largely debunked, both in the general workforce and in STEM fields (Amis, Mair, and Munir 2020; Blair-Loy and Cech 2022). However, this ideology continues to saturate how we think about earnings and other workplace rewards. The idea of the capitalist marketplace as an even playing field where individual merit will be recognized and equitably rewarded distracts from and camouflages the complex dynamics of inequal-ity that shape the workplace and the larger market.

The myth of meritocracy in a neoliberal marketplace is a fertile ground for the true lies of STEM. This is because fictions of value-free objectivity are central to STEM work itself. Research has shown, for example, that concepts like implicit bias and systemic disadvantage may be more strongly resisted by the scientific community because that community has an elevated sense of its own neutrality (Moss-Racusin et al. 2012). STEM fields are therefore not only as nonmeritocratic as any organizations, but their identification and association with disinterested neutrality amplifies the myth of indi-vidual value and meritocracy. STEM work can be seen to objectively dem-onstrate that white men simply choose higher-paying STEM occupations, are natural leaders, and justifiably earn higher salaries. Poor labor-market outcomes for others (diverse women in particular) are easily attributed to any individual's career choices or to a lack of interest or commitment.

These patterns lend legitimacy to the unfair advancement of certain groups and ensure an ongoing disconnect between the problem of eco-nomic inequity in STEM and the systemic, raced/gendered labor-market characteristics that help explain such inequities.

2. Diversity Is Not Equity.

Workplace equity naturally supports diversity. In a utopia of workplace equity (where equal access, opportunities, and wages are in place and bias and discrimination are absent), anyone and everyone could thrive. How-ever, the reverse is not true: diversity does not naturally support equity. Just because an organization boasts a proportional mix of historically underrep-resented groups or declares that it passionately desires such a mix, the pres-ence of (or wish for) diversity does not tell us anything about the experience of different workers. Diversity in STEM may indeed increase opportunity, but, as this book repeatedly shows, the opportunities involved may be disturbingly different in their outcomes.

This distinction between diversity and equity is rarely made, but it is critical. Making this distinction helps us parse out the disconcerting but unacknowledged disconnect between enthusiastic corporate commitment to STEM diversity (see the introduction for numerous examples) and the highly uneven, often disadvantaged experiences of the diverse people actually doing STEM work. The world of business touts a passion for diversity with a keen awareness of the documented economic value that diverse people bring in terms of talent, unique insights, and problem-solving abilities. Indeed, positivity about diversity is usually framed by an enthusiasm about increased profits and competitiveness—an approach that makes the expense and effort of diversity initiatives more acceptable to shareholders and other invested interests. But while it is commonplace to state that diversity is good for business, this does not mean that diversity will be economically good for workers.

Diversity opportunism can mask larger issues of exploitation because the profit-value interest in diversity easily blurs into a different understanding of the concept. This other version is committed to equity, the recognition of systemic injustices, and the more just distribution of resources. But if this equity-focused version of diversity were really part of the normative STEM diversity movement as reflected in US corporate capitalism, the true lies of STEM could not exist. The uneven fortunes of diverse women in STEM jobs would already be widely recognized, and we would already be working hard on ensuring pay equity in STEM occupations inside and outside of academia, particularly for vulnerable groups. And we are not.

The language of diversity is powerful and appealing, but without a commitment to deep systemic change, it can be a dangerously deceptive shell game. There is nothing about diversity that necessarily has anything to do with justice or equity. At its worst, the narrative of diversity can become a cover for exploiting more widely and profiting more rapaciously.

Disparate Measures: A Final Word

This book is invested in recognizing the importance of a historicized, nuanced approach to identity groups and in seeing identities as socially produced and intersectional. It also embraces quantitative data to demonstrate that while identities are in motion, they are also connected to persistent and real patterns of economic (dis)advantage. In many ways, our work has been an attempt to address to what theorist Nancy Fraser has criticized as feminism's "over-focus on recognition and under-attention to distribution" (Fraser and Schikert 2018). Our work suggests that matters of distribution must be recentered and emphasized within feminist analysis.

Looking at intersectional groups of women who are prime-age workers working full-time in STEM reveals the startling unevenness of these women's participation and earnings relative to non-Hispanic white men and destabilizes the sanguine promises of STEM work. Looking forward from this point, it will be critical to continue researching and deploying identity-driven solutions (like rooting out implicit bias) and also intervening at the organizational level (by challenging unfair workplace policies). But years of frustration around the stagnation of diversity in STEM as well as the concerning intersectional economic data we have explored here should alert us to the fact that familiar approaches are not enough. We must also consider broader market issues that are rarely raised in the context of STEM participation and equity but that are nonetheless fundamental to those conversations.

The absence of public investment in easing the many structural forms of social disadvantage makes STEM-work participation (and many other forms of paid-work participation) difficult for women and others. Women in the US work in a neoliberal economic system that lacks supportive policies at the highest levels. Mothers typically experience an onerous second shift and a shocking lack of available, affordable childcare. Native women experience poverty and violence at sickeningly high rates. Black women consistently fall through the intersectional cracks. Asian women encounter many forms of unacknowledged racialized and gendered bias. Women with disabilities often face extreme obstacles to labor-force access. Queer people labor under constant threat of stigma and violence. Higher education is, for many, unaffordable. It takes but one short step away from STEM to see how these social issues drive STEM, impacting who can work in STEM, what STEM work they will do, and what the outcomes are likely to be.

Identity issues are also distribution issues. That connection must be clearly made and vigorously sustained. Without acknowledging the link, attempts at inclusivity and equity in STEM will remain inside the STEM bubble. That bubble focuses disproportionately on academia, bolsters a naïve reliance on a systemically racialized and gendered labor market to benefit the very people it exploits, fosters unquestioning belief in the myth of meritocracy, and supports a shell game where "diversity and inclusivity" really means "more profit." STEM work is a powerful cog in a greater hierarchized, neoliberal, global marketplace. Finding ways to articulate and intervene in that larger framework may ultimately determine if we can ever move past the true lies of STEM work.

Appendix A: STEM Occupational Categories: American Community Survey and Current Population Survey

This appendix reflects the 2010 SOC occupational codes, which were refined in 2018. The 2018 adjustments are clarified in parentheses.

Computer and Math Occupations: Computer and information research scientists, Computer systems analysts, Information security analysts, Computer programmers, Software developers, applications and systems software (Software quality assurance analysts and testers), Web developers (Web and digital interface designers), Computer support specialists, Database administrators, Network and computer systems administrators, Computer network architects, Computer occupations, all other, Actuaries, Mathematicians, Operations research analysts, Statisticians, Miscellaneous mathematical science occupations

Engineering Occupations: Surveyors, cartographers, and photogrammetrists, Aerospace engineers, Agricultural engineers, Biomedical engineers, Chemical engineers, Civil engineers, Computer hardware engineers, Electrical and electronics engineers, Environmental engineers, Industrial engineers, including health and safety, Marine engineers and naval architects, Materials engineers, Mechanical engineers, Mining and geological engineers (including mining safety engineers), Nuclear engineers, Petroleum engineers, Engineers, all other, Drafters (Architectural and civil drafters, Other drafters), Engineering technicians, except drafters (Electrical and electronic engineering technologists and technicians; other Engineering technologists and technicians, except drafters), Surveying and mapping technicians, Sales engineers

Physical and Life Sciences Occupations: Agricultural and food scientists, Biological scientists, Conservation scientists and foresters, Medical scientists, Life scientists, all other, Astronomers and physicists, Atmospheric and space scientists, Chemists and materials scientists, Environmental scientists and geoscientists (Environmental scientists and specialists, including health; Geoscientists and Hydrologists, except Geographers), Physical scientists, all other, Economists, Survey researchers, Psychologists (Clinical and counseling psychologists, School psychologists, Other psychologists), Sociologists, Urban and regional planners, Miscellaneous social scientists and related workers, Agricultural and food science technicians, Biological technicians, Chemical technicians, Geological and petroleum technicians (Environmental science and geoscience technicians), Nuclear technicians, Social Science research assistants, Miscellaneous life, physical, and social science technicians

STEM Managerial Occupations: Computer and information systems managers, Architectural and Engineering managers, Natural science managers

Appendix B: STEM-Related Occupational Categories: American Community Survey and Current Population Survey

This appendix reflects the 2010 SOC occupational codes, which were refined in 2018. The 2018 adjustments are clarified in parentheses.

Manager/Other: Medical and health services managers, Architects (Architects, except landscape and Naval; Landscape architects), Miscellaneous health technologists and technicians, Other health-care practitioners and technical occupations

Professional: Chiropractors, Dentists, Dietitians and nutritionists, Optometrists, Pharmacists, Physicians and surgeons (Emergency medicine physicians, Radiologists, Other physicians, Surgeons), Physician assistants, Podiatrists, Audiologists, Veterinarians, Health diagnosing and treating practitioners, all other (Acupuncturists; Health diagnosing and treating practitioners, all other)

Therapists: Occupational therapists, Physical therapists, Radiation therapists, Recreational therapists, Respiratory therapists, Speech-language pathologists, Exercise physiologists, Therapists, all other

Professional Nurses: Registered nurses, Nurse anesthetists, Nurse midwives, Nurse practitioners

Vocational Nurses: Licensed practical and licensed vocational nurses

Medical Support: Clinical laboratory technologists and technicians, Dental hygienists, Diagnostic related technologists and technicians (Cardiovascular technologists and technicians, Diagnostic medical sonographers, Radiologic technologists and technicians, Magnetic resonance imaging technologists, Nuclear medicine technologists and medical dosimetrists), Emergency medical technicians and paramedics, Health practitioner support technologists and technicians (Emergency medical technicians, Paramedics, Pharmacy technicians, Psychiatric technicians, Surgical technologists, Veterinary technologists and technicians, Dietetic technicians and ophthalmic medical technicians), Medical records and health information technicians (Medical records specialists), Opticians, dispensing

Appendix C: STEM and STEM-Related Occupational Categories: National Health Interview Survey

Conventional STEM Occupations

Computer and Math Occupations: Computer specialists, mathematical science occupations

Engineering Occupations: Architects, surveyors, and cartographers, Engineers, Drafters, engineering, and mapping technicians

Physical and Life Sciences Occupations: Life scientists, Physical scientists, Social scientists and related workers, Life, physical, and social science technicians

STEM-Related Occupations

Professional: Health diagnosing and treating practitioners, Other health-care practitioners, and technical occupations

Therapists: Occupational and physical therapist assistants and aides

Nurses: Nursing, psychiatric, and home health aides

Medical Support: Health technologists and technicians, other health-care support occupations

References

Acker, Joan. 1990. "Hierarchies, Jobs, Bodies: A Theory of Gendered Organizations." *Gender & Society* 4, no. 2: 139–158.

Acker, Joan. 2006. *Class Questions: Feminist Answers*. Rowman & Littlefield.

Acker, Joan. 2013. "Is Capitalism Gendered and Racialized?" In *Race, Gender, Sexuality, and Social Class: Dimensions of Inequality*, edited by Susan Ferguson, 115–124. Sage.

Acuña, Rodolfo. 2003. *U.S. Latino Issues*. Greenwood Publishing Group.

Adoption Network. n.d. "US Adoption Statistics." Adoption Network. Accessed October 1, 2021. https://adoptionnetwork.com/adoption-myths-facts/domestic-us-statistics.

AFL-CIO, Department for Professional Employees. 2020. "The H-1B Temporary Visa Program's Impact on Diversity in STEM." https://www.dpeaflcio.org/factsheets/the-h-1b-temporary-visa-programs-impact-on-diversity-in-stem.

Agyemang, Charles, Raj Bhopal, and Marc Bruijnzeels. 2005. "Negro, Black, Black African, African Caribbean, African American or What? Labelling African Origin Populations in the Health Arena in the 21st Century." *Journal of Epidemiology & Community Health* 59, no. 12: 1014–1018.

Albrecht, Gary L., Katherine D. Seelman, and Michael Bury, eds. 2003. *Handbook of Disability Studies*. Sage.

Alexander, Michelle. 2010. *The New Jim Crow: Mass Incarceration in the Age of Colorblindness*. New Press.

Allard Mary D. 2011 "Asians in the US Labor Force: Profile of a Diverse Population." *Monthly Labor Review* 134 (November 1): 3–22.

Alterman, Hyman. 1969. *Counting People: The Census in History*. Harcourt, Brace & World.

Ameri, Mason, Lisa Schur, Meera Adya, F. Scott Bentley, Patrick McKay, and Douglas Kruse. 2018. "The Disability Employment Puzzle: A Field Experiment on Employer Hiring Behavior." *ILR Review* 71, no. 2: 329–364.

American Immigration Council. 2020a. "The H-1B Visa Program." https://www .americanimmigrationcouncil.org/sites/default/files/research/the_h1b_visa_program _a_primer_on_the_program_and_its_impact_on_jobs_wages_and_the_economy_0.pdf.

American Immigration Council. 2020b. "Immigrants in the United States." https:// www.americanimmigrationcouncil.org/research/immigrants-in-the-united-states.

Amis, John M., Johanna Mair, and Kamal A. Munir. 2020. "The Organizational Reproduction of Inequality." *Academy of Management Annals* 14, no. 1: 195–230.

Anand, Priyanka, and Purvi Sevak. 2017. "The Role of Workplace Accommodations in the Employment of People with Disabilities." *IZA Journal of Labor Policy* 6, no. 1: 1–20.

Anderson, Deborah, Melissa Binder, and Kate Krause. 2003. "The Motherhood Wage Penalty Revisited: Experience, Heterogeneity, Work Effort and Work-Schedule Flexibility." *Industrial and Labor Relations Review* 56, no. 2: 273–294.

Anderson, Margo J. 2015. *The American Census: A Social History.* Yale University Press.

Anderson, Margo, and Stephen E. Fienberg. 1999. *Who Counts? The Politics of Census-Taking in Contemporary America.* Russell Sage.

Anderson, Monica, and Gustavo López. 2018. "Key Facts about Black Immigrants in the U.S." Pew Research Center. https://www.pewresearch.org/fact-tank/2018/01/24 /key-facts-about-black-immigrants-in-the-u-s.

Anderson, Monica, and Andrew Perrin. 2017. "Tech Adoption Climbs among Older Adults." Pew Research Center. https://www.pewresearch.org/internet/2017/05/17 /tech-adoption-climbs-among-older-adults.

Anzaldúa, Gloria. 1987. "Borderlands/La Frontera: The New Mestiza." Aunt Lute.

Arena Jr., David F., and Kristen P. Jones. 2017 "To 'B' or Not to 'B': Assessing the Disclosure Dilemma of Bisexual Individuals at Work." *Journal of Vocational Behavior* 103: 86–98.

Armstrong, Mary A., and Jasna Jovanovic. 2015. "Starting at the Crossroads: Intersectional Approaches to Institutionally Supporting Underrepresented Minority Women STEM Faculty." *Journal of Women and Minorities in Science and Engineering* 21, no. 2: 141–157.

Armstrong, Mary A., and Jasna Jovanovic. 2017. "The Intersectional Matrix: Rethinking Institutional Change for URM Women in STEM." *Journal of Diversity in Higher Education* 10, no. 3: 216–231.

Aronson, Joshua, Michael J. Lustina, Catherine Good, Kelli Keough, Claude M. Steele, and Joseph Brown. 1999. "When White Men Can't Do Math: Necessary and Sufficient Factors in Stereotype Threat." *Journal of Experimental Social Psychology* 35, no. 1: 29–46.

Association of Women in Science. 2022. "The Association of Women in Science Condemns the Overturning of *Roe v. Wade*." https://awis.org/awis-condemns-over turning-roe.

Atherton, Timothy J., Ramon S. Barthelemy, Wouter Deconinck, Michael L. Falk, Savannah Garmon, Elena Long, Monica Plisch, Elizabeth H. Simmons, and Kyle Reeves. 2016. "LGBT Climate in Physics: Building an Inclusive Community." American Physical Society. https://www.aps.org/programs/lgbt/upload/LGBTClimatein PhysicsReport.pdf.

AT&T. 2021a. "AT&T Supports Girls and Women in STEM." https://about.att.com /newsroom/2021/women_stem.html.

AT&T. 2021b. "Diversity, Equity and Inclusion." https://about.att.com/sites/diversity /equality.

Baber, Lorenzo DuBois. 2015. "Considering the Interest-Convergence Dilemma in STEM Education." *Review of Higher Education* 38, no. 2: 251–270.

Badgett, M. V. Lee, Christopher S. Carpenter, and Dario Sansone. 2021. "LGBTQ Economics." *Journal of Economic Perspectives* 35, no. 2: 141–170.

Badgett, M. V. Lee, Soon Kyu Choi, and Bianca D. Wilson. 2019. "LGBT Poverty in the United States." Williams Institute and American Foundation for Suicide. http://williamsinstitute.law.ucla.edu/wp-content/uploads/National-LGBT-Poverty -Oct-2019.pdf.

Ballesteros, Anali Crispin. 2015. "Latino Professionals' Views on Employment Discrimination towards the Latino Immigrant Community." Master of Social Work Clinical Research Papers: St. Catherine's University. https://sophia.stkate.edu/msw _papers/434.

Banks, Nina. 2019. "Black Women's Labor Market History Reveals Deep-Seated Race and Gender Discrimination." *Working Economics Blog*. Economics Policy Institute. February 19. https://www.epi.org/blog/black-womens-labor-market-history-reveals -deep-seated-race-and-gender-discrimination.

Bargerhuff, Mary Ellen, Heidi Cowan, and Susan A. Kirch. 2010. "Working toward Equitable Opportunities for Science Students with Disabilities: Using Professional Development and Technology." *Disability and Rehabilitation: Assistive Technology* 5, no. 2: 125–135.

Barroso, Amanda. 2021. "With a Potential 'Baby Bust' on the Horizon, Key Facts about Fertility in the U.S. before the Pandemic." Pew Research Center. https://www

.pewresearch.org/fact-tank/2021/05/07/with-a-potential-baby-bust-on-the-horizon
-key-facts-about-fertility-in-the-u-s-before-the-pandemic.

Barroso, Amanda, and Juliana Menasce Horowitz. 2021. "The Pandemic Has High-
lighted Many Challenges for Mothers, but They Aren't Necessarily New." Pew
Research Center. https://www.pewresearch.org/fact-tank/2021/03/17/the-pandemic
-has-highlighted-many-challenges-for-mothers-but-they-arent-necessarily-new.

Bauer, Greta R., Siobhan M. Churchill, Mayuri Mahendran, Chantel Walwyn, Daniel
Lizotte, and Alma Angelica Villa-Rueda. 2021. "Intersectionality in Quantitative
Research: A Systematic Review of Its Emergence and Applications of Theory and
Methods." *SSM-Population Health.* https://www.sciencedirect.com/science/article/pii
/S2352827321000732.

Bauman, Carina. 2013. "Social Evaluation of Asian Accented English." *University of
Pennsylvania Working Papers in Linguistics* 19, no. 2: 9–20.

Baumle, Amanda K., and Ben Dreon. 2019. "The Demography of Sexuality." In
Handbook of Population. Handbooks of Sociology and Social Research, edited by Dudley
Poston Jr., 279–288. Springer.

Baumle, Amanda K., and Dudley L. Poston Jr. 2011. "The Economic Cost of Homosexuality: Multilevel Analyses." *Social Forces* 89, no. 3: 1005–1031.

Beede, David N., Tiffany A. Julian, Beethika Khan, Rebecca Lehrman, George McK-
ittrick, David Langdon, and Mark E. Doms. 2011. "Education Supports Racial and
Ethnic Equality in STEM." Economics and Statistics Administration Issue Brief No.
05–11.

Beemyn, Genny. 2014. "Transgender History in the United States." In *Trans Bodies,
Trans Selves: A Resource for the Transgender Community*, edited by Laura Erickson-
Schroth, 1–50. Oxford University Press.

Belkin, Lisa. 2003. "The Opt-Out Revolution." *New York Times*, October 26. https://
www.nytimes.com/2003/10/26/magazine/the-opt-out-revolution.html.

Bell, Myrtle P., Eileen Kwesiga, and Daphne P. Berry. 2010. "Immigrants: The New
'Invisible Men and Women' in Diversity Research." *Journal of Managerial Psychology*
25, no. 2: 177–188.

Benard, Stephen, In Paik, and Shelley J. Correll. 2008. "Cognitive Bias and the Motherhood Penalty." *Hastings Law Journal* 59, no. 6: 1359–1388.

Benbouzid, Bilel. 2019. "To Predict and to Manage. Predictive Policing in the United
States." *Big Data & Society* 6, no. 1: 1–13.

Bend, Gemma L., and Vincenza Priola. 2018. "What about a Career? The Intersection of Gender and Disability." In *Research Handbook of Diversity and Career*, edited

by Adlena M. Broadbridge and Sandra Fielden, 193–208. New Horizons in Management. Edward Elgar.

Bialik, Kristen. 2017. "7 Facts about Americans with Disabilities." Pew Research Center. https://www.pewresearch.org/fact-tank/2017/07/27/7-facts-about-americans-with-disabilities.

Bilge, Sirma. 2013. "Intersectionality Undone." *Du Bois Review: Social Science Research on Race* 10, no. 2: 405–424.

Bilimoria, Diana, and Abigail J. Stewart. 2009. "'Don't Ask, Don't Tell': The Academic Climate for Lesbian, Gay, Bisexual, and Transgender Faculty in Science and Engineering." *NWSA Journal* 21, no. 2: 85–103.

Binggeli, Steve, Joerg Dietz, and Franciska Krings. 2013. "Immigrants: A Forgotten Minority." *Industrial and Organizational Psychology* 6, no. 1: 107–113.

Black Girls CODE. 2021. "The Future Looks Like Me." http://www.blackgirlscode.com/about-us.

Blaine, Bruce E., and Kimberly J. McClure Brenchley. 2020. *Understanding the Psychology of Diversity*. 4th ed. Sage.

Blair-Loy, Mary, and Erin A. Cech. 2022. *Misconceiving Merit: Paradoxes of Excellence and Devotion in Academic Science and Engineering*. University of Chicago Press.

Blewett, Lynne, Julia A. Rivera Drew, Miriam L. King, Kari C.W. Williams, Natalie Del Ponte, and Pat Convey. 2022. IPUMS Health Surveys: National Health Interview Survey, version 7.2. Integrated Public Use Microdata Series. https://doi.org/10.18128/D070.V7.2.

Blickenstaff, Jacob Clark. "Women and Science Careers: Leaky Pipeline or Gender Filter?" *Gender and Education* 17, no. 4 (2005): 369–386.

Bonilla-Rodriguez, Damary. 2016. "Latinas in the Workplace: Creating a Path of Success." *Gender, Race, and Ethnicity in the Workplace: Emerging Issues and Enduring Challenges*, edited by Margaret Foegen Karsten, 339–358. Praeger.

Bound, John, Gaurav Khanna, and Nicolas Morales. 2017. "Understanding the Economic Impact of the H-1B Program on the US." Working Paper 23153. National Bureau of Economic Research. http://www.nber.org/papers/w23153.

Boustan, Leah, and William J. Collins. 2015. "The Origin and Persistence of Black-White Differences in Women's Labor Force Participation." In *Human Capital in History: The American Record*, edited by Leah Boustan, Carola Frydman, and Robert A. Margo, 205–240. University of Chicago Press.

Bradley-Geist, Jill C., and James M. Schmidtke. 2018. "Immigrants in the Workplace: Stereotyping and Discrimination." In *The Oxford Handbook of Workplace*

Discrimination, edited by Adrienne Colella and Eden B. King, 159–176. Oxford University Press.

Brandt, Carol B. 2008. "Discursive Geographies in Science: Space, Identity, and Scientific Discourse among Indigenous Women in Higher Education." *Cultural Studies of Science Education* 3, no. 3: 703–730.

Branigin, Anne, and Nick Kirkpatrick. 2022. "Anti-trans Laws Are on the Rise." *Washington Post*, October 14. https://www.washingtonpost.com/lifestyle/2022/10/14/anti -trans-bills.

Branson, Douglas M. 2018. *The Future of Tech Is Female: How to Achieve Gender Diversity*. New York University Press.

Brault, Matthew W. 2012. "Americans with Disabilities: 2010." US Bureau of the Census. https://www.census.gov/library/publications/2012/demo/p70-131.html.

Braun, Annette, Carol Vincent, and Stephen J. Ball. 2008. "'I'm So Much More Myself Now, Coming Back to Work': Working Class Mothers, Paid Work and Childcare." *Journal of Education Policy* 23, no. 5: 533–548.

Brayne, Sarah. 2017. "Big Data Surveillance: The Case of Policing." *American Sociological Review* 82, no. 5: 977–1008.

Brescoll, Victoria L., and Eric Luis Uhlmann. 2008. "Can an Angry Woman Get Ahead? Status Conferral, Gender, and Expression of Emotion in the Workplace." *Psychological Science* 19, no. 3: 268–275.

Breward, Katherine. 2020. "Privileges and Prejudices: Intersectionality and Disability Accommodation." In *The Palgrave Handbook of Disability at Work*, edited by Sandra L. Fielden, Mark Edward Moore, and Gemma L. Bend, 417–432. Palgrave Macmillan.

Bronski, Michael. 2011. *A Queer History of the United States*. Vol. 1. Beacon Press.

Broussard, Kristin A., Ruth H. Warner, and Anna R. D. Pope. 2018. "Too Many Boxes, or Not Enough? Preferences for How We Ask about Gender in Cisgender, LGB, and Gender-Diverse Samples." *Sex Roles* 78, no. 9–10: 606–624.

Brown, Anna. 2020. "The Changing Categories the U.S. Census Has Used to Measure Race." Pew Research Center. June 30. https://www.pewresearch.org/fact-tank/2020 /02/25/the-changing-categories-the-u-s-has-used-to-measure-race/#:~:text=Through out%20most%20of%20the%20history,slaves%20and%20mulatto%20slaves%20 separately.

Brown, Nicole, and Jennifer Leigh. 2020. *Ableism in Academia: Theorising Experiences of Disabilities and Chronic Illnesses in Higher Education*. UCL Press.

Brown, Scott, Jane Herr, Radha Roy, and Jacob Alex Klerman. 2020. "Employee and Worksite Perspectives of the FMLA: Who Is Eligible?" Abt Associates for the US

Department of Labor. https://www.dol.gov/sites/dolgov/files/OASP/evaluation/pdf /WHD_FMLA2018PB1WhoIsEligible_StudyBrief_Aug2020.pdf.

Bryman, Alan. 2008. "The End of the Paradigm Wars?" In *The SAGE Handbook of Social Research Methods*, edited by Alasuutari, Pertti, Leonard Bickman, and Julia Brannen, 13–25. Sage.

Bucknor, Cherie. 2016. *Hispanic Workers in the United States*. Center for Economic and Policy Research.

Budig, Michelle J., and Paula England. 2001. "The Wage Penalty for Motherhood." *American Sociological Review* 66, no. 2: 204–225.

Budig, Michelle J., and Melissa J. Hodges. 2010 "Differences in Disadvantage: Variation in the Motherhood Penalty across White Women's Earnings Distribution." *American Sociological Review* 75, no. 5: 705–728.

Budiman, Abby. 2020. "Key Findings about U.S. Immigrants." Pew Research Center. https://www.pewresearch.org/fact-tank/2020/08/20/key-findings-about-u-s-immigrants.

Budiman, Abby, and Neil G. Ruiz. 2021. *Asian Americans Are the Fastest-Growing Racial or Ethnic Group in the U.S.* Pew Research Center. https://www.pewresearch.org /fact-tank/2021/04/09/asian-americans-are-the-fastest-growing-racial-or-ethnic-group -in-the-u-s.

Burgstahler, S., and C. Chang. 2009. "Promising Interventions for Promoting STEM Fields to Students Who Have Disabilities." *Review of Disability Studies: An International Journal* 5: 29–47.

Burkus, David. 2017. "Everyone Likes Flex Time, but We Punish Women Who Use It." *Harvard Business Review*, February. https://hbr.org/2017/02/everyone-likes-flex -time-but-we-punish-women-who-use-it.

Burneson, Elizabeth Childress. 2017. "The Invisible Minority: Discrimination against Bisexuals in the Workplace." *University of Richmond Law Review* 52: 63–82.

Burnett, Nicholas P., Alyssa M. Hernandez, Emily E. King, Richelle L. Tanner, and Kathryn Wilsterman. 2022. "A Push for Inclusive Data Collection in STEM Organizations." *Science* 376, no. 6588: 37–39.

Burns, Katelyn. 2020. "Why Police Often Single Out Trans People for Violence." *Vox*. https://www.vox.com/identities/2020/6/23/21295432/police-black-trans-people -violence.

Bywater, Krista, Kristy L. Duran, Rukmani Vijayaraghavan, Claire Horner-Devine, Kelly Ramirez, and Jane Zelikova. 2017. "We Are Never Just Scientists." 2017. *Scientific American*, March 8. https://blogs.scientificamerican.com/voices/we-are-never -just-scientists.

Calvert, Cynthia Thomas. 2020. "Protecting Parents during COVID-19: State and Local FRD Laws Prohibit Discrimination at Work." Center for Worklife Law, University of California at Berkeley.

Cannady, Matthew A., Eric Greenwald, and Kimberly N. Harris. 2014. "Problematizing the STEM Pipeline Metaphor: Is the STEM Pipeline Metaphor Serving Our Students and the STEM Workforce?" *Science Education* 98, no. 3: 443–460.

Cantú, Norma. 2012. "Getting There Cuando No Hay Camino (When There Is So Path): Paths to Discovery Testimonios by Chicanas in STEM." *Equity & Excellence in Education* 45, no. 3: 472–487.

Casper, A. M. Aramati, Rebecca A. Atadero, and Linda C. Fuselier. 2022. "Revealing the Queer-Spectrum in STEM through Robust Demographic Data Collection in Undergraduate Engineering and Computer Science Courses at Four Institutions." *PLOS One* 17, no. 3: e0264267.

Catalyst. 2003a. "Advancing Asian Women in the Workplace: What Managers Need to Know." https://www.catalyst.org/research/advancing-asian-women-in-the-work place-what-managers-need-to-know.

Catalyst. 2003b. "Advancing Latina Women in the Workplace: What Managers Need to Know." https://www.catalyst.org/wp-content/uploads/2019/01/Advancing _Latinas_in_the_Workplace_What_Managers_Need_to_Know.pdf.

Catalyst. 2004. "Advancing African-American Women in the Workplace: What Managers Need to Know." https://www.catalyst.org/research/advancing-african -american-women-in-the-workplace-what-managers-need-to-know.

Catanzarite, Lisa, and Lindsey B. Trimble. 2008. "Latinos in the United States Labor Market." In *Latinos/as in the United States*, edited by Havidán Rodriguez, Rogelio Saenz, and Cecilia Menjivar, 149–167. Springer.

Cech, Erin A., and Mary Blair-Loy. 2014. "Consequences of Flexibility Stigma among Academic Scientists and Engineers." *Work and Occupations* 41, no. 1: 86–110.

Cech, Erin A., and Mary Blair-Loy. 2019. "The Changing Career Trajectories of New Parents in STEM." *Proceedings of the National Academy of Sciences* 116, no. 10: 4182–4187.

Cech, Erin A., and Tom J. Waidzunas. 2011. "Navigating the Heteronormativity of Engineering: The Experiences of Lesbian, Gay, and Bisexual Students." *Engineering Studies* 3, no. 1: 1–24.

Cech, Erin A., and Tom J. Waidzunas. 2021. "Systemic Inequalities for LGBTQ Professionals in STEM." *Science Advances* 7, no. 3.

Center for Economic and Policy Research. 2020. CPS ORG Uniform Extracts, version 2.5.

Center for Economic and Policy Research. 2021. ACS Uniform Extracts, version 1.6.

Chang, Robert S., and Jerome McCristal Culp Jr. 2002. "After Intersectionality." *University of Missouri-Kansas City Law Review* 71, no. 2: 485–491.

Charette, Robert N. 2013. "The STEM Crisis Is a Myth." *IEEE Spectrum* 50, no. 9: 44–59.

Chauncey, George. 1994. *Gay New York: Gender, Urban Culture, and the Making of the Gay Male World, 1890–1940*. Basic Books.

Chavez, Maria. 2011. *Everyday Injustice: Latino Professionals and Racism*. Rowman and Littlefield.

Chen, Grace A., and Jason Y. Buell. 2018. "Of Models and Myths: Asian (Americans) in STEM and the Neoliberal Racial Project." *Race Ethnicity and Education* 21, no. 5: 607–625.

Cho, Sumi, Kimberlé Williams Crenshaw, and Leslie McCall. 2013. "Toward a Field of Intersectionality Studies: Theory, Applications, and Praxis." *Signs: Journal of Women in Culture and Society* 38, no. 4: 785–810.

Choo, Hae Yeon, and Myra Marx Ferree. 2010. "Practicing Intersectionality in Sociological Research: A Critical Analysis of Inclusions, Interactions, and Institutions in the Study of Inequalities." *Sociological Theory* 28, no. 2: 129–149.

Clark Blickenstaff, Jacob. 2005. "Women and Science Careers: Leaky Pipeline or Gender Filter?" *Gender and Education* 17, no. 4: 369–386.

Cohn, D'Vera. 2015. "Future Immigration Will Change the Face of America by 2065." Pew Research Center. https://www.pewresearch.org/fact-tank/2015/10/05/future-immigration-will-change-the-face-of-america-by-2065.

Coleman, Jill M., Amy B. Brunell, and Ingrid M. Haugen. 2015. "Multiple Forms of Prejudice: How Gender and Disability Stereotypes Influence Judgments of Disabled Women and Men." *Current Psychology* 34, no. 1: 177–189.

Coleman, Sara B. 2017. "A Case Study on the Life Trajectories of Women with Sensory and Mobility Disabilities in Stem Careers." PhD diss., Drake University.

Collins, Patricia Hill. 1990. *Black Feminist Thought: Knowledge, Consciousness and the Politics of Empowerment*. Hyman.

Collins, Patricia Hill. 2019. *Intersectionality as Critical Social Theory*. Duke University Press.

Collins, Patricia Hill, and Sirma Bilge. 2020. *Intersectionality*. Wiley.

Colson, Elizabeth. 1986. "Political Organization in Tribal Societies: A Cross-cultural Comparison." *American Indian Quarterly* 10, no. 1: 5–19.

Combahee River Collective. 1983. "The Combahee River Collective Statement." *Home Girls: A Black Feminist Anthology*, edited by Barbara Smith, 264–274. Kitchen Table: Women of Color Press.

Conde, Ximena, 2020 "White and Black People to Get More Room on 2020 Census to Explain Their Origins." National Public Radio, WHYY. February 24. https://whyy .org/articles/white-and-black-people-to-get-more-room-on-2020-census-to-explain -their-origins.

Connley, Courtney. 2017. "Why the CEO of Black Girls CODE Turned Down a $125,000 Uber Grant." CNBC Make It. https://www.cnbc.com/2017/09/06/black -girls-code-ceo-talks-about-turning-down-a-125000-uber-grant.html.

Connolly, Michele, Mehgan Gallagher, Felicia Hodge, Mary Cwik, Victoria O'Keefe, Bette Jacobs, and Amy Adler. 2019. "Identification in a Time of Invisibility for American Indians and Alaska Natives in the United States." *Statistical Journal of the IAOS* 35, no. 1: 71–89.

Connolly, Michele, and Bette Jacobs. 2020. "Counting Indigenous American Indians and Alaska Natives in the US Census." *Statistical Journal of the IAOS* 36, no. 1: 201–210.

Connor, Phillip, and Gustavo Lopez. 2016. "5 Facts about the U.S. Rank in Worldwide Migration." Pew Research Center. https://www.pewresearch.org/fact-tank/2016 /05/18/5-facts-about-the-u-s-rank-in-worldwide-migration.

Cooper, Anna Julia. 1892. *A Voice from the South*. Aldine Printing House.

Correll, Shelley J., Stephen Bernard, and In Paik. 2007. "Getting a Job: Is There a Motherhood Penalty?" *American Journal of Sociology* 112, no. 5: 1297–1338.

Cover, Rob. 2018. *Emergent Identities: New Sexualities, Genders and Relationships in a Digital Era*. Routledge.

Crenshaw, Kimberlé Williams. 1989. "Demarginalizing the Intersection of Race and Sex: A Black Feminist Critique of Antidiscrimination Doctrine, Feminist Theory and Antiracist Politics" *University of Chicago Legal Forum* 1989, no. 1: 139–167.

Crenshaw, Kimberlé Williams. 1991. "Mapping the Margins: Identity Politics, Intersectionality, and Violence against Women." *Stanford Law Review* 43, no. 6: 1241–1299.

Crosby, Faye J., Joan C. Williams, and Monica Biernat. 2004. "The Maternal Wall." *Journal of Social Issues* 60, no. 4: 675–682.

Curtin, Sally C., and Holly Hedegaard. 2019. "Suicide Rates for Females and Males by Race and Ethnicity: United States, 1999 and 2017." National Center for Health Statistics: Health E-Stats. Centers for Disease Control and Prevention.

Cvencek, Dario, Na'ilah S. Nasir, Kathleen O'Connor, Sarah Wischnia, and Andrew N. Meltzoff. 2014. "The Development of Math-Race Stereotypes: 'They Say Chinese People Are the Best at Math.'" *Journal of Research on Adolescence* 25, no. 4: 630–637.

Data for Black Lives. 2021. "Data for Black Lives." https://d4bl.org.

Davila, Arlene. 2000. "Mapping Latinidad: Language and Culture in the Spanish TV Battlefront." *Television & New Media*. 1, no. 1: 75–94.

Davis, Angela Y. 1981. *Women, Race and Class*. Vintage.

Davis, F. James. 2010. *Who Is Black? One Nation's Definition*. Penn State Press.

Davis, Kathy. 2008. "Intersectionality as Buzzword: A Sociology of Science Perspective on What Makes a Feminist Theory Successful." *Feminist Theory* 9, no. 1: 67–85.

Dell Technologies. 2021. "2021 Diversity and Inclusion Report." https://corporate .delltechnologies.com/en-us/social-impact/reporting/2021-diversity-and-inclusion -report.htm#tab0=0.

De Welde, Kris, and Sandra L. Laursen. 2011. "The Glass Obstacle Course: Informal and Formal Barriers for Women Ph.D. Students in STEM Fields." *International Journal of Gender, Science and Technology* 3, no.: 572–595.

Dias, Felipe A., Joseph Chance, and Arianna Buchanan. 2020. "The Motherhood Penalty and the Fatherhood Premium in Employment during COVID-19: Evidence from the United States." *Research in Social Stratification and Mobility* 69. https://doi .org/10.1016/j.rssm.2020.100542.

Dietz, Jörg. 2010. "Introduction to the Special Issue on Employment Discrimination against Immigrants." *Journal of Managerial Psychology* 25, no. 2: 104–122.

D'Ignazio, Catherine, and Lauren F. Klein. 2020. *Data Feminism*. MIT Press.

Doan, Petra L. 2016. "To Count or Not to Count: Queering Measurement and the Transgender Community." *WSQ: Women's Studies Quarterly* 44, no. 3–4: 89–110.

Dolmage, Jay T. 2017. *Academic Ableism: Disability and Higher Education*. University of Michigan Press.

Dumonthier, Asha, Chandra Childers, and Jessica Milli. 2017. "Executive Summary." *The Status of Black Women in the United States*. Institute for Women's Policy Research.

Eaton, Brianna L. 2019. "Pregnancy Discrimination: Pregnant Women Need More Protection in the Workplace." *South Dakota Law Review* 64: 244–265.

Edelman, Lee. 2004. *No Future: Queer Theory and the Death Drive*. Duke University Press.

Edney, Hazel Trice. 2020. "National Urban League: 2010 Census Omitted 3.7 Million Blacks—Nearly Five Times Its Original 'Undercount' Claims." *Capital Outlook*. http://

capitaloutlook.com/site/national-urban-league-2010-census-omitted-3-7-million
-blacks-nearly-five-times-its-original-undercount-claims.

Edwards, Frank, Sara Wakefield, Kieran Healy, and Christopher Wildeman. 2021.
"Contact with Child Protective Services Is Pervasive but Unequally Distributed by
Race and Ethnicity in Large US Counties." *Proceedings of the National Academy of Sciences* 118, no. 30.

Eickmeyer, Kasey J. 2017. "American Children's Family Structure: Single-Parent
Families." National Center for Marriage and Family Research. https://www.bgsu.edu
/content/dam/BGSU/college-of-arts-and-sciences/NCFMR/documents/FP/eickmeyer
-single-parent-families-fp-17-17.pdf.

Eligon, John. 2020. "Why the Fastest Growing Population in America Is the Least
Likely to Fill Out the Census" *New York Times*, February 14. https://www.nytimes
.com/2020/02/14/us/asian-american-census.html?referringSource=articleShare.

Elliott, Diana, Robert Santos, Steven Martin, and Charmaine Runes. 2019. "Assessing Miscounts in the 2020 Census." *Urban Institute*. https://www.urban.org/research
/publication/assessing-miscounts-2020-census.

England, Kim. 2015. "Nurses across Borders: Global Migration of Registered Nurses
to the US." *Gender, Place & Culture* 22, no. 1: 143–156.

Enke, Finn, ed. 2012. *Transfeminist Perspectives in and beyond Transgender and Gender
Studies*. Temple University Press.

Eschbach, Karl, Khalil Supple, and C. Matthew Snipp. 1999. "Changes in Racial
Identification and the Educational Attainment of American Indians, 1970–1990."
Demography 35: 35–43.

Espiritu, Yen Le. 2008. *Asian American Women and Men: Labor, Laws, and Love*.
Rowman & Littlefield.

Eswaran, Vijay. 2019. "The Business Case for Diversity in the Workplace Is Now
Overwhelming." World Economic Forum. https://www.weforum.org/agenda/2019
/04/business-case-for-diversity-in-the-workplace.

Eubanks, Virginia. 2018. *Automating Inequality: How High-Tech Tools Profile, Police,
and Punish the Poor*. St. Martin's Press.

Excelencia in Education. 2015. "The Condition of Latinos in Education: 2015
Factbook."

Fayer, Stella, Alan Lacey, and Audrey Watson. 2017. "STEM Occupations: Past, Present, and Future." *Spotlight on Statistics*. US Bureau of Labor Statistics.

Feinberg, Leslie. 1996. *Transgender Warriors: Making History from Joan of Arc to Dennis
Rodman*. Beacon.

Ferree, Myra Marx. 2009. "Inequality, Intersectionality and the Politics of Discourse: Framing Feminist Alliances." In *The Discursive Politics of Gender Equality*, edited by Emanuela Lombardo, Petra Meier, and Mieke Verloo, 106–124. Routledge.

Fidas, Deena, and Liz Cooper. n.d. *A Workplace Divided: Understanding the Climate for LGBTQ Workers Nationwide.* Human Rights Campaign. Accessed May 20, 2021. https://assets2.hrc.org/files/assets/resources/AWorkplaceDivided-2018.pdf?_ga=2 .117814089.1332503278.1621437156-1869730232.1619207240.

Fine, M. 2006. "Bearing Witness: Methods for Researching Oppression and Resistance—A Textbook for Critical Research." *Social Justice Research* 19, no. 1: 83–108.

Fins, Amanda, Sarah David Heydeemann, Jasmine Tucker. 2021. "Unions Are Good for Women." Fact Sheet. National Women's Law Center. July. https://nwlc.org/wp -content/uploads/2021/07/Union-Factsheet-9.8.21.pdf.

Flores, Andrew, Ilan H. Meyer, Lynn Langton, and Jody L. Herman. 2021. "Gender Identity Disparities in Criminal Victimization: National Crime Victimization Survey, 2017–2018." Williams Institute. https://williamsinstitute.law.ucla.edu/publications /ncvs-trans-victimization/.

Floyd, Schenita. 2021. "Assessing African American Women Engineers' Workplace Sentiment within the AI Field." *International Journal of Information, Diversity, & Inclusion (IJIDI)* 5, no. 5: 1–12.

Forber-Pratt, Anjali J., Dominique A. Lyew, Carlyn Mueller, and Leah B. Samples. 2017. "Disability Identity Development: A Systematic Review of the Literature." *Rehabilitation Psychology* 62, no. 2: 198–207.

Foucault, Michel. 1978. *The History of Sexuality.* Vol. 1, *An Introduction.* Translated by Robert Hurley. Pantheon.

Fox, Mary Frank, K. Whittington, and Marcela Linkova. 2017. "Gender, (In)equity, and the Scientific Workforce." *The Handbook of Science and Technology Studies*, edited by Ulrike Felt, Rayvon Fouché, Clark A. Miller, and Laurel Smith-Doerr, 701–731. MIT Press.

Foxworth, Raymond. 2016. "Native American Women, Leadership and the Native Nonprofit Sector." First Nations Development Institute.

Francis, Leslie, and Anita Silvers. 2016. "Perspectives on the Meaning of 'Disability.'" *AMA Journal of Ethics* 18, no. 10: 1025–1033.

Fraser, Nancy, and Christine Schikert. 2018. "Feminism in Neoliberal Times: An Interview with Nancy Fraser." *Global Dialogue: Magazine of the International Sociological Association* 8, no. 3. https://globaldialogue.isa-sociology.org/articles/feminism -in-neoliberal-times-an-interview-with-nancy-fraser.

Freeman, Jonathan B. 2020 "Measuring and Resolving LGBTQ Disparities in STEM." *Policy Insights from the Behavioral and Brain Sciences* 7, no. 2: 141–148.

Freeman, Jonathan B. 2021. "STEM Disparities We Must Measure." *Science* 374, no. 6573: 1333–1334.

Friedman, Stacey R., and Carol S. Weissbrod. 2005. "Work and Family Commitment and Decision-making Status among Emerging Adults." *Sex Roles* 53, no.: 317–325.

Fry, Rick, Brian Kennedy, and Cary Funk. 2021. "STEM Jobs See Uneven Progress in Increasing Gender, Racial and Ethnic Diversity." Pew Research Center. https://www .pewresearch.org/science/2021/04/01/stem-jobs-see-uneven-progress-in-increasing -gender-racial-and-ethnic-diversity.

Frye, Jocelyn. 2018. "Valuing Black Women's Work." Center for American Progress. June 30. https://www.americanprogress.org/issues/women/news/2018/08/07/454508 /valuing-black-womens-work.

Fujiura, Glenn, and Violet Rutkowski-Kmitta. 2001. "Counting Disability." In *The Handbook of Disability Studies*, edited by G. L. Albrecht, K. D. Seelman, and M. Bury, 69–96. Sage.

Funk, Cary, and Kim Parker. 2018. "Women and Men in STEM Often at Odds over Workplace Equity." Pew Research Center. https://www.pewresearch.org/social-trends /2018/01/09/women-and-men-in-stem-often-at-odds-over-workplace-equity.

Gao, George. 2016. *The Challenges of Polling Asian Americans*. Pew Research Center. https://www.pewresearch.org/fact-tank/2016/05/11/the-challenges-of-polling-asian -americans.

Gates, Gary J. 2011. "LGBT Identity: A Demographer's Perspective." *Loyola of Los Angeles Law Review* 45: 693–714

Gates, Gary J. 2017. "LGBT Data Collection Amid Social and Demographic Shifts of the US LGBT Community." *American Journal of Public Health*: 1220–1222.

Gates, Gary J., and Jason Ost. 2004. *The Gay and Lesbian Atlas*. Urban Institute.

Gedye, Grace, and the Washington Monthly. 2019. "The (Possibly) Forthcoming Elder-Care Revolution." *The Atlantic*, July 15. https://www.theatlantic.com/family /archive/2019/07/elder-care-becoming-american-crisis/593791.

GenIUSS Group. 2014. *Best Practices for Asking Questions to Identify Transgender and Other Gender Minority Respondents on Population-Based Surveys*, edited by J. L. Herman. Williams Institute, UCLA School of Law.

Gerson, Kathleen. 2009. *The Unfinished Revolution: Coming of Age in a New Era of Gender, Work, and Family*. Oxford University Press.

Gieseking, Jen Jack. 2018. "Size Matters to Lesbians, Too: Queer Feminist Interventions into the Scale of Big Data." *Professional Geographer* 70, no. 1: 150–156.

Gillborn, David, Paul Warmington, and Sean Demack. 2018. "QuantCrit: Education, Policy, 'Big Data' and Principles for a Critical Race Theory of Statistics." *Race Ethnicity and Education* 21, no. 2: 158–179.

Girl Scouts of the United States of America. 2017. "Girl Scouts Announces Pledge to Bring 2.5 Million Girls into Stem Pipeline by 2025." Cision PR Newswire. https://www.prnewswire.com/news-releases/girl-scouts-announces-pledge-to-bring-25-million-girls-into-stem-pipeline-by-2025-300550385.html.

Girls Who Code. 2020. "Girls Who Code Annual Report 2020: Bravery in a Crisis." https://girlswhocode.com/2020report.

Glass, Jennifer L., Sharon Sassler, Yael Levitte, and Katherine M. Michelmore. 2013. "What's So Special about STEM? A Comparison of Women's Retention in STEM and Professional Occupations." *Social Forces* 92, no. 2: 723–756.

Glauber, Rebecca. 2018. "Trends in the Motherhood Wage Penalty and Fatherhood Wage Premium for Low, Middle, and High Earners." *Demography* 55, no. 5: 1663–1680.

Goldin, Claudia. 1977. "Female Labor Force Participation: The Origin of Black and White Differences, 1870 and 1880." *Journal of Economic History* 37, no. 1: 87–108.

Goldin, Claudia. 2014. "A Grand Gender Convergence: Its Last Chapter." *American Economic Review* 104, no. 4: 1091–1119.

Goldin, Claudia, Sari Pekkala Kerr, Claudia Olivetti, and Erling Barth. 2017. "The Expanding Gender Earnings Gap: Evidence from the LEHD-2000 Census." *American Economic Review* 107, no. 5: 110–114.

Goldstein, Katherine. 2018. "The Open Secret of Anti-Mom Bias at Work." *New York Times*, May 16. https://www.nytimes.com/2018/05/16/opinion/workplace-discrimination-mothers.html.

Gould, Elise, and Tanyell Cooke. 2015. "High Quality Child Care Is Out of Reach for Working Families." Economic Policy Institute. https://www.epi.org/files/2015/child-care-is-out-of-reach.pdf.

Graae, Cynthia Norris. 1973. "To Know or Not to Know: Collection and Use of Racial and Ethnic Data in Federal Assistance Programs: A Report of the US Commission on Civil Rights." US Commission on Civil Rights. https://files.eric.ed.gov/fulltext/ED091110.pdf.

Gramlich, John. 2020. "Black Imprisonment Rate in the U.S. Has Fallen by a Third since 2006." Pew Research Center. https://www.pewresearch.org/fact-tank/2020/05/06/share-of-black-white-hispanic-americans-in-prison-2018-vs-2006/.

Granovskiy, Boris. 2018. "Science, Technology, Engineering, and Mathematics (STEM) Education: An Overview." Congressional Research Service (R45223), January 8. https://sgp.fas.org/crs/misc/R45223.pdf.

Grover, Kevin. 2017. "Five Myths about Native Americans." *Washington Post,* November 22. https://www.washingtonpost.com/outlook/five-myths/five-myths-about -american-indians/2017/11/21/41081cb6-ce4f-11e7-a1a3-0d1e45a6de3d_story.html ?utm_term=.c73ca14f9617.

Grue, Jan. 2016. "The Social Meaning of Disability: A Reflection on Categorisation, Stigma and Identity." *Sociology of Health & Illness* 38, no. 6: 957–964.

Gulfo, Adele. 2017. "STEM: Helping Women Advance from Lab Bench to Boardroom." *PharmExec,* August 6. https://www.pharmexec.com/view/stem-helping-women -advance-lab-bench-boardroom.

Gurr, Barbara. 2014. *Reproductive Justice: The Politics of Health Care for Native American Women.* Rutgers University Press.

Guterl, Matthew Pratt. 2009. *The Color of Race in America, 1900–1940.* Harvard University Press.

Gutierrez Rinchiera, Lillian. 2020. "A Study of Factors Which Impact Latina Participation in Science, Technology, Engineering, and Mathematics." ETD Collection for Fordham University. https://research.library.fordham.edu/dissertations/AAI27961184.

Gutiérrez y Muhs, Gabriella, Yolanda Flores Niemann, Carmen G. González, and Angela P. Harris. 2012. *Presumed Incompetent: The Intersections of Race and Class for Women in Academia.* Utah State University Press.

Guyan, Kevin. 2021. "Constructing a Queer Population? Asking about Sexual Orientation in Scotland's 2022 Census." *Journal of Gender Studies:* 1–11.

Guzmán, Betsy, and Eileen Diaz McConnell. 2002. "The Hispanic Population: 1990–2000 Growth and Change." *Population Research and Policy Review* 21, no. 1: 109–128.

Halberstam, Jack. 2017. *Trans: A Quick and Quirky Account of Gender Variability.* University of California Press.

Hale, Kori. 2020. "Being Undercounted in the U.S. Census Costs Minority Communities Millions of Dollars." *Forbes,* March 24. https://www.forbes.com/sites /korihale/2020/03/24/being-undercounted-in-the-us-census-costs-minority-commu nities-millions-of-dollars.

Haley, Emery D. 2020. "The Invisible Minority in STEM." Gradhacker (blog). *Inside Higher Ed,* June 15. https://www.insidehighered.com/blogs/gradhacker/invisible -minority-stem.

Hamilton, Brady E., Joyce A. Martin, and Michelle J.K. Osterman. 2021. "Births: Provisional Data for 2020." Report No. 012. Division of Vital Statistics, National Center for Health Statistics. https://www.cdc.gov/nchs/data/vsrr/vsrr012-508.pdf.

Hancock, Ange-Marie. 2007. "When Multiplication Doesn't Equal Quick Addition: Examining Intersectionality as a Research Paradigm." *Perspectives on Politics* 5, no. 1: 63–79.

Hancock, Ange-Marie. 2011. *Solidarity Politics for Millennials: A Guide to Ending the Oppression Olympics*. Springer.

Hankivsky, Olena, and Renée Cormier, 2009. "Intersectionality: Moving Women's Health Research and Policy Forward." Women's Health Research Network.

Hankivsky, Olena, Daniel Grace, Gemma Hunting, Olivier Ferlatte, Natalie Clark, Alycia Fridkin, and Tarya Laviolette. 2012. "Intersectionality-Based Policy Analysis." In *An Intersectionality-Based Policy Analysis Framework*, edited by Olena Hankivsky, 33–46. Institute for Intersectionality Research and Policy.

Haraway, Donna. 1988. "Situated Knowledges: The Science Question in Feminism and the Privilege of Partial Perspective." *Feminist Studies* 14, no. 3: 575–599.

Harley, Sharon, and the Black Women in Work Collective, eds. 2002. *Sister Circle: Black Women and Work*. Rutgers University Press.

Harris, Cheryl M. 2019. "Quitting Science: Factors That Influence Exit from the STEM Workforce." *Journal of Women and Minorities in Science and Engineering* 25, no. 2: 93–118.

Haveman, Christopher D. 2016. *Rivers of Sand: Creek Indian Emigration, Forced Relocation, and Ethnic Cleansing in the American South*. University of Nebraska Press.

Hernández, Leandra Hinojosa. 2019. "I Take Something from Both Worlds." In *This Bridge We Call Communication: Anzaldúan Approaches to Theory, Method, and Praxis*, edited by Robert Gutierrez-Perez and Leandra Hinojosa Hernández, 95–120. Lexington Books

Herr, Jane, Radha Roy, and Jacob Alex Klerman. 2020. "Gender Differences in Needing and Taking Leave." Abt Associates for the US Department of Labor. https://www.dol.gov/sites/dolgov/files/OASP/evaluation/pdf/WHD_FMLAGenderShortPaper_January2021.pdf.

Hesse-Biber, Sharlene Nagy, and Gregg Lee Carter. 2000. *Working Women in America: Split Dreams*. Oxford University Press.

Hesse-Biber, Sharlene Nagy, and Gregg Lee Carter. 2005. *Working Women in America: Split Dreams*. 2nd ed. Oxford University Press.

Hill, Matthew J., Nicole Maestas, and Kathleen J. Mullen. 2016. "Employer Accommodation and Labor Supply of Disabled Workers." *Labour Economics* 41: 291–303.

Hirsch, Barry T., and David A. Macpherson. 2003. "Union Membership and Coverage Database from the Current Population Survey: Note." *Industrial and Labor Relations Review* 56, no. 2 (January): 349–354 (updated annually at unionstats.com).

Hochschild, Arlie, and Anne Machung. 2012. *The Second Shift: Working Families and the Revolution at Home*. Penguin.

Holder, Michelle, and Alan A. Aja. 2021. *Afro-Latinos in the US Economy*. Rowman & Littlefield.

Horowitz, Juliana Menasce. 2019. "Despite Challenges at Home and Work, Most Working Moms and Dads Say Being Employed Is What's Best for Them." Pew Research Center. https://www.pewresearch.org/fact-tank/2019/09/12/despite-challenges-at-home-and-work-most-working-moms-and-dads-say-being-employed-is-whats-best-for-them.

Hosoda, Megumi, Lam T. Nguyen, and Eugene F. Stone-Romero. 2012. "The Effect of Hispanic Accents on Employment Decisions." *Journal of Managerial Psychology* 27, no. 4: 347–364.

Houtenville, Andrew, Purvi Sevak, John O'Neill, and Elizabeth Cardoso. 2013. "Disability, Prevalence and Economic Outcomes." In *Career Development, Employment and Disability: From Theory to Practice*, edited by D. Strauser, 11–40. Springer.

Howard, Jacqueline. 2021. "U.S. Births Fell during the Pandemic, CDC Data Show." CNN Health, June 23. https://edition.cnn.com/2021/06/23/health/us-births-decline-pandemic-cdc-study-wellness/index.html.

Howard, Melinda A., and Anne Liu Kern. 2019. "Conceptions of Wayfinding: Decolonizing Sscience Education in Pursuit of Native American Success." *Cultural Studies of Science Education* 14, no. 4: 1135–1148.

Hullman, Jessica, and Nick Diakopoulos. 2011. "Visualization Rhetoric: Framing Effects in Narrative Visualization." *IEEE Transactions on Visualization and Computer Graphics* 17, no. 12: 2231–2240.

Human Rights Campaign. 2021. "Fatal Violence Against the Transgender and Gender-nonconfomring Community in 2021" https://www.hrc.org/resources/fatal-violence-against-the-transgender-and-gender-non-conforming-community-in-2021

Humes, Karen, and Howard Hogan. 2009. "Measurement of Race and Ethnicity in a Changing, Multicultural America." *Race and Social Problems* 1, no. 3: 111–131.

Hunt, Vivian, Lareina Yee, Sara Prince, and Sundiatu Dixon-Fyle. 2018. "Delivering through Diversity." McKinsey & Company. https://www.mckinsey.com/business-functions/people-and-organizational-performance/our-insights/delivering-through-diversity.

Hyun, Jane. 2005. *Breaking the Bamboo Ceiling: Career Strategies for Asians.* Harper Collins.

Iliadis, Andrew, and Federica Russo. 2016. "Critical Data Studies: An Introduction." *Big Data & Society* 3, no. 2: 1–7.

Impelli, Matthew. 2021. "More Americans Support LGBTQ Rights Than Ever Before, Poll Shows." *Newsweek*, May 5.

Institute for Women's Policy Research (IWPR). 2020. "Breadwinner Mothers by Race/Ethnicity and State." https://iwpr.org/wp-content/uploads/2020/05/QF-Bread winner-Mothers-by-Race-FINAL-46.pdf.

Ireland, Danyelle T., Kimberley Edelin Freeman, Cynthia E. Winston-Proctor, Kendra D. DeLaine, Stacey McDonald Lowe, and Kamilah M. Woodson. 2018. "(Un) hidden Figures: A Synthesis of Research Examining the Intersectional Experiences of Black Women and Girls in STEM Education." *Review of Research in Education* 42, no. 1: 226–254.

James, Keith 2001. "Fires Need Fuel: Merging Science Education with American Indian Community Needs." In *Science and Native American Communities: Legacies of Pain, Visions of Promise*, edited by Keith James, 1–8. University of Nebraska Press.

James, Keith, Willie Wolf, Chris Lovato, and Steve Byers. 1994. "Barriers to Work-place Advancement Experienced by Native Americans." Glass Ceiling Commission, US Department of Labor. http://citeseerx.ist.psu.edu/viewdoc/download?doi=10.1.1 .203.937&rep=rep1&type=pdf.

James, Sandy, Jody Herman, Susan Rankin, Mara Keisling, Lisa Mottet, and Ma'ayan Anafi. 2016. "The Report of the 2015 US Transgender Survey." National Center for Transgender Equality.

Jean, Vanessa A., Stephanie C. Payne, and Rebecca J. Thompson. 2015. "Women in STEM: Family-Related Challenges and Initiatives." In *Gender and the Work-Family Experience: An Intersection of Two Domains*, edited by M. Mills, 291–311. Springer.

Jee, Eunjung, Joya Misra, and Marta Murray-Close. 2019. "Motherhood Penalties in the US, 1986–2014." *Journal of Marriage and Family* 81, no. 2: 434–449.

Jobe, Margaret M. 2004. "Native Americans and the US Census: A Brief Historical Survey." *Journal of Government Information* 30, no. 1: 66–80

Johnson, Austin H. 2016. "Transnormativity: A New Concept and Its Validation through Documentary Film about Transgender Men." *Sociological Inquiry* 86, no. 4: 465–491.

Jones, Jacqueline. 2010. *Labor of Love, Labor of Sorrow: Black Women, Work, and the Family, from Slavery to the Present.* Basic Books.

Jones, Jeffrey M. 2021. "LGBT Identification Rises to 5.6% in Latest U.S. Estimate." Gallup. https://news.gallup.com/poll/329708/lgbt-identification-rises-latest-estimate .aspx.

Jones, Kelly, and Anna Bernstein. 2019. "The Economic Effects of Abortion Access: A Review of the Evidence." Fact Sheet B377. Institute for Women's Policy Research.

Jones, Nicholas, Rachel Marks, Roberto Ramirez, and Merarys Ríos-Vargas. 2021. "2020 Census Illuminates Racial and Ethnic Composition of the Country." US Bureau of the Census. https://www.census.gov/library/stories/2021/08/improved -race-ethnicity-measures-reveal-united-states-population-much-more-multiracial .html.

Kahn, Joan R., Javier García-Manglano, and Suzanne M. Bianchi. 2014. "The Motherhood Penalty at Midlife: Long-term Effects of Children on Women's Careers." *Journal of Marriage and Family* 76, no. 1: 56–72.

Kahn, Joan R., and Leslie A. Whittington. 1996. "The Labor Supply of Latinas in the USA: Comparing Labor Force Participation, Wages, and Hours Worked with Anglo and Black Women." *Population Research and Policy Review* 15, no. 1: 45–77.

Kahn, Shulamit, and Donna Ginther. 2018. "Women and Science, Technology, Engineering, and Mathematics (STEM): Are Differences in Education and Careers Due to Stereotypes, Interests, or Family?" In *The Oxford Handbook of Women and the Economy*, edited by Susan L. Averett, Laura M. Argys, and Saul D. Hoffman, 767–798. Oxford University Press.

Kanter, Rosabeth Moss. 2008. *Men and Women of the Corporation.* Rev. ed. Basic.

Kawai, Yuko. 2005. "Stereotyping Asian Americans: The Dialectic of the Model Minority and the Yellow Peril." *Howard Journal of Communications* 16: 109–130. doi:10.1080/ 10646170590948974.

Kawash, Samira. 2011. "New Directions in Motherhood Studies." *Signs* 46, no. 4: 969–1003.

Keller, Evelyn Fox. 1995. *Reflections on Gender and Science.* Yale University Press.

Kennedy, Brian, Richard Fry, and Cary Funk. 2021. "6 Facts about America's STEM Workforce and Those Training for It." Pew Research Center. https://www .pewresearch.org/fact-tank/2021/04/14/6-facts-about-americas-stem-workforce-and -those-training-for-it.

Kesslen, Ben. 2019. "Native Americans, the Census' Most Undercounted Racial Group, Fight for an Accurate Tally." NBC News. https://www.nbcnews.com/news /us-news/native-americans-census-most-undercounted-racial-group-fight-accurate -2020-n1105096.

Kessler Foundation. 2015. "Kessler Foundation National Employment & Disability Survey: Overview." https://kesslerfoundation.org/kfsurvey15.

Khubba, Shadie, Krista Heim, and Jinhee Hong. 2022. "2020 Post-Enumeration Survey Estimation Report." *National Census Coverage Estimates for People in the United States by Demographic Characteristics*. US Census Bureau PES20-G-01. US Government Publishing Office.

Kinser, Amber. 2010. *Motherhood and Feminism*. Seal Press.

Kinsey, Alfred C., Wardell B. Pomeroy, Clyde E. Martin, and Paul H. Gebhard. 1948. *Sexual Behavior in the Human Male*. W. B. Saunders.

Kramer, Jillian. 2021. "In Covid Vaccine Data, L.G.B.T.Q. People Fear Invisibility." *New York Times*, May 5. https://www.nytimes.com/2021/05/07/health/coronavirus -lgbtq.html.

Kubota, S. 2018. "Child Care Costs and Stagnating Female Labor Force Participation in the US." Semantic Scholar. https://www.semanticscholar.org/paper/Child-care -costs-and-stagnating-female-labor-force-Kubota/a668eb4794bb2ff99f5be560f5c64e 8263b9ba83.

Langdon, David, George, McKittrick, David Beede, Beethika Khan, and Mark Doms. 2011. "STEM: Good Jobs Now and for the Future." ESA Issue Brief 03-11. Economics and Statistics Administration, US Department of Commerce. https://eric .ed.gov/?id=ED522129.

Laumann, Edward O., John H. Gagnon, Robert T. Michael, and Stuart Michaels. 2000. *The Social Organization of Sexuality: Sexual Practices in the United States*. University of Chicago Press.

Laursen, Sandra, and Ann E. Austin. 2020. *Building Gender Equity in the Academy: Institutional Strategies for Change*. Johns Hopkins University Press.

Lavietes, Matt, and Elliott Ramos. 2022. "Nearly 240 Anti-LGBTQ Bills Filed in 2022 So Far, Most of Them Targeting Trans People." NBC News. https://www.nbcnews .com/nbc-out/out-politics-and-policy/nearly-240-anti-lgbtq-bills-filed-2022-far -targeting-trans-people-rcna20418.

Law, Charlie L., Larry R. Martinez, Enrica N. Ruggs, Michelle R. Hebl, and Emily Akers. 2011. "Trans-parency in the Workplace: How the Experiences of Transsexual Employees Can Be Improved." *Journal of Vocational Behavior* 79, no. 3: 710–723.

Lee, Ahlam. 2020. "A Forgotten Underrepresented Group: Students with Disabilities' Entrance into STEM Fields." *International Journal of Disability, Development and Education*: 1–18.

Leggon, Cheryl B. 2006. "Women in Science: Racial and Ethnic Differences and the Differences They Make." *Journal of Technology Transfer* 31, no. 3: 325–333.

Liebler, Carolyn A., Renuka Bhaskar, and Sonya R. Porter. 2016. "Joining, Leaving, and Staying in the American Indian/Alaska Native Race Category between 2000 and 2010." *Demography* 53, no. 2: 507–540.

Liddell, Jessica L., Catherine E. McKinley, Hannah Knipp, and Jenn Miller Scarnato. 2021. "'She's the Center of My Life, the One That Keeps My Heart Open': Roles and Expectations of Native American Women." *Affilia* 36, no. 3: 357–375.

Lin, Monica H., Virginia S. Y. Kwan, Anna Cheung, and Susan T. Fiske. 2005. "Stereotype Content Model Explains Prejudice for an Envied Outgroup: Scale of Anti-Asian American Stereotypes." *Personality and Social Psychology Bulletin* 31, no. 1: 34–47.

Lincoln, Anne E., and Elaine Howard Ecklund. 2016. *Failing Families, Failing Science: Work-Family Conflict in Academic Science*. NYU Press.

Lindstrom, Lauren, Kara Hirano, and Angela Ingram. 2020. "Finding Our Voices: Employment and Career Development for Women with Disabilities." In *The Palgrave Handbook of Disability at Work*, edited by Sandra L. Fielding, Mark E. Moore, and Gemma L. Bad, 387–402. Palgrave Macmillan.

Livingston, Gretchen. 2018a. "More Than One-in-Ten U.S. Parents Are Also Caring for an Adult." Pew Research Center. https://www.pewresearch.org/fact-tank/2018/11/29/more-than-one-in-ten-u-s-parents-are-also-caring-for-an-adult.

Livingston, Gretchen. 2018b. "They're Waiting Longer, but U.S. Women Today More Likely to Have Children Than a Decade Ago." Pew Research Center. https://www.pewresearch.org/social-trends/2018/01/18/theyre-waiting-longer-but-u-s-women-today-more-likely-to-have-children-than-a-decade-ago.

Livingston, Gretchen, and Anna Brown. 2017. "Trends and Patterns in Intermarriage." Pew Research Center. https://www.pewsocialtrends.org/2017/05/18/1-trends-and-patterns-in-intermarriage.

Lord, Susan M., Matthew W. Ohland, Richard A. Layton, and Michelle M. Camacho. 2019. "Beyond Pipeline and Pathways: Ecosystem Metrics." *Journal of Engineering Education* 108, no. 1: 32–56.

Lorde, Audre. 1983. "There Is No Hierarchy of Oppressions." In *Homophobia and Education*, edited by Leonore Gordon, 306–307. Council on Interracial Books for Children.

Lorde, Audre. 1984. "Age, Race, Class, and Sex: Women Redefining Difference." In *Sister Outsider: Essays and Speeches*, 114–123. Crossing Press.

Loukissas, Yanni Alexander. 2019. *All Data Are Local: Thinking Critically in a Data-Driven Society*. MIT Press.

Louvet, Eva. 2007. "Social Judgment toward Job Applicants with Disabilities: Perception of Personal Qualities and Competences." *Rehabilitation Psychology* 52, no. 3: 297–303.

Lubensky, Micah E., Sarah L. Holland, Carolyn Wiethoff, and Faye J. Crosby. 2004. *Diversity and Sexual Orientation: Including and Valuing Sexual Minorities in the Workplace.* In *The Psychology and Management of Workplace Diversity*, edited by M. S. Stockdale and F. J. Crosby, 206–223. Blackwell Publishing.

MacKinnon, Catharine A. 2013. "Intersectionality as Method: A Note." *Signs: Journal of Women in Culture and Society* 38, no. 4: 1019–1030.

Madden, Richard, Clare Coleman, Angela Mashford-Pringle, and Michele Connolly. 2019. "Indigenous Identification: Past, Present and a Possible Future." *Statistical Journal of the IAOS* 35, no. 1: 23–27.

Maestas, Nicole, Kathleen J. Mullen, and Alexander Strand. 2013. "Does Disability Insurance Receipt Discourage Work? Using Examiner Assignment to Estimate Causal Effects of SSDI Receipt." *American Economic Review* 103, no. 5: 1797–1829.

Magliozzi, Devon, Aliya Saperstein, and Laurel Westbrook. 2016. "Scaling Up: Representing Gender Diversity in Survey Research." *Socius: Sociological Research for a Dynamic World* 2: 1–11.

Mahowald, Lindsay, Sharita Gruberg, and John Halpin. 2020. "The State of the LGBTQ Community in 2020." Center for American Progress. https://www.american progress.org/article/state-lgbtq-community-2020.

Malcom, Shirley Mahaley, Paula Quick Hall, and Janet Welsh Brown. 1976. *The Double Bind: The Price of Being a Minority Woman in Science. Report of a Conference of Minority Women Scientists, Arlie House, Warrenton, Virginia, December 1975.* American Association for the Advancement of Science.

Margaria, Alice, 2020. "Trans Men Giving Birth and Reflections on Fatherhood: What to Expect?" *International Journal of Law, Policy and the Family* 34, no. 3: 225–246.

Martell, Michael. 2019. "Age and the New Lesbian Earnings Penalty." *International Journal of Manpower* 41, no. 6: 649–670.

Martin, Joyce A., Brady E. Hamilton, Michelle J. K. Osterman, and Anne K. Driscoll. 2019. "Births: Final Data for 2018." *National Vital Statistics Reports* 68, no. 13: 1–46.

Martin, Joyce A., Brady E. Hamilton, Michelle J. K. Osterman, and Anne K. Driscoll. "Births: Final Data for 2019." 2021. *National Vital Statistics Reports* 70, no. 2: 1–51.

Martin, Joyce A., Brady E. Hamilton, Stephanie J. Ventura, Fay Menacker, Melissa M. Park, and Paul D. Sutton. 2002. "Births: Final Data for 2001." *National Vital Statistics Reports* 51, no. 2: 1–104.

Martucci, Jessie. 2017. "Science and Disability." Science History Institute Center for Oral History. https://www.sciencehistory.org/distillations/science-and-disability.

Mattheis, Allison, Daniel Cruz-Ramírez De Arellano, and Jeremy B. Yoder. 2020. "A Model of Queer STEM Identity in the Workplace." *Journal of Homosexuality* 67, no. 13, 1839–1863.

Matthews, Madison, and Valerie Wilson. 2018. "Separate Is Still Unequal: How Patterns of Occupational Segregation Impact Pay for Black Women." Working Economics Blog, Economics Policy Institute. https://www.epi.org/blog/separate-is-still-unequal-how-patterns-of-occupational-segregation-impact-pay-for-black-women.

May, Vivian M. 2015. *Pursuing Intersectionality, Unsettling Dominant Imaginaries*. Routledge.

Mays, Vickie M., Lerita M. Coleman, and James S. Jackson. 1996. "Perceived Race-Based Discrimination, Employment Status, and Job Stress in a National Sample of Black Women: Implications for Health Outcomes." *Journal of Occupational Health Psychology* 1, no. 3: 319–329.

McGee, Ebony O. 2018. "'Black Genius, Asian Fail': The Detriment of Stereotype Lift and Stereotype Threat in High-Achieving Asian and Black STEM Students." *AERA Open* 4, no. 4: 1–16. https://doi.org/10.1177/2332858418816658.

McGee, Ebony O. 2021. *Black, Brown and Bruised: How Racialized STEM Education Stifles Innovation*. Harvard Education Press.

McGee, Ebony O., and Lydia Bentley. 2017. "The Troubled Success of Black Women in STEM." *Cognition and Instruction* 35, no. 4: 265–289.

McGee, Ebony O., and William H. Robinson. 2019. "Introduction." In *Diversifying STEM: Multidisciplinary Perspectives on Race and Gender*, edited by Ebony O. McGee and William H. Robinson, 1–16. Rutgers University Press.

McGee, Ebony O., Bhoomi K. Thakore, and Sandra S. LaBlance. 2017. "The Burden of Being 'Model': Racialized Experiences of Asian STEM College Students." *Journal of Diversity in Higher Education* 10, no. 3: 253–270.

McGlotten, Shaka. 2016. "Black Data." In *No Tea, No Shade: New Writings in Black Queer Studies*, edited by E. Patrick Johnson, 262–286. Duke University Press.

McKinley, Elizabeth. 2007. "Postcolonialism, Indigenous Students and Science Education." In *Handbook of Research on Science Education*, edited by Sandra K. Abell and Norman G. Lederman, vol. 1, 199–226. Psychology Press.

McKinsey and Co. and LeanIn.org. 2019. *Women in the Workplace Report 2019*. https://wiw-report.s3.amazonaws.com/Women_in_the_Workplace_2019.pdf.

McKinsey and Co. and LeanIn.org. 2021. "Women in the Workplace 2021." https://womenintheworkplace.com.

McWhorter, John. 2019. "Why *Latinx* Can't Catch On." *The Atlantic*. https://www.theatlantic.com/ideas/archive/2019/12/why-latinx-cant-catch-on/603943.

Mezey, Naomi. 2003. "Erasure and Recognition: The Census, Race and the National Imagination." *Northwestern University Law Review* 97, no. 4: 1701–1768.

Michelson, Joan. 2021. "The Secret Success of Women in STEM Jobs in 2020." *Forbes*. https://www.forbes.com/sites/joanmichelson2/2021/03/29/the-secret-success-of -women-in-stem-jobs-in-2020/?sh=64b7ae2436ff.

Miller, Claire Cain. 2021a. "How Other Nations Pay for Child Care. The U.S. Is an Outlier." *New York Times*, October 6. https://www.nytimes.com/2021/10/06/upshot /child-care-biden.html.

Miller, Claire Cain. 2021b. "The Pandemic Created a Child-Care Crisis. Mothers Bore the Burden." *New York Times*, May 17.

https://www.nytimes.com/interactive/2021/05/17/upshot/women-workforce -employment-covid.html.

Mizock, L., J. Riley, N. Yuen, T. D. Woodrum, E. A. Sotilleo, and A. J. Ormerod. 2018. "Transphobia in the Workplace: A Qualitative Study of Employment Stigma." *Stigma and Health* 3, no. 3: 275–282.

Mora, G. Cristina. 2014. *Making Hispanics: How Activists, Bureaucrats, and Media Constructed a New American*. University of Chicago Press.

Morello, Carol. 2013. "Demographic Research on Lesbians and Gays Emerges from Shadows." *Washington Post*, March 1. https://www-washingtonpost-com.ezproxy .lafayette.edu/local/demographic-research-on-lesbians-and-gays-emerges-from -shadows/2013/03/01/2bdb61ba-7f8d-11e2-a350-49866afab584_story.html.

Moss-Racusin, Corinne A., John F. Dovidio, Victoria L. Brescoll, Mark J. Graham, and Jo Handelsman. 2012. "Science Faculty's Subtle Gender Biases Favor Male Students." *Proceedings of the National Academy of Sciences* 109, no. 41: 16474–16479.

Movement Advancement Project, American Civil Liberties Union, and Lambda Legal. 2018. "Are LGBT Workers Protected from Discrimination?" https://www .lgbtmap.org/file/Brief-Employment-Landscape-Final.pdf.

Muhammad, Dedrick A. Rogelio Tec, and Kathy Ramirez. 2019. "Racial Wealth Snapshot: American Indians/Native Americans." National Community Reinvestment Coalition. https://ncrc.org/racial-wealth-snapshot-american-indians-native -americans.

Munsch, Christin L. 2016. "Flexible Work, Flexible Penalties: The Effect of Gender, Childcare, and Type of Request on the Flexibility Bias." *Social Forces* 94, no. 4: 1567–1591.

Murray, Pauli. 1987. *Song in a Weary Throat: Memoir of an American Pilgrimage*. HarperCollins.

Murti, Lata. 2017. "Studying the Racial Experience of Indian Doctors in Southern California through Interviews and Observations." Sage Research Methods Cases in Health. Sage Publishing.

Museus, Samuel D., and Jon Iftikar. 2013. "An Asian Critical Theory (AsianCrit) Framework." *Asian American Students in Higher Education* 31, no. 10: 18–29.

Nadal, Kevin L., Chassitty N. Whitman, Lindsey S. Davis, Tanya Erazo, and Kristin C. Davidoff. 2016. "Microaggressions toward Lesbian, Gay, Bisexual, Transgender, Queer, and Genderqueer People: A Review of the Literature." *Journal of Sex Research* 53, no. 4–5: 488–508.

Nagel, Joane. 1996. *American Indian Ethnic Renewal: Red Power and the Resurgence of Identity and Culture.* Oxford University Press.

Nagel, Joane. 2015. *Gender and Climate Change: Impacts, Science, Policy.* Routledge.

Nash, Jennifer C. 2013. "Practicing Love: Black Feminism, Love Politics, and Post-Intersectionality." *Meridians: Feminism, Race, Transnationalism* 11, no. 2: 1–24.

Nash, Jennifer. 2015. "The Institutional Lives of Intersectionality." *Economic and Political Weekly* 50, no. 38: 74–76.

Nash, Jennifer. 2019. *Black Feminism Reimagined: After Intersectionality.* Duke University Press.

National Academy of Sciences. 2007. *Rising above the Gathering Storm: Energizing and Employing America for a Brighter Economic Future.* National Academies Press.

National Academy of Sciences. 2010. *Rising above the Gathering Storm, Revised: Rapidly Approaching Category 5.* National Academies Press.

National Public Radio, Robert Wood Johnson Foundation, and Harvard T. H. Chan School of Public Health. 2017. "Discrimination in America: Experiences and Views of Native Americans, Final Report." https://cdn1.sph.harvard.edu/wp-content/uploads /sites/21/2017/11/NPR-RWJF-HSPH-Discrimination-Native-Americans-Final-Report .pdf.

National Public Radio, Robert Wood Johnson Foundation, and Harvard T. H. Chan School of Public Health. 2018. "Discrimination in America: Experiences and Views of LGBTQ Americans." https://www.rwjf.org/en/library/research/2017/10/discrimi nation-in-america--experiences-and-views.html.

National Science and Technology Council. 2000. "Ensuring a Strong U.S. Scientific, Technical, and Engineering Workforce in the 21st Century." https://clintonwhite house4.archives.gov/media/pdf/workforcerpt.pdf.

National Science Board. 2003. "The Science and Engineering Workforce: Realizing America's Potential." National Science Board. Document NSB 03–69. National Science Foundation.

National Science Board. 2015. "Revisiting the STEM Workforce: A Companion to Science and Engineering Indicators 2014." NSB-2015-10. National Science Foundation. https://www.nsf.gov/nsb/publications/2015/nsb201510.pdf.

National Science Foundation. 1951. "The First Annual Report of the National Science Foundation 1950–51." US Government Printing Office.

National Science Foundation. 2017. *Women, Minorities, and Persons with Disabilities in Science and Engineering.* NSF 17-310. National Center for Science and Engineering Statistics, January. https://www.nsf.gov/statistics/2017/nsf17310/digest/employment-status.

National Science Foundation. 2019. *Women, Minorities, and Persons with Disabilities in Science and Engineering.* NSF 19-304. National Center for Science and Engineering Statistics, March 8. https://ncses.nsf.gov/pubs/nsf19304.

National Science Foundation. 2020. "Inclusion across the Nation of Communities of Learners of Underrepresented Discoverers in Engineering and Science (INCLUDES) Program Solicitation." NSF 20–569. NSF." https://www.nsf.gov/od/broadeningparticipation/bp.jsp.

National Science Foundation. 2021. *HRD Programs.* March 3. https://www.nsf.gov/pubs/2021/nsf21054/nsf21054.pdf.

National Urban League. 2020. "Lessons from the 2020 Census: Make Black Count." https://nul.org/sites/default/files/2021-11/NUL_Census_Report_2020_final.pdf.

National Women's Law Center. 2014. "Underpaid and Overloaded: Women in Low-Wage Jobs." https://nwlc.org/wp-content/uploads/2015/08/final_nwlc_lowwagereport2014.pdf.

Naylor, Lorenda A. 2020. "Counting an Invisible Class of Citizens: The LGBT Population and the US Census." *Public Integrity* 22, no. 1: 54–72.

Nelson, Joey, Allison Mattheis, and Jeremy B. Yoder. 2022. "Nondisclosure of Queer Identities Is Associated with Reduced Scholarly Publication Rates." *PLOS One* 17, no. 3: e0263728.

New American Economy Research Fund. 2017. "Sizing Up the Gap in Our Supply of STEM Workers: Examining Job Postings and Unemployment Data from 2010–2016." https://research.newamericaneconomy.org/report/sizing-up-the-gap-in-our-supply-of-stem-workers.

Noble, Safiya Umoja. 2018. *Algorithms of Oppression.* NYU Press.

Nobles, Melissa. 2000. *Shades of Citizenship: Race and the Census in Modern Politics.* Stanford University Press.

Noe-Bustamante, Luis, Mark Hugo Lopez, and Jens Manuel Krogstad. 2020. "US Hispanic Population Surpassed 60 million in 2019, but Growth Has Slowed." Fact

Tank, News in the Numbers. Pew Research Center. https://www.pewresearch.org/fact-tank/2020/07/07/u-s-hispanic-population-surpassed-60-million-in-2019-but-growth-has-slowed.

Norris, Tina, Paula L. Vines, and Elizabeth M. Hoeffel. 2012. *The American Indian and Alaska Native Population: 2010*. US Department of Commerce, Economics and Statistics Administration, US Census Bureau.

Nunn, Ryan, Jimmy O'Donnell, and Jay Shambaugh. 2018. "A Dozen Facts about Immigration." Brookings Institute. https://www.brookings.edu/research/a-dozen-facts-about-immigration.

Oakley, Ann. 1999. "Paradigm Wars: Some Thoughts on a Personal and Public Trajectory." *International Journal of Social Research Methodology* 2, no. 3: 247–254.

O'Hara, Mary Emily. 2017. "LGBTQ Americans Won't Be Counted in 2020 U.S. Census after All." NBC News. https://www.nbcnews.com/feature/nbc-out/lgbtq-americans-won-t-be-counted-2020-u-s-census-n739911.

O'Hare, William P. 2019. *Differential Undercounts in the US Census: Who Is Missed?* Springer.

O'Neil, Cathy. 2016. *Weapons of Math Destruction: How Big Data Increases Inequality and Threatens Democracy*. Crown.

Orgad, Shani. 2019. *Heading Home: Motherhood, Work, and the Failed Promise of Equality*. Columbia University Press.

Orrell, Brent, and Daniel A. Cox. 2020. "STEM Perspectives: Attitudes, Opportunities, and Barriers in America's STEM Workforce." American Enterprise Institute for Public Policy Research.

Ortiz, Erik. 2020. "Lack of Awareness, Data Hinders Cases of Missing and Murdered Native American Women, Study Finds." NBC News. https://www.nbcnews.com/news/us-news/lack-awareness-data-hinders-cases-missing-murdered-native-american-women-n1235233.

Owens, Donna M. 2020. "The Pandemic May Leave Communities of Color Undercounted in the Census—and Cost Them Billions." *Vox*, May 12. https://www.vox.com/identities/2020/5/12/21250766/census-2020-undercount-black-latino-asian.

Page-Reeves, Janet, Ananda. Marin, Kathy DeerInWater, and Douglas Medin. 2017. "Broadening Conceptualization of Native Identity as Foundational for Success among Native Americans in STEM." *Anthropol* 5, no. 187. doi:10.4172/2332–0915.1000187.

Page-Reeves, Janet, Ananda Marin, Maurice Moffett, Kathy DeerInWater, and Douglas Medin. 2019. "Wayfinding as a Concept for Understanding Success among Native Americans in STEM: 'Learning How to Map through Life.'" *Cultural Studies of Science Education* 14, no. 1: 177–197.

Parker, Kim. 2015. "Women More Than Men Adjust Their Careers for Family Life." Pew Research Center. https://www.pewresearch.org/fact-tank/2015/10/01/women-more-than-men-adjust-their-careers-for-family-life.

Patil, Vrushali. 2013. "From Patriarchy to Intersectionality: A Transnational Feminist Assessment of How Far We've Really Come." *Signs* 38, no.4: 847–867.

Passel, Jeffrey S. 1996. "The Growing American Indian Population, 1960–1990: Beyond Demography." In *Changing Numbers, Changing Needs: American Indian Demography and Public Health*, edited by G. D. Sandefur, R. R. Rindfuss, and B. Cohen, 79–112. National Academy Press.

Peñaloza, Marisa. 2020. "Latinx Is a Term Many Still Can't Embrace." National Public Radio, October 1. https://www.npr.org/2020/10/01/916441659/latinx-is-a-term-many-still-cant-embrace.

Peplau, Letitia Anne, and Adam Fingerhut. 2004. "The Paradox of the Lesbian Worker." *Journal of Social Issues* 60, no. 4: 719–735.

Perlmann, Joel. 2018. *America Classifies the Immigrants: From Ellis Island to the 2020 Census*. Harvard University Press.

Pepping, Amanda, and Balasundram Maniam. 2020. "The Motherhood Penalty." *Journal of Business and Behavioral Sciences* 32, no. 2: 110–125.

Petrosky, Emiko, Laura M. Mercer Kollar, Megan C. Kearns, Sharon G. Smith, Carter J. Betz, Katherine A. Fowler, and Delight E. Satter. 2021. "Homicides of American Indians/Alaska Natives—National Violent Death Reporting System, United States, 2003–2018." *MMWR Surveillance Summaries* 70, no. 8: 1–19.

Pettit, Becky, and Carmen Gutierrez. 2018. "Mass Incarceration and Racial Inequality." *American Journal of Economics and Sociology* 77, no. 3–4: 1153–1182.

Pew Research Center. 2020. "What Census Calls Us." February 6. https://www.pewresearch.org/interactives/what-census-calls-us.

Pichler, Shaun, and Erica L. Ruggs. 2018. "LGBT Workers." In *The Oxford Handbook of Workplace Discrimination*, edited by Adrienne J. Colella and Eden B. King, 117–195. Oxford University Press.

Poo, Ei-jen. 2015. *The Age of Dignity: Preparing for the Elder Boom in a Changing America* New Press.

Popova, Milena. 2018. "Inactionable/Unspeakable: Bisexuality in the Workplace." *Journal of Bisexuality* 18, no. 1: 54–66.

Posner, Mariam. 2016. "What's Next: The Radical, Unrealized Potential of Digital Humanities." In *Debates in the Digital Humanities 2016*, edited by Matthew K. Gold and Lauren F. Klein, 32–41. University of Minnesota Press.

President's Council of Advisors on Science and Technology. 2012. "Engage to Excel: Producing One Million Additional College Graduates with Degrees in Science, Technology, Engineering, and Mathematics." https://obamawhitehouse.archives.gov /sites/default/files/microsites/ostp/pcast-engage-to-excel-final_2-25-12.pdf.

Prewitt, Kenneth. 2013. *What Is Your Race? The Census and Our Flawed Efforts to Classify Americans*. Princeton University Press.

Purdie-Vaughns, Valerie, and Richard P. Eibach. 2008. "Intersectional Invisibility: The Distinctive Advantages and Disadvantages of Multiple Subordinate-Group Identities." *Sex Roles* 59, no. 5: 377–391.

Ravaud, Jean-François, Béatrice Madiot, and Isabelle Ville. 1992. "Discrimination towards Disabled People Seeking Employment." *Social Science & Medicine* 35, no. 8: 951–958.

Reskin, Barbara, and Irene Padavic. 1999. "Sex, Race and Ethnic Inequality in U.S. Workplaces." In *Handbook of the Sociology of Gender*, edited by Janet Saltzman Chafetz, 343–374. Kluwer Academic.

Restar, Arjee J., and Don Operario. 2019. "The Missing Trans Women of Science, Medicine, and Global Health." *The Lancet* 393, no. 10171: 506–508.

Reynolds, Tracey. 2001. "Black Mothering, Paid Work and Identity." *Ethnic and Racial Studies* 24, no. 6: 1046–1064.

Rice, Carla, Elisabeth Harrison, and May Friedman. 2019. "Doing Justice to Intersectionality in Research." *Cultural Studies ↔ Critical Methodologies* 19, no. 6: 409–420.

Rich, Adrienne. 1976. *Of Woman Born: Motherhood as Experience and Institution*. Norton.

Ridgeway, Cecilia L. 2011. *Framed by Gender: How Gender Inequality Persists in the Modern World*. Oxford University Press.

Rinderle, Susana, and Montoya, Danielle. 2008. "Hispanic/Latino Identity Labels: An Examination of Cultural Values and Personal Experiences." *Howard Journal of Communication* 19, no. 2: 144–164.

Ro, Christine. 2019. "Parental Leave: How Rich Countries Compare." BBC. https://www.bbc.com/worklife/article/20190615-parental-leave-how-rich-countries-compare.

Roberts, Dorothy. 2002. *Shattered Bonds: The Color of Child Welfare*. Civitas Books.

Rohmer, Odile, and Eva Louvet. 2012. "Implicit Measures of the Stereotype Content Associated with Disability." *British Journal of Social Psychology* 51, no. 4: 732–740.

Romero, Mary. 2016. *Maid in the USA*. Routledge.

Rosay, André B. 2016. "Violence against American Indian and Alaska Native Women and Men." US Department of Justice. https://www.ncjrs.gov/pdffiles1/nij/249736.pdf.

Ross, Loretta, and Rickie Solinger. 2017. *Reproductive Justice*. University of California Press.

Ross, Monique S., and Allison Godwin. 2016. "Engineering Identity Implications on the Retention of Black Women in the Engineering Industry." 2016 ASEE Annual Conference & Exposition, American Society for Engineering Education.

Rosser, Sue V. 2017. *Academic Women in STEM Faculty*. Springer.

Rothwell, Jonathan. 2013. *The Hidden Stem Economy*. Brookings Institute. https://www.brookings.edu/wp-content/uploads/2016/06/TheHiddenSTEMEconomy610.pdf.

Ruberg, Bonnie, and Spencer Ruelos. 2020. "Data for Queer Lives: How LGBTQ Gender and Sexuality Identities Challenge Norms of Demographics." *Big Data & Society* 7, no. 1: 1–13.

Rubin, Gayle. 2006. "Of Catamites and Kings." In *The Transgender Studies Reader*, edited by Susan Stryker and Stephen Whittle, 471–481. Routledge.

Sandberg, Sheryl. 2013. *Lean In: Women, Work, and the Will to Lead*. Random House.

Sansone, Dario, and Christopher S. Carpenter. 2020. "Turing's Children: Representation of Sexual Minorities in STEM." *PLOS One* 15, no. 11.

Sassler, Sharon, Jennifer Glass, Yael Levitte, and Katherine M. Michelmore. 2017 "The Missing Women in STEM? Assessing Gender Differentials in the Factors Associated with Transition to First Jobs." *Social Science Research* 63: 192–208.

Saujani, Reshma. 2017. "Girls Who Code Turns Five: What I've Learned since Our Founding." Girls Who Code. https://medium.com/girls-who-code/girls-who-code-turns-five-what-ive-learned-since-our-founding-4c70861e6769.

Schilt, Kristen, and Matthew Wiswall. 2008. "Before and After: Gender Transitions, Human Capital, and Workplace Experiences." *BE Journal of Economic Analysis & Policy* 8, no. 1: 1–28.

Schmidt, Ronald, Rodney E. Hero, Andrew L. Aoki, and Yvette M. Alex-Assensoh. 2009. *Newcomers, Outsiders, and Insiders: Immigrants and American Racial Politics in the Early Twenty-first Century*. University of Michigan Press.

Schochet, Leila. 2019. "The Child Care Crisis Is Keeping Women out of the Workforce." Center for American Progress. https://www.americanprogress.org/issues/early-childhood/reports/2019/03/28/467488/child-care-crisis-keeping-women-workforce/.

Schor, Paul. 2017. *Counting Americans: How the US Census Classified the Nation*. Oxford University Press.

Schuster, Mark A., Artem Osherov, and Paul J. Chung. 2020. "Why Counting Black Lives Matters: The 2020 Census." *New England Journal of Medicine*. https://www.nejm.org/doi/full/10.1056/NEJMp2022162.

Seidman, Steven. 2010. *The Social Construction of Sexuality*. Norton.

Seo, Eunjin, Yishan Shen, and Edna C. Alfaro. 2019. "Adolescents' Beliefs about Math Ability and Their Relations to STEM Career Attainment: Joint Consideration of Race/Ethnicity and Gender." *Journal of Youth and Adolescence* 48, no. 2: 306–325.

Serpe, Christine R., and Kevin L. Nadal. 2017. "Perceptions of Police: Experiences in the Trans* Community." *Journal of Gay & Lesbian Social Services* 29, no. 3: 280–299.

Servon, Lisa J., and M. Anne Visser. 2011. "Progress Hindered: The Retention and Advancement of Women in Science, Engineering and Technology Careers." *Human Resource Management Journal* 21, no. 3: 272–284.

Shah, Niral. 2019. "'Asians Are Good at Math' Is Not a Compliment: STEM Success as a Threat to Personhood." *Harvard Educational Review* 89, no. 4: 661–686.

Shanahan, Jesse. 2016. "Disability Is Not a Disqualification." *Science* 351, no. 6271.

Shanahan, Jesse. 2017. "The Cost of Disclosure: One Being a Woman with a Disability in Geophysics." *Lady Science*. https://www.ladyscience.com/cost-of-disclosure/no35.

Sharma, G. 2018. "BP's Chief Scientist Says Boosting Gender Diversity and STEM Pathways Crucial for 'Big Oil.'" *Forbes*, March 6. https://www.forbes.com/sites/gauravsharma/2018/03/06/bp-chief-scientist-says-boosting-gender-diversity-and-stem-pathways-crucial-for-big-oil/#7fcaea875256.

Sharpe, Rhonda Vonshay. 2019. "Disaggregating Data by Race Allows for More Accurate Research." *Nature Human Behavior* 3, no. 12: 1240.

Sheppard, Donald Lee. 2018. "The Dividends of Diversity: The Win-Win-Win Model Is Taking Over Business and It Necessitates Diversity." *Strategic HR Review*.

Sheridan, Vanessa. 2016. "Navigating Transgender Issues in the Workplace." In *Gender, Race, and Ethnicity in the Workplace: Emerging Issues and Enduring Challenges*, edited by Margaret Foegen Karsten, 43–58. Praeger.

Siegel, Reva B. 2018. "Pregnancy as a Normal Condition of Employment: Comparative and Role-based Accounts of Discrimination." *William & Mary Law Review* 59, no. 3: 969–1006.

Simms, Margaret. 2018. "Say African American or Black, but First Acknowledge the Persistence of Structural Racism." *Urban Institute*. https://www.urban.org/urban-wire/say-african-american-or-black-first-acknowledge-persistence-structural-racism.

Singer, Bennett, and David Deschamps. 2017. *LGBTQ Stats: Lesbian, Gay, Bisexual, Transgender, and Queer People by the Numbers*. New Press.

Sinton, Matthew C., Katie Nicoll Baines, Kiri A. Thornalley, Vinodh Ilangovan, and Mehmet Kurt. 2021. "Increasing the Visibility of LGBTQ+ Researchers in STEM." *The Lancet* 397, no. 10269: 77–79.

Slaughter, Christine M., and Chelsea N. Jones. 2022. "How Black Women Will Be Especially Affected by the Loss of *Roe*." *Washington Post*, June 25. https://www.washingtonpost.com/politics/2022/06/25/dobbs-roe-black-racism-disparate-maternal-health.

Smith, Andrea. 2006. "Without Bureaucracy, Beyond Inclusion: Re-centering Feminism." *Leftturn*, June 1. http://leftturn.org/without-bureaucracy-beyond-inclusion-re-centering-feminism.

Smith, David. 2014. "No Sexuality Please, We're Scientists." *Chemistry World*. https://www.chemistryworld.com/opinion/no-sexuality-please-were-scientists/7197.article.

Snorton, C. Riley. 2017. *Black on Both Sides: A Racial History of Trans Identity*. University of Minnesota Press.

Society of Women Engineers. 2022. "SWE's Statement on U.S. Supreme Court Ruling on *Dobbs v. Jackson Women's Health*, Which Overturns the 1973 *Roe v. Wade* Decision." https://swe.org/swes-statement-on-u-s-supreme-court-ruling-on-dobbs-v-jackson-womens-health-which-overturns-the-1973-roe-v-wade-decision/.

Söder, Mårten. 1990. "Prejudice or Ambivalence? Attitudes toward Persons with Disabilities." *Disability, Handicap & Society* 5, no. 3: 227–241.

Spade, Dean. 2006. "Mutilating Gender." *The Transgender Studies Reader*, edited by Susan Stryker and Stephen Whittle, 315–332. Routledge.

Spade, Dean. 2012. "What's Wrong with Trans Rights?" In *Transfeminist Perspectives in and beyond Transgender and Gender Studies*, edited by Finn Enke, 184–194. Temple University Press.

Spivak, Gayatri Chakravorty. (1985) 1996. "Subaltern Studies: Deconstructing Historiography." In *The Spivak Reader*, edited by Donna Landry and Gerald MacLean, 203–236. Routledge.

Spruhan, Paul. 2006. "A Legal History of Blood Quantum in Federal Indian Law to 1935." *South Dakota Law Review* 51, no. 1: 1–50.

Stewart, Abigail J., Janet E. Malley, and Danielle LaVaque-Manty. 2007. *Transforming Science and Engineering: Advancing Academic Women*. University of Michigan Press.

Staff, Jeremy, and Jaylen Mortimer. 2012. "Explaining the Motherhood Penalty during the Early Occupational Career." *Demography* 49, no. 1: 1–21.

Stiker, Henri-Jacques. (1999) 2019. *A History of Disability*. University of Michigan Press.

Stone, Pamela. 2007. *Opting Out? Why Women Really Quit Careers and Head Home*. University of California Press.

Strmic-Pawl, Hephzibah V., Brandon A. Jackson, and Steve Garner. 2018. "Race Counts: Racial and Ethnic Data on the US Census and the Implications for Tracking Inequality." *Sociology of Race and Ethnicity* 4, no. 1: 1–13.

Stryker, Susan, and Stephen Whittle, eds. 2006. *The Transgender Studies Reader*. Taylor & Francis.

Stryker, Susan. 2017. *Transgender History: The Roots of Today's Revolution*. 2nd ed. Hachette UK.

Tan-Wilson, Anna, and Nancy Stamp. 2015. "College Students' Views of Work-Life Balance in STEM Research Careers: Addressing Negative Preconceptions." *CBE—Life Sciences Education* 14, no. 3: 1–13.

Tashman, Brian. 2018. "Trump Is Undermining the 2020 Census: Marginalized Communities Will Bear the Brunt." *American Civil Liberties Union*, May 7.

Taylor, Linnet. 2017. "What Is Data Justice? The Case for Connecting Digital Rights and Freedoms Globally." *Big Data & Society* 4, no. 2: 1–14.

Teitelbaum, Michael S. 2014. *Falling Behind? Boom, Bust, and the Global Race for Scientific Talent*. Princeton University Press.

Thébaud, Sarah, and Catherine J. Taylor. 2021. "The Specter of Motherhood: Culture and the Production of Gendered Career Aspirations in Science and Engineering." *Gender & Society* 35, no. 3: 395–421.

Thompson, Derek. 2017. "Is the H-1B Program a Cynical Attempt to Undercut American Workers?" *The Atlantic*. https://www.theatlantic.com/business/archive/2017/02/the-dark-side-of-the-h-1b-program/516813.

Thoreson, Ryan. 2021. "'I Just Try to Make It Home Safe': Violence and the Human Rights of Transgender People in the United States." Human Rights Watch.

Thornton, Russell. 1987. *American Indian Holocaust and Survival: A Population History since 1492*. University of Oklahoma Press.

Tinkler, Justine, Jun Zhao, Yan Li, and Cecilia L. Ridgeway. 2019. "Honorary Whites? Asian American Women and the Dominance Penalty." *Socius* 5. doi: 2378023119836000.

Tomaskovic-Devey, Donald, and Dustin Avent-Holt. 2019. *Relational Inequalities: An Organizational Approach*. Oxford University Press.

Tompkins, Kyla Wazana. 2021. "The Shush." *PMLA* 136, no. 3: 417–423.

Torpey, Elka. 2021. "Effects of the Pandemic on Projected Employment in Selected Industries, 2019–29." *Career Outlook*. US Bureau of Labor Statistics.

Torres, Nicole. 2017. "The H-1B Visa Debate, Explained." *Harvard Business Review*. https://hbr.org/2017/05/the-h-1b-visa-debate-explained.

Towler, Annette J., and David J. Schneider. 2005. "Distinctions among Stigmatized Groups 1." *Journal of Applied Social Psychology* 35, no. 1: 1–14.

TransPop. 2021. "U.S. Transgender Population Health Survey." http://www.trans pop.org/.

Traustadóttir, Rannveig. 2006. "Disability and Gender: Introduction to the Special Issue." *Scandinavian Journal of Disability Research* 8, no. 2–3: 81–84.

Tso, Tiffany Diane. 2018. "The Bamboo Glass Ceiling." *Slate*. https://slate.com /human-interest/2018/08/asian-american-women-face-a-glass-ceiling-and-a-bamboo -ceiling-at-work.html.

Tucker, Jasmine. 2019. "Equal Pay for Native Women." National Women's Law Center. https://nwlc.org/wp-content/uploads/2018/11/Native-Women-Equal-Pay-2019.pdf.

Tweedy, Ann E., and Karen Yescavage. 2014. "Employment Discrimination against Bisexuals: An Empirical Study." *William and Mary Journal of Women and Law* 21, no. 3: 699–741.

United Nations. 2019. "International Migrant Stock 2019." United Nations Department of Economic and Social Affairs, Population Division. https://www.un.org/en /development/desa/population/migration/data/estimates2/estimatesmaps.asp?1t1.

US Bureau of Labor Statistics. 2019. "Report: Labor Force Characteristics by Race and Ethnicity, 2018." https://www.bls.gov/opub/reports/race-and-ethnicity/2018/home .htm.

US Bureau of Labor Statistics. 2020a. "BLS Data Viewer: Child Care and Nursery School in U.S. City Average, All Urban Consumers, Seasonally Adjusted." https:// beta.bls.gov/dataViewer/view/timeseries/CUSR0000SEEB03.

US Bureau of Labor Statistics. 2020b. "Labor Force Characteristics by Race and Ethnicity, 2019." Report 1088. https://www.bls.gov/opub/reports/race-and-ethnicity/2019 /home.htm.

US Bureau of the Census. 2012a. "Census Bureau Releases Estimates of Undercount and Overcount in the 2010 Census." https://www.census.gov/newsroom/releases /archives/2010_census/cb12-95.html.

US Bureau of the Census. 2012b. "2010 Census Coverage Measurement Estimation Report: Summary of Estimates of Coverage of Persons in the United States." *DSSD 2010 Census Coverage Measurement Memorandum Series 2012*. 2010-G-01.

US Bureau of the Census. 2018. *2020 Census Operational Plan: A New Design for the 21st Century.* https://www2.census.gov/programs-surveys/decennial/2020/program-management/planning-docs/2020-oper-plan4.pdf.

US Bureau of the Census. 2019a. "American Community Survey: Educational Attainment." https://data.census.gov/cedsci/table?q=education&tid=ACSST1Y2019.S1501.

US Bureau of the Census. 2019b. "Censuses of American Indians." https://www.census.gov/history/www/genealogy/decennial_census_records/censuses_of_american_indians.html.

US Bureau of the Census. 2020a. "Disability Characteristics." American Community Survey 2018. https://data.census.gov/cedsci/table?t=Disability&tid=ACSST1Y2018.S1810&hidePreview=true.

US Bureau of the Census. 2020b. "Why We Ask Questions About . . . Disability." https://www.census.gov/acs/www/about/why-we-ask-each-question/disability.

US Bureau of the Census. 2021. "How Disability Data Are Collected from the American Community Survey." https://www.census.gov/topics/health/disability/guidance/data-collection-acs.html#:~:text=The%20American%20Community%20Survey%20(ACS),-History&text=The%20ACS%20began%20in%20the,complexity%20of%20the%20decennial%20census.

US Centers for Disease Control and Prevention. 2021a. "Disability and Health Overview." https://www.cdc.gov/ncbddd/disabilityandhealth/disability.html.

US Centers for Disease Control and Prevention. 2021b. "Disability Impacts All of US." https://www.cdc.gov/ncbddd/disabilityandhealth/infographic-disability-impacts-all.html.

US Citizenship and Immigration Services. 2021. "H-1B Specialty Occupations, DOD Cooperative Research and Development Project Workers, and Fashion Models." https://www.uscis.gov/working-in-the-united-states/h-1b-specialty-occupations.

US Department of Defense, Defense Industry Board. 2021. "Industrial Capabilities Report to Congress: 2020 Annual Report." https://media.defense.gov/2021/Jan/14/2002565311/-1/-1/0/FY20-INDUSTRIAL-CAPABILITIES-REPORT.PDF.

US Department of Homeland Security, Office of Immigration Statistics. 2020. *Yearbook of Immigration Statistics 2019.*

US Department of Labor. 2021 "Family and Medical Leave Act (FMLA)." https://www.dol.gov/general/topic/benefits-leave/fmla.

US Department of Justice. 2021. "Information and Technical Assistance on the Americans with Disabilities Act." https://www.ada.gov.

US Department of Labor, Office of Disability Employment Policy. n.d. "Women." https://www.dol.gov/agencies/odep/program-areas/individuals/Women.

US Department of the Interior, Census Office. 1894. *Report on Indians Taxed and Not Taxed in the United States (Except Alaska) at the Eleventh Census: 1890*. Government Printing Office. https://www2.census.gov/prod2/decennial/documents/1890a_v10 -01.pdf.

Valentine, David. 2007. *Imagining Transgender: An Ethnography of a Category*. Duke University Press.

van derMeulen, Marjolein C. H., Jennifer S. Wayne, Naomi C. Chesler, and Lori A. Setton. 2022. "Maintaining Inclusion in Engineering in a Post-*Dobbs* World." *Inside Higher Ed*. https://www.insidehighered.com/advice/2022/10/14/keeping-stem -fields-inclusive-post-dobbs-world-opinion.

Varma, Roli, and Vanessa Galindo-Sanchez. 2006. "Native American Women in Computing." In *Encyclopedia of Gender and Information Technology*, edited by Eileen M. Trauth, 914–919. IGI Global.

Velte, Kyle C. 2020. "Straightwashing the Census." *Boston College Law Review* 61, no. 1: 69–127.

Verloo, Mieke. 2006. "Multiple Inequalities, Intersectionality and the European Union." *European Journal of Women's Studies* 13, no. 3: 211–228.

Verniers, Catherine, and Jorge Vala. 2018. "Justifying Gender Discrimination in the Workplace: The Mediating Role of Motherhood Myths." *PLOS One* 13, no. 1.

Võ, Linda T. 2012. "Navigating the Academic Terrain: The Racial and Gender Politics of Elusive Belonging." In *Presumed Incompetent: The Intersections of Race and Class for Women in Academia*, edited by Gabriella Gutiérrez y Muhs, Yolanda Flores Niemann, Carmen G. González, and Angela P. Harris, 93–109. Colorado University Press.

Wallace, Phyllis.1980. *Black Women in the Labor Force*. MIT Press.

Warbelow, Sarah, Courtnay Avant, and Colin Kutney. 2020. "2020 State Equality Index: A Review of State Legislation Affection the Lesbian, Gay, Bisexual, Transgender and Queer Community and a Look Ahead in 2021." Human Rights Campaign.

Warner, Leah R. 2008. "A Best Practices Guide to Intersectional Approaches in Psychological Research." *Sex Roles* 59, no. 5: 454–463.

Waterman, Stephanie J., and Lorinda S. Lindley. 2013. "Cultural Strengths to Persevere: Native American Women in Higher Education." *NASPA Journal about Women in Higher Education* 6, no. 2: 139–165.

Weisgram, Erica S., and Amanda B. Diekman. 2017. "Making STEM 'Family Friendly': The Impact of Perceiving Science Careers as Family-Compatible." *Social Sciences* 6, no. 2.

Weller, Christian E. 2019. "African Americans Face Systemic Obstacles to Getting Good Jobs." Center for American Progress. December 5. https://www.american

progress.org/issues/economy/reports/2019/12/05/478150/african-americans-face
-systematic-obstacles-getting-good-jobs.

Wernimont, Jacqueline. 2019. *Numbered Lives: Life and Death in Quantum Media*. MIT Press.

Wilkerson, Isabel. 1989. "'African American' Favored by Many of America's Blacks." *New York Times*, January 31. https://www.nytimes.com/1989/01/31/us/african-american -favored-by-many-of-america-s-blacks.html.

Wilkie, Dana. 2014. "Challenges Confront Disabled Who Pursue STEM Careers." Society for Human Resource Management. https://www.shrm.org/resourcesandtools /hr-topics/behavioral-competencies/global-and-cultural-effectiveness/pages/disabled -in-stem-careers.aspx.

Williams, Joan C. 2010. *Reshaping the Work-Family Debate: Why Men and Class Matter*. Harvard University Press.

Williams, Joan C. 2014. "Double Jeopardy? An Empirical Study with Implications for the Debates over Implicit Bias and Intersectionality." *Harvard Journal of Law & Gender* 37: 185–242.

Williams, Joan C., Mary Blair-Loy, and Jennifer L. Berdahl. 2013. "Cultural Schemas, Social Class, and the Flexibility Stigma." *Journal of Social Issues* 69, no. 2: 209–234.

Williams, Joan C., Marina Multhaups, and Rachel Korn. 2018. "The Problem with 'Asians Are Good at Science.'" *The Atlantic*, January. https://www.theatlantic.com /science/archive/2018/01/asian-americans-science-math-bias/551903.

Williams, Joan C., Katherine W. Phillips, and Erika V. Hall. 2014. "Double Jeopardy: Gender Bias against Women in Science." University of California Hastings College of Law. https://worklifelaw.org/publications/Double-Jeopardy-Report_v6_full_web-sm.pdf.

Wilson, Bianca D. M., and Ilan H. Meyer. 2021. "Nonbinary LGBTQ Adults in the United States." Williams Institute. https://williamsinstitute.law.ucla.edu/wp-content /uploads/Nonbinary-LGBTQ-Adults-Jun-2021.pdf.

Windchief, Sweeney, and Blakely Brown. 2017. "Conceptualizing a Mentoring Program for American Indian/Alaska Native Students in the STEM Fields: A Review of the Literature." *Mentoring & Tutoring: Partnership in Learning* 25, no. 3: 329–345.

Wingfield, Nick, and Mike Isaac 2017. "Tech Industry Frets over Visa Program." *New York Times*, January 28. https://www.nytimes.com/2017/01/27/business/technology -h-1b-visa-immigration.html.

Wolfe, Patrick. 2016. *Traces of History: Elementary Structures of Race*. Verso.

World Health Organization. 2021. "Measuring Health and Disability: Manual for WHO Disability Assessment Schedule." https://www.who.int/publications/i/item

/measuring-health-and-disability-manual-for-who-disability-assessment-schedule
-(-whodas-2.0).

Wu, Lilian, and Wei Jing. 2011. "Asian Women in STEM Careers: An Invisible Minority in a Double Bind." *Issues in Science & Technology* 28, no. 1: 82–87.

Wyss, Vanessa L., and Robert H. Tai. 2010. "Conflicts between Graduate Study in Science and Family Life." *College Student Journal* 44, no. 2: 475–492.

Xu, Yonghong Jade. 2017. "Attrition of Women in STEM: Examining Job/Major Congruence in the Career Choices of College Graduates." *Journal of Career Development* 44, no. 1: 3–19.

Xue, Yi, and Richard C. Larson. 2015. "STEM Crisis or STEM Surplus? Yes and Yes." *Monthly Labor Review*. US Bureau of Labor Statistics. https://www.bls.gov/opub/mlr/2015/article/stem-crisis-or-stem-surplus-yes-and-yes.htm.

Yavorsky, Jill E., Claire M. Kamp Dush, and Sarah J. Schoppe-Sullivan. 2015. "The Production of Inequality: The Gender Division of Labor across the Transition to Parenthood." *Journal of Marriage and Family* 77, no. 3: 662–679.

Yoder, Jeremy B., and Allison Mattheis. 2016. "Queer in STEM: Workplace Experiences Reported in a National Survey of LGBTQA Individuals in Science, Technology, Engineering, and Mathematics Careers." *Journal of Homosexuality* 63, no. 1: 1–27.

Yoshino, Kenji. 2016. "The Epistemic Contract of Bisexual Erasure." In *Feminist and Queer Legal Theory: Intimate Encounters, Uncomfortable Conversations*, edited by Martha Albertson Fineman, Jack E. Jackson, and Adam P. Romero, 215–236. Routledge.

Yu, Helen H. 2020. "Revisiting the Bamboo Ceiling: Perceptions from Asian Americans on Experiencing Workplace Discrimination." *Asian American Journal of Psychology* 11, no. 3: 158–167.

Zamarro, Gema, and María J. Prados. 2021. "Gender Differences in Couples' Division of Childcare, Work and Mental Health during COVID-19." *Review of Economics of the Household* 19, no. 1: 11–40.

Index